To the memory of AMAZIAH MORGAN (1787–1839),
Major General of Indiana Militia, who served
as Private of United States Rangers and as
Ensign of Ohio Militia on the northwestern
frontier in 1812 and 1813

THE DEMOCRATIC REPUBLIC

1801 ★ 1815

By MARSHALL SMELSER

ILLUSTRATED

1817

HARPER & ROW, PUBLISHERS

NEW YORK, EVANSTON, AND LONDON

Contents

Illustrations

*These illustrations, grouped in a separate section,
will be found following page 82*

1. Thomas Jefferson
2. Monticello, 1809
3. Bank of the United States, Philadelphia, 1799
4. Dolley Payne Madison
5. James Madison, 1805
6. The United States Capitol, before the fire of August 24, 1814
7. The United States Capitol after the fire
8. James Monroe
9. "The Hartford Convention or Leap No Leap"
10. The Capture and Destruction of Washington, August 24, 1814
11. Construction of a warship—the U.S.F. *Philadelphia*
12. The burning of the United States Frigate *Philadelphia* in the harbor of Tripoli
13. Dedicatory page of Hezekiah Niles's *Weekly Register* (Baltimore)
14. Facsimile of title page of Zadok Cramer's *Navigator*
15. Fort Harrison on the Wabash River, 1812
16. New York in 1800, as seen from the Jersey shore
17. "A View of the Bombardment of Fort McHenry," Baltimore, 1814
18. *Constitution* capturing *Guerrière*, 1813
19. "The fall of Washington or Maddy in full flight"
20. General Winchester humiliated by his Indian captors after the massacre of the Raisin River
21. Journal of William Clark, open at entry for October 15, 1805

MAPS

Editors' Introduction

HOWEVER much historians admire the genius of Henry Adams and his perspicacious portrayal of American society in the Age of the Jeffersonians, they are disinclined to take at face value his rather harsh judgment of the Jeffersonian Presidents. To Adams, Jefferson's policy of "peaceable coercion" not only involved withdrawal without dignity but proved to be a mistaken one. Even measured by Jefferson's own states' rights yardstick, it was not constitutional. In Adams' account, Jefferson's administration, beginning under such happy auguries, comes to an end with a whimper.

With these judgments Marshall Smelser emphatically disagrees. With other revisionists he is prepared to overlook Jefferson's faults because the President was in the main (and there were some glaring exceptions!) on the side of liberty. Mr. Smelser's sympathetic portrait presents the better side of Jefferson without overlooking the flaws. He recognizes Jefferson's spoilsmanship, but considers it a part of his consummate political art. While showing partiality to friends, the President kept his administration free of serious scandals. Committed at the start to fiscal frugality and to de-emphasizing the military (save for his bellicose posture toward the Barbary States and Santo Domingo), world events beyond the control of the United States proved the futility of his policies. Indeed, one might argue that Jefferson's passion for peace, to which the nation's military weakness must be attributed in large measure, provoked the contempt of Europe. Mr. Smelser carefully plots the steps by which the United States was led into a European war, bringing to an abrupt end the rapprochement with Great Britain, initiated in 1795 by John Jay.

The Jefferson who emerges in these pages is no flaming radical, but instead a Whiggish moderate, a friend of liberty rather than democracy, a strong executive who overreached himself only in his embargo policy, a "Scholar Boss," if not a Philosopher King. Mr. Smelser is prepared, too, to see the better side of Madison, and to reject the conventional view of him as an "incapable President" who "mismanaged an unnecessary war." While rescuing Mr. Madison from the long-standing charges of incompetence, the author concedes that Jefferson's successor lacked both the instincts and the talents to exert leadership in wartime. Aside from shortcomings of personality, Madison's views about the division of powers under the Constitution prevented him from exercising the control and direction of Congress that might have been expected of so adroit a politician. That very "constitutional republicanism" of which Madison stands as the ablest champion hobbled all his operations as a war president.

Mr. Smelser's account of the disunity of the nation at the time of the War of 1812, of his scathing criticism of the Radical Right who flirted with disunion and treason and brought the Federalist party into disrepute, serve as a reminder of the perils of leading a divided nation into war.

A procession of colorful individualists march through these pages —the eccentric Randolph, the deceitful Burr, the waspish Pickering. In addition, the author has much to tell that is fresh and instructive. His scrutiny of the House roll calls provokes doubt that the declaration of war was prompted either by expansionism or the Indian menace. Instead, Smelser shows how states that produced for export generally favored the War of 1812, while the freighting states opposed it. The story of how a third-rate power conducted a war against a naval colossus, managed, after enormous bungling and incompetence, to avoid other than local disasters and to emerge from the conflict with its independence vindicated and confirmed, secures herein a fresh and authoritative re-telling.

The Democratic Republic, 1801–1815 constitutes a volume in The New American Nation Series, a comprehensive and cooperative survey of the history of the area now embraced in the United States, from the days of discovery to our own time. Constitutional issues, alluded to in this book, will be separately dealt with and at length; the rise of the West is the theme of Francis S. Philbrick's account of expansion during these years, while Russel B. Nye has examined the cultural life of the era.

HENRY STEELE COMMAGER
RICHARD B. MORRIS

Prefatory Note

THE purpose of this book is to organize the abundant learning of the writers and editors who have written so many specialized studies and perfected so many documents of the history of the United States from 1801 to 1815. The work of the scholars who have labored in the half century which has elapsed since the appearance of the last one-volume treatment of the subject has seemed to deserve special attention. The task has been mainly the blending of the very large corpus of monographs and documents in such order as will, it is hoped, tell a coherent and illuminating story. The earlier sources—press, polemics, reports, correspondence, and memoirs—have not been neglected.

The author's indebtedness is large. The John Simon Guggenheim Foundation awarded him a fellowship in the academic year 1963–64, and aid came from the Notre Dame Faculty Development Fund and the Notre Dame Committee on Research in the Humanities. Colleagues Julius W. Pratt, Thomas Stritch, and Samuel Shapiro read parts of the manuscript and tried, with incomplete success, to persuade the author to mend some of his ways. Vice-President Chester A. Soleta, and Deans Paul E. Beichner and Charles E. Sheedy, all of Notre Dame, removed many obstacles. Irving Brant, Alexander Balinky, Vincent P. DeSantis, Adrienne Koch, Leonard W. Levy, Thomas T. McAvoy, and Merrill Peterson contributed insights in conversation and correspondence which the author has appropriated shamelessly; for any distortions of their views, they are in no way responsible. Warren H. Goodman and the Department of

History of Duke University kindly permitted the use of unpublished matter from a graduate thesis by Mr. Goodman. At the risk of omitting many helpful librarians, gratitude must be expressed for the assistance of the librarians and staffs of the Memorial Library of Notre Dame, the Library of Congress, Yale University Library, the Alderman Library of the University of Virginia, the Chicago Historical Society, the Connecticut Historical Society, the Historical Society of Pennsylvania, the Widener Library of Harvard College, the Massachusetts Historical Society, the Boston Public Library, and the New York Public Library. Several generations of student assistants—James P. Murphy, Patrick Bowers, Ronald J. Dvorak, Robert Noe, the late John F. Hickey, Jr., and Arnold Klingenberg—all tolerated the author's crotchets and accurately performed many drudging tasks. The elite corps of manuscript typists in the faculty stenographic pool of Notre Dame, directed by Carmela Rulli, were severally kind, swift, and efficient. The writer's wife, Anna Padberg Smelser, who luckily for him remembers everything he ever mentioned having learned (which is more than he can say for himself), was his kindest, most perspicacious, and ablest collaborator.

MARSHALL SMELSER

South Bend, Indiana

CHAPTER 1

Mr. Jefferson in 1801

A T least we know what he looked like.[1] He was tall and slender, framed of large, loosely shackled bones. His clothes, including a cherished scarlet vest and a pair of run-over slippers, never seemed quite to fit. He struck one observer as a man who was all ends and angles. A Federalist senator, William Plumer of New Hampshire, on calling at the White House, mistook him for "a servant" and carefully noted that he wore a dirty shirt. The senator was fair-minded enough to record the wearing of a clean shirt at a dinner some time later.

Mr. Jefferson's usual manner was good-humored, even sunny, although occasionally abstracted or cynical. His disposition fitted a country squire whose excellent health and enviable digestion gave him a lifelong euphoria, interrupted only by periodic headaches and occasional rheumatic twinges. He had the typical complexion of the freckled gray-eyed Celt. His hair was cut short and powdered. Its color we know, because a correspondent saluted him in a letter, carefully preserved by the recipient, as "You red-headed son of a bitch."[2]

[1] This description is compounded from William Maclay, *Journal*, ed. E. S. Maclay (New York, 1890), p. 272; Dumas Malone, "Thomas Jefferson," *Dictionary of American Biography* (11 vols., New York, 1927–58), hereafter cited as Malone, *DAB*; Dumas Malone, *Jefferson the Virginian* (New York, 1948), p. xviii; an unsigned review of the unpublished Augustus Foster, "Notes on the United States," *The Quarterly Review*, CXXXVI (1841), p. 24; and William Plumer, quoted in Lynn W. Turner, *William Plumer of New Hampshire, 1759–1850* (Chapel Hill, 1962), p. 94.
[2] E. Millicent Sowerby, "Thomas Jefferson and His Library," Bibliographical Society of America, *Papers*, L (1956), 221–222.

His small talk was built as loosely as his lounging body. Although often brilliant, his conversation was usually rambling and diffuse. It might range from weather and crops to the ingenuity of the Senate in finding excuses to recess during the local race meetings. Following the ponies was a lesser vice than dice; it gave the gentlemen "time for reflection," as he put it, between investments of their risk capital.[3]

That was the exterior Jefferson as seen by the casual caller, but his personality had layers like an onion. His intimate friends knew the next layer, his family knew the third, but no one except God and Thomas Jefferson knew what lay farther inside this sensitive, unsentimental violinist, bird watcher, and horticulturist. We do know that forgiveness of his enemies did not come to him easily.

He broke the precedent of delivering messages orally to the Congress, which was set by George Washington and carried on by John Adams. Jefferson sent his messages to Capitol Hill to be read by a clerk. He said it was to save time, but we know he hated to speak in public, and he was only entirely at ease in the company of kinfolk, artists, savants, and a few Republican leaders.[4] Margaret Bayard Smith, daughter of a warm Federalist and wife of the Republican editor of the new *National Intelligencer,* expected to meet a fanatical boor. To her surprise he was "so meek and mild, yet dignified in his manners, with a voice so soft and low, with a countenance so benignant and intelligent. . . ."[5] But Anthony Merry, the British minister, and his wife did not think the President so dignified and benignant. When Jefferson, lacking a hostess, disregarded all protocol at state dinners, saying "pele-mele is our law," they felt literally degraded and quit coming to the White House. The Spanish minister joined the banquet boycott.[6]

The absence of the diplomatic corps was not of first importance.

3 Lynn W. Turner, "Thomas Jefferson Through the Eyes of a New Hampshire Politician," *Mississippi Valley Historical Review,* XXX (1943), 205. The politician was William Plumer.

4 Henry Adams, *History of the United States During the Administrations of Jefferson and Madison* (9 vols., New York, 1889–91), I, 143–146. Hereafter cited as Adams, *United States.*

5 Gaillard Hunt (ed.), *The First Forty Years of Washington Society Portrayed by the Family Letters of Mrs. Samuel Harrison Smith (Margaret Bayard) from the Collection of Her Grandson J. Henley Smith* (New York, 1906), p. 6.

6 "Jefferson to William Short on Mr. and Mrs. Merry, 1804," *American Historical Review,* XXXIII (1928), 832–833; Joel Larus, "Pell Mell Along the Potomac," *William and Mary Quarterly,* Third Series, XVII (1960), 349–357.

To Jefferson the dinner party—particularly the stag dinner party—was a principal domestic political tool. Inviting not more than a dozen legislators at a time, he managed to get through the whole list more than once a session. The groups were chosen for compatibility. He seated them at a round table where he would be only first among equals and where private conversations would be difficult. He served his guests himself from a dumb-waiter to preclude the presence of eavesdropping servants. His French chef has been rated highly and his cellar must have been superb. Never dominating the conversation, he guided it away from the shoptalk in which congressmen found themselves already too much immersed, and planted the seeds of his political philosophy by indirection, letting his charm and his menu carry things along. The diplomatic corps knew well enough what he was doing, since it was the customary procedure of European courts, but to the political community in the raw new capital it seems to have been dazzling, and it showed Thomas Jefferson at his guileful best in the tactics of politics.[7]

The contrast between his manner with Mrs. Smith across a tea table and his treatment of the diplomatic corps makes clear the split between his private life and his public bearing as the chief of state of a democratic republic. In private, the gentle introvert; in public matters, the incarnation of a stormy nation of freemen, willing to provoke contention, even though he found controversy painful.[8] When relaxed with friends or family, his simple carriage was obviously not the way of a clod, but was more the manner of a negligent, self-assured nobleman, correctly confident of his status and of his own good taste. Yet, in a conference on the public's business, a senator could notice his "stiff gentility or lofty gravity."[9]

It seems very unlikely that such an undramatic and diffident man, whose charm was felt only in private, could have reached the White House in any later generation. His merits were publicized only by his friends. Not for him was the alley fighting of ballot politics. Once he warned his grandson to avoid two kinds of disputants: self-assured young intellectuals with more confidence than knowledge,

7 James Sterling Young, *The Washington Community, 1800–1828* (New York, 1966), pp. 168–170. Mr. Young's perspicacious book is a study of the ruling group in Washington by the methods we call behavioral science.

8 Adams, *United States*, I, 143–145.

9 Maclay, *Journal*, p. 310.

and bad-tempered, passionate politicians—these latter needed "medical more than moral counsel."[10]

Now peel down to the third layer. There one sees a homesick widower with chronic money troubles, yearning for his children and his grandchildren. His was a great career but rarely a happy life. Between 1772 and 1782, four of his six children died. In 1781 a British army devastated his farm, and the difficulties of his term as governor of Virginia left a faint smear on his reputation. Then in 1782 Mrs. Jefferson died. At the age of forty his life had become a vacuum. It is almost enough to explain his later career to say that political, scientific, and intellectual projects rushed into his vacant soul to fill that vacuum and to make him the man we remember instead of the reclusive squire he wished to be. His two surviving daughters married young. One, Polly Jefferson Eppes, died in childbirth. He had a brief hope of something approaching normal family life when both of his sons-in-law were elected to the House of Representatives, but each of the girls was advanced in pregnancy and dared not risk the rigors of travel to Washington.[11]

After assuming the debts of his father-in-law, his personal finances were forever out of control. In old age he owed $107,000. When his daughters married, there was nothing left for him to take pleasure in except the talk of his intellectual friends, and the forty years of building and rebuilding Palladian Monticello. What he liked about Washington was that it lay between Monticello[12] and "The American Philosophical Society Held at Philadelphia for the Diffusion of Useful Knowledge."

II

All men claim to be Jeffersonians today. It is doubtful whether the study of any other public man in our national story has been equally absorbing to so many minds. Jefferson's popularity has

[10] Malone, *DAB;* Charles A. Beard, "Thomas Jefferson: A Civilized Man," *Mississippi Valley Historical Review,* XXX (1943) , 160.

[11] Sarah N. Randolph, *The Domestic Life of Thomas Jefferson* (New York, 1871) ; Julian P. Boyd *et al.* (eds.) , *The Papers of Thomas Jefferson* (15 vols., Princeton, 1950–61) , VI, VII; Dumas Malone, "Polly Jefferson and Her Father," *Virginia Quarterly Review,* VII (1931) , 81–95.

[12] Rayford W. Logan (ed.) , "Memoirs of a Monticello Slave, As Dictated to Charles Campbell in the 1840's by Isaac, One of Thomas Jefferson's Slaves," *William and Mary Quarterly,* Third Series, VIII (1951) , 561–582.

reached its zenith since 1920. The published evaluations differ so widely that they tell us more about their writers than about Jefferson.[13] There is so much to see, so much to understand about this man of many flashing facets that it requires more self-discipline than most students have been willing to exercise in order to get the emphases in the right places.[14] He would, perhaps, be easier to understand except for the monument of literary evidence he left us—fifty thousand items, dated from 1760 to 1826, one of the richest left by any man.[15] It has not yet been completely mastered.

Thomas Jefferson's work has been scrutinized and searched not so much for understanding as to justify positions which often contradict each other. As the pendulum of public favor swings from generation to generation, he and Alexander Hamilton exchange the roles of Saint Michael and Lucifer. Laissez faire, states' rights, isolationism, agrarianism, rationalism, civil liberty, and constitutional democracy have all been fiercely defended by the use of quotations from Jefferson's writings, regardless of context. On a more sophisticated level of scholarship, professors drub each other with Jeffersonian tags to prove mutually exclusive generalizations. To get all of the academic theorizers under Jefferson's roof, we must label him the Agrarian Commercial Industrial Democratic Federalist. Fortunately for the history of the republic, the Jeffersonian administration, because of its optimistic evaluation of the public's common sense, was keen on explaining everything to the people. The wholly public business, despite the inner personal subtleties and complexities of the leaders, was very well documented, although one must read the public statements with the usual disciplined skepticism.[16]

---

[13] Malone, *Jefferson the Virginian*, pp. viii–xi; H. Hale Bellot, "Thomas Jefferson in American Historiography," Royal Historical Society, *Transactions*, IV (1954).

[14] Vernon Louis Parrington, *Main Currents in American Thought* (3 vols., New York, 1927–30), I, 342–356, an idolatrous portrait, is a fine thing, but not done from life; evidence is used frugally and predilections govern.

[15] Jeffersonian bibliography is a career in itself: "If I may say so, I think one of his really outstanding achievements and contributions to humanity is the number of people, including of course myself, whom he has helped to support since his death." Sowerby, "Jefferson and His Library," p. 213.

[16] Bernard Mayo, *Myths and Men: Patrick Henry, George Washington, Thomas Jefferson* (Athens, Ga., 1959), pp. 49–71; Clinton Rossiter, "Which Jefferson Do You Quote?" *The Reporter*, XIII, No. 10 (Dec. 15, 1955), pp. 33–36.

III

Nothing that promised the ultimate physical or moral improvement of mankind was alien to the polygonal mind of Thomas Jefferson. With the Adamses and Woodrow Wilson he was one of the four most intellectual of the Presidents of the United States, and he and Wilson are still the objects of hero worship by some Americans. His own heroes were Francis Bacon, Isaac Newton, and John Locke, a "trinity of the three greatest men the world had ever produced." His nominal occupations were farmer and lawyer. He was close to being a true scientist of agriculture, and he was a much more active and successful lawyer, at least up to 1771, when public affairs began to take more and more of his time, than has been generally known.[17]

He mastered Greek and Latin before he was eighteen. Thereafter his reading revolved around the classical authors like a wheel around its hub. Because so few of us nowadays know the classics, we miss much in his mind. He not only knew Greek but he tried to reform its pronunciation by an essay in which he leaned more toward eighteenth-century Greek pronunciation than toward the Italian style then in vogue. He spoke French and Italian, although not fluently, and he had looked into, and had some acquaintance with, forty Indian languages. He also tried to reform the spelling of English. Although he was surely a first-rate writer of his own language, he thought of himself only as a discriminating reader. Omnivorous would be as good an adjective as discriminating. By 1794 he could honestly say he had the best library in the United States. Its 6,500 volumes, all of them collected since a fire destroyed his first library in 1770, formed the nucleus of the Library of Congress.[18]

[17] There are twenty lines of references in Merle Curti, *The Growth of American Thought* (New York, 1945), under index: "Jefferson, Thomas"; Dumas Malone, *Jefferson and the Rights of Man* (Boston, 1951), p. 287; Roland S. Morris, "Jefferson as a Lawyer," American Philosophical Society, *Proceedings*, LXXXVII (1944), 211–215—Attorney Jefferson had 227 cases in 1771.

[18] Malone, *DAB;* Louis B. Wright, "Thomas Jefferson and the Classics," American Philosophical Society, *Proceedings*, LXXXVII (1944), 223–233; Gilbert Chinard, "Jefferson Among the Philosophers," *Ethics,* LIII (1942–43), 255–268; Van Wyck Brooks, "Thomas Jefferson, Man of Letters," American Academy of Arts and Letters, *Academy Papers,* II (1951), 174–182; E. Millicent Sowerby, *Catalogue of the Library of Thomas Jefferson* (5 vols., Washington, 1952–59); Sowerby, "Jefferson and His Library," pp. 213–214.

He must have been a pretty fair violinist or he could not have endured to practice as much as he did, and he certainly has won praise as an architect,[19] but his attitude toward the arts was the attitude of his age. Artists were craftsmen who succeeded if their works pleasantly filled the leisure of the connoisseur by giving him something animating, interesting, attractive to contemplate.[20] Jefferson would not have understood the phrase "art for art's sake," nor could he have approved of the self-appointed Great Tormented Souls who floridly dominated the next generation's lush romanticism.

Thomas Jefferson was more inclined toward science than toward politics. He knew more of applied science, and he knew more scientists, than any of his American contemporaries. He was *the* American agricultural student of his day. For forty-seven years he belonged to the American Philosophical Society; for nearly twenty years he was its president and may have contributed more to its greatness than Benjamin Franklin.[21] Not only was his *Notes on the State of Virginia* (1784–85) a respectable contribution, but his stimulation of the researches of other men, for example, Lewis and Clark, is an influence still felt.[22] His scientific methods will still pass close scrutiny.[23] If the Revolution had failed, and if he had escaped the gallows, he would probably have been barred from public life; in the seclusion of Albemarle County, Virginia, he likely would have become the father of American agricultural chemistry.

Early in life he lost his faith, but not his morals; nevertheless, he had his children baptized in the Anglican Church, attended Anglican services, and had all of his relatives buried according to the

19 Fiske Kimball, "Jefferson and the Arts," American Philosophical Society, *Proceedings*, LXXXVII (1944), 238–245. Jefferson said he practiced the violin three hours daily for an eight-year stretch. In pre-Paganini days this expenditure of energy might have made virtuosity of even a meager talent.

20 H. M. Kallen, "The Arts and Thomas Jefferson," *Ethics*, LIII (1942–43), 269–283.

21 Charles A. Browne, "Thomas Jefferson and the Scientific Trends of His Time," *Chronica Botanica*, VIII (1944), 363–418; Daniel Joseph Boorstin, *The Lost World of Thomas Jefferson* (New York, 1948), pp. 8–26.

22 Dwight Boehm and Edward Schwartz, "Jefferson and the Theory of Degeneracy," *American Quarterly*, IX (1957), 448–453. While on the Board of Visitors of William and Mary College, Governor Jefferson helped to found the chairs of anatomy and medicine.

23 Harlow Shapley, "Notes on Thomas Jefferson as a Natural Philosopher," American Philosophical Society, *Proceedings*, LXXXVII (1944), 234–237.

Anglican rites. In Pennsylvania, he was Unitarian; in Virginia, Episcopalian; and in the District of Columbia, who-knows-what. He ended as a deist after enduring a lifetime of fierce, intemperate, even slanderous attacks on his infidelity from many who became Unitarians, that is, deists, themselves. According to his home-made theology, Saint Paul corrupted Christianity to prove Christ divine. Better, he said, that men should apply reason to the Book of Nature in order to discover the laws of God.[24]

This remarkable virtuoso, nationally honored for the virtues of the intellect before the time of the establishment of the federal government, was a talented connoisseur of all the arts. In some he had a taste and dexterity which approached professional standards. He was neither pure scientist nor pure philosopher.[25]

IV

Thomas Jefferson's prefederal political career was the career of a man who hated contention, who was better at counsel than at execution, who was better in committee than on the floor. As the scribe of Independence he had drawn together the feelings of his fellow countrymen into superb but prudently circumscribed prose. He gained no glory as revolutionary governor of Virginia and, indeed, barely escaped the censure of the Virginia legislature at the end of his term. The famous legislative reforms in Virginia, which were enacted under his leadership, were merely reforms of the squirearchy.

His mild and conversationally uncontentious liberalism, and his diplomatic experience as minister to France, made him seem the natural choice for Secretary of State in President George Washington's new administration. Jefferson accepted the appointment reluctantly and assumed the office in March, 1790. At that moment in the story, the President and the Secretary were cordial friends, but their relations chilled in the late 1790's. When the new Secretary of State came to New York, he was walking on to a political battle-

[24] Malone, *DAB;* George H. Knoles, "The Religious Ideas of Thomas Jefferson," *Mississippi Valley Historical Review,* XXX (1943), 187–204; Herbert W. Schneider, "The Enlightenment in Thomas Jefferson," *Ethics,* LIII (1942–43), 246–254; Henry Wilder Foote, *The Religion of Thomas Jefferson* (Boston, 1960).
[25] Dr. Jefferson held the following honorary degrees: D.C.L., William and Mary, 1783; LL.D., Yale, 1786; LL.D., Harvard, 1788. Malone, *Jefferson the Virginian,* pp. 422, 422 n. Any list of his "scientific" accomplishments will mainly comprise items of inventive genius rather than advances in pure science.

field. He did not take a place in the array immediately. Indeed, as late as 1792, he still recoiled from direct political action.

An opposition had emerged in the Congress, led by Representative James Madison of Virginia. It was hotly opposed to the Treasury policies of Alexander Hamilton. Madison and John Beckley, the Clerk of the House, carried the antiadministration banner. From early 1791 they had Jefferson's sympathy, but he did not create their faction. It recognized and claimed him as its leader. Not until 1796, during the fierce wrangle over the Jay Treaty, did Jefferson become the public partisan head of antifederalism. The notion that Jefferson founded the opposition was an invention of the Hamiltonians, to suit their short-range vote-getting purposes.[26]

True, Jefferson disapproved of Hamilton's policies because Hamilton influenced the Congress to favor finance and commerce over farming. By late 1792 he was so stirred that he could describe Hamilton's career to the uneasy Washington as "a tissue of machinations against the liberty of the country," but the explanation of the history of the Federalist period as a struggle between Jefferson and Hamilton is useful only as what Broadus Mitchell called "a sociological shorthand." It was Madison and Beckley who organized the group that later made Jefferson its idol. The squire of Monticello has been sketched as a shadowy *provocateur* from 1790 to 1795, holding other men's coats while they smote the enemy in the public prints, but this picture too is a Hamiltonian caricature. Only twice did Jefferson urge men to take up their quills and stab Hamilton, and in each instance it was in a public debate on a question of deep importance. Jefferson was always available at the elbows of the front-rank anti-Hamiltonians, but he did not march in public. The famous liberal sentiments which are so venerated by modern democrats were—after 1776—all written in private letters, not for publication. Even during the campaign of 1800 he stayed at Monticello to supervise the baking of bricks, while letting his political views filter out to the public through letters to his friends.[27]

[26] Joseph Charles, *The Origins of the American Party System, Three Essays* (Williamsburg, 1956), pp. 74–90. On Madison's political leadership in these years, see Irving Brant, *James Madison, Father of the Constitution* (Indianapolis, 1950).

[27] Jefferson to Washington, Sept. 9, 1792, Gertrude Atherton (ed.), *A Few of Hamilton's Letters* (New York, 1903), pp. 162, 175; Broadus Mitchell, "The Secret of Alexander Hamilton," *Virginia Quarterly Review*, XXIX (1953), 595–609; Noble E. Cunningham, Jr., "John Beckley: An Early American Party

Thomas Jefferson was never a flaming radical. His environment made it impossible, although there is a monumental Jeffersonian mythology which makes him out a doctrinaire democrat. In truth, he believed in getting what seemed best for the public good with as little painful acrimony and criticism as possible. He had no oratorical talent as a crowd pleaser and he never made a speech that brought cheers. The energy and admiration of his friends, not his own qualities of leadership, put him in the White House.

If the French Revolution had not caused a recanvass of fundamental libertarian principles, he and his supporters probably could not have pulled off the electoral coup of 1800. Nor was his election a victory for infidel rationalism. It was the counterattack of theologically conservative farmers against the Federalists' aristocratic contempt for America's sunburned agricultural drudges. They thought they were voting for electors, or assemblymen who would choose electors, who would favor Thomas Jefferson, a Whiggish moderate, whose only controversial publications had been the Declaration of Independence and the Virginia Statute for Religious Freedom long, long before. And they were right.

V

Thomas Jefferson never wrote a formal comprehensive treatise of political philosophy.[28] His views were expressed in parts—in the Declaration of Independence, in his *Notes on Virginia*, his arguments for legal reform in Virginia, the Kentucky Resolutions of 1798 (the authorship of which was unknown when he was elected), inaugural addresses, messages to the Congress, and, most of all, in private correspondence and conversation. Friends and enemies, with little public help from him, pushed him forward to accept the Federalists' label which tagged him as the chief symbol of opposition to Hamiltonian Federalism. Liberty, not democracy, was the

---

Manager," *William and Mary Quarterly*, Third Series, XIII (1956), 41–45; Philip Marsh, "Jefferson and Journalism," *Huntington Library Quarterly*, IX (1946), 209–212.

28 When Adrienne Koch writes, "he is, I believe, the greatest philosopher of domestic society and government in the modern world," her heart rules her head unless she means he was the greatest man who attempted philosophy in modern times. Adrienne Koch, "Power and Morals and the Founding Fathers," *Review of Politics*, XV (1953), 472.

key word in his sometimes inconsistent political talk and correspondence.[29]

When faced by a political problem, he went to printed classical
and modern sources for solutions which harmonized with his broad
political experience and observation. He can properly be called a
professional scholar of legal history and of the political history of
the seventeenth century, but his historical method was utilitarian
and servile. It was not used for pure understanding and liberal
learning.[30] Theoretical treatises which could not be applied immediately to concrete and present questions had little appeal for
him. His intellectual pedigree included the Epicureans; the Stoics;
a purely human Jesus Christ; John Locke; the Scottish common-
sense philosophers; Adam Smith; Henry St. John, Viscount Boling-
broke; Henry Home, Lord Kames; and Dugald Stewart. Because the
French *philosophes* venerated some of the same masters, Jefferson
was at ease when he talked with them in France.[31] In a sense,
Jefferson's outlook in 1801 was reactionary. He consistently pressed
for a return to the pure republicanism of the years of the American
Revolution.[32]

How much his mind owed to France is a fair question. His
Commonplace Book shows his views were pretty well formed long
before the French Revolution. The only French author who was
extensively quoted in it was Charles Secondat de Montesquieu, but
Jefferson only copied out the parts he already agreed with. No
doubt his residence in France broadened his political outlook and,
at the same time, stiffened his repugnance to monarchy, aristocracy,
land monopoly, and urbanism. What he saw in France alerted him

[29] A good explanation of the difficulty of defining Jeffersonian democracy is in
Russell Amos Kirk, "Jefferson and the Faithless," *South Atlantic Quarterly*, XL
(1941), 220–227.

[30] Sowerby, *Catalogue.*

[31] Adrienne Koch, *The Philosophy of Thomas Jefferson* (New York, 1943).
There is a theory that Jefferson owed something to the thinking of Robert
Bellarmine, whose views he is said to have learned from Robert Filmer's attempted refutations of Bellarmine in his *Patriarcha.* Jefferson owned two copies
of *Patriarcha,* but there is no proof that he read it, nor did he mention it in his
writings, at least not as late as 1789. Sowerby, *Catalogue,* III, 11–12; *Papers of
Jefferson,* I–XII.

[32] David Savile Muzzey, *Thomas Jefferson* (New York, 1918), p. 133, says:
"Jefferson's 'democracy' was based less on the reading of Rousseau than on the
behavior of George III."

to the necessity for certain political safeguards to guarantee and to preserve agrarian republicanism.[33] But he remained more Whig than *philosophe.*

Jefferson's faith in reason, education, and the future of America was fixed, but his procedures were adjustable. Unlike most of his contemporaries, he had a constitutional theory of change—"the earth," he said, "always belongs to the living." His political thought was a search for intellectual props for the democratic republican state. Such thinking is the method of an eclectic utilitarian rather than the method of a political philosopher. Because he was optimistically working for something new in the world's limitless future, his philosophical affirmations were necessarily a little indefinite. But certainly he was no doctrinaire.[34] He studied history to learn the traps into which Great Britain had fallen. From his study he concluded that all had gone wrong since the Norman Conquest. Studying the age before the Norman Conquest, he thought he discovered an Anglo-Saxon utopia, an antifeudal utopia, which might be re-established in North America by directed progress toward the perfection of the past.[35] Although he was a materialist in science, he accepted the notion of moral responsibility in man. Because he erroneously assumed that all men were as interested in public concerns as he was,[36] he believed the United States could be as perfect as King Alfred's England, if every child were taught history as Thomas Jefferson understood it.

By a careful selection of his most liberal remarks, a specious case can be constructed to support a Jeffersonian anarchism, or something near it. The people, he said, if they had the proper education

33 R. R. Palmer, "A Neglected Work: Otto Vossler on Jefferson and the Revolutionary Era," *William and Mary Quarterly,* Third Series, XII (1955), 462–471. Vossler's work appears as Beiheft 17 of *Historischen Zeitschrift,* as *Die amerikanischen Revolutionsideale in ihrem Verhältnis zu den europäischen: Untersuch an Thomas Jefferson* (München, 1929). Both Jefferson's influence and the intellectual character of the Revolution seem to have been overrated by Vossler.

34 Charles Maurice Wiltse, *The Jeffersonian Tradition in American Democracy* (Chapel Hill, 1935), especially passages on pp. 5, 38, 51, 90, 177; Charles, *Origins of the Party System,* pp. 75–80.

35 H. Trevor Colbourn, "Thomas Jefferson's Use of the Past," *William and Mary Quarterly,* Third Series, XV (1958), 56–70. Jefferson tried to promote the study of his historical interpretation by preparing a simplified grammar of Anglo-Saxon.

36 Koch, *Philosophy of Jefferson.*

and the correct public information, were the only sure reliance for
the preservation of liberty. A rebellion every twenty years might be
a good thing. Constitutions and laws should periodically expire.
"The tree of liberty must be refreshed from time to time with the
blood of patriots and tyrants. It is it's [sic] natural manure."[37] No
men were congenitally of the governing or the governed classes. The
Constitution must be changed only by amendment, not by interpretation. He even exceeded Locke in toleration, because he believed
ridicule would kill opinions which were morally harmful to society.
And, finally, there is the classic, much-quoted, but not authentic
aphorism, "that government is best which governs least."

All of these politically relaxed apothegms can be matched by
seemingly antagonistic opinions and legislative proposals: tax-
supported schools, public libraries, and dispensaries, subsidized
newspaper circulation, subdivision of great landholdings and the
legal frustration of land speculators by geometrically proportional
taxation, a literacy test for voting, a national transport system. He
did not believe in simple, direct government, but wished for a sharp
separation of powers and difficult methods of amending constitutions. Some of his views on the vigor of the powers of the President,
written or spoken privately to George Washington during the
1790's, would have surprised his followers if they had been published.[38]

The apparent paradox can be reconciled by remembering that
liberty was his navigating star, even though there were cloudy
nights in his career when he steered in another direction. He did
not fear any act of the state except encroachment on civil liberty.
Civil liberty comprised those rights guaranteed in the several American bills of rights which were drawn and ratified between 1776 and
1791. He would support any other use of that political power and
authority which had been *delegated* by constitutional compact, if it
seemed for the common good, and if it did not limit civil liberty.[39]
This liberalism had a strong agrarian color, which limits its rele-

[37] Jefferson to W. S. Smith, Nov. 13, 1787, *Papers of Jefferson*, XII, 356. He
could not free his slaves because he was in debt. Virginia law would not allow
him to injure his creditors by manumitting his assets.
[38] Elisha P. Douglass, *Rebels and Democrats* (Chapel Hill, 1955) ; Frank P.
Bourgin and Charles E. Merriam, "Jefferson as a Planner of National Resources,"
Ethics, LIII (1942–43) , 284–292.
[39] A good analysis is Julian P. Boyd, "Thomas Jefferson and the Police State,"
North Carolina Historical Review, XXV (1948) , 233–253.

vance to the problems of a later industrial society. When he spoke
of the people as the guardians of liberty, he meant farmers, who
comprised nearly the whole people of the United States. City mobs
were easily corruptible by largesse from the public funds. Landowning farmers were unlikely to tax themselves in order to corrupt
themselves. Like the several varieties of physiocrats, he opposed
mercantilism, and his high opinion of Adam Smith's *Wealth of
Nations*—"of money and commerce . . . the best book . . ."—
suggests Smith as the source of his opposition. In sum, he thought if
land were fairly distributed, and the business community (meaning
the Federalists) could be prevented from manipulating the economy in its own interest, liberty was safe.[40]

His thinking had already contributed to the form of the United
States. His pamphlet *A Summary View* (1774) was among the first
by a native American to forecast sharply the division of power and
authority now found in our federal arrangement. By interpretation
or misinterpretation, the implicit theory of state nullification of
federal law, as written in his then anonymous "Kentucky Resolutions" of 1798, was to have catastrophic consequences long after his
death. As a social-contract theorist, he believed the state of nature
to be a state of peace. Applying this theory to international relations, he concluded that war was unnatural, peace natural. Therefore, he had sought and would continue to seek peace by every
means possible.[41]

Jefferson would have been more than human if he had always
practiced what he preached. In private life he showed a certain
meanness of spirit by carefully recording much of the derogatory
gossip he heard about his political rivals and enemies, and having
the manuscript bound as a literary monument to the difficulties of
his cause. He also privately slandered his opponents by ungrounded
accusations of monarchism. As a public official, at one time or other
he supported or countenanced loyalty oaths for those of doubtful
fidelity to the Revolution and internment camps for political
suspects, drafted a bill of attainder, championed a peace process of
outlawry (there being no process of extradition of fugitives), urged

40 Richard Hofstadter, *The American Political Tradition and the Men Who
Made It* (New York, 1958), pp. 26–42, analyzes, *inter alia*, Jefferson's agrarian
liberalism. On Adam Smith, Jefferson to Norvell, June 11, 1807, A. A. Lipscomb
et al. (eds.), *The Writings of Thomas Jefferson* (20 vols., Washington, 1904–5),
XI, 223.

41 Anthony M. Lewis, "Jefferson's *Summary View* as a Chart of Political
Union," *William and Mary Quarterly*, Third Series, V (1948), 34–51.

prosecutions for seditious libel, left himself open to charges of unconstitutional search and seizure, censored reading, and rated pro-
spective professors according to their political orthodoxy.[42] Of these
lapses it can be said that they were in character for a man who so
admired seventeenth-century Whiggery. He was never committed to
the tyrannical side of his opponents, he aided the victory of liberty,
and his abstract and formal teachings became the enduring positions while his concrete departures from his own principles were
temporary.

On the immediate problems facing the union in the year of his
inauguration as President, he appears to have joined with Edmund
Pendleton and John Taylor of Caroline in a proposal to amend the
federal Constitution (published in Richmond in October, 1801)
which would have prohibited the re-election of the President, have
given the Congress the appointment of judges and ambassadors,
have shortened the terms of senators or have made them removable
by their constituents, have prevented the appointment of judges
and members of the Congress to other offices, have made judges
removable by vote of the Congress, and have limited the federal
borrowing power.[43]

The proposals to "reform" the Constitution were not the proposals of the library politician. They were the reactions of Virginia
Republicans as they looked back in anger at the Federalist policies
which enacted the Hamiltonian fiscal program and the Alien and
Sedition Acts. If the Republicans had remained in the minority for
another decade or so, we would have heard more about these
propositions.

VI

The lanky lord of Monticello came to Washington in November,
1800, to wait out the electoral vote. He called on John Adams and
soothed the rude and angry loser, who wore his defeat like a knife

42 Jefferson's departures from his libertarian creed are meticulously documented in Leonard W. Levy, *Jefferson & Civil Liberties: The Darker Side*
(Cambridge, Mass., 1963) ; on the extent of monarchism in the Federalist party,
see D. H. Fischer, *The Revolution of American Conservatism: The Federalist
Party in the Era of Jeffersonian Democracy* (New York, 1965) , pp. 22–25.

43 H. H. Simms, *The Life of John Taylor* (Richmond, 1932) , p. 100. The
proposed amendments would also have required House concurrence in treaties
concerning war, peace, commerce, and appropriations, have listed powers prohibited to the Congress, and have more sharply drawn the line between state and
federal power.

in the ribs, by blaming the outcome of the election on the unpopularity of Adams' enemies in the Federalist party. Jefferson spent the
winter in "Mayfair in the mud," which he had helped to lay out, as
a lodger in Conrad and McMunn's boardinghouse—$15 a week,
American Plan—where he modestly dined at the chilly foot of the
long table, far from a seat of honor near the fire.[44]

At noon on March 4, 1801, Jefferson took the oath of office in
purposely, almost ostentatiously, simple circumstances intended to
emphasize the Republican "revolution." He walked to the unfinished Capitol accompanied by two of Adams' cabinet officers, a
handful of representatives, and a battery of Maryland militia
gunners. In the Senate chamber he took his place with Vice-
President Aaron Burr, the American Catiline who could never
quite pull off any of his imperial schemes, and with cousin John
Marshall, the Chief Justice and Jefferson's inveterate but honorable
political foe. It was an interesting tableau. Each of the three men
deeply distrusted the other two. There were two noticeable ab-
sences. John Adams had driven out of town into retirement by
daybreak. Theodore Sedgwick, the arch-Federalist Speaker of the
House, stayed away in fuming exasperation.

Probably no American presidential inaugural address has been
heard by fewer people. The hall was packed, but Jefferson spoke his
happily phrased remarks in a voice barely above a whisper. Perhaps
only Marshall and Burr heard it all; however, printed copies were
immediately distributed to the strained listeners.

The speech stated the Republican principles of that instant:
justice for all, friendship with all nations and "entangling alliances
with none," the support of state governments as "the surest bul-
warks against antirepublican tendencies," the preservation of the
strength of the union, "a jealous care of the right of election,"
majority rule, economy in government, individualism, payment of
the public debts, "encouragement of agriculture and of commerce
as its handmaid," dissemination of information, freedom of religion, press, and person. The cooled-off ex-democrat John Marshall
must have winced internally at the President's remark, "I believe

[44] For the electoral contest of 1800–1801, see John C. Miller, *The Federalist
Era, 1789–1801* (New York, 1960); Claude Bowers, *Jefferson in Power* (Boston,
1936); Dumas Malone, *Jefferson and the Ordeal of Liberty* (Boston, 1963).
Jefferson lived at Conrad and McMunn's from Nov. 27, 1800, until Mar. 19,
1801.

CHAPTER 2

The United States in 1801

THE Americans were a few people in a vast space, but they were certainly prolific. They had increased in number by more than a quarter since 1790, and they were to grow in the same proportion between 1800 and 1810—from five and a third million to seven and a quarter million. About a sixth of the Americans were slaves. Subtracting the slaves from the free, we can deduce that the burden of occupying and governing 888,000 square miles (soon to be doubled by the Louisiana Purchase) was carried by two million free adults, aided by half a million dark-skinned drudges. They were joined by a few immigrants. Could the job be done? We know it was, but detached observers then would have had reason to be pessimistic about their prospects for success in unity.[1]

It takes an effort of the imagination to conjure up the feel of so remote a time and culture as early nineteenth-century America. Outside the few towns, according to season the roving eye fell on the green, gold, and drab of farm fields, the gaudy flicker of orchard fruits, and, everywhere, woodland colors—green or scarlet, or winter's wood. The nose sniffed the organic, yeasty smells of farmyards and barns, the sweet fragrance of new-cut timothy and clover, the

[1] United States Bureau of the Census, *Historical Statistics of the United States, Colonial Times to 1957* (Washington, 1960), pp. 7, 8, 12. Because of the opportunity afforded by the Peace of Amiens, the year 1801 saw the heaviest flow of immigration of many years before or after. Marcus L. Hansen, *The Atlantic Migration, 1607–1860* (Cambridge, Mass., 1940), pp. 68–70. Carl F. Wittke, *We Who Built America* (New York, 1939), p. 101, estimated 250,000 immigrants, 1790–1820; this might allow a guess at fewer than 10,000 yearly, 1800–1812.

damp, fresh smells of forests, woodsmoke, the weak perfume of wild flowers. From sunburn, sweat trickles, insect bites, and frost-chapped knuckles, every man knew that he, his skin, and his surroundings were one. The range of tastes was narrow: salty or smoked meats, rare natural sweets, bitter coffee and tea, and the emphatic warmth of strong drink or the sour foaming of small beer. Rural sounds were few: animal cries, ax blows, birdcalls, children's voices, and always the wind in the trees, sometimes provoked to gales and blizzards. The forests receded steadily before the ax. The people mistakenly believed the climate had changed considerably and for the better as the great wooded tracts of the eastern seaboard disappeared.[2]

Only one of each twenty-five Americans lived in a city, that is, 202,000 out of 5 million. The cities were really but small towns. It was an even chance the rare town dweller lived in a center with a population somewhere between five and twenty-five thousand. Not yet had American industrialism betrayed President Thomas Jefferson's vision of a farmers' culture. The leading cities, with their population totals, were:

	1800	1810	1820
Boston	25,000	33,000	43,000
New York	60,000	96,000	124,000
Philadelphia	69,000	92,000	113,000
Baltimore	26,000	36,000	63,000
Charleston	20,000	25,000	25,000
New Orleans	—	17,000	27,000

2 Ralph Hall Brown, *Mirror for Americans: Likeness of the Eastern Seaboard, 1810* (New York, 1943), pp. 13–22, and *Historical Geography of the United States* (New York, 1948), pp. 93–96. The American insistence on an improvement of the climate was more patriotic than scientific. The subject of human relationships with the environment of the past has produced a considerable literature. A useful introduction is Paul B. Sears, "Climate and Civilization," in Harlow Shapley (ed.), *Climatic Change: Evidence, Causes, and Effects* (Cambridge, Mass., 1963), pp. 35–50. In the same collection, John H. Conover, "Climatic Changes as Interpreted from Meteorological Data," pp. 222–230, distinguishes between "real" and "apparent" temperature changes over a long period. Botanical changes alter local wind velocities and transpirational cooling, but the study is difficult owing to the lack of homogeneity in the data, which, of necessity, were recorded at different times and places by different observers using differing instruments in different ways. Judging from C. E. P. Brooks, *Climate Through the Ages* (New York, 1949), pp. 342–356, the only truly reliable studies of climatological history of the lands in the present United States concern the far western states and generalize on periods of five hundred to a thousand years.

Obviously, the southern cities were languishing. Baltimore, which is nowadays consciously southern for the tourist trade, belonged to the middle states in political orientation and economic interest.

The commercial wealth of Boston, just swelling in the 1790's, was to allow rebuilding in the next twenty-five years. Polyglot New York had a Negro population of one-ninth, of whom two-thirds were slaves. Philadelphia, the heterogeneous cultural center, compared favorably with any English out-port.[3] A seventeen-year-old visitor had celebrated its gridiron street plan,

> Hail, Philadelphia, I now behold
> Thy regularity, as I've been told,
>
> . . . .
>
> The streets are wide, and in a line direct,
> The angles right where they do intersect.[4]

Baltimore was a boom town with a bustling port and hustling shippers.

Municipal governments had many regulations and collected many fees, if all their ordinances were enforced, but many municipal responsibilities were exercised by private citizens, or not at all. Philadelphia had public sewerage and water systems by 1801. Most towns had organized volunteer fire departments. And most of them smelled terrible, especially during hot dry spells, when garbage and excrement accumulated in the rat-infested, pig-ridden streets.

Washington, now a city of magnificent distances, was then a new, raw, unfinished, swampy village of vexing vistas. There were five clusters of mean houses, separated by broad, stump-blocked boulevards, in which wagons sank hub-deep in mud or raised choking clouds of dust. Few of the citizens could afford to meet the requirements of the building code, which demanded exterior masonry walls between thirty-five and forty feet high; President Jefferson waived the rule in 1801. The Capitol, its pillars prone, had barely enough finished space in which to accommodate the Congress. Oliver Wolcott, Jr., who had been John Adams' Secretary of the Treasury, despised the place. "The people are poor," he wrote to Mrs.

[3] John Allen Krout and Dixon Ryan Fox, *The Completion of Independence, 1790–1830* (New York, 1944), pp. 5–29; Brown, *Mirror for Americans*, pp. 42, 270.

[4] *Ibid.*, p. 37 n.

Wolcott, "and as far as I can judge, they live like fishes, by eating each other."[5]

The Congress had all of the glorious highlands of the East to choose from, but the assumption deal dictated a southern site. George Washington, deputized by the Congress for the purpose, selected the head of navigation of the Potomac River, where nature provided a humid river bottom with saucerlike sides to concenter the summer heat, surrounded by low rises which were too low for natural splendor, but high enough to impede the movement of air. According to Margaret Bayard Smith's vivacious letters and reminiscences, the most admirable features of the landscape at the moment were the figures in it: "Never were there a plainer set of men, and I think I may add a more virtuous and enlightened one, than at present forms our administration."[6]

This proves only that Mrs. Smith was a very cheerful woman. It is hard to see how life in Washington then could have been endured. Members of the smaller executive branch of the government huddled west of Tiber Creek, while the larger legislative group gathered around the Capitol in shabby boardinghouses without privacy. Capitol Hill was a travesty of a New England town, with the Capitol as its meetinghouse—for both state and church—and the houses for transient legislators as its village settlement. The ties of true community life were lacking. Its institutions were deliberately designed to make contention easy by encouraging opposing interests to neutralize each other, fraternity was impossible, and a heterogeneous band of comparative strangers lived in forced intimacy whether they liked it or not. The Congress was a true microcosm of the United States, but nowhere else in the country did antipathetic spokesmen have to spend the greater part of every day together, perhaps even as messmates and roommates. Not only were the

5 George Gibbs, *Memoirs of the Administrations of Washington and John Adams* (2 vols., New York, 1846), II, 377. The most recent description of life in Washington in the early nineteenth century is James Sterling Young, *The Washington Community, 1800–1808* (New York, 1966). Its most important contribution is a convincing picture of the ruling elements as a single group.

6 In 1790, the rivalry of northern and southern states for the government capital was ended when Jeffersonians supported Hamilton's program for federal assumption of state debts and Hamilton's followers in return voted to locate the capital on the Potomac. Gaillard Hunt (ed.), *The First Forty Years of Washington Society* (New York, 1906), p. 29. These are memoirs of life in Washington as seen by Margaret Bayard Smith (Mrs. Samuel Harrison Smith), wife of the editor of the administration paper *The National Intelligencer*.

economic and political interests of the nation drawn to a common center but also the animosities and acerbities.[7] But, of course, the good-natured Mrs. Smith had a house of her own.

II

The intellectual life of the United States was a minor consideration of its people. As Benjamin Henry Latrobe wrote to Constantin de Chasseboeuf, Comte de Volney, ". . . with us the labor of the hand has precedence over that of the mind."[8] This, of course, was stark necessity, but there was a cerebral climate, so to speak, affected by the eighteenth century's ideas of benevolence, morality, and classical simplicity, compounded with what was thought of as a primitive or a purified Christianity.

Americans imported most of their arts and ideas from England, whether medical, scientific, artistic, or literary, although they were on the edge of declaring intellectual independence. After the French revolutionary attacks on persons, property, and religion, a great many of the farmers of the United States were in a conservative reaction. Most people experienced this reaction as a great fundamentalist religious revival, almost a Protestant Counter Reformation, which, curiously enough, coincided with the inauguration of the "infidel" Jefferson.[9]

There was more enthusiasm for education as the method of perfecting man than there was achievement. Education was not yet secularized. Few people, except for the President and his circle, dreamed of separating sacred and profane learning at any level. Professors were nearly all clergymen, Federalists, and orthodox in their opposition to Jefferson, Unitarianism, deism, skepticism, scriptural criticism, and religious equality. Their political and scientific influence was slight. They were not riding the crest of the wave of the future.[10]

---

[7] Young, *Washington Community*, pp. 87–95.

[8] Quoted in Henry Adams, *A History of the United States of America During the Administrations of Jefferson and Madison* (9 vols., New York, 1889–90), I, 130.

[9] Robert Ernest Spiller *et al.*, *Literary History of the United States* (3 vols., New York, 1948), I, 122–125; Merle Curti, *The Growth of American Thought* (New York, 1943), pp. 185–204.

[10] Krout and Fox, *Completion of Independence*, pp. 179–184; Joseph Dorfman, *The Economic Mind in American Civilization* (5 vols., New York, 1946–59), II, 503–506.

Samuel Miller, a contemporary critic of the quality of American intellectual life at the turn of the century, rated its quality low because of the lack of money and because of the lack of leisure. One of the most articulate critics of education was Noah Webster, the dictionary man. He praised little except the literacy rate of New England and the quality of American political writing. He said higher learning was "superficial, to a shameful degree." The neglect of science he also blamed on the lack of leisure and money. American libraries were next to contemptible. The people were intelligent enough—they just lacked the means. The self-made American rich man "avoids a man of learning as you would a tiger."[11] But Miller and Webster were cultural primitivists looking backward with longing to an age of aristocratic learning and princely patronage. The American republic had the highest standard of literacy in the world—no accomplishment to be minimized— and had a higher proportion of first-rate minds engaged in statecraft than any other country.

American creative writing was in its childhood, but it was a vigorous infant, anxious to exert its independent will. Like all babes, it was beginning to eye, touch, smell, and taste what was closest to hand. There were as yet no full-grown, first-rate American creative writers. In Jefferson's first year as President, the big three of the next generation were but boys. Washington Irving was eighteen years old, James Fenimore Cooper eleven, and William Cullen Bryant seven.

The Hartford Wits (or Connecticut Wits, or Yale Poets, or Connecticut Choir) had an undeserved popularity from 1780 to 1800, from their poetical, or, occasionally, doggerel work, some of it scoffing, because of alleged Frenchiness, at the aspirations which infused the Declaration of Independence. They had pretty well petered out by 1800, as their members devoted themselves to their several professions, businesses, and services. Timothy Dwight was the coldly reactionary president of Yale; Noah Webster was deep in lexicography and journalism; David Humphreys and Joel Barlow went abroad in diplomacy and business. Barlow, the radical among

11 Samuel Miller, "A Sketch of the Revolution and Improvements in Science, Arts, and Literature. Reprinted from . . . *Brief Retrospect of the Eighteenth Century* (1803) ," with introduction and notes by L. H. Butterfield, *William and Mary Quarterly*, Third Series, X (1953) , 624–627; Webster to Priestley, 1800, Harry R. Warfel (ed.) , *Letters of Noah Webster* (New York, 1953) , pp. 210–213.

them, more interested in materialism than in poetry, expanded his "Vision of Columbus" (1787) to the much longer and somewhat gassy *Columbiad* (1807),[12] only to become the butt of critics.

The truest poet of the age, fiercely democratic Philip Freneau, author of "The Indian Burying Ground" and "To a Wild Honeysuckle," was still rated somewhat below several of the Hartford Wits by his contemporaries, but they were probably evaluating his Jeffersonian politics rather than his verses. Freneau, a classmate of James Madison, Aaron Burr, and Hugh Henry Brackenridge at Princeton, could and did earn his living as translator, printer, editor, or master of a merchant ship. He did not take his poetry very seriously.[13] George Washington had called him "that rascal," and Irving later called him "a barking cur," but Jefferson said he saved the Constitution when it was "galloping fast into monarchy." All three exaggerated, but they proved that Freneau had more than poetry on his mind. He contributed "a poet's share" to the founding of the republic.[14] He was a romanticist, influenced by the same ideas that influenced his English opposite numbers, but he was original, and in idea and image often anticipated the English romantics. His vice was overproduction, but he gave up poetical polemics when Jefferson's inauguration assured the cause on which he had spent so much ink and nervous energy. Unsentimental, unfashionable, he was, for maturity and promise, the only American poet of 1801 who was really worthy of the name.[15]

If all American fiction in circulation on Jefferson's inauguration day were erased by some chemical mischance, not much of it would be missed. Only one novelist of the day—not William Brown Hill, not Susanna Rowson, not Hannah Foster, not Charles Brockden Brown, but only Hugh Henry Brackenridge—would leave a gap, and he would be missed, not for literary artistry, but for his picture of rough-and-rowdy daily life in America.

The others, except Brown, were diluted, synthetic Samuel Rich-

[12] Spiller, *Literary History*, I, 162–168; Theodore A. Zunder and Stanley Thomas Williams, "Joel Barlow," *Dictionary of American Biography* (11 vols., New York, 1927–58). Other printings are in twenty volumes with two supplementary volumes.

[13] Russel Blaine Nye, *The Cultural Life of the New Nation, 1776–1830* (New York, 1960), pp. 120, 259–264; Lewis Leary, *That Rascal Freneau, A Study in Literary Failure* (New Brunswick, 1941), pp. 318–319, 338.

[14] *Ibid.*, pp. 3–4, 363–364.

[15] Nye, *Cultural Life*, pp. 259–261; Spiller, *Literary History*, I, 169–175.

ardsons, exploiting the sure-fire theme of the damsel in distress in a cruel, cruel world. Brown stands a little apart. He was the first American to try to support himself entirely by creative writing. (It did not work.) He was the only American who can be fairly called a professional novelist before Cooper. His *Wieland* (1798), a study of murder and religious hallucination, has been called his best work, but *Ormond* (1799) and *Arthur Mervyn* (1799–1800) were eaten up by the same fright-seeking readership that devoured the English Gothic novels. *Edgar Huntley* (1799) was the first American detective story. Thereafter, Brown turned to love stories (*Clara Howard* and *Jane Talbot,* both 1801), but he quit novelizing in 1804. He obviously had the gift, but just as Freneau force-fed his fire of talent to save the country from the Federalists, so Brown wrote hurriedly to pay for provender.[16]

Brown's very first book was *Alcuin; or, The Rights of Women* (1798), an attempt to popularize William Godwin's radical feminism. Not even Brown's best friends were interested. Brown himself kept up with the latest in science, manners, customs, agrarianism, and literary criticism. In a later generation he might have been an influential literary editor, a powerful critic, even a columnist. His aim was to decide what in American life was peculiarly American, but he never found the satisfactory criterion by which to measure.[17]

Hugh Henry Brackenridge, a western Pennsylvania lawyer and politician, worked out his long *Modern Chivalry* from 1792 until 1815, seriatim. John Quincy Adams, who would have liked to be a novelist, praised Brackenridge as a legitimate heir of Miguel Cervantes. In the adventures of Brackenridge's Captain Farrago, and his grotesque squire, Teague O'Regan, he satirized the legal profession, the clergy, education, the press, the code duello, science, and Jeffersonian agrarianism. Most of all he was concerned with how democracy worked in practice. Brackenridge was a good literary workman who nourished his rationalist mind on the classics, modeled his writing on Jonathan Swift's, and made clarity his ideal. His

16 *Ibid.,* I, 125, 177–178, 181–184; Carl Van Doren, "Fiction, I: Brown, Cooper," William P. Trent *et al.* (eds.), *The Cambridge History of American Literature* (4 vols., New York, 1917–21), I, 284–292. Charles Brockden Brown, in 1798, hinted that the Indians provided material for American writers, but a generation passed before James Fenimore Cooper began to mine that vein; Nye, *Cultural Life,* p. 244.

17 David Lee Clark, *Charles Brockden Brown, Pioneer Voice of America* (Durham, N.C., 1952), pp. 108–154.

sense of humor saved him from the cynicism that might have infected him on falling short of greatness as writer and statesman.[18]

The American theater had been an established institution since the 1750's, except for the turbulent years of the War for Independence. From 1783 to 1812, Americans wrote at least 149 plays. Except that the dramatists were rather more interested in abolition and religion than their audiences were, they faithfully reflected their country. Unlike the novelists, they focused on the American scene, because a synthetic English play could not compete with the genuine article. Their models were often French and German. Not *all* of the plays were written by the leading impresario, William Dunlap; it just seemed that way, for he wrote fully fifty of the 149, and translated and adapted many French and German plays for his American Company (1796–1805), including twelve by August Kotzebue alone. Royall Tyler had already created the stage Yankee in 1787, but by 1801 Dunlap, with his opposition to the star system, with his close attention to the details of production and stage management, bestrode the narrow theatrical world like a colossus— which he was not quite.[19]

The formal essay, as an art form, lived in newspapers, wearing what Robert Ernest Spiller called "strange patchworks of Yankee homespun with Addisonian finery." Far, far more creditable were the published and private prose writings of the statesmen, closely argued, flexibly idiomatic, passionately republican.[20]

There were about two hundred newspapers in 1801. After the Bible and the sermons, they probably had more influence on the American mind than all of the novels, plays, and essays put together. The newspaper was almost the only literature the American yeoman had time for. The tone of the press was usually bitter and often libelous. Duels between editors were common. News collecting was unsystematic and fiercely partisan. Publishers did not even think of giving lip service to the ideal of impartial reporting. Their loyalty was given without limit to their political parties.

[18] Claude Milton Newlin, *The Life and Writings of Hugh Henry Brackenridge* (Princeton, 1932), pp. 189–191, 305–307; Spiller, *Literary History*, I, 178–180.

[19] *Ibid.*, I, 184–190; Joseph Aaron Elfenbein, "American Drama, 1782–1812, as an Index to Socio-political Thought," thesis, New York University, Pub. 3444 of University Microfilms (Ann Arbor, 1951), digested in *Dissertation Abstracts*, XII (1952), 140; A. H. Quinn, "The Early Drama, 1756–1860," *Cambridge Hist. Am. Lit.*, I, 215–219, 232.

[20] Spiller, *Literary History*, I, 146–161.

Every faction of each party had its organ. The new administration in Washington favored *The National Intelligencer and Washington Advertiser,* founded in 1800. The *Port Folio,* founded in 1801 at Philadelphia, was the most sophisticated newspaper of its day. Its editor was prim, patronizing, conservative, alcoholic Joseph Dennie, who was not original or imaginative, but who was a fairly good literary critic. He printed long excerpts from British authors, and recognized William Wordsworth early. Either sloth or the bottle kept Dennie from greatness, although he was entirely confident that only the barbaric taste of the Americans kept him poor.

Architecture was still an art, governed by rule of thumb. That synthesis of scientific, engineering, mathematical, and artistic talents, which was necessary to create architectural engineering, hardly existed before 1810. After all, the nail cutter was not invented until 1777, and the circular saw did not exist until 1814. Building was wholly dependent on the skills of carpenters and masons, but it was very good. By 1800, large-scale wood framing, needed to get large interior spaces, was perfected. In its externals, American architecture paralleled European. When executed under the direction of able designers, the classical revival well fitted the needs of the young republic, and emerged as the Federal Style, which was a good expression of the best of American culture.[21]

Charles Bulfinch, nineteen years a selectman of Boston, was just in the first phase of his career. In 1800 he finished the second Harrison Gray Otis house in Boston. Benjamin Henry Latrobe was then the country's leading architect. He had just completed the building for the Bank of Pennsylvania (1798–1800), the first Greek Revival structure in America. Because of him, many American bankers are still making change and practicing their more esoteric monetary mysteries in miniature Parthenons. At the moment of Jefferson's inauguration, Latrobe was arranging to have Philadelphia's water supply moved about by steam pumps, but he was to come to Washington in the following year to help make the Capitol what it is. More than any other American he was the founder of architecture as a profession. Up in Salem, Massachusetts, a foremost domestic architect, Samuel McIntire, was at the height of his

21 Carl W. Condit, *American Building Art: The Nineteenth Century* (New York, 1960), pp. 6–7, 16, 17, 265.

powers, and was also establishing himself as the greatest of American wood carvers.[22]

The country was full of portrait painters, men of real merit, equal in all ways to their European confreres, but portraiture was rather an industry than an art. The respectable, the intellectual painting was either historico-mythologico-documentary painting or landscapes. America's only widely popular practitioner, the one-eyed John Trumbull, had temporarily abandoned painting for diplomacy, and sat in London, sifting Tory claims against the Treasury of the United States, by authority of Jay's Treaty.[23]

The current of American thought was diked-in by the environmentalism of some of the minor French *philosophes*. If the environment were perfected, progress would inexorably follow. Democracy, science, and rationalistic education were to be the tools for perfecting the environment of the American. The improvement of education required that knowledge be unlocked from the vault of dead languages. Therefore, modern languages must be taught. Science promised the most speedy liberation. Already it was at odds with orthodox theologies, a set of systems which radical leaders regarded as manacles on mankind. The almost inevitable result of applying science and classical liberalism simultaneously was ultimately to create a savagely competitive materialistic economic order, but this was hardly foreseen, because the Americans read and thought little about theoretical economics in the next two decades. Anti-intellectualism was at the moment more influential than these ideas of the environmentalists. A method of learning, an attitude of mind, called science could not be correct as conservatives saw the matter because it was promoted by adherents of democracy and deism, although anti-intellectuals, as always, used ridicule rather than analysis and evaluation.[24]

William Bartram, Quaker-bred scientist, rationalist, and quasi-

---

[22] C. A. Place, *Charles Bulfinch, Architect and Citizen* (Boston, 1925), pp. 1–168; Talbot Hamlin, "Benjamin Henry Latrobe: The Man and the Architect," *Maryland History Magazine*, XXXVII (1942), 339–345, and *Benjamin Henry Latrobe* (New York, 1955), pp. 3–167; Frank Cousins and P. M. Riley, *The Wood Carver of Salem, Samuel McIntire* (Boston, 1916), pp. 17–30.

[23] Theodore Sizer (ed.), *The Autobiography of Colonel John Trumbull, Patriot-Artist, 1756–1843* (New Haven, 1953), pp. xvi–xvii, 179 n.

[24] Curti, *American Thought*, pp. 171–184, 204–210; Dorfman, *Economic Mind*, II, 512–514.

pantheist, had traveled the southwestern states and territories in the previous decades. His *Travels* (1791) was spreading over Europe at the turn of the century (republished in Ireland, England, the Netherlands, Germany, and France), where it influenced romantic poets and helped to perpetuate the myth of the Noble Savage. Bartram trained and helped Alexander Wilson, the first distinguished American ornithologist, who began his studies in 1803, in the same year John James Audubon arrived in the country.[25]

Charles Willson Peale could as well be classed with the painters as with the scientists. He, his brother, his three sons, and two of his nieces all became notable painters. But in 1801, Peale was absorbed by his scientific museum at Philadelphia, where he displayed dioramas of mounted animals in their native habitats, arranged according to the Linnaean scheme of classification. What Peale was doing was scientific, but his exhibition sired the dime museum of later generations. The sensation of 1801 was his showing of the reconstructed skeleton of a mammoth, recovered from the swamps of New Jersey. A dinner with Peale's stoutly Jeffersonian friends celebrated the discovery, and gave the occasion for confounding Federalist scoffers by a toast to "Success to these *boney parts* in Europe."[26]

In 1800, Noah Webster was beginning his three dictionaries, one for schools, one for business offices, and the ancestor of the great unabridged. He was satirized and ridiculed for his presumption. Newspaper editors published many letters which pretended to offer newly coined words as gifts, or for sale in bulk. These lampoons were needles to prick a controversial Federalist, which proved that anti-intellectualism was bipartisan.[27]

The 1790's had heard many charges of French revolutionary infidelity and deism, but, actually, Americans were more interested in French political liberalism than in French rationalism. Nevertheless, there were two religious movements which were at once rationalist, fashionable among opinion leaders, and subversive of orthodoxy. They were Unitarianism and Universalism. The one was an

25 Ernest Earnest, *John and William Bartram* (Philadelphia, 1940), pp. 84–180.
26 Charles Coleman Sellers, *Charles Willson Peale* (2 vols., Philadelphia, 1947), II, 124–145.
27 Harry R. Warfel, *Noah Webster, Schoolmaster to America* (New York, 1936), pp. 289–294. Webster's first dictionary came out in 1806.

institutionalized deism, the other much the same except (in reaction to the dour Calvinism of the time) that it emphasized the
doctrine of universal salvation. Unitarians, in effect, said God was
too good to damn man; Universalists said man was too good to be
damned, a very comforting notion. The adherents of these movements were only a molecule of society, when compared with the tens
of thousands who were then going through the spiritual and
physical rigors of the western fundamentalist revival.[28] In 1801,
Elihu Palmer, the blind Dartmouth alumnus and ex-Baptist
preacher, was writing his *Principles of Nature* (1802), which was an
attempt to popularize natural ethics divorced from the Christian
revelation.

Materialism was more typically European than these bland and
respectable heterodoxies. Joseph Priestley, notable chemist and
Unitarian minister, was its important contemporary importer, bal-
ancing himself between deism in theology and materialism in
science. But materialism became no popular American fad. The
idea of the immortality of the soul was too attractive an idea to be
put down. Environmentalism among English-speaking Protestants
led logically to humanitarianism, a substitute for the supernatural
virtue of charity. Environmentalism, applied to social evils, was the
application of human reason to such social problems as slavery and
crime by humanely improving the environment so as to eradicate,
or at least mitigate, the evils.[29]

Not much touched by these swirling currents—at least not consciously—was the tiny Roman Catholic minority. It was chiefly an
Anglo-American minority, with small reinforcements, on the pe-
rimeter, of French and Irish. Culturally the Catholics were indis-
tinguishably American. The three marked qualities of American
Catholicism in 1801 were, first, its full membership in the Anglo-
American culture; second, the attempt—eventually successful—to
assert episcopal authority over lay trustees in ecclesiastical concerns;
and, third, its freedom from foreign intrigues, a freedom made
plain by Rome's acceptance of Bishop John Carroll for the American primacy, when nominated by the few American priests.[30]

28 Krout and Fox, *Completion of Independence*, pp. 162–175.
29 Curti, *American Thought*, pp. 155–171.
30 Thomas T. McAvoy, "The Catholic Minority in the United States, 1789–
1821," United States Catholic Historical Society, *Records and Studies*, XXXIX–
XL (1952), 33–50.

III

The American standard of material life included more of the animal necessities than a European laborer had, but primitive technology did not yet permit the full exploitation of resources. Simplicity of material life was about the only physical habit common to all parts of the nation.

At the turn of the century, Salem, Massachusetts, showed the finest examples of new urban domestic housing. The new houses were most often three-story, square, somewhat severe wooden buildings. The owners called on the woodcarvers of the local shipyards to relieve the severity. Of these carvers Samuel McIntire was the ablest. His mantels, chimney pieces, and other works have been compared favorably with those of the brothers Adam, who worked in London in the 1790's. The Derby-Crowninshield-Rogers house, built about 1800, well illustrates the best of town architecture of the time, and shows McIntire's eye for line. Elias Haskett Derby's mercantile enterprises and his privateering prizes permitted him to spend about $80,000 to build the structure, which was also a monument to McIntire's genius.[31]

Money built the stairway to the social heights. In manners, at the top of the stairs, the influence of the British aristocracy was still strong. Just as the idle English frequented Bath, so their American emulators visited spas. It was not unknown that British labels were sewn into American clothes. American hostesses lionized upper-class European visitors, whether tourists, officials, or refugees. The admiration was not returned. Beginning about 1800, English travelers' books on America showed a distaste for lower-class vulgarity, which was really part of the Englishry of the American vulgus. The coarseness and brutality of rough-and-tumble fighting, and public drunkenness, came to America with the English rural immigrant. But the more sophisticated vices of Britain and Europe were not known in the United States.[32]

Although no scientifically acceptable statistics are available, the worth of the family holdings of the American people as of about 1800 has been estimated by Henry Adams at $1,800 million, which

---

31 Cousins and Riley, *Woodcarver of Salem*, pp. 1–11, 71–80, 93–94, 102–105.

32 Krout and Fox, *Completion of Independence*, pp. 28–40; Lane Cooper, "Travelers and Observers, 1763–1846," *Cambridge Hist. Am. Lit.*, I, 202–214.

would work out to about $2,000 per five-member free family. Whatever the figure, the difference between the poorest and richest free men was much smaller than at any time since.

The avaricious American was already a stereotype of foreign critics, but it has always been impossible for Americans to outdo Europeans in rapacity and greed. Charles Maurice de Talleyrand-Périgord, perhaps the most squalidly extortionate public figure of modern history, took careful note of the American hunger for money when he visited the United States—just as fat men often comment on the obesity of passers-by. Avarice served to explain what was peculiar in America, but the Duc de La Rochefoucauld-Liancourt, from his observations of the 1790's, was kind enough to say it was not a manifestation of miserliness. Europeans were baffled, really. Americans hustled for money, not to hoard it, but to spend it liberally and to speculate audaciously. This was not the European pattern of greed. Travelers re-embarked for Europe, shaking their heads at the puzzle of an energetic people as interested in spending and risking as in getting.[33]

IV

Subsistence farming was the American way of life. American farmers worked their lands cruelly, but, although they got less yield per acre than English farmers did, they usually got more yield per man-hour, which was their necessary goal in a country short of labor. A few, very few, well-read farmers practiced a field-rotation system and knew the fertilizing value of legumes. A list of men interested in improving agriculture by scientific methods would be practically identical with a list of the leading landowning public figures. In the state of chemistry and metallurgy, there was not much they could do. The iron-covered curved plowshare was just about two years old when Jefferson became President.[34]

Most farmers conserved labor at the expense of land, neglecting fertilization, crop rotation, and selective animal breeding, even though these practices could have been adopted without much increase in the expenditure of their capital. Little could be done about insect pests and other blights, except to grumble. In six Massachusetts counties, in 1801, two-thirds of the fields were

33 Adams, *United States,* I, 164–166.
34 Krout and Fox, *Completion of Independence,* pp. 92–121.

planted in corn. The Middle States relied on wheat as their cash crop. Farmers made twenty to twenty-five bushels of corn per acre, ten to fifteen bushels of wheat, and the same yield of rye.[35]

American domestic animals were nothing to be proud of. Northern farmers usually kept one or two horses, three to six cows, seven to nine sheep, and from one to fifteen pigs. A two-hundred-acre farm in Bucks County, Pennsylvania, could support twelve cows (six of them fresh at all times), twenty sheep, ten hogs, and 120 hens and cocks. Only because American farmers ignored known principles of selective breeding, American farm animals had mostly degenerated below the quality of European imports. The only distinctive American development was the Conestoga draft horse, improved by the Germans of Pennsylvania from English stock. Animals require hay. A ten-acre hayfield in Massachusetts would produce from seven to eight and a half tons of clover or timothy.[36]

The self-containment of the rural economy required the northern farmer to practice many skills. Despite the visions of the past in the dreams of romantic agrarians, his textiles, his blacksmithing, and his carpentry were crude, and were unlikely to improve in the circumstances, the more especially because the relatively low price of land and the scarcity of labor tempted him to overexpand his holdings at a time when farm machinery was most primitive.[37]

The Land Act of 1800, drafted by William Henry Harrison with the help of Albert Gallatin, provided for the sale of minimum tracts of 320 acres—half a square mile—at a minimum price of two dollars an acre. The buyer paid at least a fourth down, and the balance in four years. There were men who voted for it who lived to regret its effect on the speculative spirit of their fellow citizens.

Southern agriculture is better known to readers because of the many exhaustive analyses of ante-bellum life. It is worth noting that the average southern acre of cotton received, in 1800, about three times the manual labor that an acre of wheat received, and twice what an acre of corn got. Generalizing roughly, four hours of work would produce a bushel of wheat, a bushel and a half of corn, or three and a quarter pounds of cotton lint. The South was in the

35 Percy W. Bidwell and J. I. Falconer, *History of Agriculture in the Northern United States, 1620–1860* (Washington, 1941), pp. 84–101. The authors make it quite clear that they are writing of Indian corn, or maize.

36 *Ibid.*, pp. 102–114.

37 *Ibid.*, pp. 115–131.

early boom stage of the cotton revolution: 3,000 bales in 1790, 73,000 bales in 1800, 178,000 bales in 1810, 272,000 bales in 1820. The expansive effect of cotton on the land and labor of the South is obvious.

Free labor, of course, was scarce. There are no adequate figures for 1801, but resident aliens were required to register in June, 1812. Ten thousand presented themselves, of whom three thousand were industrial workers of all kinds. A fourth of the industrial workers were in textile industries. One may conclude that there was a small but steady immigration from 1783, mostly to the benefit of the country's infant industries. (As for domestic help, there was more competition for servants than for jobs.) The indentured-servant system was dying. The best figures on personal income are from 1815, when wages ranged from eighty cents a day in the rural parts to a top of $1.50 in the towns. A day's work, from sun to sun, would feed a wife and four children for three days.[38] Town workers may have made up as little as 2 or 3 per cent of the population of the United States.

Although the United States had a respectable postal system (used but little as compared with the present) and a prosperous merchant fleet, it desperately needed roads and amenities for travelers. Hotels and inns served the northern traveler, but in the South he had to depend on the hospitality of the residents.[39]

The trans-Appalachian settlers were still very isolated, and as of 1801 the federal government was doing little about it. Where rivers did not run, the migrants westward followed trails which often were no more than rude paths. Privately operated toll bridges and ferries carried travelers across some of the streams. The bridges were often quite precarious, but the Cayuga Bridge in New York, which was completed in 1800, was a mile and a quarter long and could accommodate three lanes of wagon traffic. This was far from being typical. Between Monticello and the White House, Thomas Jefferson had to cross eight rivers, five of which entirely lacked either bridges or ferries. Even friendly travelers rated American roads from fair down to wretched, and ranked the inns on the same scale.

[38] Herbert Heaton, "The Industrial Immigrant in the United States, 1783–1812," American Philosophical Society, *Proceedings*, LXXXXV (1951), 519–527; Krout and Fox, *Completion of Independence*, pp. 40–46; *Niles' Weekly Register*, IX (Dec. 2, 1815), 230.

[39] Krout and Fox, *Completion of Independence*, pp. 74–90.

The beginning of the turnpikes was the only auspicious note in the life of the saddle sore American wayfarer.[40] And even the turnpikes held out no promise of good clean food and plenty of it, or of single beds, free of bedbugs.

Such crude roads depressed business. A ferryman might charge twenty-five cents for a wagon and the same for a hogshead. A Conestoga wagoner might pay ten cents a mile on a toll road. Canal rates were cheaper, but canals were very few. The business community's support of the movement to have the federal government undertake internal improvements can be easily understood when illuminated by the fact that nine dollars would pay the cost of moving a ton of goods brought three thousand miles from Europe, and another nine dollars would pay to carry it—the same ton—only thirty miles inland from the port of arrival.

Once past the Appalachian barrier, the rivers provided good transportation, but downstream only. Ninety per cent of western waterborne freight at the turn of the century went with the currents; only 10 per cent fought its way upstream. The Westerners used packhorses to move freight over crude trails unless the rivers ran where they were going. Meanwhile the Westerners waited for Robert Fulton to apply the power of vaporized water to commercial purposes. So long as the great American common market could not be exploited because of the primitive inland distribution system, inland trade had to remain merely trivial market-town trade, and the big concerns of commerce were its rolling, creaking wind-driven coastal and oceanic ships. The only important change in travel yet inaugurated by the Americans was to shift the traffic from the left to the right side of the road. The Conestoga wagoner, leading his large-muscled six-horse team, walked on their left side, perhaps because most men are right-handed. This put him on the same side as the steering wheel of the modern American automobile.[41]

Although small by European standards, American business and finance throve under the security of the commerce power and contract clauses of the Constitution, the encouragement of Alexander Hamilton's fiscal policies, and the stimulation of foreign wars. During the wars of the French Revolution, the United States had

40 B. H. Meyer et al., *History of Transportation in the United States Before 1860* (Washington, 1917), pp. 3–64.
41 *Ibid.*, pp. 65–82, 94–121; Bidwell and Falconer, *Agriculture*, pp. 132–144. A Conestoga rig, including the horses, was about sixty feet long.

been the only important neutral carrying nation. At the same time, the China trade made profits of 100 per cent per venture. Manufacturing was not yet important, nationally, in 1801; manufacturers stood lower in the social scale than the merchant shippers. In such manufacturing as there was, New England led the way with household industries, Yankee notions, and shipbuilding.[42]

The original thinking about the economy was not done in the ragged farm clearings, nor in Monticello's magnificent library, but in the cities. The five largest were all seaports; they were all culturally tied to Britain; they were all intellectual, financial, and commercial links with the Old World.

New York was the oldest and the least English of the three largest cities. The Dutch business capability seems to have been absorbed by New York's population, which had always spoken many tongues. The New Yorkers, with liberal shipping laws, were the best in the country at raising risk capital and promoting trade. Philadelphia had a longer banking experience than any other community. It dated back to Robert Morris' Bank of America (1781) and it matured during the decade of experience of serving as the home office of the first Bank of the United States, to which Philadelphians had subscribed heavily. Baltimore's population doubled in the 1790's. Its tubby freighters carried its tobacco, rye, rye whisky, and wheat down the Patapsco, bound for lesser coastal towns, or steering through the capes off soundings and outbound for distant harbors. Already Baltimore was famous for fine food and beautiful women. Charleston, with the only golf course in America, was an urbane "congeries of able families," where the servile population outnumbered the free. The rice trade and the cotton explosion were to cause South Carolina to reopen the slave trade in 1804, after a recess beginning in 1800.[43] Bostonians, as Oliver Wendell Holmes said, still thought the "Boston State-House is the hub of the solar system."[44] They sold cod to the Catholic countries, carried back the heavy wines of the Mediterranean littoral and the Atlantic islands, and built staunch ships. Marine insurance was a Boston specialty.

[42] Krout and Fox, *Completion of Independence*, pp. 47–73; Thomas Slater's cotton mill, 1798, was only the seed. Harvey Wish, *Society and Thought in America* (2 vols., New York, 1950–52) , I, 259–269.

[43] Constance McLaughlin Green, *American Cities in the Growth of the Nation* (New York, 1957) , pp. 6–25.

[44] Oliver Wendell Holmes, *The Autocrat of the Breakfast Table* (Boston, 1888) , p. 125.

After 1798, the Massachusetts Mutual Insurance Company guaranteed against losses by fire, although Philadelphia had been selling fire insurance for decades.[45]

V

What of America's place in the world? We know that in the balance of power the United States tipped the scales in the same bantamweight class with the Netherlands or Switzerland, but that evaluation is only to say that the acorn is less than the oak. The American scene, from across the ocean, was blurred by the haze of distance. The French had imagined an American utopia, but the image cracked during the French Revolution's reign of terror, as a picture window might crack in a hailstorm. Thereafter, French reactionaries hated the United States, democrats yearned for the ideal but were skeptical of the reality, and nationalists scorned the place. The fraternity of the days of Benjamin Franklin was washed away by the blood flood from the guillotine. In England the sometimes opaque liberal poet William Blake wrote:

> Tho' born on the cheating banks of Thames,
> Tho' his waters bathèd my infant limbs,
> The Ohio shall wash his stains from me:
> I was born a slave, but I go to be free.[46]

As one would expect, European tourists and officials in America disagreed among themselves. Some saw the country as utopia. Others concentrated on the Noble Savage. George Washington and Benjamin Franklin were symbols of liberty. In 1801 it was too early for them to judge Jefferson, and his only book, *Notes on the State of Virginia* (1784), was not widely known. A Swiss traveler thought the Americans, unlike some Europeans, had been wise to establish a government strong enough to preserve their liberty. There was enough European interest in America to encourage Christopher Ebeling to compile information on the United States (Hamburg, 1793–99). Priestley, fleeing his mob-burned house in England, declared New York the best place he had seen, and meditated on

45 *Ibid.*, p. 27–35.
46 John Sampson (ed.), *The Poetical Works of William Blake* (Oxford, 1905), p. 165; Dr. Richard Price, whose politics were within hailing distance of Blake's, was America's greatest European admirer, reckoning the American Revolution second only to the founding of Christianity. Spiller, *Literary History*, I, 197.

the question whether "the effect of general liberty" or other causes made for such intelligence, freedom and the astonishing absence of beggars.[47]

From this rotating kaleidoscope of foreign observation it would be hard to draw any generalization unless it be "wait and see." But a most perspicacious observer was Alexandre de Lanautte, Comte d'Hautrive, a French spy in the late 1790's who said the people were "neither admirable nor detestable." He noticed how the frontiersmen were narrowed in their outlook by their backbreaking drudgery. The United States, he thought, was not yet a nation, but "its progressive growth . . . before a century has elapsed will have changed the . . . colonial system of the universe and the relative position of all civilized society."[48] One may doubt that the French Foreign Ministry was keen on getting century-long forecasts, but Hautrive had etched the picture exactly.

The views of transatlantic poets, of *philosophes,* of tourists, even of spies, were probably less important than the opinion of the regrettably inarticulate immigrants who came in a small but steady stream to a place where all white men started even. The cheap lands, the economic opportunities, the few taxes, and the breeze of freedom brought them to a country where the people "were always trading in futures." If it had not been for European obstacles, we can be sure the immigrants would have been more numerous.[49]

Except for the desolate Federalist elders who expected the worst from that shallow, shifty infidel in the White House, the native-born Americans were pretty cocky about their future. Most of those who had not favored the elevation of Jefferson judged from his inaugural address that he might turn out to be a pretty fair American President, and that the sloop of state would survive the transfer of the tiller from the hand of Adams to the hand of Jefferson. The Jeffersonians themselves were sure of it. The re-canvass of American principles, provoked by the necessity for forming judgments on the French Revolution, convinced them again, if they needed reassurance, of the greatness and rightness of the

[47] Spiller, *Literary History,* I, 192–208; Anne Holt, *A Life of Joseph Priestley* (London, 1931), pp. 182–184. Many other travelers expressed surprise at the absence of beggars.

[48] Frances S. Childs, "A Secret Agent's Advice on America, 1797," in Edward Meade Earle (ed.), *Nationalism and Internationalism: Essays Inscribed to Carlton J. H. Hayes* (New York, 1950), pp. 19, 43.

[49] Krout and Fox, *Completion of Independence,* pp. 1–5.

American mission, which had been proclaimed in the Declaration of Independence, amplified in the liberty clauses of the Constitution and Bill of Rights, and ratified by the election of Jefferson. Jefferson did not found the American ideal. Its roots went deep into English constitutional history. But he and his circle scored political points when they pointed out to their restless, optimistic fellow citizens the democratic vista that could be clearly seen ahead, a democracy which promised benefits to most white men.

VI

The loosely aggregated population of the country had a long way to go before it truly became "We the people of the United States." The self-contained, self-satisfied sections were remote from each other. The distances were vast, the people few, the landmass great, the labor scarce. The French spy Hautrive had seen the point: the national character of the United States was "as yet unformed."[50]

With the benefit of more than a century and a half of experience with the American experiment, we can see that the chief obstacle to the attainment of nationality was what we now call racism.

Slavery was declining in the North but not in the South. The last quarter of the eighteenth century had been, in the South, a period of sentimental emancipationism, but that feeling had reached its zenith in 1800 and declined steadily thereafter. The Negro population grew more rapidly than the white, probably because of the cotton boom. The market value of a prime field hand rose from $400 to $800 while Jefferson and Madison executed the federal government. It was possible to be a vocal opponent of slavery in the South, because dispassionate discussion of leading issues was still a public ideal, but the hard-core slavery apologetics had already been heard in the land. Among prominent Southerners on record as opposing slavery were Jefferson, Washington, Luther Martin, and James Madison. Jefferson urged the manumission of children of slaves born after a chosen date, predicted universal emancipation, and said the two races, if equally free, could not live in the same country.[51] Governor James Monroe suppressed Gabriel's uprising near Richmond in August, 1800. During a state of neighborhood hysteria, somewhere between sixteen and thirty-five Negroes were

50 Childs, "Secret Agent's Advice," p. 34.

51 John Lofton, "The Enslavement of the Southern Mind," *Journal of Negro History*, XLIII (1958), 132–140; George Livermore, "An Historical Research

killed. On hearing the news, candidate Jefferson sadly said, "We are truly to be pitied."[52]

Jefferson, in his heart, was torn between the apparent inferiority of the Negro in many respects (e.g., ideal skin was, of course, "white") and a feeling of shame at the existence of slavery. He believed mulatto children were superior to their Negro parents, and that Negroes were peers of whites only in memory, natural musical talent, and courage. Even their physical bravery, he thought, was more the product of recklessness than of anything else. His conscience would have been less troubled if he could have attributed the Negro to a separate creation, but his adherence to the Linnaean scheme of biological classification precluded that solution, because such differences as Jefferson could observe must be understood as variations within a species rather than differences of species. While he could not think slavery compatible with free institutions, he apologetically declined in 1814 to head an antislavery movement.[53] One can almost sense the relief with which he complimented the free Negro Benjamin Banneker on the compilation of an excellent almanac in 1791: "No body wishes more than I do to see such proofs as you exhibit, that nature has given to our black brethren, talents equal to those of other colors of men, and that the appearance of want of them is owing merely to the degraded condition of their existence, both in Africa & America."[54] He described Banneker and his work to Jean de Caritat, Marquis de Condorcet, adding, "I have seen very elegant solutions of Geometrical problems by him."[55]

The international slave trade had been opposed in the eighteenth century by most Americans who lived north of South Carolina. As late as 1800, even South Carolina prohibited the import of slaves, except that persons from other states might bring in as many as ten if they had owned them at least two years. Whether motivated by

Respecting the Opinions of the Founders . . . on Negroes as Slaves, as Citizens, and as Soldiers," Massachusetts Historical Society, *Proceedings, 1862–1863,* pp. 86–171.

52 Jefferson to Rush, Sept. 23, 1800, A. A. Lipscomb *et al.* (eds.), *The Writings of Thomas Jefferson* (20 vols., Washington, 1903–4), X, 176.

53 Curti, *American Thought,* pp. 169, 170, 198; William Peden (ed.), *Notes on the State of Virginia by Thomas Jefferson* (Chapel Hill, 1955), pp. 137–143; Daniel J. Boorstin, *The Lost World of Thomas Jefferson* (New York, 1948), pp. 92–98.

54 Jefferson to Banneker, Aug. 30, 1791, Paul Leicester Ford (ed.), *The Writings of Thomas Jefferson* (10 vols., New York, 1892–99), V, 377.

55 Jefferson to Condorcet, Aug. 30, 1791, *ibid.,* V, 379.

justice or by fear of the kind of revolution which had ravaged San Domingo, this statute represents the humane ante-bellum high-water mark in the racial history of the South, although it benefited no Negro already in America.

Nowhere in the country, except possibly in Quaker neighborhoods, was the Negro, whether slave or free, truly at home. He was feared and suspected, both North and South. Some southern states barred free Negroes from residence. Massachusetts, with 6,000 free Negroes counted in the census of 1800, had, in 1788, prohibited the entry of free Negroes from foreign parts. Uneasy Philadelphia had 6,880 free Negroes in 1800, and was to endure a race riot in 1804. Therefore, white people always linked emancipation with colonization or deportation of the freedmen in public discussion of the issue. The word "abolitionist" then meant a believer in colonization, whether in the Far West or in Africa. The concepts were practically never separated, except among the Quakers, simply because the Negro was not thought even potentially equal to the white.[56]

The seedling democracy of Jefferson's and Madison's republic in 1801 was a rough-hewn, unfinished place, with little patina of refinement, nor much of any kind of learning except what pertained to lawbooks and to politics. Its people were not closely knit, nor did their manners call forth praise from visitors. Their arts were primitive—except for portraiture and architecture—and their theologies were wildly divergent. They owned a wealthy land, and they were beginning to scratch and hack at the obstacles which would be overcome to make them the richest people ever seen on the planet. Their country puzzled foreign critics, but Americans cared nothing about that. They were growing swiftly, mostly by natural increase. Except for the unstable compound of races, the explosive quality of which they usually ignored, they believed they had the formula for making free government work. To mix indigenous metaphors, they thought they had the world on a string, on a downhill pull.

[56] Edward Channing, *A History of the United States* (6 vols., New York, 1905–25), V, 133–134. Channing (no statistician he) cited reports to show a greater incidence of crime and insanity in the free Negro population than in the white population. Such studies, which compare a single restricted and depressed group with all strata of another and socially dominant group, produce easily predictable results. Henry N. Sherwood, "Early Negro Deportation Projects," *Mississippi Valley Historical Review*, II (1915–16), 484–508.

CHAPTER 3

The Jeffersonians Take the Tiller

IN a time of peril—real or imagined—when men feared disorder and destruction, the Federalists had enjoyed power. Now, as it proved, they were swept from the federal executive branch and replaced by the optimistic Republicans, who were more popular, and who trusted more in the common sense of the free white male voter.[1]

As President Thomas Jefferson's political principles were applied, one by one, it could be seen that his theme in federal public administration was all stated in the phrase limited government. As means to this goal he sought harmony of the parts of government, simplicity of federal powers, adaptability of policy, decentralization of function, and personal responsibility in execution. His was an informal administration, in which the President did much of the paper work with his own hands, looked after many petty details, and transacted a good deal of the public's business while cracking the nuts and passing the Madeira around his dinner table.[2] He

[1] A good account of the popular moods affecting political life at the turn of the century is in John A. Krout and Dixon Ryan Fox, *The Completion of Independence, 1790–1830* (New York, 1944), pp. 150–162. For a sample of Jeffersonian optimism, see Dr. Ames's attitudes as revealed in "Squire Ames and Dr. Ames," Samuel Eliot Morison, *By Land and by Sea, Essays and Addresses* (New York, 1954).

[2] Lynton K. Caldwell, *The Administrative Theories of Hamilton & Jefferson: Their Contribution to Thought on Public Administration* (Chicago, 1944), pp. 129–141; Leonard D. White, *The Jeffersonians: A Study in Administrative History, 1801–1829* (New York, 1951), pp. 71–72, 71 n., 74. President Jefferson absented himself from Washington one day in four during his eight years as President.

refused to spend his summers in Washington. As he wrote to Albert Gallatin, "Grumble who will, I will never pass those two months on tidewater."[3] Those who know Washington in July and August will think him wise.

He organized his administrative family in a leisurely manner, leaving affairs of the first few weeks in the hands of his new Attorney General, Levi Lincoln of Massachusetts, helped by a few Adams holdovers. The other new department heads were to be James Madison of Virginia as Secretary of State, Albert Gallatin of Pennsylvania as Secretary of the Treasury, Henry Dearborn of Massachusetts as Secretary of War, and Robert Smith of Maryland as Secretary of the Navy. Geography did not govern the choices of Madison and Gallatin, but the appointments of Dearborn and Lincoln were undoubtedly anti-Federalist gestures and assurances against northern jealousy of Virginia.[4] Smith's appointment was simple desperation.

Both his long-enduring personal link with the President and his obvious ability made the choice of the small, precise, wise, persistent Madison inevitable. He was easily confirmed to his miniature agency which dealt with such colossal problems.[5] As early as 1790, Jefferson told Benjamin Rush he believed Madison "was the greatest man in the world,"[6] and a leading student of their relationship has well said, "The two men needed each other in order to achieve the victory of their joint political philosophy."[7] Although Federal-

---

[3] Quoted in Allen Johnson, *Jefferson and His Colleagues: A Chronicle of the Virginia Dynasty* (New Haven, 1921), p. 11. Johnson's little book is the highest kind of popularization.

[4] The State and Treasury offices paid $5,000 annually, the War and Navy posts $4,500. On the distribution of appointments by geography, Irving Brant, *James Madison: Secretary of State, 1800–1809* (Indianapolis, 1953), p. 56. Brant's multivolume biography of Madison takes a sharply different view from that of Henry Adams, who is eloquently tendentious in 750,000 words of damningly faint praise. In fairness to the reader, one ought to summarize a dissenting opinion of Brant's work by Nathan Schachner, *American Historical Review*, LX (1954), 126–127. Schachner thought Brant's book a work of idolatry, exalting Madison at the expense of his contemporaries, especially the "completely overshadowed" Albert Gallatin, and too hard on Aaron Burr. This writer sides with Brant.

[5] From 1801 to 1821, the Department's staff grew from nine to fourteen clerks.

[6] George W. Corner (ed.), *The Autobiography of Benjamin Rush* (Princeton, 1948), p. 181.

[7] Adrienne Koch, *Jefferson and Madison: The Great Collaboration* (New York, 1950), p. 221.

ists slandered him as merely the pliable accomplice of villainous Tom, they knew better. Unfortunately for historical understanding, posterity has swallowed the opposition polemics.[8]

Equally logical was the choice of Gallatin, the only Republican with authoritative legislative experience in public finance (in the Pennsylvania Assembly), with local political deftness, with an understanding of the federal Treasury accounting and fiscal system, and with an informed alternative financial program of his own. His mind was first rate, his integrity stainless, but he had suffered such painful Federalist libels that the President gave him an interim appointment to dodge the possibility of senatorial rejection. Unlike Madison, posterity has been kind to Gallatin. While a hard-money, balance-the-budget, cut-taxes, pay-the-debt Secretary, he advocated the merit system in civil service, and was also a sturdy defender of civil liberty. Some part of his record is admirable to every inquirer.[9]

Robert Smith of Maryland, who lived in the shadow of his brother Samuel, was Jefferson's fifth choice for the office of Secretary of the Navy. Like Madison's, his reputation has suffered from Federalist belittling, but, surely, he might at least be memorialized for substituting bourbon whisky in place of rum in the Navy ration, and Navy men could be found to cry, "Robert Smith, *si;* Josephus Daniels, *no.*"[10] The Attorney General had a tiny stipend, little to do, no official headquarters, no clerical help, no control over the district attorneys, no departmental budget, no library, no letter books.[11]

Of the five chief officers, only Madison and Gallatin had intellectual powers that could rival the President's, and they were immovably loyal to their chief. The three were an executive trium-

8 Charles E. Hill, "James Madison," in Samuel Flagg Bemis (ed.), *The American Secretaries of State and Their Diplomacy* (10 vols. in 5, New York, 1958), III, 6–8; Irving Brant, "James Madison and His Times," *American Historical Review*, LVII (1952), 853–870. This short piece states the theme of Brant's Madison symphony.

9 For examples of such libels on Gallatin, see Claude Milton Newlin, *The Life and Writings of Hugh Henry Brackenridge* (Princeton, 1932), pp. 201–207; Jay C. Henlein, "Albert Gallatin: A Pioneer in Public Administration," *William and Mary Quarterly*, Third Series, VII (1950), 64–94.

10 Secretary of the Navy Josephus Daniels barred alcoholic beverages from naval vessels during the prohibitionist wave which crested during Woodrow Wilson's administration.

11 White, *Jeffersonians,* pp. 336–338.

virate, except that Madison had little to do directly with legislation. The President supervised their every act, used their advice on broad policy questions to guard himself against impulsive error, and had, withal, the most harmonious cabinet yet.[12]

Having formed his official family, the President next faced up to the painful problem of what he called the "midnight appointments, to wit, all after Dec. 12,"[13] by which date President Adams must have known he had not been re-elected. As Jefferson wrote to Abigail Adams, these appointments "laid me under the embarrasment [sic] of acting thro' men whose views were to defeat mine; or to encounter the odium of putting others in their places." He thought it an unjustly imposed dilemma,[14] and chose to encounter the odium, knowing that his public policies would be more acceptable than his removal policy. The new Judiciary Act of 1801, and a special organization law for the District of Columbia, signed respectively on February 13 and 27, 1801, had intrinsic merits, but they provided rather more lavish staffing than necessary. Twenty-three new judges were created, with their retinues of marshals, attorneys, bailiffs, and messengers. They and all men newly appointed as revenue surveyors and collectors, postmasters, port officers, and bankruptcy commissioners were Federalists. After consulting Madison, Jefferson stonily vacated the midnight appointments, and asked the Congress to reconsider the Judiciary Act of 1801.[15]

Now, what of Federalist officeholders of longer standing, whose places were coveted by deserving Republicans? Office seekers flooded the Washington-bound mails with lists of their public talents and their influential friends, with statements of their financial straits and narratives of their loyal services. The Federalists believed, with some reason, that Jefferson, during the electoral crisis of 1801, had

[12] *Ibid.*, p. 61; Jefferson to Destutt de Tracy, Jan. 26, 1811, in A. A. Lipscomb *et al.* (eds.), *The Writings of Thomas Jefferson* (20 vols., Washington, 1903–4), XIII, 17–18.

[13] Quoted without citation in Edward Channing, *A History of the United States* (6 vols., New York, 1905–25), IV, 253 n.

[14] Jefferson to Abigail Adams, June 13, 1804, in Lester J. Cappon (ed.), *The Adams-Jefferson Letters: The Complete Correspondence Between Thomas Jefferson and Abigail and John Adams* (2 vols., Chapel Hill, 1959), I, 270.

[15] Channing, *United States*, IV, 276–279; Nathan Schachner, *Thomas Jefferson, A Biography* (2 vols., New York, 1951), II, 670–672. Adams appointed forty-two justices of the peace in and for the District of Columbia.

agreed not to disturb the lesser federal officials. Jefferson's decision on removals was matured during his first month in office. Tories of 1776–83, arch-Hamiltonians and monarchists, and men who had abused their power, especially in enforcing the Sedition Act, must go. None were to be removed for difference of principle only. Vacancies would be filled by Republicans, quite properly he thought, until they had half the places. Federalists were bitter as they gradually learned the President's opinion, but their own record weakened their position. Jefferson estimated that Washington and Adams had appointed about six hundred federal officers, yet only six known Republicans were in the federal civil service when he took the oath of office. Could it be that Federalists entirely monopolized merit? The new President thought not. He asked Levi Lincoln for a list of arch-Federalists in federal office in New England, in order to remove them. He was ready to thrash the shepherds while trying to lure the Federalist flock.[16]

The customs collectors were the most vulnerable. Their fees, in the larger ports, were handsome. They had patronage to give out. They comprised a good system of political intelligence. Postmasters, it may be noted with some surprise, were not much molested. The Congress, in 1802, made the Treasury and Post Office jobs somewhat less attractive by placing ceilings on their income ranging from $2,000 to $5,000.[17] The removal of Elizur Goodrich, the collector at New Haven, and his replacement by the elderly Samuel Bishop was the *cause célèbre* of the removal policy. New Haven was the Vatican City of New England Federalism, under Pope Timothy Dwight, whose younger brother Theodore, writing of a New Haven Republican meeting led by a reputable clergyman, had described "Ye Ragged Throng of Democrats" as "Drunkards and Whores/And rogues in scores."[18] In a widely circulated remonstrance, New Haven merchants protested the firing. This gave the President a chance to make his views widely known. He wrote to the remon-

[16] Only United States marshals had a status approaching tenure. They were appointed for four-year terms. Morton Borden, *The Federalism of James A. Bayard* (New York, 1955), pp. 86–93, 95, 221 (note 99); Jefferson to T. M. Randolph, Mar. 12, 1801, Jefferson Papers, Library of Congress; Jefferson to Eppes, Mar. 27, 1801, photostat in New York Public Library, cited by permission of the Buist family of Charleston, S.C., owners of the original.

[17] White, *Jeffersonians*, pp. 148–151, 153, 326, 403–404.

[18] Quoted in David Hackett Fischer, *The Revolution of American Conservatism* (New York, 1965), p. 147.

strants that few died and none resigned. They must expect Federalists to lose government jobs at a rate faster than that of death and resignations, until half the posts were held by Republicans. Noah Webster, the spokesman of what passed for moderate Federalism east of the Hudson River, was so outraged by the Bishop affair that he wrote eighteen printed "Letters to the President of the United States," seventy-six pages of artistically constructed invective, vituperation, and abuse. But a careful distribution of offices, from that of Gideon Granger, Postmaster General, down to the lowest federal jobs, made the Connecticut Republicans a true party, as subsequent elections proved.[19]

There were a few specific botcheries. John Quincy Adams was relieved of his duties as commissioner in bankruptcies, and the Adamses resented it for years. Yet the chief clerk of the Department of State, which meant *de facto* undersecretary, a man devoted to the Jefferson-hating Timothy Pickering, was kept on. James Thomson Callender, an editor convicted under the Sedition Act of libeling John Adams, failed of his ambition to replace the postmaster of Richmond, and vindictively printed the only scandal of Jefferson's life.[20]

Nevertheless, by July, 1803, of 316 offices in the gift of the President, only 130 were held by Federalists. The principle of equalization had been applied. In New York a working arrangement let the Clintonian Republican faction have its way in state politics, while the Livingstonian faction was taken care of by the appointment of Edward as district attorney and the successive offers of a cabinet post and the Paris legation to Robert R. Thereby the Burrites were tightly fenced out of the plum orchard; they got no benefit from their leader's peculiarly won Vice-Presidency.[21]

19 Samuel Bishop died in 1803, a year after his appointment. His son Abraham, a dauntless Republican, succeeded him and served until 1829. For a warm specimen of Webster's critiques of the administration (privately communicated), see Webster to Jefferson, October, 1801, in Harry R. Warfel (ed.), *Letters of Noah Webster* (New York, 1953), pp. 240–245. For the growth of Connecticut Republicanism, Richard J. Purcell, *Connecticut in Transition, 1775–1818* (Washington, 1918), pp. 240–243.

20 Schachner, *Jefferson*, II, 677–678, 762–766. Callender was reaching back more than thirty years for a "news" story, since Jefferson's frankly and humbly admitted impropriety occurred in 1768.

21 Brant, *Madison, 1800–1809*, pp. 53–55. One Burrite became district attorney before the patronage fence was completed.

Only one highly placed Republican opposed political preferment. Albert Gallatin wished to initiate the merit system in the Treasury, but he was easily persuaded to table the proposition indefinitely. Jefferson's spoilsmanship was part of his consummate political art. While he aimed to make federal office the goal of a man's political action, he made his appointments with a due regard for the integrity and reputation of the service. Standards of performance remained high. He showed partiality to friends, but no scandals stained his administration.[22]

The reorganized executive branch had to do business with a revolutionized Congress. In the Seventh Congress, the Republicans outnumbered the Federalists in the House, 69–36; and in the Senate, 18–13. The congressional Republicans have been described as badly organized, but it may be noted that all the key leaders were lieutenants of the President, which could hardly happen by accident. Jefferson had the first administration floor leader in congressional history, the ambitious but somewhat distracted and inattentive William Branch Giles of Virginia. The House chose Nathaniel Macon of North Carolina as its Speaker from 1801 to 1807. The severe Macon suffered from chronic low-grade obstructionitis during his thirty-seven years of congressional service, and his record ranks near the top in the all-time record of "no" votes. A colleague said if Macon drowned he would look for the body upstream. In Macon's day the speakership amounted to a good deal less than it did after Henry Clay exalted it, and Giles was more influential than Macon, but Macon saw to it that his favorite representative, John Randolph, ennobled with the suffix "of Roanoke," headed the Committee on Ways and Means. Unfortunate, eccentric Randolph had a hormonal deficiency, and remained all his life the aging, beardless boy soprano, who might remind one of the sharpest lad in a good elementary school, whose mind was improved by acquiring information, but whose judgment was not refined by maturity. God did not mold Randolph to be in any majority. He was only at ease in opposition, a fact which helped him to carry his constituency with regularity, cast in the role of the original political Honest John.[23]

[22] *Ibid.*; Caldwell, *Hamilton and Jefferson*, pp. 200–202.

[23] Ralph Volney Harlow, *The History of Legislative Methods in the Period before 1825* (New Haven, 1917), pp. 166–169, 171–172; Wilfred E. Binkley, *President and Congress* (Garden City, 1947), pp. 49–55; Noble E. Cunningham,

The lives of Macon and Randolph remind us that an easy way for a legislator to get a reputation for virtue and probity is to confine himself to negative voting and destructive criticism.

The talkative but weak Federalist opposition was led by James A. Bayard of Delaware, the key man of the 1801 electoral crisis, and by the unstable Roger Griswold of Connecticut.[24]

There were several minor but not supernumerary characters on the Washington stage. Samuel Harrison Smith edited the *National Intelligencer*, selected by the President to be the administration's voice.[25] The appointment of Gideon Granger to be Postmaster General, an office under the Secretary of State, was ominous for New England Federalism, although he was not popular with Southerners. William Thornton, the quasi Leonardo who was architect of the Capitol, ran the Patent Office for twenty-eight years with but a single clerk. The Department of the Navy struck gold when it appointed Charles W. Goldsborough to be chief clerk. The great chemist, Professor Samuel Latham Mitchill of Columbia College, sat in one or other of the chambers of the Congress almost continuously from 1801 to 1813. Since he was deprived of laboratory facilities, he amused himself during dull moments at his congressional desk by rewriting nursery rhymes to Americanize them and to correct their scientific errors.[26] John Beckley, the first American to

Jr., "Nathaniel Macon and the Southern Protest Against National Consolidation," *North Carolina Historical Review*, XXXII (1955), 376–377, 377 n.

Several biographers have tried their hands at carving a likeness of John Randolph, but none has improved on the monumental William Cabell Bruce, *John Randolph of Roanoke, 1773–1833* (2 vols., New York, 1922). Mason Daly, "The Political Oratory of John Randolph of Roanoke," Ph.D. thesis, Northwestern University, summarized in Northwestern University, *Summaries of Doctoral Dissertations*, XIX (1951), 105–110, illuminates specific facets of Randolph's eccentric career.

24 Borden, *Bayard*, pp. 96–101. Griswold had been in a slugging match on the floor of the House with Matthew Lyon, "The Beast of Vermont." Some of Griswold's votes in the previous decade cannot be analyzed logically.

25 "I recommend to you to pay not the least credit to pretended appointments in any paper, till you see it in Smith's." Jefferson to Eppes, Mar. 27, 1801, photostat in New York Public Library.

26 Lyman C. Newell, "Samuel Latham Mitchill," *Dictionary of American Biography* (22 vols. in 11, New York, 1927–58). Edgar F. Smith, *Samuel Latham Mitchill* (New York, 1922), gives one historico-scientific revision:

> "When the pie was opened,
> The birds they were songless;
> Was that not a pretty dish
> To set before Congress?"

THE JEFFERSONIANS TAKE THE TILLER 53

function as a national party chairman, although the office had not been formalized, was reinstated as Clerk of the House after several years of Federalist-imposed exile for un-Federalist activities in the election of 1796.[27] Jefferson completed casting for the drama he was to direct with the appointment of his young Virginian neighbor, Lieutenant Meriwether Lewis, United States Army, to be his private secretary. Exalted in the public eye, but completely isolated from power, was the enigmatic Vice-President Aaron Burr, for whom no lines were written. The Jeffersonian circle saw to it that he had little to do except to preside over the Senate and to dream inscrutable imperial dreams.

II

The Seventh Congress of the United States received its first presidential message in December, 1801. Its author intended it to strengthen and gladden the agrarians without alarming the men of business. Jefferson prepared a draft and circulated it among his department heads (asking Madison to verify the grammar). On reflection the President cut out an attack on the Sedition Act. It was due to expire, and, anyway, all of the convicts had been pardoned. In its final form, the First Annual Message turned out to be a rather tranquilizing description of the utopia in which Americans would live when taxes and expenditures were cut. The President also inserted a reassuring clause praising free enterprise, which was probably the work of his Massachusetts lieutenant, Levi Lincoln. Federalist litmus paper showed no trace of acid in this bland syrup. The Federalist critics had to stoop to sneering at the cowardice of a President who feared to come down to the Capitol and say his piece like a man, and to pointing at the Frenchiness of the opening salutation, "Fellow Citizens . . ." After the Lucifer-Michael match of 1800, this tame Republican program seemed an anticlimax perpetrated—as it was in fact—by the mildest, smoothest statesman of the day. No nuance threatened violence to that Federalist monument which was the federal government.[28]

[27] Noble E. Cunningham, Jr., "John Beckley: An Early American Party Manager," *William and Mary Quarterly,* Third Series, XIII (1956), 40–52.
[28] Charles A. Beard, *Economic Origins of Jeffersonian Democracy* (New York, 1927), pp. 435–438, 442–445; Jefferson to Gallatin, Nov. 14, 1801, Gallatin Papers, New-York Historical Society; Schachner, *Jefferson,* II, 693–696; J. D. Richardson

Could the Republicans in the Congress convert this undemanding program into actual legislation? They had never shown any legislative genius, even in their rare seasons of majority. Individualism and separatism were their badges of honor. In the 1790's many of them (but not Gallatin) had seemed to believe a legislature should do its work in the manner of a seventeenth-century Quaker meeting, sitting in brooding silence until the Holy Ghost moved a member to present a resolution. But they soon began legislating, and they went at it in the shameful fashion they had decried in the foul fiends of Federalism. They fell to caucusing.[29]

Thomas Jefferson had a wonderfully simple theory of public finance. The United States should pay its frugal way entirely by tariff revenues, because customs duties fell wholly on the rich and because they did not burden production. He and Secretary Gallatin worked out the fiscal program. To Gallatin, the national debt was an unmitigated evil. Debt was the brand of the spendthrift. When you came right down to it, federal spending was evil in itself. It never occurred to him that the United States was an underdeveloped nation which needed to make capital outlays larger than its current revenue. He even opposed financial preparedness for military emergencies because, on the one hand, overflowing treasuries tempted nations to war and, on the other hand, public borrowing permitted warfare at no cost except to posterity.[30]

Gallatin knew he had been brought into the administration to help the President cut spending and cut the national debt. The debt was about $82 million. He proposed to cut spending so as to pay the national debt by 1817.[31] The publicly frugal but privately spendthrift President and his Secretary relied on geographic re-

---

(ed.), *A Compilation of the Messages and Papers of the Presidents* (20 vols., Washington, 1897–1917), I, 314–320. Jefferson was sensitive to charges of Jacobinism: the next twenty-five special messages each began, "Gentlemen . . ." *ibid.*, I, 320–330.

[29] Harlow, *Legislative Methods*, pp. 163–167, 183–191.

[30] Alexander Balinky, *Albert Gallatin: Fiscal Theories and Policy* (New Brunswick, 1958), pp. 29–48.

[31] From 1801 to 1812, federal expenditures were annually less than in 1800. A hypothetical amortization of the debt at 4 per cent interest, by the writer's calculations, shows that it would have been cut about 42 per cent by Jefferson's eighth year if the plan had worked perfectly. In practice, that goal was reached in 1811. By 1814, it had risen to about the sum it had been on Inauguration Day, 1801, and by 1816 the debt was 50 per cent greater than in 1801.

moteness and diplomatic isolation to preserve the peace necessary to make the program work. Together they managed the Congress in order to get their system through.[32] In practice, Gallatin's design was the application of Pennsylvanian fiscal methods to the federal government. The ideals were transparent financial reports, specific appropriations, hostility to debt, hostility to excises.[33]

Where to start cutting? The armed forces spent the most money. Q.E.D. The Army was less vulnerable to the pruning knife than the Navy, because Westerners could always point to the near and present danger of Indians. But the Navy had been founded against the will of the congressional Republicans, led by Gallatin, who believed it unnecessary, beyond the financial capacity of the country, and, as Patrick Henry said in 1788, a temptation to substitute glory for liberty as the prime goal of the American people. As for cutting taxes, the tax on whisky was the black beast of the western country because of the unpleasant memory of the armed suppression of the Whisky Rebellion, although there is no evidence that the tax hurt very much in 1801.[34] Without the whisky excise, the remaining excises would hardly be worth the expense of collection, and for that reason alone Gallatin wished to keep it for awhile. Jefferson's political instinct dictated its repeal.[35] By an act so awkwardly drafted by John Randolph that it required a clarifying amendment twice as long as the bill, the Congress repealed all internal taxes, arguing, mostly, the disproportionate expense of collection.

Now they turned to the armed forces. Gallatin, Smith, and Dearborn agreed to a military budget of $1,900,000, which was about half what the Federalists appropriated for 1801. The Regular Army, that potential tool of tyranny, was set, on paper, at 3,350 officers and men. Junior officers foresaw a dismal professional future

[32] Balinky, *Gallatin*, pp. 19–22, 24–26; Harlow, *Legislative Methods*, pp. 181–183.

[33] Gallatin had contributed a specific recommendation for specific appropriations to Jefferson's message of 1801.

[34] Leland D. Baldwin, *Whiskey Rebels; The Story of a Frontier Uprising* (Pittsburgh, 1939), pp. 104–106, 264.

[35] Balinky, *Gallatin*, pp. 53–64. What might be considered an anti-intellectual tariff on books was kept on by this intellectualist administration. Rollo Gabriel Silver, "The Book Trade and the Protective Tariff, 1800–1804," Bibliographical Society of America, *Papers*, XLVI (1952), 33–44. John Randolph helped to beat a move to abolish a tariff on educational books in 1804.

when they looked above them at ten generals. Gallatin hoped to keep the soldiers in the woods where they belonged, and never to see them in the cities. So far as the Navy was concerned, the last Federalist Congress had provided a reduction in officers and men, and had retained only thirteen ships from the undeclared war with France, of which seven could be taken out of service. Jefferson, not unwisely, proposed to lay them up at Washington in covered dry-docks, but Gallatin and the Congress decided it would cost too much to build the drydocks. All things considered, the United States Navy has had no greater domestic enemy than Albert Gallatin. The result of his meditations was a cut in the Federalist recommendations from $3,500,000 to $1,000,000 for 1802.[36]

The President made minor but symbolic savings by closing the United States legations in The Hague and Berlin, leaving ministers only in London, Paris, and Madrid.[37] The Mint, which produced trivial results at a trivial cost, narrowly escaped abolition during the thrift drive.[38]

In his own dominion, Gallatin got his way in every Treasury matter he felt strongly about, except the merit system. Specific appropriations became the congressional practice, beginning in 1802. Strict, detailed accounting became the rule in every office except the armed forces, where things moved too fast to allow it. (Jefferson himself thought lump-sum appropriations to these departments were safe enough under a system of annual appropriations.) For the first time in their lives the Federalists felt the crushing pain of the legislative power roller. Despondent elder Federalists, accustomed to deference, sank deeper into despair as the enemy rose in strength and popular esteem. Despite their murmurs of pessimism, the republic endured, the people lived in respectable tranquillity, and business—after a brief sag—began to improve. Some Federalists tried to make a national association of their

36 White, *Jeffersonians*, pp. 211–214; Harold and Margaret Sprout, *The Rise of American Naval Power, 1776–1918* (rev. ed., Princeton, 1942), pp. 52–53, 55; Alexander Balinky, "Albert Gallatin, Naval Foe," *Pennsylvania Magazine of History and Biography*, LXXXII (1958), 293–304.

37 Rufus King stayed in London, Robert R. Livingston eventually went to Paris, and "Blackguard Charlie" Pinckney, the Republican renegade of his family, became minister to Madrid. The consuls in the Barbary States were kept on—on salaries—and the other consuls were retained on the fee system.

38 George Adams Boyd, *Elias Boudinot, Patriot and Statesman, 1740–1821* (Princeton, 1952), pp. 238–245.

scattered state elements, but the steady succession of Republican congressional and hustings victories through 1804 disheartened most erstwhile Federalist leaders. A few sturdily persevered in the Congress, but if the future of the Federalist cause depended entirely on the efforts of Federalist veterans, there could be no national opposition party. Until Jefferson's election, and through his first term, the Federalists had been a loose league of men who classed themselves as gentlemen. Their bonds were the memory of George Washington and the constitutional revolution, hostility to democracy and Jefferson, and fear of organized opposition, which they called "faction." Thus inhibited, they could not organize themselves if they tried, which they infrequently did. Bayard, Griswold, and company resisted bravely in the Congress, but the Republican members ignored the bills they sponsored, and refused even to answer their forlorn forensics.[39]

The Jeffersonian administration, in its first acts, had made it clear that the federal government was to do as little as possible. The hindsight strategist can see the military and naval policies as only hazardous, almost reckless, but the parsimony of the Republicans allowed the retirement by 1807 of all federal bonds which could lawfully be called by that year. The tariff policy at the moment was merely a continuation of Federalist tariff policy, except that it was now, with the negligible exception of public-land sales, the sole reliance for national revenue.

III

It took four headstrong despots on the Barbary coast of the Mediterranean Sea to provoke President Jefferson into showing that his policies were more flexible than they seemed, and that he was no more a pacifist than George Washington or John Adams, if as much.[40] The rulers of Morocco, Algiers, Tunis, and Tripoli relied on piracy or extortion for their cash income. After the War for Independence, American ships, no longer protected by British extortion payments, were seized in the Mediterranean, their crews

[39] Balinky, *Gallatin*, pp. 78–83; Borden, *Bayard*, pp. 101–105; Fischer, *Revolution of American Conservatism*, pp. 28, 52, 83–84.

[40] J. G. de Roulhac Hamilton, "The Pacifism of Thomas Jefferson," *Virginia Quarterly Review*, XXXI (1955), 607–620. Merle E. Curti, *Peace or War: The American Struggle, 1636–1936* (New York, 1936), p. 28, sees it this way: "Devoted to the ideal of social justice, he was willing to see it advanced by force."

enslaved, and their Mediterranean trade extinguished. When the pirates sallied into the Atlantic Ocean and took more American ships, the Congress, in 1794, voted to build a Navy against them, as Thomas Jefferson had been urging for years. In 1795, Joel Barlow concluded a typical extortion treaty with the Dey of Algiers, the strongest of the four marine-bandit leaders,[41] and similar treaties were made in 1797 with Tripoli and Tunis. These treaties protected the trade of about a hundred American ships a year at a cost of about $100,000 annually.[42] In 1801, the tribute to Algiers was three years in arrears, and the Dey, becoming impatient, publicly humiliated Captain William Bainbridge of the frigate *George Washington* by sending him on an errand as if he were a temporary captain in what one could call the Algerine Naval Reserve.[43] Meanwhile the Pasha of Tripoli, Yusuf Karamanli, raised his demands, and declared war on the United States by the usual North African gesture of chopping down the flagstaff at the United States Consulate. Consul James T. Cathcart escaped to Leghorn.[44]

The insolence of the Barbary pirates had called the Navy into being in 1794. Because Jefferson detested the pirates more than the Navy, the avarice of the Barbary corsairs saved the Navy from extinction in 1801. Before the Tripolitan declaration was known in Washington, the President had been studying consular and naval reports of the restlessness of the Barbary miscreants. He sent Commodore Richard Dale with four vessels to the Mediterranean to make a reconnaissance in force, and to punish any insults to the flag. While the Pasha of Tripoli sat securely defended by his massive walls, built by generations of Christian slaves, Dale's force accomplished nothing much in a year's tour except to capture one surprised Tripolitan rover, and to bottle up two others in Gibraltar.[45]

41 Marshall Smelser, *The Congress Founds the Navy, 1787–1798* (Notre Dame, 1959), pp. 35–44, 49–59, 77. A treaty had been made with Morocco in 1786. The Algerine peace cost nearly a million dollars to secure, and $144,000 in the next two years.

42 In twelve years of Federalism the United States had paid nearly $10 million in tribute and ransom to the Barbary pirates. The Tripolitan and Tunisian treaties cost about $163,000 in all.

43 Johnson, *Jefferson and Colleagues*, pp. 35–37.

44 Cathcart had been an Algerine slave, which probably explains why he showed what the turf press might describe as good early foot.

45 Dale had been John Paul Jones's lieutenant.

William Eaton, the United States consul at Tunis, had declared a blockade of Tripoli. Dale enforced it in 1801 and 1802, but his "idle & inactive" successor, Commodore Richard V. Morris, bungled the job in 1802 and 1803. (He was tried and dismissed from the service.) [46] Commodore Edward Preble came out to command in 1803 and 1804, with *Constitution, Philadelphia,* and six smaller vessels. Preble sent Captain Bainbridge ahead to Tripoli in *Philadelphia,* while he himself successfully overawed the truculent Sultan of Morocco. Disaster followed. Bainbridge, chasing pirates, ran his ship aground. He, his crew (mostly British subjects), and his ship were taken by the pirates. Lieutenant Stephen Decatur, on February 16, 1804, heroically steered a captured vessel into Tripoli harbor and burned the sun-dried *Philadelphia* by night. He was promoted to captain on the spot.[47] Decatur's pyrotechnical but Pyrrhic victory, Preble's maintenance of the blockade, the premature self-destruction of an American fire ship sent into Tripoli harbor, and some theatrical but indecisive bombardments of Tripoli were all that could be accomplished with the reduced force, even though Preble augmented his squadron with galleys, called "gunboats," from home and from the sympathetic King of Naples and the Two Sicilies. (Preble loved those galleys.) [48] Meanwhile there was some heroic and barely credible action on the land side.

William Eaton got reluctant permission from Madison and Jefferson to attack Tripoli by land, with the ostensible aim of restoring usurper Yusuf's elder exiled brother Hamet to the throne of Tripoli. In Egypt, after refuting French denunciations that he was a British spy,[49] Eaton, with Hamet's timorous help, organized a

46 Felix Howland, "The Blockade of Tripoli, 1801–1802," United States Naval Institute, *Proceedings,* LXIII (1937), 1702–4; Mary Lewis Cooke and Charles Lee Lewis, "An American Naval Officer in the Mediterranean, 1802–1807," *ibid.,* LXVII (1941), 1535.

47 Bainbridge to Preble, Dec. 5, 1803, in Dudley W. Knox (ed.), *Naval Documents Relating to the United States Wars with the Barbary Powers, 1785–1807* (6 vols., Washington, 1935–44), III, 253. An animated account of the Philadelphia episode by a participant is in *ibid.,* III, 417–420, as are all other necessary documents, in the same volume.

48 Charles Moran, "Commodore Preble's Sicilian Auxiliaries," United States Naval Institute, *Proceedings,* LXV (1939), 80–82.

49 Hull to Eaton, Jan. 5, 29; Eaton to Hull, Jan. 8, 31, 1805, in Charles Henry Lincoln (ed.), "The Hull-Eaton Correspondence During the Expedition Against Tripoli, 1804–1805," American Antiquarian Society, *Proceedings,* New Series, XXI (1911), 121–125.

rabble army. He had seven United States Marines, some Greek soldiers, and a band of restive, unhappy Arabs. Eaton showed a fine gift for understatement when, thirty days' march from Alexandria, his men near starvation, his Arabs talking mutiny, he wrote, "We have a difficult undertaking!"[50] Yet this unpromising mob success-fully stormed Derna in a two-hour action. The seven Marines behaved splendidly on the shores of Tripoli.[51] The fall of Derna, according to Eaton and a few admirers, shocked Pasha Yusuf into making the peace the Navy had failed to force, although it seems doubtful that he could have pressed his attack across the hundreds of miles of desiccated landscape yet to be crossed without more logistical help than Preble's force could have provided. Probably a further penetration of Tripoli (Derna is less than halfway from Alexandria to Tripoli port) would only have provoked the mas-sacre of *Philadelphia*'s languishing crew, and have ended in Eaton's own destruction.[52]

To the pain of the frugal-minded Republicans, all this sort of thing cost money. At the beginning the Navy waged a small war four thousand miles from home on a budget intended to support a three-ship American coastal patrol. To raise enough to carry out the commitment, a stingy surtax was put on the tariff in 1804. The Congress earmarked the proceeds as the Mediterranean Fund, to discourage posterity from thinking it a permanent fiscal fixture. The Congress's penny-pinching policy was plainly defective, but the Navy Department also showed an extraordinary view of warfare by changing commanding officers for each new sailing season.[53] Con-tinuity of tactical method was lacking, and the operation resembled a cluster of small-unit training problems with live ammunition more than strategically planned warfare. But at any rate, it was a superb training school for "Preble's Boys," and created a true officer corps which was to show its steel in the War of 1812.

[50] Quoted without citation in Meade Minnigerode, *Lives and Times: Four Informal American Biographies* (New York, 1925), p. 85.
[51] Lieutenant Presley N. O'Bannon, U.S.M.C., received a commendation but no promotion, upon which he resigned his commission. No signal honor was paid to him until the naming of the destroyer *O'Bannon* in 1917. C. H. Metcalf, *A History of the United States Marine Corps* (New York, 1939), pp. 45–47.
[52] Louis B. Wright and Julia H. McLeod, *The First Americans in North Africa; William Eaton's Struggle for a Vigorous Policy Against the Barbary Pirates, 1799–1805* (Princeton, 1945).
[53] Dudley W. Knox, *A History of the United States Navy* (rev. ed., New York, 1948), pp. 62–73.

Tobias Lear, George Washington's sometime private secretary, now made peace with Tripoli (1805), with naval advice and encouragement, but with the threat of the slaughter of *Philadelphia's* crew always at the back of his mind. He and Yusuf settled for $60,000 (to Yusuf). Eaton attacked the treaty as contemptible.[54] Men born later condemned the treaty as a yielding to extortion, and Ray W. Irwin has doubted whether *Philadelphia's* people could "have died in a nobler cause."[55] Inasmuch as they were mostly subjects of King George III, they may have had another opinion on that point. The American civil and military officers who were on the scene with Lear unanimously applauded his work. It was a conventional western-style treaty of amity and commerce, certainly the best treaty any power had extracted from a Pasha of Tripoli up to that time. As for spending $60,000 to sweeten Yusuf's disposition, Gallatin had somberly watched the Navy's spending for combat climb from $900,000 in 1802 to $1,600,000 in 1806. For once, it was both the principle of the thing *and* the money.

IV

The Tripolitan War had shown the utility of small gunboats (more properly, galleys), about fifty feet long, for shallow protected waters and in calms. Commodore Preble praised them warmly. They had been used in southern bays and estuaries during the War for Independence, and Republicans, even some Federalists, argued for them in the 1790's as economical defense tools.[56] Being almost wholly defensive, they were attractive to backwoods naval theorists. With seventy-four-gun ships costing a third of a million to build, and a fifth of a million a year to keep up, President Jefferson was strongly drawn to galleys, which cost only about $10,000 apiece. Although Gallatin always thought their building could wait until the moment of danger, the President tucked away in his capacious memory the notion of one day asking the Congress for a couple of hundred galleys. As auxiliaries, they had value. As the main naval defense, they were tragicomic.

In 1802, the President signed the act which founded the United States Military Academy at West Point, New York. This was the

54 Hill, "Madison," in *Secretaries of State*, III, 75–77.
55 Ray W. Irwin, *The Diplomatic Relations of the United States with the Barbary Powers, 1776–1816* (Chapel Hill, 1931), p. 158.
56 Smelser, *Navy, 1787–1798*, pp. 75–76, 78, 87, 118, 143, 147–148.

fruition of a seed planted in the minds of the members of the
Continental Congress during the War for Independence. The
Academy amounted to little until after the War of 1812, but no
fortification erected by its alumni was carried by the enemy during
that war, and its United States Military Philosophical Society
(1802–13) gave the military arts and sciences a respectable intellectual standing.[57]

The Constitution prohibited the Congress from abolishing the
international slave trade before 1808. In the constitutional debates,
slavery had been usually presented as at best a necessary evil, but a
few polemicists had begun to use the positive-good theory that
early. In 1803, South Carolina opened its previously enjoined trade
and, in the next four years, admitted about 36,000 slaves, of whom
approximately a third appear to have arrived in Rhode Island
ships. President Jefferson in 1806 suggested a federal law to prohibit
the international trade, beginning January 1, 1808. Britain, where
the slave trade had become a branch of finance rather than of
agriculture, abolished the trade in 1807, not so much for humani-
tarian reasons as to protect the prior owners from new competition.
The British law did not affect the interisland, intraimperial slave
trade.[58]

The United States Congress prohibited the international slave
trade by an Act of 1807, without attempting to regulate interstate
commerce in slaves. The debate was strongly sectional only on
matters of detail. The central problem was how to dispose of slaves
who were confiscated by enforcement officers. Northerners would
not agree that they be sold, because that would mean that the
United States was giving title to human beings. The insipid compromise was that they be disposed of according to local law. It has
been thought that the law worked fairly well, but documents in
Havana show that the trade from the United States to Cuba was
immediately reversed after 1808, and the Louisiana importation of

57 White, *Jeffersonians*, pp. 251–253, 259–260; Sidney Forman, *West Point, A History of the United States Military Academy* (New York, 1950), pp. 20–35.

58 Ulrich Bonnell Phillips, *American Negro Slavery* (New York, 1952), pp. 135–138; R. B. Sheridan, "The Commercial and Financial Organization of the British Slave Trade, 1750–1807," *Economic History Review*, XI (1958), 249–263; Eric Williams, "The British West Indian Slave Trade After Its Abolition in 1807," *Journal of Negro History*, XXVII (1942), 175–191. The Preface to Phil-lips' book, which has long dominated the field, shows that he belonged to the happy-darky-strummin'-on-the-ol'-banjo school of history.

slaves was probably greater after 1808 than before.[59] The trade continued in the next few years after its prohibition, as an underground railroad to carry Negroes into slavery.[60] The law benefited no Negro living in the United States. On the contrary, it encouraged slave owners to demoralize their charges by encouraging them to breed under any circumstances. Female Negro fertility became a quality transcending most traditional virtues.[61]

[59] Phillips, *Slavery*, pp. 145–147; D. C. Corbitt, "Shipments of Slaves from the United States to Cuba, 1789–1807," *Journal of Southern History*, VII (1941), 540–549.

[60] E. Franklin Frazier, *The Negro in the United States* (rev. ed., New York, 1957), pp. 38–39, estimates that perhaps as many as 300,000 Negroes were smuggled into the United States after 1808. That would be an average of 5,650 a year until 1861, hardly an inconspicuous number of illegal entries.

[61] See Frederic Bancroft, *Slave Trading in the Old South* (Baltimore, 1931), p. 8, and index, "Breeders and Breeding."

CHAPTER 4

Republicans vs. *Federalists*

LOOKING back a hundred and sixty-odd years one sees that the differences between Republicans and Federalists have been overemphasized at the expense of their similarities,[1] and that the differences were more of temperament than of principle. But in the decade before Thomas Jefferson's inauguration, there had been a bitter struggle for power which could not be quickly forgotten. The Republicans had won. Now many of the Republicans, thinking rightly that they had been infamously treated by the Federalists wished to chase the enemy force into its last redoubts, giving no quarter to the Federalist captains.

I

Although dislodged from the White House, losing a war of attrition in the executive branch, and hopelessly outnumbered on Capitol Hill, the Federalists were solidly entrenched in the judiciary, from where, as Jefferson wrote, they could turn their "guns on those they were meant to defend." Jefferson had a personal aversion to John Marshall. (Indeed, Marshall was not, at the moment, very popular among Federalists.) Marshall, who was as plain and unostentatious as the President—his favorite sport was pitching quoits—was contemptuous of Jefferson, whom he described as one of the "speculative theorists." The Republicans had several reasonable objections in principle to Federalist jurisprudence, which had a decidedly

---

[1] Richard Hofstadter, *The American Political Tradition and the Men Who Made It* (New York, 1958) , Chap. II.

British cast, but the assault on the judicial bastion which soon followed the Republican ascendancy was a matter of practical politics, aimed at the judges, not at the judicial power. The judges were antidemocratic, many were arrogant, many were snobs, all were Federalists. Those were reasons enough. The Republican regiments advanced to the attack.[2]

The Judiciary Act of 1801, signed during John Adams' last months as President, was the first target of the Republicans. The law had real merits. Its predecessor, the Act of 1789, had real defects which had thrice provoked serious proposals for amendment in the 1790's. The basic change made by the Act of 1801 was to relieve the justices of the Supreme Court of the hardship of riding the circuits. The Act of 1801 would probably have been immune from attack except that its passage coincided with the passions of the day, and John Adams, after defeat, had seized the opportunity to fill all of the newly created places with Federalists. The new Judiciary Act also had what appeared to be an anti-Republican needle built in: when the next vacancy occurred in the Supreme Court, the authorized number of justices would be reduced to five, a change which would delay Jefferson's first chance to make an appointment. The judiciary was also behaving provocatively: first, the District of Columbia Circuit Court told the district attorney to prosecute the editor of the administration's paper, the *National Intelligencer,* for slander against the judges; second, it told its clerk to ignore a directive from the President (good law, bad politics) ; third, the Supreme Court set a date for the hearing which later became famous as *Marbury* v. *Madison.* Jefferson told John Breckinridge the judiciary must be checked. On January 6, 1802, Senator Breckinridge (a future Attorney General) moved to repeal the Act of 1801.[3]

Although the Congress argued the abstract right of the matter, it

2 Jefferson to Eppes, May 28, 1807, in Paul Leicester Ford (ed.) , *The Writings of Thomas Jefferson* (10 vols., New York, 1892–99) , IX, 68; Charles Warren, *The Supreme Court in United States History* (rev. ed., 2 vols., Boston, 1937) , I, 175–184, 190–194, 211–239. Caleb Perry Patterson, *The Constitutional Principles of Thomas Jefferson* (Austin, 1953) , pp. 118–125, observes that Jefferson approved a qualified judicial review *per se* as part of his constitutional philosophy. Edward S. Corwin, *John Marshall and the Constitution* (New Haven, 1919) , Chap. VIII, gives a sympathetic description of Marshall's private life.

3 Warren, *Supreme Court,* I, 185–188, 194–208; Erwin C. Surrency, "The Judiciary Act of 1801," *American Journal of Legal History,* II (1958) , 53–65.

was not a contest of idea against idea but of Republican Congress against Federalist judges. The repealer skinned through the Senate by one vote and triumphed in the House by twenty-seven votes. Federalists cried "Unconstitutional!" but had the situation been reversed the idea would not have occurred to them; if the Congress can create inferior courts, the Congress can abolish inferior courts. Some Republicans feared political damage to themselves, but there was none, except to Aaron Burr, whose temporizing on a tie vote to recommit in the Senate cost him the last shred of Jefferson's good will. The Act of 1789 was restored as of March, 1802, and the Supreme Court justices renewed their saddlesores as they went their rounds of the circuit courts' sittings. The Federalist Hartford *Courant* printed the news of the repeal in a black frame of mourning,[4] but the Republicans had won another battlestreamer at no real cost.

The next action in the campaign was a sortie from the bench of the Supreme Court, a skirmish known to posterity as the intrinsically trivial but historically monumental case of *Marbury* v. *Madison,* 1 Cranch 137 (1803). William Marbury was one of forty-two justices of the peace in and for the sparsely populated District of Columbia, nominated by John Adams, but—by the intervention of President Jefferson—never commissioned. The Judiciary Act of 1789 gave power to the Supreme Court to require the Secretary of State to appear to show cause why a mandamus, or court order, should not compel him to hand over the commission. Marbury got a lawyer and went to court. Could the Court compel an executive officer to perform his "duty"? John Marshall, with feigned reluctance, answered for the Court: No. The reason was that the Act

4 Warren, *Supreme Court,* I, 189–194, 208–214; Morton Borden, *The Federalism of James A. Bayard* (New York, 1955), pp. 106–124; A. C. McLaughlin, *A Constitutional History of the United States* (New York, 1935), pp. 289–293; Dallas to Burr, Feb. 3, 1802, in W. C. Ford (ed.), "Some Papers of Aaron Burr," American Antiquarian Society, *Proceedings,* New Series, XXIX (1919), 109–112; Nathan Schachner, *Thomas Jefferson, A Biography* (2 vols. in 1, New York, 1960), II, 702–704; James E. Smith, *One Hundred Years of Hartford's Courant* (New Haven, 1949), p. 81. In Stuart *v.* Laird, 1 Cranch 298 (1803), the Court accepted the constitutionality of the abolition of the circuit courts created in 1801. In 1802, the Congress passed another Judiciary Act, which changed the system in some details, and which provided that the Supreme Court sit but once a year, the next sitting to be in February, 1803. McLaughlin, *Constitutional History,* pp. 292–293, 293 n.

of 1789 gave this power in original jurisdiction, although the original jurisdiction of the Court, as explicitly described in the Constitution, included no such power or remedy. Therefore, that section of the act of the Congress was unconstitutional. The Court had never before thrown out, in a court action, a piece of federal legislation, and was not to do so again for fifty-four years. The tall, thin, black-eyed Chief Justice, reading the opinion of the Court in his hard, dry voice,[5] had audaciously pronounced what his greatest admirer has called "America's original contribution to the science of law," using a dubious decision to found an enduring principle.[6] Having left Marbury utterly without remedy, Marshall could have declared the Court adjourned. But no—he went on for another twenty pages to say that Marbury had been duly appointed, should have his commission, and was the abused victim of James Madison, who should know better than to "sport away the vested rights of others."[7] This sermon—called an obiter dictum—was entirely gratuitous.

There is no reason to think, as some have thought, that the case was rigged to give Marshall a chance to define judicial review and to excoriate the administration, but his opinion was certainly long premeditated and craftily drafted, and his heart must have leaped when he beheld Marbury's petition. Judicial review had long been talked about, had been accepted as dogma by many, and had even been used in Virginia by Jefferson's favorite jurist, Spencer Roane, to strike down a Virginia statute.[8] Marshall certainly knew what he was doing; as Rufus King had said in 1796, "His head is one of the best organized of any one that I have known."[9] The Republicans had expected him to grant the court order, and thereby to open himself to ridicule as a judge powerless to enforce his mandamus.

5 Carl Brent Swisher, *American Constitutional Development* (2nd ed., Boston, 1954), pp. 101–109. Marshall's appearance is described in William Wirt, *Letters of the British Spy*, much quoted. It may most conveniently be found in Corwin, *Marshall*, pp. 39–42.

6 Albert J. Beveridge, *The Life of John Marshall* (4 vols., Boston, 1916–19), III, 142. Beveridge gives the best detailed account of the judiciary struggle, but is somewhat biased in favor of Marshall. As he points out, pp. 136–137, a reasonable man could believe that the Congress could add to but not subtract from the original jurisdiction of the Court.

7 1 Cranch 137, 166 (1803).

8 McLaughlin, *Constitutional History*, pp. 303–306.

9 Quoted in Corwin, *Marshall*, p. 44.

Instead, he denied his power, while orally flogging the administration for a frivolous attitude toward justice.[10]

Jefferson never agreed that Marshall had established the Supreme Court's monopoly of judgments of constitutionality; the branches of government were equal, and the people in the states were the final judges. For the rest of his long life he resented the Chief Justice's homily on the duties of the executive. The Republican press boiled over briefly, but other pressing problems soon distracted public attention from the case.[11] In depriving poor Marbury of his sinecure and status, the administration had won a battle, but Marshall, while pulling off a partisan coup, had also written a bare, didactic argument which, in generations to come, was to establish the Supreme Court, and the federal judiciary as a whole, in the position Marshall thought it should occupy, even though, as one commentator has written, his strongest remarks were "somewhat beside the point."[12]

Marshall's dictum in *Marbury* v. *Madison* was essentially a defensive action, as Clausewitz has defined all small raids. At Jefferson's suggestion the Republicans moved again to the assault, this time to test the utility of the ancient technique of impeachment, which had already been used successfully by Pennsylvania Republicans to rid their commonwealth of an obnoxious judge. The first victim selected by the United States House of Representatives was the emotionally disturbed and alcoholic Federal District Judge John Pickering of New Hampshire. Jefferson thought impeachment was the correct way to remove any officer who was unacceptable to two-thirds of the senators. Federalists doubted whether an insane man could be tried, but Jefferson insisted that to prove habitual drunkenness was sufficient. Pickering, patently psychotic, was convicted and removed from the bench in March, 1804.[13] On that very day, the House of Representatives impeached

[10] Beveridge, *Marshall*, III, 112, 126–127.

[11] Adrienne Koch, *Jefferson and Madison: The Great Collaboration* (New York, 1950), pp. 227–232; Warren, *Supreme Court*, I, 248–253.

[12] Barbara Barlin, "John Marshall: Usurper or Grantee?" *Social Education*, XXII (1958), 116–118, 121; J. P. Cotton, *Constitutional Decisions of John Marshall* (2 vols., New York, 1905), I, 6, who reprints the case, pp. 7–43. Much of the commentary on Marbury *v.* Madison was quickly dated, as tracts for the times. Both friends and foes of judicial review used the case as a premise to prove it a good thing or a bad thing.

[13] Louis Boudin, *Government by Judiciary* (2 vols., New York, 1932), I, 247–249.

the injudicious, acrimonious Associate Justice Samuel Chase of the Supreme Court, a native of Annapolis and a signer of the Declaration of Independence, who was the narrowest-minded arch-Federalist in a place of national power.

There is no doubt that Chase had disgraced the bench, but he was too opinionated and insensitive to know it. In the previous administration's term, this massively built, white-haired, brown-skinned judge had been the Jeffreys of the Sedition Act prosecutions, in which he showed "oppressive and disgusting" partisanship. Provoked by the repeal of the Judiciary Act of 1801, he exploded before the Baltimore Grand Jury with characteristic turbulence in May, 1803, denouncing the administration as incompetent and as lusting for power. Jefferson asked Maryland Representative Joseph H. Nicholson whether the Congress should allow Chase to go unpunished. Impeachment followed, in January, 1805.[14] The House charged Chase with misconduct in one trial, coercion in another, an attempt (at Baltimore) to inflame the people against their government, and lesser offenses. The Republican theory behind the impeachment was Jefferson's—that it was the way to make the judiciary responsive to the public will. Chase's highly skilled team of defense counsel insisted that an officer was removable only for a criminal act which was indictable.[15]

Aaron Burr, as president of the Senate, presided, and rather well. John Randolph led the prosecution, but, owing to his rustiness at law, tried to get a conviction by rhetoric rather than by reason. The trial was the best show yet produced in Washington. In the crowded Senate Chamber, which was draped with crimson, blue, and green, Randolph tried eloquently but unsuccessfully to convince the senators that impeachment was not a criminal proceeding, but merely a removal. When the eight charges were finally read off, and the roll was called on each, the House managers got a simple majority to convict on three charges but failed to get the necessary two-thirds on any.[16] Federalists were jubilant; most Republicans were bitter.

14 The quoted adjectives are Senator Stevens T. Mason's, quoted in Irving Brant, *James Madison, Secretary of State, 1800–1809* (Indianapolis, 1953), p. 14; Warren, *Supreme Court*, I, 273–279; Edward S. Corwin, "Samuel Chase," *DAB*.

15 Charles Grove Haines and Foster H. Sherwood, *The Role of the Supreme Court in American Government and Politics* (2 vols., Berkeley, 1944–57), I, 259–264; Borden, *Bayard*, pp. 145–148.

16 William Cabell Bruce, *John Randolph of Roanoke* (2 vols., New York, 1922), I, 200–221; Beveridge, *Marshall*, III, 169–219, covers the trials; Warren, *Supreme Court*, I, 289–291.

The Raleigh *Register* said Chase escaped only by "The *Mercy* of our constitution." Randolph was humiliated—which did not sadden *all* of his colleagues—and blamed the White House circle for not invoking party discipline. For other reasons he had reached the point of breaking with the administration. After Chase's acquittal, he was more abusive but less dangerous. John Marshall was temporarily shaken by the crisis and suspense. Some think that if Chase had been convicted, John Marshall would also have been removed. On that, of course, one can only speculate. As for Jefferson, the Senate voted Chase's acquittal only three days before his second inauguration, which made the acquittal, in a sense, a personal defeat for the President. He had learned that impeachment was not a useful lever for prying opponents out of office, although he remained convinced that the Federalists in the judiciary were a band of marplots who were determined to frustrate the people.[17]

Louis Boudin believed the Chase trial was far more important for posterity than the case of *Marbury* v. *Madison*. Albert Beveridge called it "one of the few really great crises in American history." We can say for sure that Chase's successors have been better-mannered, and politically more restrained, and that loose construction of the impeachment clause died right there on that March day in the Senate Chamber.[18]

Thus the Supreme Court remained intact and devoutly Federalist (five to one Federalist at the moment), but before Jefferson moved out of the White House he had the opportunity of appointing three Republicans. In 1804, Jefferson named William Johnson of South Carolina, vice Alfred Moore, resigned. Johnson was strong, bold, and tough-minded—no puppet he. Henry Brockholst Livingston of New York succeeded William Paterson of New Jersey when Paterson died in 1806. Livingston specialized in maritime and commercial law. The creation of a new western circuit in 1807 required the enlargement of the Supreme Court by one member, to seven. After consulting the congressmen from the West, Jefferson filled the vacancy by appointing Thomas Todd, the chief justice of Kentucky, aged 41, who was an expert in land law. As for sour Samuel Chase,

17 *Ibid.*, pp. 291–299; Robert Neal Elliott, Jr., *The Raleigh Register, 1799–1863* (Chapel Hill, 1955), p. 23; Beveridge, *Marshall*, III, 158–162.
18 Boudin, *Government by Judiciary*, I, 254.

between attacks of gout he continued to sit until his death in 1811. Of the new judges, only Johnson's work was memorable, and his nationalist-republican mind resembled more that of the James Madison of the Constitutional Convention than it resembled the minds of the Republicans who annually bombed the judiciary in the Congress and in the press from 1802 to 1805.[19]

John Marshall, the dominant personality of the Supreme Court, resembled his fellow Virginian, George Washington, in that he was moderate in his Federalism and not learned, but he had a dedicated nationalism, a great perseverance, and the ability to use the learning of other men. To John Marshall law was the common law plus the cases which explained its principles, although he knew it would be poor politics to cite explicitly the principles of the common law because of its anglicism and unpopularity. For case law he drew on his colleagues and on the learning of the sparkling assembly of lawyers, mostly Virginians and Marylanders, who practiced before the Supreme Court. His task was not laborious. There were only ninety-eight cases docketed for the February term of 1810.[20]

Except for *Marbury* v. *Madison,* the most celebrated opinions of the Marshall Court came after the administrations of Jefferson and Madison, but two important cases may be briefly noticed to show the steady pressure of nationalism exerted by the Supreme Court. In *United States v. Judge Peters,* the Court compelled the payment of a congressionally ordered privateering prize award, despite a Pennsylvania statute to the contrary, and despite a mobilization of Pennsylvania militia to prevent service of the writ. In *Fletcher* v. *Peck,* the Court refused to let the Georgia legislature impair the obligation of a contract made by an earlier legislature, even though the contract had been secured by bribing the legislators. In this decision Marshall drew on the earlier thinking of Alexander Ham-

[19] Warren, *Supreme Court,* I, 286–288, 299–301. All of the justices mentioned above are well sketched in *DAB.* The standard life of Johnson is Donald G. Morgan, *Justice William Johnson, The First Dissenter* (Columbia, S.C., 1954); matters herein are treated in pp. 41–54, 157–162. A shorter account is Henry F. Bedford, "William Johnson and the Marshall Court," *South Carolina Historical Magazine,* LXII (1961), 165–171.

[20] McLaughlin, *Constitutional History,* pp. 299–301; Julius Goebel, Jr., "The Common Law and the Constitution," in W. Melville Jones (ed.), *Chief Justice John Marshall: A Reappraisal* (Ithaca, 1956), pp. 101–123; Charles Warren, *A History of the American Bar* (Boston, 1911), pp. 256–263.

ilton,[21] as he was to do again in the later case of *McCulloch* v. *Maryland* (1819).

There is no fixed consensus on the value and effect of Marshall's work. The pendulum has alternated between praise and damnation ever since. John Taylor of Caroline thought the Supreme Court, by 1814, stood in relation to the people of the United States as the British Parliament had stood before 1776: aristocratic, uninformed, legislative in fact, not shaped by law but a shaper of law. This was the classic Old Republican position. On the other hand, a more recent student, William Winslow Crosskey, thought Marshall was great but in a losing cause, since (to oversimplify Mr. Crosskey's argument brutally) he failed to destroy states' rights. In between these extreme views are the more widely held conclusions that the Marshall Court, and not Marshall alone, established judicial limits on legislative powers, and made the Supreme Court a great national organ which construed a nationalistic instrument in a nationalistic way. The Constitution being national in essence, and the Court national in function, it is hard to see how any other result could be expected.[22]

II

After their first year in office, the Republicans had won far more popularity than the Federalists had ever achieved. In an age of primitive communications, the election politics of the national capital was congressional politics—particularly House politics. In directing the important social aspect of political affairs at the center, Jefferson had little help. Madison's hands were full of diplomatic dispatches. The thoroughly domesticated Albert Galla-

[21] United States *v.* Judge Peters, 5 Cranch 115 (1809); Hampton L. Carson, "The Case of the Sloop 'Active,'" *Pennsylvania Magazine of History and Biography*, XVI (1892), 385–389; Fletcher *v.* Peck, 6 Cranch 87 (1810), which will be treated in more detail later.
[22] E. T. Mudge, *The Social Philosophy of John Taylor of Caroline* (New York, 1939), pp. 120–130; Benjamin F. Wright, Jr., "The Philosopher of Jeffersonian Democracy," *American Political Science Review*, XXII (1928), 870–892, and H. H. Simms, *Life of John Taylor* (Richmond, 1932), help in understanding Taylor's dry, angular mind; William Winslow Crosskey, "Mr. Justice Marshall," in Allison Dunham and Philip B. Kurland (eds.), *Mr. Justice* (Chicago, 1956), pp. 17–46; Robert E. Cushman, "Marshall and the Constitution," *Minnesota Law Review*, V (1920), 1–31, reviews Beveridge's and Corwin's works on Marshall, both of which were completed in that year; Robert G. McCloskey, *The American Supreme Court* (Chicago, 1960), pp. 61–62, 78–80.

tin stayed at home with his Hannah as much as possible, and saw
few people except on Treasury business. For the necessary foot-and-
mouth work needed in Washington to win votes elsewhere, Jefferson, in the first couple of years, relied on John Randolph, who had
temporarily become the most politically effective representative,
and on his friend John Beckley, reappointed as Clerk of the House
with the added post of Librarian of Congress. Beckley had "the
keenest pair of ears in the country," while Randolph had the
glibbest tongue. So partisan was Beckley that he contrived to make
it difficult for Federalists to use the Library.[23] Randolph and
Beckley provided the political information and channels to the
members of the Congress, who, in their turn, preached the gospel in
their home districts. Jefferson provided the brains, the judgments of
his executive officers, and the indispensable symbol of headship.

Cracks began to appear in the walls of Federalist New England.
By the spring of 1802, Republicans were winning local elections.
Religious pluralism hurt Federalism, as Connecticut Baptists and
Methodists voted Republican against their Congregationalist bet-
ters. Except for the deservedly dying Burrite faction, New York
Republicanism was in good health. By 1802 the Pennsylvania
Federalist Party had almost committed suicide by antagonizing the
Germans and the Scots-Irish.[24] As John Adams wrote years later to
Jefferson, "Pennsylvania is a contest between German, Irish and old
English families. When Germans and Irish unite, they give 30,000
majorities."[25] In the off-year election of 1802, the Federalists could
not find a real cudgel to flourish. Jefferson's program had been
deliberately sedative, to quiet the old fears of his Jacobinism and to
lure popular support from under the Federalist leaders. His theories
pleased the small farmers. His practices conciliated the mercantile
men. He himself put it well when he wrote that if an election could
be held without personalities—that is, simply Republicanism

[23] J. Q. Adams to King, Oct. 8, 1802, in W. C. Ford (ed.), *The Writings of
John Quincy Adams* (7 vols., New York, 1913–17), III, 9; Philip M. Marsh, "John
Beckley: Mystery Man of the Early Jeffersonians," *Pennsylvania Magazine of
History*, LXXII (1948), 54–69; Gloria Jahoda, "John Beckley: Jefferson's Cam-
paign Manager," New York Public Library, *Bulletin*, LXIV (1960), 247–260.

[24] Richard J. Purcell, *Connecticut in Transition, 1775–1818* (Washington,
1918), pp. 79, 89, 97; Sanford W. Higginbotham, *The Keystone in the Democratic
Arch: Pennsylvania Politics, 1800–1816* (Harrisburg, 1952), pp. 1–47.

[25] J. Adams to Jefferson, Nov. 15, 1813, in Lester J. Cappon (ed.), *The Adams-
Jefferson Letters* (2 vols., Chapel Hill, 1959), II, 401.

against Federalism—the Federalists would get not a single electoral vote. As we have seen, Hamilton, in April, 1802, tried to promote a Christian Constitutional Society to crusade against the infidel Republicans, but few were interested. Even a series of pro-Jefferson letters by Thomas Paine, which would have been deadly kisses in 1798, could not provoke a strong anti-Jacobin reaction in the Federalist rank and file. The election of 1802 was not a battle; it was a rout. The desolation of Federalism was well reflected in the Congress. The House had been enlarged from 105 to 141 seats. In the Seventh Congress the Republican-Federalist ratio was 69:36. After the election of 1802 it was 102:39, an increase from 66 per cent of the seats to 72 per cent for the Republicans. In the Senate the Republican advantage had been 18:13; now it was 25:9. Even the moderate Representative James A. Bayard of Delaware lost to his friend Caesar A. Rodney by fifteen votes, while the quite immoderate Timothy Pickering failed to win a House seat, although he was then elected to the Senate by the Great and General Court of Massachusetts.[26] It was the most convincing endorsement of an administration the American voter can give—an increased congressional majority in the off-year balloting.

The Eighth Congress, which convened in October, 1803, prepared the way for the presidential election of 1804 by initiating the Twelfth Amendment to provide that each presidential elector vote separately for President and for Vice-President. This would prevent a repetition of the dangerous intraparty tie of 1800, and, more important at the moment, would preclude any huggermugger among Federalist electors to promote the Republican vice-presidential candidate over Jefferson's head. Such a change in the mode of election had been argued as early as 1799. Federalists in the Congress opposed it. They said it would alter the nature of the union, would make it difficult for a citizen of a small state to rise to either office, and would make the Vice-Presidency the prize of intrigue. The Republicans paid no attention. For them the chief difficulty was in agreeing on one of the numerous plans which were ready in Republican pockets when the Congress convened. Gallatin and Senator DeWitt Clinton of New York reminded Republicans that Federalists, under the old system, could support any Republi-

[26] Borden, *Bayard*, pp. 127-131; William A. Robinson, "Timothy Pickering," *DAB*.

can vice-presidential choice, including—God forbid!—even Aaron Burr if he were named, in order to depose Jefferson. That was sufficient motive to get quick agreement. The amendment was sent to the state legislatures in December, 1803, and ratified by the following September, in time to govern the presidential election of 1804.[27]

Jefferson might have liked to retire after one term. Quidnuncs hinted that Madison might lead in 1804, but Jefferson said slanders prevented his retirement. (Also, he needed the salary.) The only problem was the Vice-Presidency, for which the Congressional Caucus (the first held for such a purpose) nominated George Clinton of New York, aged 67, as a way of keeping up the New York alliance without putting a new heir apparent in Madison's way.[28]

South of Pennsylvania the Republican prospects for 1804 were wholly cheerful. In New England some ground might be gained. But in Pennsylvania and in New York there were factions which required special attention. Burr had been eclipsed, deserted by Gallatin's father-in-law, the influential Commodore James Nicholson, and even by his faction's truculent editor, James Cheetham. Senator DeWitt Clinton led the party in alliance with the Livingston clan. This was clear for all to read in the news of the nomination of DeWitt's played-out uncle George for the office of Vice-President.[29]

Pennsylvania's party had suffered a simple fracture, which did not affect the presidential contest but which made life unpleasant for Republicans of principle. Ideological differences were slight, but cliquishness was serious. The legislature was trying to remodel the judiciary and to impeach nearly all of the judges. Governor Thomas McKean, Gallatin, judge-novelist Hugh Henry Brackenridge, Dr. George Logan, and Alexander James Dallas—all of whom except Dallas had been at least once denounced as subversive tools of Jacobin anarchy—found themselves associated as conservatives in opposition to the legislature. The exquisite, powdered, perfumed demagogue, Dr. Michael Leib, and editor William

[27] Edward Stanwood, *History of the Presidency from 1788 to 1897* (new ed., Boston, 1924), pp. 77–82; Uriah Tracy, "Amendment of the Constitution [1802]," in Frank Moore, *American Eloquence* (2 vols., New York, 1856–57), I, 432–442.
[28] Stanwood, *Presidency*, pp. 74–85.
[29] Mary Atwell Moore, "James Cheetham," *DAB*.

Duane, the erstwhile paladin of the free press, led the radicals, chiefly in order to control Philadelphia and to avenge themselves for an insufficiency of federal patronage and federal printing. Luckily for the Republicans, the comatose Federalist group could not call up enough strength to exploit this dissension in their enemies' array.[30]

Indeed, the Federalist element—it could hardly be called a national party any more—was suffering a malaise. A general practitioner of politics might have diagnosed it as deteriorating popularity, complicated by doctrinaire unteachability, prognosis poor. Doctrinaire Federalists—to shift metaphors—believed they had lost the ship of state to a gang of envious, shiftless, or demented mutineers, who would first tumble into anarchy and who would then cheer some military despot who would rise from the crew. The Federalist thinkers only proved they had studied the French Revolution better than they had studied their own countrymen.

Differences of political doctrine were intensified by the measurable loss of political power. In the reapportionment of the House, and the increase in the number of seats from 105 to 141, New England gained but six seats, and two of them were in untrustworthy Vermont. Tennessee, Kentucky, and Ohio (after 1803) gained seven seats between them, while the wild west of New York and Georgia added more. The Louisiana Purchase guaranteed a further lightening of New England's relative weight in the national scale.[31] Although the Federalists had once been a national party, they had no formidable following in the optimistic West.

Furthermore, organized orthodox religion seemed to weaken in direct proportion to the decline of New England Federalism. For example, in Vermont, where Republicans calculated that 95 per cent of the clergy were Federalists, a temporary upsurge of Federalist strength in 1799 had subsided by 1802. The Republican legislature then showed what the faithful might expect: it exempted dissenters from taxes for the support of organized religion. The President himself had written to a Baptist congregation to condemn the union of church and state (which was not a federal question before the ratification of the Fourteenth Amendment). He used the much-quoted phrase "wall of separation" between church and state

[30] Higginbotham, *Keystone*, pp. 49–75; Claude M. Newlin, *The Life and Writings of Hugh Henry Brackenridge* (Princeton, 1932), pp. 241–250.
[31] The Louisiana Purchase is the subject of Chapter 5.

to describe what he believed to be the intention of the First Amendment.

Paradoxically, those who loved Federalism best now seemed determined upon its destruction. These men are usually lumped together as the so-called Essex Junto, a term used by John Hancock to describe a group in Essex County, Massachusetts, during the War for Independence and by Thomas Jefferson, while President, to mark out his most abusive Massachusetts enemies. They included lawyer Theophilus Parsons, Senator Timothy Pickering, ex-Representative Fisher Ames, who was their most skilled vituperator, and others of like minds. Except for Pickering and Parsons, who was to become chief justice of Massachusetts, the older leaders were too fastidious for the squalid work of getting into office. Most of them lived in semiretirement, enjoying their dark forebodings of the future of the republic. Those who worked actively in politics daintily determined Federalist nominations in self-appointed and sometimes secret caucuses of rich gentlemen or by mail, while the bulk of the neglected voters drifted into the handshaking, cigar-awarding, storytelling, barbecue-promoting Republican party.[32] There were Federalists of the same temper in Connecticut, that most intransigent of states, where Senator Uriah Tracy, poet John Trumbull, lexicographer Noah Webster, and their allies stared in dismay at the spread of radicalism, while deploring the assault on the judicial bastion. In Connecticut the legislature let the Twelfth Amendment go unratified, but removed the chief judge of the County Court at Hartford for celebrating the Louisiana Purchase.[33]

Fisher Ames well expressed the New England arch-Federalist feeling in a sentence when he wrote that New England held its place in the union "not as the guarded treasure of freemen, but as the pittance, which the disdain of conquerors has left to their captives."[34] Hatred of democracy had become hatred of the United

[32] Elisha P. Douglass, "Fisher Ames, Spokesman for New England Federalism," American Philosophical Society, *Proceedings*, CIII (1959), 693–715; Samuel Eliot Morison, *By Land and by Sea* (New York, 1954), pp. 210–213, and *Life and Letters of Harrison Gray Otis, Federalist, 1765–1848* (2 vols., Boston, 1913), I, 286–317. There are good profiles of Parsons, Pickering, and Ames in *DAB*.

[33] Norman L. Stamps, "Party Government in Connecticut, 1800–1816," *Historian*, XVII (1955), 181–184.

[34] "The Republican," No. I, July, 1804, in Seth Ames (ed.), *Works of Fisher Ames* (2 vols., Boston, 1854), II, 252. Fisher Ames summarized all of the ideological grievances and despotic portents in "The Dangers of Liberty," 1805, *ibid.*, pp. 344–399.

States. From this position it was a short step to thinking of secession—secession by conspiratorial *coup d'état* if possible, but secession in any case.[35]

Secession was the most frequently discussed federal question before 1865. Even Jefferson briefly toyed with the notion of writing it into the Kentucky Resolutions of 1798 as a state's right. In 1804 the immediate catalyst of the secession reaction was the Louisiana Purchase. Senator Pickering and the Connecticut congressional delegation discussed secession. Pickering then developed a plan for a Northern Confederacy. Ames and George Cabot, who had the best brain but the least energy in the group, disapproved of the scheme, thinking it would be wiser to await a fatal mistake by Jefferson, while working through state governments and through the press. Alexander Hamilton urged instead the organization of a truly national Federalist party. The Federalist governor of Massachusetts, Caleb Strong, appears to have known nothing of the conspiracy. British Minister Anthony Merry listened politely, reported it to his government, but offered the conspirators no help. Jefferson learned of it privately, and said it would not work because it was against the trend of affairs. Nevertheless, Pickering pressed his first step successfully: a resolution by the Massachusetts legislature to abolish the three-fifths compromise in the Constitution, which provided that three-fifths of the slaves be counted as population for the purpose of determining the apportionment of seats in the House of Representatives. Unhappily for Pickering and friends, not even Connecticut joined in throwing this challenge to the South. Undiscouraged, the secessionists continued to dream of a Confederacy including Nova Scotia, New York, and even Pennsylvania, with New England. How could one bring in New York? With the help, of course, of Aaron Burr, who would also be handy as a commander in chief if it came to fighting.[36]

---

[35] The absolutely indispensable collection of materials on Federalist dissatisfaction and maneuverings is Henry Adams (ed.), *Documents Relating to New England Federalism, 1800–1815* (Boston, 1877). Pages 1–329 comprise ten retrospective letters and documents of 1825–29, reopening old wounds. The Appendix, from p. 331, has contemporary documents. The relevant materials for Jefferson's first term will be found in pp. 331–365.

[36] Jefferson to Granger, April 16, 1804, *Writings of Jefferson*, VIII, 298–300; James Truslow Adams, *New England in the Republic, 1776–1850* (Boston, 1926), pp. 237–239; John C. Miller, *Alexander Hamilton* (New York, 1959), pp. 564–566.

The opportunity seemed to lie in the election of Burr as governor of New York in 1804. The Republicans had nominated mild, respectable Morgan Lewis. The feeble, factious New York Federalists rallied behind Burr and his dwindling faction of Republican malcontents. Burr's only qualification for Federalist support seemed to be that he had, in 1802, attended a Federalist dinner in New York, where he offered the bizarre toast, "To the union of all honest men!" The naïve New England conspirators had no assurances from New York's Machiavellian prince except that his administration would be satisfactory to Federalists. It made no difference anyway. Lewis and the efficient Clintonian-Livingstonian Republicans, with the help of Alexander Hamilton, crushed the Burrite sulkers and Federalists with dispatch, getting 58 per cent of the vote. The failure of the so-called northern conspiracy showed the political weakness of the man who has mistakenly been regarded as the leader of New England Federalists, Timothy Pickering. Although he originated the separatist scheme as the only remaining defense against democracy, he did not convince many other Federalists. All in all, he was merely a figurehead, rather more ornamental than useful to the younger working Federalists. His value to them was that he was a living symbol of the Washington administration in which he had held—without distinction—two cabinet posts.[37]

Hamilton had played Joan of Arc against this offensive alliance. He had continuously opposed Burr on grounds of personality and character since 1791. In 1804, dreading a Burr victory, he told his views of Burr's unfitness for public office to all who would listen. His words were paraphrased in print as his "despicable opinion . . . of Mr. Burr." When this appeared, the duelists' code required Burr to challenge Hamilton. Burr's second was William P. Van Ness, his political lieutenant, who believed in dueling as a gentlemanly way of getting rid of political enemies. At Weehawken, New Jersey, on July 11, 1804, Hamilton intended to miss in the hope

[37] Charles Worthen Spencer, "Morgan Lewis," *DAB;* Dixon Ryan Fox, *The Decline of Aristocracy in the Politics of New York* (New York, 1919), pp. 57–83, explains the decay of Federalism in New York; J. C. Hamilton (ed.), *History of the Republic of the United States as Traced in the Writings of Alexander Hamilton* (7 vols., New York, 1859), VII, 769–836, gives the details of 1804 from the Hamiltonian viewpoint. On Pickering and secession, see D. H. Fischer, *The Revolution of American Conservatism: The Federalist Party in the Era of Jeffersonian Democracy* (New York, 1965), pp. 28, 175–176.

that Burr would also miss, but Burr shot to kill. Thus died, at the height of his intellectual powers, a man who fell short of greatness only by the margin of his distrust of the American people.[38]

And thus also died the Northern Confederacy project, the overt political career of Vice-President Aaron Burr, and the only possible rivalry with Jefferson for the White House. Burr's smoothness, his strong appeal to women, and the admiration he aroused in younger men helped him no more in legitimate politics. He lived out his term almost alone. If he had forced Jefferson's prompt election in 1801, as he certainly could, he would have had a strong claim as heir, at least in 1808.[39] It is hard to say a kindly word at the graveside of this curious career, except that Burr never held a public post that demanded all of his intelligence, energy, and charm. Now his life as a public servant was finished, but not his life as a servant of Aaron Burr.

Except for the manic reaction of a few old-time Federalist leaders and editors, the presidential election of 1804 was one of the calmest. True issues hardly existed. The party of nationalism tried to persuade the people that the Louisiana Purchase was not a national triumph, but hardly anyone listened, even though it was said to have cost every inhabitant of Massachusetts the incredible sum of four dollars. Jefferson's administration had not been dynamic in other directions. The Seventh and Eighth Congresses, between them, passed only 173 public bills. The Virginia legislature spoke for the South when it countered the Massachusetts call to repeal the three-fifths compromise by approving a weak, contrived, barely intelligible resolution, carefully written to offend or excite nobody. The Federalist press went back to the 1790's and tried to blacken the Republicans as ignorant, opportunistic members of a sinister worldwide conspiracy, and to defame Jefferson as a physical coward and a libertine, but few readers were moved. The President, himself, began to see more merit in the law of libel than he had seen in, say, 1798, but the death of one of his two living children, Mary

38 Nathan Schachner, *Alexander Hamilton* (New York, 1946), pp. 419–430; William E. Smith, "William Peter Van Ness," *DAB;* John A. Krout, "Alexander Hamilton's Place in the Founding of the Nation," American Philosophical Society, *Proceedings,* CII (1958), 124–128.
39 Samuel H. Wandell and Meade Minnigerode, *Aaron Burr* (2 vols., New York, 1925), I, 336–339.

Jefferson Eppes, pained him much more than the Federalists could.[40]

For the decaying Federalists the election was a catastrophe which proved their sometime party was but a weathered scarecrow. Jefferson received 162 electoral votes, leaving his relatively unknown opponent, Charles Cotesworth Pinckney, a miserable fourteen. From Connecticut (which abolished the paper ballot) Pinckney received nine, from Delaware three, and from Maryland two of its eleven. Massachusetts Republicans could luxuriate in the favor of the people, for the commonwealth gave Jefferson a plurality of 3,052 in a poll of 55,222. Connecticut Federalism won because it had a warm local issue (and perhaps because of oral voting) ; the local issue was whether to call a state constitutional convention. In Pennsylvania the ecological relics of Federalism were trampled to death in a rough scrimmage between the Republican factions. In South Carolina there were barely enough Federalists left in office to make up an adequate Virginia Reel. Only in Delaware, the home of the teachable Federalists, did the Federalist element actually gain in strength. Federalist depression at the national result was typically phrased by one who wrote " . . . I believe that sooner or later we must all go thro the Democratic mill." The ferment was bubbling. At the White House reception after the President's second inauguration, it was noticed that "dirty boys" and Negroes drank wine and sat in the presence of their superiors.[41]

As in every other American presidential election, the decision was reached in 1804 for a variety of reasons. In New England, only Connecticut had a real local issue which worked for Federalism. Elsewhere, national prosperity, the failure of Jefferson to be as bestial as his advance billing, the extension of the privilege of voting, the obvious sectionalism of the Federalists, the increase in the number of states which chose their presidential electors by direct election, the national pride in the Louisiana Purchase, the

[40] Morison, *Otis,* I, 261–263. For examples of political lampoons, see George L. Roth, "Verse Satire on 'Faction,' 1790–1815," *William and Mary Quarterly,* Third Series, XVII (1960) , 473–485.

[41] Purcell, *Connecticut,* pp. 227–261; John Munroe, *Federalist Delaware, 1775–1815* (New Brunswick, 1954) , pp. 235–241; Borden, *Bayard,* pp. 141–143; George Henry Haynes (ed.), "Letters of Samuel Taggart, Representative in Congress, 1803–1814," Nov. 17, 1804, American Antiquarian Society, *Proceedings,* New Series, XXXIII (1923) , p. 133.

southern and western admiration for Jeffersonian agrarianism—all these helped to form a national consensus in favor of continuing the moderate Jeffersonian administration in power.

The Federalists had really finished their job by the time the federal government was organized. They had stayed in power because their talents were immediately available, because of gratitude, and because of the popular veneration of George Washington. By the time of Jefferson's first election, their vitality and popularity had been dissipated by snobbery, by internal quarrels, and by their open distrust of the people they governed. In 1804, a detached observer might have thought they were finished, although the label "Federalist" was successfully used in politics, as in Delaware, for example, as late as the 1820's,[42] because of a spirited Young Federalist revival which began to make itself felt during Jefferson's second term.

On March 4, 1805, the successful President delivered his second inaudible inaugural address. On foreign policy, he limited himself mainly to moral aphorisms. On domestic politics, it has been said that he obliquely satirized the Federalists in a parable in which he pretended to be talking of the Indian problem. The Indians (i.e., the Federalists) were capable of civilization but were held back by the malignant influence of their medicine men (i.e., their clergy). He proposed to spend the Treasury surplus on peacetime public works. "War will then be but a suspension of useful works, and a return to a state of peace a return to the progress of improvement."[43] Thomas Jefferson had moved some distance in the time since he appointed the parsimonious Gallatin to oppose federal spending. The responsibilities and, perhaps more important, the opportunities of federal leadership had changed him to the man who bought Louisiana and who now (with Gallatin's approval) advocated public works. Some of the Old Republicans muttered that he had been Federalized. They were to be troublesome. The second term would not end as pleasantly as the first.

42 William A. Robinson, *Jeffersonian Democracy in New England* (New Haven, 1916), pp. 36–51, 74–75; D. H. Gilpatrick, *Jeffersonian Democracy in North Carolina* (New York, 1931), pp. 234–239; Wilfred E. Binkley, *American Political Parties, Their Natural History* (3rd ed., New York, 1959), pp. 86–89.

43 J. D. Richardson (ed.), *A Compilation of the Messages and Papers of the Presidents* (20 vols., Washington, 1897–1917), I, 367.

1. Thomas Jefferson by Thomas Sully

(Illustrations are from the Library of Congress unless otherwise attributed.)

2.   Monticello, 1809, by Jane Bradick Petticolas

(Permission of T. J. Coolidge, Jr.)

3.   Bank of the United States. Philadelphia, 1799

Engraving, William Birch and Son, *The City of Philadelphia . . . as It Appeared in the Year 1800, Philadelphia, 1800*

4. Dolley Payne Madison
   by Gilbert Stuart

5. James Madison, 1805,
   by Gilbert Stuart

(Permission Colonial Williamsburg, Inc. The original hangs in the Joint Committee Room of the Capitol, Williamsburg, Virginia.)

6. The United States Capitol, before the fire of August 24, 1814

Watercolor, Benjamin H. Latrobe (?) . The scene is from Pennsylvania Avenue and shows the poplars planted at Jefferson's suggestion.

7. The United States Capitol after the fire

Tinted engraving by William Strickland, after a drawing by George Munger

8.   James Monroe by Thomas Sully

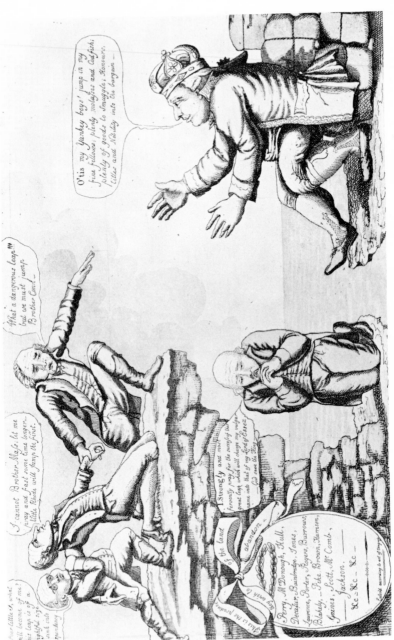

9. "The Hartford Convention or Leap No Leap." Etching by William Charles

Massachusetts tries to persuade Connecticut and Rhode Island to leap into the arms of King George, who promises profits and privilege; a Federalist leader prays for success, which will raise him to the peerage as Lord Essex.

10. The capture and destruction of Washington, August 24, 1814. Anonymous English engraving, 1814

The artist has compressed the events of several days on a line of operations extending more than fifty miles into one climactic moment on an imagined water front. The unlikely gunboats in the foreground were destroyed by their Commodore, Joshua Barney, on the Patuxent River, far to the southeast of Washington. There was no naval combat on the Potomac on this occasion.

11. Construction of a warship—the U.S.F. *Philadelphia*

Engraving, William Birch and Son, *The City of Philadelphia . . . as It Appeared in the Year 1800*, *Philadelphia, 1800*

12. The burning of the United States Frigate *Philadelphia* in the harbor of Tripoli, by a party under the command of Stephen Decatur

Engraving, John Guerazzi, 1805 (?)

TO REMEMBRANCE

OF THE

BALTIMORE MILITIA,

WHO MET, OR WITHSTOOD, THE CHOICEST TROOPS OF THE FOE,

SEPTEMBER 13, 1814,

And died in defence of their altars and fire sides, their
"wives and their little ones;"

WHOSE GALLANT HEARTS SHIELDED THE VIRGIN FROM POLLUTION, AND THE
MATRON FROM INSULT;

𝕎ho preserved this City from plunder and conflagration

AND

ALL THE MURDERING BUSINESS OF WAR,

WAGED BY A

NEW RACE OF GOTHS

OUTRAGING THE ORDINANCES OF GOD, AND THE LAWS OF HUMANITY:

THIS VOLUME OF THE WEEKLY REGISTER

IS REVERENTIALLY DEDICATED,

BY THE EDITOR.

13. (Above) Dedicatory page of
Hezekiah Niles's *Weekly Register*
(Baltimore), volume VI (March-
September, 1814)

(Memorial Library,
University of Notre Dame)

THE

NAVIGATOR

CONTAINING DIRECTIONS FOR NAVIGATING

THE MONONGAHELA, ALLEGHENY, OHIO AND MISSISSIPPI RIVERS

WITH AN AMPLE ACCOUNT
OF THESE MUCH ADMIRED WATERS
FROM THE HEAD OF THE FORMER TO THE MOUTH
OF THE LATTER;

AND A CONCISE DESCRIPTION

OF THEIR

TOWNS, VILLAGES, HARBORS, SETTLEMENTS, &c

WITH MAPS OF THE OHIO

TO WHICH IS ADDED

AN APPENDIX

CONTAINING AN ACCOUNT OF LOUISIANA, AND OF THE
COLUMBIA RIVER AS DISCOVERED BY THE VOYAGE UNDER
CAPTS. LEWIS AND CLARK

Eighth Edition—Improved and Enlarged

PITTSBURGH

PUBLISHED AND SOLD

By CRAMER, SPEAR and EICHBAUM

FRANKLIN HEAD, MARKET
STREET

ROBERT FERGUSON & CO.   *PRINTERS*

1814

14. Facsimile of title page of Zadok
Cramer's *Navigator,* the most popular guide for emigrants of the period

(Memorial Library,
University of Notre Dame)

15. Fort Harrison on the Wabash River, 1812, near present Terre Haute, Indiana. Anonymous lithograph, 1848

During the War of 1812 Fort Harrison was commanded and successfully defended by Captain Zachary Taylor, U.S.A.

16. New York in 1800, as seen from the Jersey shore. Aquatint, Francis Jukes after Alexander Robertson

17. "A View of the Bombardment of Fort McHenry," Baltimore, 1814. From an original print in the collection of Franklin D. Roosevelt

18. *Constitution* capturing *Guerrière*, 1813. Engraving by C. Tiebout after T. Birch

Constitution has her yards hauled so that she stands still in the water while pounding the helpless and uncontrollable British frigate.

19. "The fall of Washington or Maddy in full flight." Anonymous English etching, 1814

President Madison and *de facto* Secretary of War Monroe run from the flaming Capitol, mocked by British seamen and suspected of planning to join Napoleon on Elba.

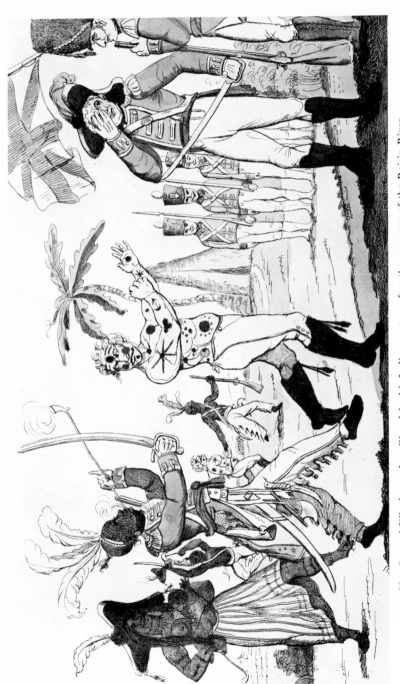

20. General Winchester humiliated by his Indian captors after the massacre of the Raisin River. Anonymous English engraving, 1813

21. Journal of William Clark, open at entry for October 15, 1805

(Missouri Historical Society)

22. Flag flown by Commodore Oliver Hazard Perry in the Battle
of Lake Erie, 1813

(Permission of U.S. Naval Academy Museum)

23. "Andrew Jackson, The Hero of New-Orleans"

This lithograph, made near the end of his second term as President, showed that Jackson helped to meet the need of a young nation for heroes in its pantheon.

twenty fourth day of December one
thousand eight hundred and fourteen.

Gambier.

Henry Goulburn.

William Adams

John Quincy Adams.

J. A. Bayard

H. Clay

Jon. Russell,

Albert Gallatin

24.   The signatures to the Treaty of Ghent, 1814

(The National Archives)

CHAPTER 5

The Purchase of a Trackless World

AT the close of the Great War for Empire, in 1763, the diplomatic servants of a humiliated France deeded the Louisiana country and New Orleans to the Spanish, their partners in defeat. The conveyance was not a kind of booby prize but, more selfishly, was done to encourage Spain to make peace quickly and to rid France of an expensive encumbrance.[1] In the next twenty-five years the French court had no serious intention of trying to recover the country. It had never paid its way. Furthermore, French diplomatists valued the friendship of both Spain and the United States too highly to think of such an annoyance to both, although France would have taken whatever steps necessary to prevent British expansion in that direction.[2] Then the age of the French Revolution brought dreams of military glory. Grandiose schemes inextricably linked Louisiana with Saint-Domingue.[3] But Americans could dream and scheme, too. In American publications, and in somewhat agitated political reports from New Orleans to Spain, there was ample warning of an apparently irresistible American pressure westward.[4]

[1] E. Wilson Lyon, *Louisiana in French Diplomacy, 1759–1804* (Norman, Okla., 1934), tells the story of the Louisiana Purchase exhaustively (but not exhaustingly), especially from the French side. This chapter draws heavily on the work.

[2] Mildred Stahl Fletcher, "Louisiana as a Factor in French Diplomacy," *Mississippi Valley Historical Review*, XVII (1930–31), 367–376.

[3] Rayford W. Logan, *The Diplomatic Relations of the United States with Haiti, 1776–1891* (Chapel Hill, 1941), pp. 40–60.

[4] John Carl Parish, *The Emergence of the Idea of Manifest Destiny* (Los Angeles, 1932), pp. 13–23.

The conversion of the French Revolution into a world war naturally brought the situation of the Louisiana country into question. The uncertainties of the future occasioned a profusion of American plots to seize or to subvert Louisiana. None bore fruit. Therefore, when Thomas Jefferson became President of the United States, he could correctly speak of amity with Spain,[5] but in the labyrinthine mind of Charles Maurice de Talleyrand-Périgord, Foreign Minister of France, a conviction formed: the sprawling United States ought to be kept east of the tawny Mississippi, in order to keep the new republic small and dependent on European friends. Spain was not strong enough to hold the line. France was. When Talleyrand sent Louis André Pichon as minister to Washington in 1801, he learned that Mr. Jefferson would like to have Louisiana or some part of it, but was in no hurry so long as spineless Spain controlled, in a manner of speaking, the area.[6]

As the West grew prodigiously, so did its trade with the world by way of New Orleans. The police power of Spain in Louisiana shrank in the same proportion. Spain could keep neither its wilderness orderly nor its customs officers honest. Imperial mercantilism was locally tempered by graft, nonfeasance, and civic demoralization. The leather-clad squirrel shooters of Kentucky and Tennessee could take the place when they chose, if no other government interfered, but, for the moment, they had no motive.

As early as 1789, Frenchmen, unofficially, had begun to think of retaking Louisiana. Eléonore François Elie Moustier, a French representative in the United States from 1787 to 1789, wrote a three-hundred-page *aide-mémoire* telling his government how and why it might be recovered. French officials read and reread this paper in the next ten years. Moustier's suggestion was probably the seed of

<hr />

[5] Arthur Preston Whitaker, *The Mississippi Question, 1795–1803* (New York, 1934), thoroughly covers the western problem of the United States to which the Louisiana Purchase was a solution. Much in this chapter has been derived from the study.

[6] Arthur Burr Darling, *Our Rising Empire, 1763–1803* (New Haven, 1940), pp. 413–420. Robert S. Smith (ed.), "A Proposal for the Barter and Sale of Spanish America in 1800," *Hispanic American Historical Review*, XLI (1961), 275–286, presents the proposal of Valentin Tadeo Echavarri de Foronda, writer, professor, and Spanish consul general at Philadelphia in 1801, who concluded that Spain should voluntarily dispose of all of its overseas empire by sale and barter—the influence of his notion is unknown, but any price would have been better than what Spain ended by getting.

Edmond Charles Genêt's frustrated plans to reconquer the region in the early 1790's with an American army under George Rogers Clark. Some have thought France's interest in these years was only to secure a pawn for diplomatic chess, but her steadfast policy was to keep a strong government out of the Mississippi Valley and, if possible, to make that empty waste turn a commercial profit. In the same decade the Directory of France unsuccessfully tried several complicated approaches to both the Portuguese and Spanish courts, with the intention of recovering Louisiana in some roundabout way as the termination of a series of swaps. Pierre Auguste Adet, French minister to the United States, directed some very obvious, incompetent, and uninformative espionage in 1796, trying to discover possible western disloyalty to the United States and to get some empirical data on the potential value of the great valley.

The intrigues of Frenchmen availed not. Success waited on the elevation of a Corsican. When Napoleon Bonaparte's phantasms of oriental splendor blew away with the smoke of British guns in the Battle of the Nile (1798), he seems to have begun to dream of another French empire bordering the Caribbean and the Gulf of Mexico. As First Consul, in 1800, he told the slippery Talleyrand to reopen the Louisiana matter in Madrid.

The Spanish royal family had a princess who was married to a titular but unemployed Duke of Parma. Napoleon proposed to enlarge Tuscany as the "Kingdom of Etruria," with this young couple as its sovereigns, in exchange for Louisiana, which had real value to Spain only as a buffer between the riches of Mexico and the tobacco-spitting rowdies of the United States. The fruit of the talks was the Treaty of San Ildefonso (October 1, 1800), drawn according to Napoleon's wishes in all respects but one—the court of Spain dug in its heels and refused to throw in Florida to boot. It was not a bad arrangement for the royal Spaniards, nor was it necessary to bully them into agreement. Louisiana had proved unmanageable, four-fifths of the cost of its government came from the royal Spanish coffers, and it would need even larger expenditures to be made militarily defensible. The Spanish government issued the necessary orders for its formal transfer to France after the Peace of Amiens (1802). Although Napoleon had promised not to transfer Louisiana to a third party, true to his character he had already sold the region to a very interested third party, even before taking possession.[7] For that matter, he never delivered the "Kingdom of Etruria" in a condition which satisfied the Spanish. Louisiana could be described as a Hot Province. Spain had been defrauded in all important details by a glittering confidence man.

II

Reliable but unofficial information that Louisiana had been ceded came to Washington only in May, 1801. Jefferson and James Madison told the perspicacious Pichon that the presence of France at the mouth of the Mississippi could only mean trouble. Pichon replied circumlocutionally and uninformatively, but reported their views accurately to Paris. Hoping to forestall the closing of the deal, Jefferson speeded the departure of the new American minister to France, Robert R. Livingston.[8] Considering the fragmentary character of information available in Washington, Livingston's instructions were intelligently drafted: if the transaction was not complete, try to talk them out of it. If it was complete, speak of American unhappiness, and suggest that West Florida be ceded to the United States directly from France or, if it had not become French, with French help. Leave unspoken, but manifest, the threat of Anglo-American co-operation if trouble came. There was nothing in Livingston's instructions about getting Louisiana, or even New Orleans. What was hoped was the donation of West Florida. The matter was not publicized by Livingston's superiors. President Jefferson's first public statement on the matter came more than a year later in a message to the Congress (December 15, 1802), in which he cryptically and rather casually mentioned "a change in

[7] Nobody polled the Louisiana creoles, but some of them who admired the French philosophical ideals, which they believed still animated French policy, were pleased at the retrocession. André Lafargue, "The Louisiana Purchase: The French Viewpoint," *Louisiana Historical Quarterly*, XXIII (1940), 107–117.

[8] Irving Brant, *James Madison, Secretary of State, 1800–1809* (Indianapolis, 1953), pp. 65–70. George Dangerfield, *Chancellor Robert R. Livingston of New York, 1746–1813* (New York, 1960), remedies the long-felt need for a biography of Livingston in a book which deserves only superlatives. This chapter draws too heavily on Dangerfield to cite it in each instance. Livingston, King's College '65, headed his powerful clan in New York. His national career dated from 1776. As Secretary for Foreign Affairs, appointed by the Continental Congress, he was not new to western questions. See also Robert C. Hayes, "Robert R. Livingston," *DAB*.

the aspect of our foreign relations."[9] Since the 1780's he had feared that the lilies of France or the Union Jack would flap over the West. The Pacific coast was not too remote for him to consider; a Panama canal would be a fine thing; a free United States of North and South America was not beyond imagination. If only the Spanish could hold Louisiana until the United States was ready to take over, "peice by peice [sic]."[10] He did not propose to found an empire of liberty by force of arms, but he had every confidence that the growing American population would eventually spill over both continents.[11]

Now the United States could no longer await the slow decay of the Spanish Empire. An energetic government would sit in New Orleans. It was time to enlarge the empire of liberty by a small parcel. Jefferson was serene about the long-run effects. Either Napoleon would be ensnared in a European web of his own spinning or the western Americans would become numerous and strong enough to overwhelm Louisiana. There was no need to worry about the larger panorama, but some small act must be done more quickly. At this moment Thomas Paine and Samuel du Pont de Nemours independently brought forward the notion of buying an outlet for western produce. Du Pont advised trying to buy an easement to the Gulf, or to ask for a bit of territory as an earnest of a future Franco-American project to help recover Canada for France; in any case, the touch of magnificence was called for—a very generous offer would impress the French, and would still be a good deal cheaper than a war.[12]

The administration also had a British problem. Considering that Great Britain, with its superiority at sea, could have taken Louisi-

[9] Brant, *Madison*, pp. 70–72; J. D. Richardson (ed.), *A Compilation of the Messages and Papers of the Presidents* (20 vols., Washington, 1897–1917), I, 331; Seymour H. Fersh, *The View From the White House* (Washington, 1961), analyzes Jefferson's message techniques, pp. 15–20.

[10] Jefferson to Stuart, Jan. 25, 1786, Julian P. Boyd (ed.), *The Papers of Thomas Jefferson* (16 vols., Princeton, 1950–), IX, 217–218.

[11] Gilbert Chinard, *Thomas Jefferson* (2nd ed., Ann Arbor, 1960), pp. 396–403; R. W. Van Alstyne, *The Rising American Empire* (New York, 1960), pp. 78–88; Darling, *Empire*, pp. 390–396; Parish, *Manifest Destiny*.

[12] David Savile Muzzey, *Thomas Jefferson* (New York, 1918), pp. 222–226; Adrienne Koch, *Jefferson and Madison, The Great Collaboration* (New York, 1950), pp. 235–237; du Pont to Jefferson, May 12, 1802, Dumas Malone (ed.), *Correspondence Between Thomas Jefferson and Pierre Samuel du Pont de Nemours, 1798–1817* (Boston, 1930), pp. 61–65.

ana almost painlessly at any time before 1804, it is hard to understand British restraint. Having Canada, Britain might deliberately encircle the United States, and, as Madison wrote, "she is the last of Neighbours that would be agreeable. . . ."[13] Great Britain could have scored one or more real gains. A consolidation of influence over the northwestern Indians, expansion of British trade in the Missouri and upper Mississippi valleys, a compact with France for a free hand in the Mediterranean in exchange for turning eyes away from Napoleonic adventures in America, even the overt conquest of Louisiana from France as a granary for British factory workers—all of these chimeras cavorted in American night thoughts. Certainly the United States was on its own in the Louisiana affair, with not a trusty friend. If William Pitt's group had been in office in Britain, there might have been active resistance to the retrocession of Louisiana to France, but, in the end, the British, who were bent on making peace at Amiens, let the applecart trundle undisturbed. The Louisiana cession seemed *a fait accompli*. Britons did not realize the Jefferson administration absolutely would not tolerate a French bar to the Gulf of Mexico, or they might have speculated in diplomatic futures. As it was, Louisiana was not even mentioned at Amiens.[14]

On the French side, Pichon correctly reported that the United States was so annoyed by the Louisiana business that it might seize the province or a necessary part of it. He suggested that the Paris government resign itself to the fact of America's growing strength, and do something to assure that its strength would not in the future be found as a weight on the British side of the scale.[15]

Livingston's arrival in Paris was only a stitch in Napoleon's imperial tapestry. The American was physiologically deaf; the French were diplomatically deaf. Not until late in 1802 could he get

13 Madison to King, July 24, 1801, Gaillard Hunt (ed.), *The Writings of James Madison* (9 vols., New York, 1900–1910), VI, 434–435.

14 William Windham, Nov. 3, 1802, *The Windham Papers* (2 vols., Boston, 1913), II, 200–202; Darling, *Empire*, pp. 394–407, 410, 419, 423; Bradford Perkins, "England and the Louisiana Question," *Huntington Library Quarterly*, XVIII (1954–55), 279–295, and *First Rapprochement: England and the United States, 1795–1805* (Philadelphia, 1955), pp. 159–170; King to Livingston, Jan. 15, 1802, Charles R. King (ed.), *The Life and Correspondence of Rufus King* (6 vols., New York, 1894–1900), IV, 56 (perhaps not sent, but the gist reached Livingston, IV, 86).

15 Brant, *Madison*, pp. 73–78, 89–93.

a clear understanding of the San Ildefonso terms. Only a self-assured Hudson Valley baron, which is what he was, would have persevered. Meanwhile the French were having troubles of their own.

In the island of Saint-Domingue, the parts of which are now known as Haiti and the Dominican Republic, a Napoleonic cast was acting out a tropical tragedy. France had lost control of the place in a bloody slave rebellion during the 1790's. The Negro statesman, Toussaint l'Ouverture, autonomously governed Saint-Domingue under color of a French commission. The island figured in the foreground of Napoleon's imagined New World empire. Louisiana had been cozened from Spain to be its breadbasket. To achieve Napoleon's New World ambitions, it was necessary to reassert control over the island and to re-establish slavery. An army of about 30,000, under Napoleon's brother-in-law, Victor Emmanuel Leclerc, managed to take Toussaint alone by knavery, but managed thereafter only to die of fever in appalling numbers. Saint-Domingue remained under its victorious former slaves, who owed their independence only to their own exertions and to their morbid climate. No white man consciously helped them to implement the French or American liberal slogans (except to sell food to them, C.O.D.) for fear the place would become a Caribbean Algiers.[16]

While Napoleon's soldiers died painfully in the West Indies and their illustrious leader fumed at their impotence in imperial luxury at home, the Spanish intendant in New Orleans aroused the bewildered anger of the Americans by issuing an order which was the most provocative and offensive decree he could write, short of a declaration of war. On October 18, 1802, he suspended the privilege of depositing American produce at New Orleans for transshipment to foreign parts. The intendant acted on direct orders from Madrid, but was required by the same orders to make the cloture appear to be his own decision. Both Spaniards in America and the Americans themselves thought it outrageous. That the always harassed and hindered traders did not rise up and take over New Orleans can

[16] Charles Callan Tansill, *The United States and Santo Domingo, 1798–1873* (Baltimore, 1938), pp. 70–109; Brant, *Madison*, pp. 62–65, 78–83; Jefferson tacitly approved the French attempt to reduce the island to obedience, Carl Ludwig Lokke, "Jefferson and the Leclerc Expedition," *American Historical Review*, XXXIII (1928), 322–328.

only be explained by the fact that they understandably blamed Napoleon. This attribution to Napoleon governed American re-action and policy thereafter and provoked Jefferson's much-quoted letter to Livingston in which he said, "The day that France takes possession of N. Orleans . . . we must marry ourselves to the British fleet and nation." Although Talleyrand would have liked to have been the author of the Mississippi cloture, and said of the decree "the nations of Europe can only applaud,"[17] he learned of it not from Madrid but from Pichon in Washington. The Spanish motive is not wholly clear. The abuse of the privilege of deposit by American smugglers, particularly smugglers of specie in defiance of all mercantilist theorizing, and the mistreatment of Spanish seamen in American ports, both of which were alleged as reasons, seem disproportionate to the audacity of the affront. Perhaps royal Spanish pride moved the Spaniards to exit from the Louisiana stage with a resounding ad lib. curtain line which, they hoped, might embarrass impresario Bonaparte.[18]

Back in Paris, Livingston had many intriguing—the word is chosen carefully—private conversations, but could get no official word from the French government for about a year. Talleyrand blocked him from access to Napoleon until Livingston wisely en-gaged the interest of the temperamentally conspiratorial Joseph Bonaparte, after learning of the suspension of deposit at New Orleans. By this time the Saint-Domingue disaster was known in Paris, and no succor could be sent. Now Livingston very boldly proposed the cession of West Florida, if it were French, and of that part of Louisiana which lay above the Arkansas River, for cash and for the assumption by the United States of claims against France (including the claims of a couple of Livingstons). For the first time an American official, in his public capacity, had proposed drawing the boundary of the United States somewhere west of the Father of Waters. Talleyrand listened with interest, partly to avoid provoking

17 Jefferson to Livingston, April 18, 1802, Paul Leicester Ford (ed.), *The Writings of Thomas Jefferson* (10 vols., New York, 1892–99), VIII, 145; E. Wilson Lyon, "The Closing of the Port of New Orleans," *American Historical Review*, XXXVII (1932), 283 n.

18 The mood of the Americans in New Orleans was made plain in "Despatches from the United States Consulate in New Orleans," *American Historical Review*, XXXII (1926–27), 801–824, XXXIII (1927–28), 331–359. The Pinckney Treaty, 1795, allowed Spain to close the deposit in New Orleans after three years if another was opened. None was.

Livingston to further fraternizing with Joseph Bonaparte, and partly because Livingston's remarks smelled of money for somebody.[19]

The scene now shifts to Washington. On January 11, 1803, Jefferson officially announced the retrocession of Louisiana, nominated James Monroe to join Livingston to treat with the French (if necessary he was to travel to Madrid, too), and arranged the introduction of a motion in the House to appropriate $2 million to settle things. Randolph of Roanoke steered the appropriation through the House with no difficulty. Jefferson's motives for these gestures at Washington were political, not diplomatic. Livingston had things moving fairly well in Paris. The trouble was in Washington, where the Federalists had seized on the Mississippi question to try to gain popularity in the West. They urged war. Jefferson's counter was the nomination of Monroe, who had the confidence of the Westerners. The President did not need Hamilton's simultaneously expressed opinion to see that two alternatives were open: to negotiate for an outlet or to seize an outlet and to negotiate later.[20]

James Monroe, the confidante of Jefferson and Madison for ten years, was an obvious choice for an envoy whose nomination would tranquilize the Westerners. Tall, gray-eyed, grave, he was sectionalist, partisan, and ambitious, and he had been more successful at politics than at diplomacy. Edward Channing coldly described him as "one of those men of persistent mediocrity from whom useful and attractive Presidents have been made."[21] His instructions directed him, with Livingston, to learn the boundaries of the retrocession, to get New Orleans and as much of the Floridas as possible, and to

[19] Brant, *Madison*, pp. 93–103, in which he cautions against reliance on Livingston's reports as printed in *American State Papers: Foreign Relations;* Charles E. Hill, "James Madison," in Samuel Flagg Bemis (ed.), *The American Secretaries of State and Their Diplomacy* (10 vols. in 5, New York, 1958), III, 9–24. Dangerfield, *Livingston*, pp. 349–350, politely contradicts Brant's view that Livingston's behavior in Paris was part of a campaign intended to lead him to the Vice-Presidency.

[20] *The Debates and Proceedings in the Congress of the United States* (42 vols., Washington, 1834–56), 7th Congress, 2nd Session, pp. 22–23, 352–368; Richard B. Morris (ed.), *Alexander Hamilton and the Founding of the Nation* (New York, 1957), pp. 117–121; François-Xavier Martin, *The History of Louisiana* (2 vols. in 1, New Orleans, 1882), I, 288–290.

[21] Edward Channing, *A History of the United States* (6 vols., New York, 1905–25), IV, 314.

convince the French that the United States would accept the presence of neither France nor Britain at the mouth of the Mississippi. He was not to mention that he should, at the minimum, get at least part of New Orleans and a guarantee of the use of the rivers draining through Florida.[22]

The President and his circle hoped for an alliance with Britain if it came to the worst. They did not know the British were actively meddling in the Louisiana business by offering cash rewards to the willing Joseph Bonaparte and Talleyrand to block the sale of Louisiana in order to entangle Napoleon more deeply in colonialism, so that he could not take time for more warfare in Europe. Despite this mummery in his own household, the senior Corsican decided, in March, 1803, not to try to reinforce his new province. This was significant. A third of the merchant traders, and two-thirds of the tonnage leaving New Orleans outbound that year, were American.[23] As Jefferson had foreseen, without an energetic government there, the place would be Americanized by default. All that was needed for the time being was this little easement or outlet.

Monroe had no reason to write from Paris, "having wonderful time." Napoleon treated him coldly. Livingston thought his presence unnecessary, and Monroe found Livingston reserved and cryptic. Livingston had good reason to be reticent. His proposal that the United States assume claims against France had become a scheme whereby speculators could profit from inside knowledge by buying up claims in advance. These speculators could just as well be straw men for Talleyrand. This was a typical way to deal in Parisian diplomacy, and a good deal more refined than the crudity of the XYZ Affair, but Livingston could hardly open it up to Monroe, what with Livingstons among the claimants.[24]

22 Dexter Perkins, "James Monroe," *DAB; American State Papers* (38 vols., Washington, 1832–61): *Foreign Relations,* II, 540–544; Brant, *Madison,* pp. 104–109. Monroe was the republic's first important professional politician. In forty-odd years he served fifteen terms of various offices by appointment or election.
23 Perkins, "England and Louisiana Question," and *First Rapprochement,* pp. 159–170. Dangerfield, *Livingston,* gives a lively and credible account of the French leaders' attitude, reducing it to its proper proportion: three brigands intriguing for larger shares of the loot.
24 Beckles Willson, *America's Ambassadors to France (1777–1927)* (London, 1928), pp. 86–92; William Penn Cresson, *James Monroe* (Chapel Hill, 1946), pp. 183–186, 195–196; Monroe to Madison, Apr.15, 1803, in Stanislaus M. Hamil-

When the great coup came, it came suddenly. Two days after Monroe's arrival, before he had even been presented to Napoleon, Napoleon decided to sell the whole of his Louisiana province. Livingston heard the staggering proposition from Talleyrand, as Talleyrand's idea, but, in the actual transaction, François de Barbé-Marbois, the Minister of Finance, represented Napoleon because the First Consul had read in the London *Times* of the $2 million American appropriation. Viewing politics as he did, he naturally thought the money was intended to bribe his counselors, of whom he rightly trusted Talleyrand least. In justice to Talleyrand, it should be added that he encouraged Napoleon's original American adventure because he, unlike Napoleon, thought Napoleon's career would be best served by peace rather than by a European war.

On the evening of the first day Monroe and Livingston were together (April 12, 1803), Livingston and Barbé-Marbois privately arrived at the terms, not for New Orleans alone, not for New Orleans and West Florida, but for New Orleans and all of Louisiana: 60 million francs and the outstanding American claims against France up to another 20 million francs. Livingston hurried from the minister's office that night and sent the word to Madison, apparently before he mentioned it to Monroe. Incidentally, Napoleon knew, by the optical telegraph, that Monroe was already in France at the time he told Talleyrand to offer Louisiana to Livingston.

Why the Americans snapped at the offer is easy enough to understand, but why the Corsican initiated this spectacular transaction is not a simple question. It properly belongs as much to European history as to American, but it will be answered, if at all, by American students. The Louisiana Purchase echoes like a thunderclap in America's story. If measured by historical influence, it was a major act of Napoleon's career, but to Europeans it is a tiny episode, almost lost in the sparkling tinsel of the Napoleonic cavalcade. The question is unanswerable with certainty, because the only "sources" of the answer are statements by Talleyrand in 1803

ton (ed.), *The Writings of James Monroe* (7 vols., New York, 1898–1903), IV, 10–12. Monroe and Livingston later each claimed prime credit for the outcome. Monroe thought his opportune arrival as the special envoy of a chilly government did it; Livingston gave credit to his scheme of including the claims. Actually, Napoleon did it. If anyone influenced Napoleon, it was his man in Washington, Pichon, who told him the truth about the United States. Brant, *Madison*, pp. 119, 134–140.

and 1806, and brief remarks by Napoleon much later.[25] Who would believe either, without polygraph or cross-examination?

Many theories explaining Napoleon's impulse have been constructed from the events rather than the words. They range from the commonly accepted notion that he sold Louisiana to get money for the "inevitable" coming war to a statement that Napoleon's loss of interest in Louisiana caused that war. The field is wide open for reappraisal.

Napoleon was cut out for soldiering, not civil administration. The shock of the Saint-Domingue disaster induced in him a profound revulsion against continuing the attempt to rebuild the French empire in America. Saint-Domingue had also been a laboratory in which it was proved that a French colony could not exist next door to an unfriendly United States. As a soldier he knew Louisiana was defenseless without the Floridas. Spain had made it clear the Floridas could not be had except by conquest. He knew Great Britain could and probably would best him in any military contest for the Floridas. Having in 1802 spent the anticipated revenues of 1803, he needed money. The peace which then temporarily blessed Europe was distasteful to him, because peace gave him no personal luster, and because it seemed to free his enemies to conspire undisturbed. Meanwhile, Louisiana had become a bore. He wished to get back to his glorious drums and trumpets, his drilling and killing of the fittest youth of Europe. To let Britain take Louisiana would be weak. To turn it back to Spain would be derisory. Robert R. Livingston's steady pressure reminded him that a profit could yet be turned. The perennial French problem, since 1799, had been to satisfy the Americans, that is, to keep them out of the British camp, without spending any money. Here was a chance to get, not spend, to the same end. Thus his offer.

If his goal had been solely to keep Britain out of Louisiana, the cession of New Orleans alone to the United States would have done the trick. He sold the whole for three probable reasons: a higher capital gain in francs, the tedium of the American problem, and the

25 E. Wilson Lyon, *The Man Who Sold Louisiana . . . François Barbé-Marbois* (Norman, Okla., 1942), pp. 118–122; Whitaker, *Mississippi Question*, pp. 234–236. My thanks are due to Eugene Joseph McFadden, U.S.N., for advice based on a close reading of the *Correspondance* of Napoleon I, whose letters, written in duplicity and edited for political effect, reveal more about the two Napoleons than about history.

effective diplomacy of Livingston. Then he challenged the British to get out of Malta (as they had promised at Amiens) or to fight. They chose to fight. Napoleon went happily back to his reshaping of Europe with powder, ball, and bayonet.[26]

III

The Jefferson administration, which had been thinking steadily darker and more truculent thoughts about France and Spain, let no scruple stand in the way of accepting the treaties when they arrived. By agreement the United States received whatever France had swindled from Spain under the name of Louisiana, plus New Orleans. For reasons not recorded, the French insisted on writing into the contract a provision that the *habitants* of Louisiana would be incorporated into the American people. The terms guaranteed existing Indian rights, protected private property, and gave certain commercial privileges for twelve years to French traders. Payment was to be in bonds of the United States, in the sum of $11.5 million (at 6 per cent), irredeemable for fifteen years, plus the payment of American claims against France, with interest, up to 20 million francs. All documents were antedated to April 30, 1803.[27]

The Spanish government complained to the United States. Napoleon had not paid for the place. He had promised not to alienate it to a third party. Secretary Madison suggested that the remedy lay in complaint to Napoleon. The Spaniards, with some gagging, swallowed their pride. Hispano-American relations were outwardly (but only outwardly) amicable by 1804.

[26] Practically every writer on the period has given reasons for the sale of Louisiana. Following is a list of the chief monographs: William M. Sloane, "The World Aspects of the Louisiana Purchase," *American Historical Review,* IX (1903–4), 507–521; F. P. Renaut, *La Question de la Louisiane, 1796–1806* (Paris, 1918) pp. 107–127; R. A. McLemore, "Jeffersonian Diplomacy in the Purchase of Louisiana," *Louisiana Historical Quarterly,* XVIII (1935), 346–353; Richard R. Stenberg, "Napoleon's Cession of Louisiana," *ibid.,* XXI (1938), 354–361; William C. Holmes, "The Exalted Enterprise," *ibid.,* XXIII (1940), 78–106; Lyon, *Man Who Sold Louisiana;* Carl Ludwig Lokke, "Secret Negotiations to Maintain the Peace of Amiens," *American Historical Review,* XLIX (1943–44), 55–64; Oscar Handlin, "The Louisiana Purchase: Chance or Destiny?" *The Atlantic Monthly,* CVC (Jan. 1955, No. 1), 44–49. Briefer references will be found in every work on the general or diplomatic history of the United States.

[27] Brant, *Madison,* pp. 131–134; James Monroe, "Journal or Memoranda— Louisiana, April 27," *Writings of Monroe,* IV, 14–15 (the only minutes of the negotiations); Hill, "Madison," in *Secretaries of State,* III, 25–40.

Gallatin financed the transaction as skillfully as the contract allowed. (He did not like the "irredeemable" character of the bonds.) This extraordinary transaction increased the area of the country about 140 per cent, while Gallatin was able to pay more than a quarter of the cost in cash and met the remainder without change in the tax laws. As for Napoleon, he was not interested in "growth" investments. He cashed the bonds in Amsterdam and London, at 78½, not holding them long enough to draw any interest. The brokers made $2.5 million.[28] Most of the debts owed by France to Americans dated back to the quasi war of 1798. The mixed commission liquidated the claims querulously, under regulations imposed by Napoleon, because of disagreement on procedure. Most of the claims money went to speculators who had bought the claims up in advance at low prices.[29]

Now, just what had the United States acquired? The boundaries were those of the retrocession to France. Those boundaries were the boundaries of whatever the French had ceded to Spain in the 1760's. The French refused to be more precise, and, indeed, seem to have been somewhat amused at their own cleverness in disposing of such a vaguely bounded parcel of real estate. Only the Spanish government could document a boundary assertion, and it could authenticate, so to speak, almost any limits it chose by a judicious selection of ancient yellowed papers. Although much demarcation remained to be done in the future, the immediately critical question of geography was how far the new tract ran eastward of New Orleans. Livingston and Monroe each studied the question separately, then compared notes, and unilaterally decided for the United States that they had bought the sands and marshes lying south of 31 degrees and running from New Orleans to the Perdido River.[30]

When envoys are sent to try to buy New Orleans and West

[28] Raymond Walters, Jr., *Albert Gallatin: Jeffersonian Financier and Diplomat* (New York, 1957), pp. 152–154; B. Perkins, "England and Louisiana Question," pp. 293–294. The cash and the credit transactions are minutely documented in J. E. Winston and R. W. Colomb, "How the Louisiana Purchase Was Financed," *Louisiana Historical Quarterly*, XII (1929), 189–237.

[29] Ulane Bonnel, *La France, les États-Unis, et la Guerre de Course, 1797–1815* (Paris, 1961), pp. 161–163.

[30] Francis P. Burns, "West Florida and the Louisiana Purchase; An Examination into the Question of Whether It Was Included in the Territory Ceded by the Treaty of 1803," *Louisiana Historical Quarterly*, XV (1932), 391–416. The Perdido River is the western boundary of the present State of Florida.

Florida at most, for not more than $10 million, and they mail back
a deed for New Orleans, an undefined empire of vast extent, 50,000
new citizens, and perhaps 150,000 Indians, at near $16 million, it
will cause talk. Talk there was—a rather one-sided political argument perfumed with constitutional issues. Many questions of constitutionality were ventilated, but the only really grave constitutional problem was whether the United States, by executive action,
could incorporate foreigners into the union as citizens.[31]

The debates, public and private, revealed fissures in Federalism.
The Federalist party could not present an unbroken array to its
foes. The Federalists most proudly remembered today all favored
acquiring Louisiana at one time or other, for one reason or other,
by one means or other. Doctrinaire pessimism could not defeat
natural buoyancy and national pride. And there was money in it.
The New Orleans trade with the eastern seaports was very profitable. So—the title was cloudy? Lawyers and courts had always spent
much of their time in perfecting land titles. Spain was cheated?
Spain deserved no better; the Spanish had probably sold to Napoleon just to make things hard for the Americans, as was their
chief delight in that part of the world. The United States was
already too large? A confining idea prevalent only among certain
provincial Yankees, to whom the Berkshires were 'way out West.
One by one, Rufus King, John Quincy Adams, Alexander Hamilton (who would have warred for it), John Adams, and, finally,
John Marshall concluded seriatim that it was a good thing, or at
least tolerable. Most southern Federalists in the Congress did not
boggle. They did not dare to flout the public satisfaction.[32]

[31] The Louisiana documents arrived from France on July 14, 1803. Two days
later the President called a special session of the Congress to meet on Oct. 17, and
went to Monticello. When the Congress gathered, the treaties were sent to the
Senate, which consented promptly. With the French ratifications in hand, the
closing date was Oct. 21. The papers were then published. The constitutional
questions were closely considered in Everett Somerville Brown, *The Constitutional History of the Louisiana Purchase, 1803–1812* (Berkeley, 1920), pp. 14–83,
and, more generally, in Charles Kellogg Burdick, *The Law of the American
Constitution* (New York, 1929), pp. 272–305. Madison's instructions to Monroe
and Livingston had twice noted that incorporation of the population would not
be immediately possible. *American State Papers: Foreign Relations*, II, 540–544.

[32] King to Livingston, Mar. 11, 1803, *Life and Correspondence of King*, IV,
226–227, and his "Cession of Louisiana," *ibid.*, pp. 571–575; John Quincy Adams,
1828, 1829, in Henry Adams (ed.), *Documents Relating to New England Federalism, 1800–1815* (Boston, 1877), pp. 52–55, 148, 155–156; John C. Miller,

Many of the Federalists who opposed the purchase were talkers
and writers, not doers, which may be the reason why their opposition has been somewhat overemphasized. One of the few doers
among them, John Rutledge, a representative out of step with most
of his fellow South Carolinians and a leader of the incipient Young
Federalist movement, wrote to deplore "the purchase of a trackless
world" as "a miserably calamitous business" which "must result in a
disunion of these States."[33] Fisher Ames thought "the acquiring of
territory with money is mean and despicable,"[34] a curious evaluation from a man who was born in 1758, and who had but one short
militia hitch on his military record. Ames, George Cabot, and the
Hartford *Courant* malevolently hinted that the deal was an accommodation to extricate Napoleon from an embarrassment and to
finance more French warfare against Great Britain, although Jefferson had been disenchanted with France since Napoleon had
elbowed and shot his way to the top. Other Federalists—quickly
proved mistaken—thought it would be impossible to market Treasury bonds now that the internal taxes no longer existed to inspire
the confidence of investors.[35] All of these prudential arguments
were strained.

The strong argument against the purchase was that it made
citizens by incorporation, a method of naturalization not earlier
contemplated. But hardly anyone really cared. The Federalist doctrine of implied powers made it hard for Federalists to sound
convincing when they tried to utter a tight construction of the

---

Alexander Hamilton: Portrait in Paradox (New York, 1959), pp. 560–563 (a good
analysis of Hamilton's thought processes on the subject); "Hamilton on the
Louisiana Purchase: A Newly Identified Editorial From the *New-York Evening
Post*," *William and Mary Quarterly*, Third Series, XII (1955), 268–281; John
Adams to Quincy, Feb. 9, 1811, in Charles Francis Adams (ed.), *The Works of
John Adams* (10 vols., Boston, 1854–56), IX, 631–632; American Insurance
Company *v.* Cantor, 1 Peters 511, at 541 (1828); Delbert Harold Gilpatrick,
Jeffersonian Democracy in North Carolina, 1789–1816 (New York, 1931), pp. 155–
156, 160.

[33] Rutledge to Otis, Oct. 1, 1803, in Samuel Eliot Morison, *Life and Letters of
Harrison Gray Otis, Federalist, 1765–1848* (2 vols., Boston, 1913), I, 279.

[34] Ames to Gore, Oct. 3, 1803, in Seth Ames (ed.), *Works of Fisher Ames* (2
vols., Boston, 1854), I, 323, and see other remarks, pp. 328, 329, 330.

[35] James Eugene Smith, *One Hundred Years of Hartford's Courant* (New
Haven, 1949), pp. 82–83; Lawrence S. Kaplan, "Jefferson's Foreign Policy and
Napoleon's Idéologues," *William and Mary Quarterly*, Third Series, XIX (1962),
344–359; Jefferson to J. Adams, July 5, 1814, in Lester J. Cappon (ed.), *The
Adams-Jefferson Letters* (2 vols., Chapel Hill, 1959), II, 431.

delegated powers. Today the treaty power is believed to cover all of the constitutional questions then raised, except the incorporation of new citizens. John Quincy Adams, newly arrived in the Senate, concerned himself with the incorporation problem only. He did not like joining the creoles to the United States without their consent, and found no delegated power which allowed such incorporation. He proposed an amendment to justify it. Madison told him he would support a particular amendment to take care of the Louisiana Purchase alone, but not a general statement as Adams had proposed. Nor could Adams get support in the Congress. He then bowed to the judgment of his peers, and, in later years, dated his defection from Federalism to 1803 rather than a subsequent date selected by his enemies.[36] Few Republicans, except Jefferson himself, had scruples about the purchase. Surely, if the Federalists had been willing to go to war to blast an exit for western traders, they could not be sincere in objecting to the achievement of the same object without bloodshed, and within the country's fiscal means. In the opinion of most Republicans the treaty power amply clothed the bargain in legality.

The President's personal interior struggle came to climax in his private correspondence in August, 1803. Before the Congress convened, he had concluded that a general power to annex land and to embody people might well be written into the Constitution. He dismissed as a paltry evasion Attorney General Levi Lincoln's proposal to revise the agreement with Napoleon to phrase it as a simple boundary correction, after which the unorganized part could be quietly added to Mississippi Territory or to Georgia.

Jefferson's states' rights views were not at issue. He had never been antinational, but he had asserted states' rights as a defense of liberty. Now, in 1803, he began to work out his theory of the empire of liberty. National power existed to protect peaceful freemen from aggression. That had been done by the Louisiana Purchase. A President, he thought, must sometimes leap ahead, and trust to popular approval after the event. It would be best to perfect and to

---

[36] Lynn W. Turner, *William Plumer of New Hampshire, 1759–1850* (Chapel Hill, 1962), pp. 109–113; Andrew C. McLaughlin, *A Constitutional History of the United States* (New York, 1935), pp. 294–298; Thomas M. Cooley, *The Acquisition of Louisiana* (Indianapolis, 1887); Homer C. Hockett, *The Constitutional History of the United States* (2 vols., New York, 1939), I, 314–320; H. Adams, *Documents of Federalism*, pp. 54, 154–160.

ratify the leap with an amendment (certainly not by judical construction!). His moral justification, we now see, is a sprig of the natural-law root from which evolved the law of nations on the subject of national security. In this instance the purchase was essential to security. In later years the constitutional commentator Joseph Story, who disliked Jefferson and his works, wrote with irony of how the strict-constructionist President used the implied powers officially canonized by John Marshall, but Story did not indict Jefferson for unconstitutionality. Actually, Jefferson never said the purchase was constitutional. He left it to the people to act to approve or to repudiate. The people did neither. They relied upon the delegated treaty power. Jefferson might have pressed the matter, but erroneous dispatches from Livingston said the French might change their minds. At this the Congress completed the bargain quickly.[37]

To Federalist arguments of defective title, affront to Spain, and the exercise of undelegated power, the congressional Republicans, led by Senator John Breckinridge, replied laconically that the Federalists had been willing to go to war but were now unwilling to go to market, that to acquire land is an attribute of sovereignty, that the bargain was a masterpiece of statesmanship. They ratified, appropriated, and provided temporary executive government. They did it all easily.[38]

The President thought the Louisiana creoles—who in levity or grotesque error calculated they had been bought for eleven sous a head, including slaves and cattle—might resist, but the transfer went off without trouble. The people of New Orleans universally detested the French agent, Pierre Clément Laussat, who ruled them

[37] Jefferson to Breckinridge, Aug. 12, to Madison, Aug. 25, 1803, in Andrew A. Lipscomb (ed.), *The Writings of Thomas Jefferson* (20 vols., Washington, 1903–4), X, 407–411, 412–415, Koch, *Jefferson and Madison*, pp. 238–246; Charles Grove Haines and Foster H. Sherwood, *The Role of the Supreme Court in American Government and Politics* (2 vols., Berkeley, 1944–57), I, 209–211; A. K. Weinberg, *Manifest Destiny* (Baltimore, 1935); Caleb Perry Patterson, *The Constitutional Principles of Thomas Jefferson* (Austin, 1953), pp. 140–146; Charles M. Wiltse, *The Jeffersonian Tradition in American Democracy* (Chapel Hill, 1935), pp. 171–173; Brant, *Madison*, pp. 141–145.

[38] "Breckinridge and the Louisiana Purchase," *Magazine of History* (Extra Number 192), XLVIII (1934), 188–190; Lowell H. Harrison, "John Breckinridge: Western Statesman," *Journal of Southern History*, XVIII (1952), 144–147. Holmes, "Exalted Enterprise," gave the legislative history of the purchase in detail.

only three weeks. A locally raised United States militia force stood by while Governor W. C. C. Claiborne and Brigadier General James Wilkinson, a classic sharper, took charge on December 20. Spanish officials in Upper Louisiana, at St. Louis, handed over to Captain Amos Stoddard, U.S.A., acting for France, on March 9, 1804, who went through the form of transferring it to himself, acting for the United States, on the next day.[39]

IV

The Louisiana Purchase was grand in area, natural riches, and potential growth. In 1803 its population, including Indians, was two hundred thousand at the very most. Today it has about twenty-five million people, who pay nearly $8 billion yearly in federal taxes alone. When the purchase was ratified, it made the United States the second nation in total area, the first nation in tillable area. The value of its farmland must today be reckoned in tens of billions, to say nothing of the front-foot prices of land in the central districts of its great cities, such as New Orleans, St. Louis, Kansas City, Omaha, Minneapolis. Its people, nearly all remote from the sea lanes, are among the most determinedly continentalist and least internationalist of Americans.[40]

The West has fascinated men from Homer to Frederick Jackson Turner, from Horace to Horace Greeley. Good things, interesting things, lie west in the European-American imagination. The Louisiana Purchase fitted into this optimistic vision perfectly, and no quibbles about strict and loose construction have ever been allowed to cloud the imaginations of men responsible for the American westing. True, Napoleon handed this empire on a golden plate, but all of the American actors in the scene were tough-minded enough to stare at the apocalyptic light without blinking.[41]

Thomas Jefferson had done a great deed. It is now regarded as

[39] A. P. Whitaker (ed.), "Another Dispatch from the United States Consulate in New Orleans," *American Historical Review*, XXXVIII (1932–33), 291–295; Amos Stoddard, "Transfer of Upper Louisiana," *Glimpses of the Past*, II (1935), 78–122.

[40] Sloane, "World Aspects"; an unforeseen result of the purchase was prosperity for Mexicans as Louisiana changed from a stagnant backwater to a depot for enterprising overland trade. Lauro A. De Rojas, "A Consequence of the Louisiana Purchase," *Louisiana Historical Quarterly*, XXI (1938), 362–366.

[41] Loren Baritz, "The Idea of the West," *American Historical Review*, LXVI (1960–61), 618–640; Darling, *Empire*.

the chief constructive act of his Presidency, but he wrote of it with
restraint. He did what was wanted, drubbing the Federalists, who
believed in constitutionality by implication while they split straws
of legal logic in a way that seems today ignoble. Thomas Jefferson,
to repeat, was a unionist because he identified the United States
with human liberty (a concept marred by his racism). Not knowing
that he was a Jeffersonian Democrat, he did not feel bound by any
of the systematic and often contradictory codes of exacting standards now called Jeffersonian Democracy. His phrasing of the Declaration of Independence, his influence on the Northwest Ordinance,
and his purchase of Louisiana were all consistent with his endeavor
to preserve the republican experiment. He did not complete the
purchase primarily as a victory for Jeffersonian agrarianism. To
increase the area which could be plowed was desirable, to be sure,
but it was the commerce of the Mississippi that was at the moment
needed to preserve the republic. Eastern merchants and shippers
were as keenly interested in that commerce as were the western corn
and hog growers.[42] Paradoxically, the Louisiana Purchase, in the
long run, was antiagrarianist. Only heavy industry could produce
the steel, the rails, and the machinery needed to exploit satisfactorily a land as large as Jefferson left to posterity.

The diplomatic kaleidoscope turned a few degrees and produced
a new pattern. American affairs declined in importance in British
eyes. As for Napoleon, it was not too bad a deal. He got a price for a
defenseless province which had no precise metes and bounds, and
threw a steak to a terrier snarling at his ankles. Looking farther
ahead, an episode in a struggle for Europe had made the United
States potentially strong enough to deal with European powers on
the same level. The Louisiana Purchase was a step on the path to
the floor where the Clerk of the House read aloud the Monroe
Doctrine.[43]

The curious constitutional decision—which was the decision not
to decide the constitutional question until a generation had passed
—was powerfully influential on American polity. Louisiana was, as

42 Dumas Malone, "Thomas Jefferson," *DAB;* Cooley, *Acquisition of Louisiana;*
Julian P. Boyd, "Thomas Jefferson's 'Empire of Liberty,'" *Virginia Quarterly
Review,* XXIV (1948), 546–554. It has been suggested that Jefferson was moved
to accept the purchase from fear that if he vacillated, Aaron Burr might rise as
hero of the West.
43 Van Alstyne, *American Empire,* pp. 87–99.

Turner wrote, "a region where nature herself had decreed unity of institutions."[44] The arbitrary straight lines and ninety-degree angles of trans-Mississippi state boundaries are cartographic evidence of what the Louisiana Purchase later did to the hitherto sacred concept of the natural character of statehood. More immediately, Jefferson had advanced his program of conciliating Federalists. The only powerful intransigents on the Louisiana question were in New England. Arch-Federalism, unteachable Federalism, had now become sectional. But ominous portents of another, more dangerous sectionalism passed unnoticed. The *habitants* of Louisiana had a guarantee of property in their slaves. Furthermore, at the time of the purchase, more Southerners than Northerners were interested in actually settling west of the Mississippi. The Northerners still had the Old Northwest to occupy them, while the State of Tennessee already bordered the Great River. These were gigantic but undiscerned shadows cast by futurity.

[44] Frederick Jackson Turner, "The Significance of the Louisiana Purchase," *Review of Reviews*, XXVII (1903), 584.

CHAPTER 6

To the Borders and Beyond

TRACING the uncertain borders of the suddenly expanded American nation occupied a large part of the attention and energies of a young people in love with their West. Much of that energy was spent on a partial solution of the perplexing Florida question. The Spaniards had grudgingly accepted the Louisiana Purchase, but they said nothing of boundaries, except to deny that Louisiana included their anarchic, decaying province of Florida, from which Indians raided the United States at whim. The boundary and Indian issues were complicated by the existence of $8 million in private American damage claims against Spain.[1]

President Thomas Jefferson claimed all land between the Perdido River and Matagorda Bay, or the Rio Grande, and whatever territory could be acquired west to the Pacific between 42 and 49 degrees. He wished to create a new state astride the mouth of the Mississippi, and eventually to get East Florida and the payment of the private claims. Secretary of State James Madison thought time worked for the United States. Secretary of the Treasury Albert Gallatin was converted to Jefferson's assertions. Although Jefferson

---

1 Jefferson to the Congress, Nov. 8, 1804, J. D. Richardson (ed.), *A Compilation of the Messages and Papers of the Presidents* (20 vols., Washington, 1897–1917), I, 358; Charles W. Arnade, "The Failure of Spanish Florida," *Americas*, XVI (1959–60), 271–281; Indian turbulence was promoted by the adventurer William Bowles, who tried to establish the sovereign nation of Muskogee, 1778–1803, Duvon C. Corbitt and John Tate Lanning, "A Letter of Marque Issued by William Augustus Bowles," *Journal of Southern History*, XI (1945), 246–261; Charles E. Hill, "James Madison," in Samuel Flagg Bemis (ed.), *The American Secretaries of State and Their Diplomacy* (10 vols. in 5, New York, 1958), III, 48–50.

was skeptical of Spanish diplomacy, James Monroe was sent to join Charles Pinckney to try negotiations at Madrid.[2]

Anticipated French support in Madrid was insultingly withheld because French ministers could see no cash profit for themselves. The mistakenly overconfident Spanish Foreign Office insisted on re-examining every detail of the Louisiana Purchase. Monroe, getting nowhere, left in May, 1805. Napoleon himself did not think he had sold West Florida, and the new American minister in Paris, John Armstrong, was rebuked by the French for claiming West Florida as part of Louisiana. Spain appeared to try to provoke war by keeping pugnacious civil administrators functioning in Baton Rouge and New Orleans as late as 1806. Secretary of the Navy Robert Smith accurately estimated that the Navy, if augmented, could easily take the Floridas from Spain.[3] But war was not necessary. As Madison knew, time made success inevitable.

Before Monroe had gone to Madrid, the Congress had passed the Mobile Act (February 24, 1804), erecting a customs district east of New Orleans, with boundaries to be defined by the President. Jefferson circumspectly set the port of entry at Fort Stoddert above Mobile, on indisputably United States soil. Thus the Mobile Act was merely a unilateral statutory claim to the navigation of rivers traversing West Florida.[4]

After Monroe left Spain, the French hinted slyly that Florida

[2] George Dangerfield, *Chancellor Robert R. Livingston of New York, 1746–1813* (New York, 1960), pp. 367, 374, 392; Jefferson to Breckinridge, Aug. 12, to Madison, Aug. 25, 1803, Paul Leicester Ford (ed.), *The Writings of Thomas Jefferson* (10 vols., New York, 1892–99), VIII, 242–243, 245 n.; Jefferson to du Pont de Nemours, Nov. 1, 1803, Dumas Malone (ed.), *Correspondence Between Thomas Jefferson and Pierre Samuel du Pont de Nemours, 1798–1817* (Boston, 1930), p. 79; Madison to Monroe, July 29, 1803, Gaillard Hunt (ed.), *The Writings of James Madison* (9 vols., New York, 1900–1910), VII, 57–58; Raymond Walters, Jr., *Albert Gallatin: Jeffersonian Financier and Diplomat* (New York, 1957), pp. 170, 186–187.

[3] Arthur Preston Whitaker, *The Mississippi Question, 1795–1803* (New York, 1934), pp. 266, 325–326 (note 14); Stuart Gerry Brown (ed.), *The Autobiography of James Monroe* (Syracuse, 1959), pp. 203–205; Arthur Burr Darling, *Our Rising Empire, 1763–1803* (New Haven, 1940), pp. 535–542; William Penn Cresson, *James Monroe* (Chapel Hill, 1946), pp. 211–213; Dexter Perkins, "James Monroe," *Dictionary of American Biography*; Talleyrand to Armstrong, Dec. 21, 1804, *American State Papers: Documents Legislative and Executive* (38 vols., Washington, 1832–61): *Foreign Relations*, II, 635–636 (hereafter, *ASP*).

[4] Act of Feb. 24, 1804, Sec. 11, *Annals, The Debates and Proceedings in the Congress of the United States* (42 vols., Washington, 1834–56), 8th Congress, 1st Session, Appendix, pp. 1257–1258; Richardson, *Messages and Papers*, I, 357; Darling, *Rising Empire*, pp. 521–524.

might be bought with French help. Jefferson got the point. In a truculent public message and a calculating private message to the Congress, he overtly denounced Spain and covertly suggested a settlement for cash. Some pacific Republicans mournfully followed him, but John Randolph of Roanoke exploded at the appearance of voting a bribe to French rulers. Nevertheless, Jefferson won, by roughly two to one, a tactical victory pushed home without Randolph or John Breckinridge, the men who had guided the Louisiana Purchase through the Congress. However, it was a strategic failure. Napoleon was too distracted by bloody glory to keep up his interest, and Jefferson lost prestige and power in the Congress.[5] With the rebellion of Randolph and the vindictive demotion of Speaker Nathaniel Macon for general Randolphian obstinacy, the Republican congressional front was shattered.

Relations with Spain were not eased by a filibustering expedition to Venezuela in 1806 led by Francisco de Miranda, based on New York, and aided by John Adams' futile son-in-law W. S. Smith (a customs officer), along with other New Yorkers. Miranda's American collaborators were indicted but capriciously acquitted, and the expedition failed utterly. The federal government had behaved correctly, but got no credit for its propriety. For economic reasons Miranda had secret British sympathy. His success would have been welcomed by Britain more than by the United States.[6]

Florida remained a perplexity. Napoleon could have extorted it from Spain for the United States and for a few millions of pocket money if peace had come to Europe, but a severe attack of victory disease influenced him to try to annex the whole Spanish Empire. Besides, why should an emperor help the United States, that republican reproach to the standing order? On the other side, Britain had no sympathy for the American republic which was its

5 Richardson, *Messages and Papers*, I, 372–373, 376–378; Frederick B. Tolles, *George Logan of Philadelphia* (New York, 1953), pp. 256–262; Morton Borden, *The Federalism of James A. Bayard* (New York, 1955), pp. 149–152; Lowell H. Harrison, "Attorney General John Breckinridge," *Filson Club History Quarterly*, XXXVI (1962), 319–328; Dumas Malone, "Thomas Jefferson," *DAB*.

6 William S. Robertson, *The Life of Miranda* (2 vols., Chapel Hill, 1929), I, 293–327; the economic interest of Great Britain in Latin America is explained in I. A. Langnas, "Relations Between Great Britain and the Spanish Colonies," Institute of Historical Research, *Bulletin* (Summaries of Theses, CLXXI), XVI (1939), 195–197, and Charles F. Mullett (ed.), "British Schemes Against Spanish America in 1806," *Hispanic American Historical Review*, XXVII (1947), 269–278.

chief rival for the trade of an emerging Latin America. If the Navy were strengthened somewhat, Jefferson could have taken the Floridas by force, but that might have involved the country in the world war, a hazard out of proportion to the prize. Better to let the teeming western migrants tip the balance of power in North America.[7]

Napoleon seized the throne of Spain for his brother Joseph in 1808. Spanish colonial administrators, including the officials of West Florida, were agitated and confused about their allegiance. American settlers and adventurers in West Florida revolted in 1810 and proclaimed the Republic of West Florida. They had grievances (remediable) and arbitrary government (tolerable), but their hope was to become part of the United States, and their fear was the Napoleonic menace. The United States later paid the expenses of the revolutionaries. In the pitiable condition of ravaged Spain, the Spanish loyalists could not reverse the West Florida revolution. Indeed, in 1811, United States troops camped near Mobile after President Madison proclaimed jurisdiction over all land east to the Perdido River. Only the British could have helped Spain to recover West Florida, and Britain had its own preoccupations.[8]

The boundaries of the new state of Louisiana, drawn in 1812, included the sometime Republic of West Florida. The land be-

[7] Samuel Flagg Bemis, *A Diplomatic History of the United States* (rev. ed., New York, 1950), pp. 185–186, 185 n.; Henry Adams, *The Life of Albert Gallatin* (New York, 1943), pp. 335–337; A. P. Whitaker, *The United States and the Independence of Latin America, 1800–1830* (Baltimore, 1941), pp. 31–33; Isaac Joslin Cox, *The West Florida Controversy, 1798–1813* (Baltimore, 1918), pp. 138, 265; on the influence of American westward migration and population growth, *ibid.*, Chap. XVII.

[8] James A. Padgett (ed.), "The Constitution of the West Florida Republic," *Louisiana Historical Quarterly*, XX (1937), 881–883—for the text of the constitution (minus the last page), pp. 883–894; John S. Kendall (ed.), "Documents Concerning the West Florida Revolution of 1810," *ibid.*, XVII (1934), 80–95, 306–314, 474–501; Cox, *Florida Controversy*, pp. 355–357, 435–436, 483–484, 520–521; Padgett (ed.), "The Documents Showing That the United States Ultimately Financed the West Florida Revolution of 1810," *Louisiana Historical Quarterly*, XXV (1942), 943–970; the surviving correspondence of the revolutionaries is printed in Padgett (ed.), "West Florida Revolution of 1810," *ibid.*, XXI (1938), 76–202; Philip Brooks, "Spain's Farewell to Louisiana, 1803–1821," *Mississippi Valley Historical Review*, XXVII (1940–41), 31–33; Richardson, *Messages and Papers*, I, 465–466; Wellesley to Foster, April 10, 1811, Bernard Mayo (ed.), "Instructions to the British Ministers to the United States, 1791–1812," American Historical Association, *Annual Report 1936*, III (Washington, 1941), pp. 319–321, 319 n.

tween the Pearl and the Perdido Rivers became a county of Mississippi Territory. United States regulars moved into Mobile in 1813. West Florida was all *de facto* United States soil then, and American courts have assumed ever since that West Florida land was always part of the Louisiana Purchase.[9]

East Florida had its allure, too. President Madison, hinting at possible British invasion of East Florida, received congressional authority to annex it if local officials asked help. What followed was raw aggression. George Mathews of Georgia, with a presidential commission, a band of Georgia "patriots," and United States naval help, seized Amelia Island. Except for the courage and intelligence of Florida Indians and Negroes, the whole province might have been taken easily, but the operation was too odious to be acknowledged publicly. Mathews was repudiated and dismissed.[10] Indians and Negroes relieved a siege of St. Augustine. United States troops left east Florida in 1814.

West of the Mississippi the moribund, neglected province of Texas slept in the sun. Only the sudden appearance of the Stars and Stripes in Louisiana revived Spanish interest in Texas. The Louisiana-Texas border became a squall line between contending cultures. To keep peace, General James Wilkinson, on Governor William C. C. Claiborne's authority, agreed with the local Spanish soldiery to establish a neutral ground between the Sabine River and Arroyo Hondo. This diplomatic improvisation promoted tranquillity, except when violated by glory-hunting or acre-hungry freebooters seeking to exploit Mexican internal stresses by making

[9] Cox, *Florida Controversy*, 604–619; Francis P. Burns, "West Florida and the Louisiana Purchase," *Louisiana Historical Quarterly*, XV (1932), 391–416. As John Marshall said, a land claim there was "more a political than a legal question," *ibid.*, p. 411.

[10] Dexter Perkins, "James Monroe," *DAB;* Madison appears to have been influenced by Senator William H. Crawford of Georgia, whose interest in East Florida was sharp, Paul Kruse, "A Secret Agent in East Florida," *Journal of Southern History*, XVIII (1952), 193–217; Richardson, *Messages and Papers*, II, 473, 491–495; Rembert W. Patrick, *Florida Fiasco* (Athens, Ga., 1954); Kenneth Wiggins Porter, "Negroes and the East Florida Annexation Plot, 1811–1813," *Journal of Negro History*, XXX (1945), 10–29; the material and moral decay of the United States forces in East Florida can be traced through the correspondence of senior officers in Davis T. Frederick (ed.), "United States Troops in East Florida, 1812–1813," *Florida Historical Society Quarterly*, IX (1930), 3–23, 96–116.

reputations or cotton in Texas.[11] Certainly the neutral-ground agreement was most un-Spanish in character, but the local dons were daunted by the ceaseless buzzing activity of aggressive Americans in Orleans and Louisiana Territories. As will be seen, the neutral-ground understanding freed Wilkinson to betray his confederate, Aaron Burr.[12] Filibusters against Texas in 1812, 1813, and 1814 by assorted patriots and conspirators had help from William Shaler, a federal agent accredited to Veracruz but ambitious for high rank in a Mexican republic. Bloodshed and atrocities ceased only when Secretary of War Monroe promised to prosecute leaders of filibusters based on American soil. Needing peace with Spain, the United States left Texas to the future.[13]

The only consistent United States policy toward Latin America before 1815 seems to have been to promote the river traffic of the Gulf littoral. Many Americans knew the United States had an interest and an opportunity in the emergence of Latin America, but few knew how to defend the interest or how to exploit the opportunity.[14]

Behind the newly expanded border, the United States had to provide a government for the Louisiana Purchase, and to avoid

[11] J. Villasana Haggard, "The Neutral Ground Between Louisiana and Texas, 1806–1821," *Louisiana Historical Quarterly*, XXVIII (1945), 1001–1128, and "The Counter-Revolution of Béxar, 1811," *Southwestern Historical Quarterly*, XLIII (1939–40), 222–235; Brooks, "Spain's Farewell."

[12] The Burr conspiracy is treated at length below.

[13] I. J. Cox, "The Louisiana-Texas Frontier During the Burr Conspiracy," *Mississippi Valley Historical Review*, X (1923–24), 274–284; the earliest "contemporary" record of the Magee-Gutierrez filibuster was a reminiscent publication in 1860–61, Henry P. Walker (ed.), "William McLane's Narrative," *Southwestern Historical Quarterly*, LXVI (1961–62), 234–251; Roy Franklin Nichols, *Advance Agents of American Destiny* (Philadelphia, 1956), pp. 83–102.

A case for the Spanish boundary claims was compiled in Mexico by José Antonio Pichardo, of the suppressed Society of Jesus, in the years 1808–12. It has a good deal of the history of Spanish America not easily available elsewhere, Charles Wilson Hackett (ed.), *Pichardo's Treatise on the Limits of Louisiana and Texas* (4 vols., Austin, 1931–46).

There was yet another obscure boundary. As early as 1792 it was known that the boundary set in 1783 from the Lake of the Woods "west" to the Mississippi River was a geographical anomaly. That region lay far beyond the most remote American flag, and the British were too entangled in Europe after 1792 to be able to give it much thought. The solution, correctly forecast by Jefferson, awaited a later generation of diplomatists. "Instructions to British Ministers," p. 29 n., and Darling, *Rising Empire*, pp. 525–527. See Chapter 7.

[14] Whitaker, *Independence of Latin America*, pp. 35–38.

giving the Federalists an issue in the process. By authority of the Congress, Jefferson set up a crown-colony type of government, choosing as governor the unimpressive but impeccably Republican William C. C. Claiborne, whose most obvious merit was the patronage of Tennessee's influential Andrew Jackson. From the beginning Claiborne had trouble with French and American immigrants. It had not occurred to Jefferson that the philosophy of the Declaration of Independence applied to Louisiana. Specific rights were to be confirmed by the Congress seriatim if and when Louisiana was ripe for liberty. Meanwhile, the French-speaking, politically inexperienced creoles would have to accept President Thomas of Monticello in place of King Charles of Bourbon.[15]

The Louisianians disliked several American novelties: systematic and impartial taxation, prohibition of the slave trade, mandatory proofs of land titles, and the use of English as the official language, but they were most vexed at favoritism to newcomers. Nevertheless, it was the newcomers, led by Edward Livingston, late of New York, who spoke out. They wrote a memorial in the name of the people, and in the style and mood of the Declaration of Independence, asking statehood and liberty, especially the liberty of every man to buy and sell human beings in international commerce. Three urbane emissaries from New Orleans, all born in France, were warmly received in Washington as lobbyists for Louisiana. Apparently only Thomas Paine publicly noticed the irony of their slave-trade appeal, although Albert Gallatin despised them, and tried to enforce the slave-trade prohibition.[16]

The Congress showed little interest in abstract natural rights, but was much concerned with the tacit imperialism in the idea of natural boundaries for national security. It gave representative government to the Territory of Orleans, and created a Territory of

15 Roger Griswold counted on southwestern troubles to disgrace the Virginia Republicans, Griswold to ———, Nov. 11, 1804, in Connecticut Historical Society; Jefferson to Gallatin, Nov. 9, 1803, *Writings of Jefferson*, VIII, 275 n.–276 n.

16 François-Xavier Martin, *The History of Louisiana* (2 vols. in 1, New Orleans, 1882); Claiborne to Madison, July 13, 1804, Madison Papers, Library of Congress. The memorial is in *Annals*, 8th Congress, 2nd Session, pp. 1597–1608, and one from Upper Louisiana, *ibid.*, pp. 1608–1620. W. B. Hatcher, *Edward Livingston* (University, La., 1940), pp. 111–114; Philip Foner (ed.), *The Complete Writings of Thomas Paine* (2 vols., New York, 1945), II, 963–968. Despite Jefferson's misgivings, Gallatin gave New Orleans a branch of the Bank of the United States.

Louisiana with St. Louis as its capital. Edward Livingston grew in local popularity as he successfully pressed for the retention of as much Spanish and French law as possible. For governor at St. Louis, Jefferson made about the worst possible choice—James Wilkinson. In both of the new territories a dangerously large proportion of federal appointments went to men close to Wilkinson and Burr.[17]

II

The personality and temperament of Aaron Burr charmed many of his contemporaries but repelled others. He was short, bald, hatchet-faced, with a military carriage and a somewhat dandified dress. One lady described his bright black eyes as "terrible"; another called them "persuasive."[18] The record—with both ladies and gentlemen—supports the adjective "persuasive." Descended from a distinguished line of Puritan divines, including Jonathan Edwards,[19] his piercing intelligence, sharpened at Princeton, found no intellectual satisfaction in the rigorous family Calvinism. In reaction he threw out all traditional morality, and adopted hedonism and the posturing fakery of the code of honor. Many years after Burr passed the nadir of his notoriety, John Quincy Adams accurately noted, "Ambition of military fame, ambition of conquest over female virtue, was the duplicate ruling passion of his life."[20] He had his share of dignities, but never a post which gave him full scope. He felt he owed nothing to his party because it had betrayed him in the

[17] Everett Somerville Brown, *Constitutional History of the Louisiana Purchase, 1803–1812* (Berkeley, 1920), explained the theoretical argument, pp. 84–146. John Quincy Adams failed to interest the executive or the Congress in a bill to allow the creoles to vote on their incorporation, and he got but four votes in the Senate for a resolution against taxing them without their consent. Henry Adams (ed.), *Documents relating to New England Federalism, 1800–1815* (Boston, 1877), pp. 157–160; on this point, see also A. K. Weinberg, *Manifest Destiny* (Baltimore, 1935), pp. 37, 41, 46–47, 385.

Thomas P. Abernethy, *The South in the New Nation, 1789–1819* (Baton Rouge, 1961), pp. 263–267; Hatcher, *Livingston*, pp. 117–120; Elizabeth Gaspar Brown, "Law and Government in the 'Louisiana Purchase,' 1803–1804," *Wayne Law Review*, II (1956), 169–189, and "Legal Systems in Conflict: Orleans Territory, 1804–1812," *American Journal of Legal History*, I (1957), 35–75. The Senate consented to Wilkinson's appointment by the close vote of 17–14.

[18] Gordon L. Thomas, "Aaron Burr's Farewell Address," *Quarterly Journal of Speech*, XXXIX (1953), 277.

[19] I. J. Cox, "Aaron Burr," *DAB*.

[20] Charles Francis Adams (ed.), *Memoirs of John Quincy Adams* (12 vols., Philadelphia, 1874–77), IX, 433.

election of 1796—except in Kentucky and Tennessee. Having failed of the Presidency, having failed of election as governor of New York, and having been indicted in New York and New Jersey for murdering Alexander Hamilton, at the end of his term as Vice-President this out-of-time renaissance princeling began to meditate imperially. Where could friends and opportunities be found? In the friendly West, of course. What followed is known as the Burr conspiracy, an intricate melodrama with a cast of characters as large as a modern small-town telephone directory.[21]

Augustus had Antony and Lepidus as long as he needed them, Lenin had Trotsky, but Burr had only General James Wilkinson, U.S.A. This backstairs brigadier, lately restored to the Spanish pension roll as Agent Number 13,[22] was trusted by Washington, Adams, Jefferson, Madison, and Burr, but was accurately described by John Randolph as "from the bark to the very core a villain."[23] While Burr hungered for fame and glory (and girls), Wilkinson panned the dregs of international intrigue for easy money, which he used for inconspicuous consumption. Quite inadvertently, his humbug and avarice may have saved his country.[24]

[21] Stephen Kurtz, *The Presidency of John Adams* (Philadelphia, 1957), pp. 197–199; Noble E. Cunningham, Jr., *The Jeffersonian Republicans* (Chapel Hill, 1957), pp. 91–92; Manning J. Dauer, *The Adams Federalists* (Baltimore, 1953), p. 106, gives the figures: south of Pennsylvania the electoral vote of 1796 was Jefferson 54, Burr 17. Gallatin tried to form a plan to exclude Burr from future advancement in the late summer of 1801, Gallatin to Jefferson, Sept. 14, 1801, Henry Adams (ed.), *The Writings of Albert Gallatin* (3 vols., Philadelphia, 1879), I, 51–53.

T. P. Abernethy, *The Burr Conspiracy* (New York, 1954), has succeeded W. F. McCaleb, *The Aaron Burr Conspiracy* (New York, 1903, 1936). McCaleb too easily resolves too many doubts in Burr's favor. The most useful and accessible collection of the documents is in *ASP: Misc.*, I, 468–645, 701–713. The Library of Congress has a collection of "Letters in Relation to Burr's Conspiracy," of which a photostatic copy is in the Newberry Library, Chicago. Chap. XI of Abernethy's *South in the New Nation* summarizes the conspiracy, and adds what the author has learned since 1954.

[22] I. J. Cox, "General Wilkinson and His Later Intrigues with the Spaniards," *American Historical Review*, XIX (1913–14), 794–812.

[23] Quoted by Abernethy in *South in the New Nation*, p. 294.

[24] A grandson's defense of Wilkinson, the most complete possible, showed that he, his brother, and his male descendants add up to ten commissioned United States and Confederate officers, of whom two were killed in combat (to which one might unkindly add that a descendant of Benedict Arnold won the Victoria Cross). James Wilkinson, "General James Wilkinson," *Louisiana Historical Quarterly*, I (1917), 79–165. His service record, so to speak, may be traced in Mary P. Adams, "Jefferson's Military Policy," Ph.D. thesis, University of Virginia,

After publicly receiving Louisiana in the name of the United States, he privately told his Spanish employers several useful ways to thwart the United States (e.g., arrest Lewis and Clark) and then went East. Burr had taken refuge from his indictments with Charles Biddle of Philadelphia, a close friend of Wilkinson's. Wilkinson had once been Burr's house guest in New York. They now met *chez* Biddle with one Charles Williamson who had potentially useful British political connections. Williamson later unsuccessfully represented the Burr imperial enterprise in London.[25]

Burr and Wilkinson also worked together in Washington during the next session of the Congress, when Burr last presided over the Senate. They copied maps of the Southwest and corresponded with several confiding Westerners. Burr brought the Federalist Senator Jonathan Dayton of New Jersey into the circle, an association which impressed British Minister Anthony Merry. He sought potential accomplices so talkatively that even Postmaster General Gideon Granger and Captain Thomas Truxtun, U.S.N. (ret.), the hero of 1799, later appeared to be involved. After talks with Edward Livingston's Louisiana lobbyists, Burr told Merry that Louisiana was on fire for independence, needing only British gold, British ships, and American riflemen. Merry, interested, showed a partisanship which may have cost him his post. He could not know that Burr would try to milk the French and Spanish governments, too, but the more farsighted British Foreign Secretary on receiving Merry's report recorded his perspicacious opinion that trust in Burr would be misplaced.[26]

1958, pp. 41–119. Another apologist wrote an essay in moral relativism to the effect that we must not judge Secret Agent No. 13 too harshly, but should evaluate him by the moral atmosphere of the time; Thomas Robson Hay, "Some Reflections on the Career of General James Wilkinson," *Mississippi Valley Historical Review*, XXI (1934–35), 471–494—by this standard Bishops Seabury, Asbury, and Carroll must have been anachronistic freaks. Washington Irving satirizes Wilkinson as the windy General Jacobus Van Poffenburgh in *Knickerbocker's History of New York* (2 vols., New York, 1895–97), II, 118–130.

Wilkinson collected three cash rewards from Spain for denunciations of un-Hispanic activities of Colonel John Connolly, Dr. James O'Fallon, and George Rogers Clark; see James Ripley Jacobs, *Tarnished Warrior* (New York, 1938), p. 231. T. R. Hay and M. R. Werner wrote their undocumented and unnecessary *Admirable Trumpeter* (Garden City, 1941) after Jacobs had satisfied the need.

25 I. J. Cox, "Hispanic American Phases of the 'Burr Conspiracy,'" *Hispanic American Historical Review*, XII (1932), 142–175.

26 Philadelphia *Aurora*, Nov. 27, 1806; "Instructions to British Ministers," pp. xvi, 220, 220 n.; T. R. Hay, "Charles Williamson and the Burr Conspiracy,"

By this time Monroe's failure at Madrid was known. War with Spain seemed inevitable early in 1805, and seemed a glittering opportunity for Burr's ambition. He left Washington, after an eloquent farewell to the Senate, to spy out a land of glory and to enlist associates. He visited eminent Westerners, telling somewhat different tales to each. Among others he called on Senator John Brown of Kentucky, alleged to be a former pro-Spanish conspirator; Senator John Smith of Ohio, Wilkinson's Army contractor; Andrew Jackson, to whom he said he had Secretary of War Henry Dearborn's blessing; Governor Robert Williams of Mississippi Territory; and Stephen Minor, formerly an officer in the Spanish Army. Late in June he was in New Orleans distributing uninhibited letters of introduction from Wilkinson, one of which described Governor Claiborne as an "idiot blackguard." He flattered the dissident critics of the Orleans territorial administration, and fraternized with enemies of the Viceroyalty of New Spain. He was friendly with Edward Livingston, but was mistaken in his man; Livingston was desperate for money, but he was an aggressive opposition politician, not a traitor.[27] Burr really should have known that able, insolvent, unhappy American politicians usually fight with ballots, not bullets.

By September, 1805, Burr was upstream at Wilkinson's St. Louis headquarters, trying to charm soldiers and civilians. According to their later testimony, his plan contemplated simultaneous attacks on Mexico from St. Louis and New Orleans, and the secession of the western states. Wilkinson had provided transportation, introductions, and an attempt to subvert his own proconsulship of Upper Louisiana by telling its people their land titles were jeopardized by incorporation in the United States.[28]

Journal of Southern History, II (1935), 207–209. In 1796 Dayton had proposed the election of Burr over Adams as the only way to beat Jefferson. In 1802 Truxtun wrote that he hoped to see Burr elected President.

27 Even the French minister in Washington, on March 9, 1805, reported to France that Burr, sponsored by Wilkinson and with his way paved by Edward Livingston, was leaving to intrigue in Louisiana. Elizabeth Warren, "Senator John Brown's Role in the Kentucky Spanish Conspiracy," *Filson Club Historical Quarterly,* XXXVI (1962), 158–176; Francis Rawle, "Edward Livingston," in Bemis (ed.), *Secretaries of State,* IV, 211–214; Hatcher, *Livingston,* pp. 114–115, 126–135.

28 Wilkinson to John Brown, Jan. 7, 1806 (dated 1805), John Mason Brown Papers, Yale University Library. Upper Louisiana had useful lead deposits and

When Burr returned from his western tour of 1805, he found the British minister unable to promise ships or sterling. A syllabus of treason, including the armed seizure of Washington, outlined to the late Spanish Minister Yrujo and to disappointed William Eaton, the unpaid hero of the shores of Tripoli, got $10,000 from the Spaniard, but only aroused abhorrence in Eaton. From Jefferson, Burr learned in November that war with Spain was now unlikely, a bit of bad news Burr relayed to Wilkinson; but early in 1806, the Spanish began to strengthen the defenses of Texas, upon which Jefferson ordered Wilkinson from St. Louis to the Sabine River frontier. War might inject new fuel into Burr's misfiring conspiratorial engine. But war with Spain would be a cash loss to Wilkinson. Perhaps as insurance or a hedge, one of Wilkinson's closest friends tipped off the Viceroy of New Spain in general terms about an American conspiracy aimed at Mexico. Wilkinson ignored Jefferson's movement order for the nonce, but sent Lieutenant Zebulon Montgomery Pike to explore the Arkansas River, not necessarily for the advancement of pure science. Wilkinson may also, for reasons yet unknown, have sent a large armed band up the Missouri River.[29]

Wilkinson seems to have decided to keep his Spanish connection and to betray Burr. Although Burr proved his fund-raising ability, he was plainly unable to get money out of foreign treasuries as regularly as Wilkinson could. The General liked to work in the dark, but this thing was beginning to glow. A Philadelphia newspaper, in August, 1805, asked embarrassing questions, and New Orleans gossips gabbled freely of the secession of the West.[30] If Wilkinson sat idle while Burr tried a *Putsch*, the soldier would be incriminated as nonfeasant at best, as an accomplice at worst. In short, Wilkinson stood by Burr until it seemed Burr might just pull it off, to the hazard of Wilkinson's Spanish dishonorarium.

Burr announced his advent in a falsely gasconading letter to Wilkinson in July. Thinking he had the anti-Claiborne faction

---

some hard characters who could have been useful to aim the lead. Clarence E. Carter, "The Burr-Wilkinson Intrigue in St. Louis," *Missouri Historical Society, Bulletin*, X (1954), 447–464.

29 Abernethy, *South in the New Nation*, pp. 272–279; Burr to Wilkinson (deciphered), Dec. 12, 1805, Wilkinson Papers, Chicago Historical Society. Pike's explorations are treated below.

30 Abernethy, *South in the New Nation*, pp. 271–272, 275–276.

primed for treason, he also sent his agents Dr. Justus Erich Bollman and Samuel Swartwout to Louisiana with letters for Wilkinson and others. At the Ohio River island of Burr's guileless but rich Irish refugee friend, Harman Blennerhassett, who was an easily duped romantic, boatbuilding began and recruits were enrolled. Letters by Blennerhassett on the need to complete the American revolution appeared in the Marietta *Gazette*. Burr visited Jackson again, to tell him he sailed against Mexico. Jackson, enchanted, promptly offered a surprised Jefferson several regiments of Tennessee militia for use in the halls of Montezuma, whereupon Burr asked Governor William Henry Harrison of Indiana Territory for some of *his* militia. Burr now had money, including $25,000 borrowed from the prudent investment counselors of a Kentucky insurance company. For $5,000 he bought the dubious Bastrop claim to vast lands thirty miles west of the Mississippi. The site would make a useful military staging area.[31]

Kentucky Federalists now seized an opportunity. Joseph A. Daveiss, district attorney, and ex-Senator Humphrey Marshall tried to indict Burr and to impeach his friend Associate Justice Ben Sebastian, a Spanish pensioner. Burr, defended by Henry Clay, got off, but Sebastian resigned the bench in disgrace. After this episode, Jackson dropped Burr like a hot brick, sharpening the point that, in the long run, latent western nationalism made Burr's grand design hopeless.[32] With Wilkinson as praetorian commandant, Burr could have crowned himself at New Orleans, but bellicose border captains like Jackson and Harrison were soon to prove their invincibility in the West.

In the first ten months of 1806, Jefferson received at least eight conscious or unconscious notices from substantial men who knew of Burr's project. Perhaps he riskily delayed action against an obviously weak force to await the overt act which would make conviction sure. Finally, in October, he ordered Marines to New Orleans, and sent Orleans Territorial Secretary John Graham to sniff along Burr's path. Graham was a good sleuth. He tricked Blennerhassett

31 *Ibid.*, pp. 279–283. For a sample of Blennerhassett's futile agitation, W. H. Safford (ed.), *The Blennerhassett Papers* (Cincinnati, 1864), pp. 132–140.
32 Carter, "Burr-Wilkinson Intrigue": I. J. Cox, "Western Reaction to the Burr Conspiracy," Illinois State Historical Society, *Transactions* (1928), pp. 73–87.

into blabbing all he knew, although Blennerhassett escaped downstream to join Burr.[33]

Having received notice from Burr that it was nearly time to act, Wilkinson, now on the Sabine, decided to play hero, and concluded his neutral-ground agreement with the Spanish. Agent Number 13 then wrote an alarmist letter to Jefferson (November 7), and a little note to the Viceroy of New Spain suggesting that $200,000 would be a suitable reward for his virtue. As Wilkinson moved to New Orleans to save his country, Jefferson issued a proclamation on November 27, prejudging Burr guilty of crime and ordering his arrest. The President took further precautions which might prevent the fall of New Orleans or, at the least, allow of its early reoccupation.[34]

At first Burr thought Wilkinson's move to New Orleans was counterfeit obedience to orders from Washington, but when he neared Natchez in January, 1807, with his terrifying horde of three-score unstable amateurs in small boats, he learned Wilkinson had denounced him and had ordered his arrest. Fearing military detention more than loss of dignity, he raced for Pensacola, probably on his way to Europe, but was intercepted and carried to Richmond. Wilkinson went about New Orleans like a roaring lion seeking whom he might devour, proving his hyperloyalty by arbitrary arrests, by ignoring writs of habeas corpus, and by decreeing unauthorized and unnecessary martial law, all to Jefferson's satisfaction.[35]

[33] Abernethy, *South in the New Nation*, pp. 281, 282, 285–289; Carter, "Burr-Wilkinson Intrigue"; Morgan to Neville, Sept. 2, 1806, University of Virginia MSS., Alderman Library, Charlottesville; Adams, "Jefferson's Military Policy," pp. 1–40.

[34] Dearborn opposed the announcement, but Jefferson approved and took credit for it after the fact, Richardson, *Messages and Papers*, I, 392–394, 401. The affair now appeared in the press in some detail, Philadelphia *Aurora*, Nov. 26, 27, 1806.

[35] Abernethy, *South in the New Nation*, pp. 291–293. What the Spaniards of the Floridas expected from Burr, a genuine, registered, pedigreed chimera of horrid mien, seen through Wilkinson's skillfully distorted camera obscura, was set out in Cox, *Florida Controversy*, pp. 193–210. James E. Winston (ed.), "A Faithful Picture of the Political Situation in New Orleans . . . 1807" (by James Workman or Edward Livingston), *Louisiana Historical Quarterly*, XI (1928), 359–433, although partisan, seems to be a useful record of Wilkinson's bloodless but galling quasi terror.

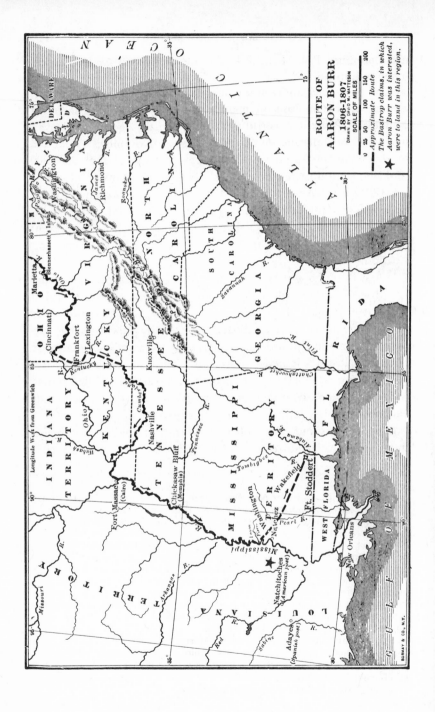

ROUTE OF
AARON BURR
1806-1807
DRAWN BY DAVID M. MATTESON
SCALE OF MILES
0 25 50   100   150   200
- - - Approximate Route ★
The Bastrop claims, in which
Aaron Burr was interested,
were to land in this region.

BURNAY & CO., N.Y.

In December, Robert Smith had advised the President to take the Congress into his confidence, and to ask for the suspension of the writ of habeas corpus. Jefferson's message to the Congress, on January 22, 1807, insisted on Burr's guilt, praised Wilkinson's "honor" and "fidelity," and justified the arbitrary arrests. He asked for *ex post facto* suspension of the writ for three months. The House was hostile; it rejected the request at first opportunity, almost unanimously. Randolph made the most caustic speech, naturally.[36]

Aaron Burr, whose last public court appearance had been as theatrical producer and president of the showy trial of Samuel Chase, now found himself charged with treason in an atmosphere of similarly warm partisanship. Chief Justice Marshall, on circuit in Richmond, heard the arraignment on March 30, 1807, alleging merely the misdemeanor of organizing an anti-Spanish filibuster. Marshall freed Burr on bond to appear before the grand jury,[37] with an unjudicial remark about the "hand of malignity" "capriciously" grasping Burr's collar.[38] Wrangling over the selection of jurors (no Virginian was unbiased) took much time. Then Luther Martin, leader of the six defense counsel, called on Marshall—in heated argument—to subpoena Jefferson and his interesting Wilkinson manuscripts. Marshall, in a political speech, acceded. Jefferson correctly refused, on straight constitutional grounds, to make reply.[39]

When witnesses had been heard, John Randolph, foreman of the grand jury (who was acceptable to the defense because he hated

36 Smith to Jefferson, Dec. 22, 1806, Jefferson Papers, Library of Congress; *Annals,* 9th Congress, 2nd Session, pp. 39–44, 402–405; for the outraged feelings of an able Federalist out of office, see Charles R. King (ed.), *The Life and Correspondence of Rufus King* (6 vols., New York, 1894–1900), IV, 544–549; see also Boston *Columbian Centinel,* Feb. 4, 7, 11, 1807. In the Senate, John Quincy Adams "was *passionately* zealous for its passage," and Henry Clay voted for it. E. S. Brown (ed.), *William Plumer's Memorandum of Proceedings in the Senate, 1803–1807* (New York, 1923), p. 589.

37 In addition to Abernethy's work, previously cited, a most convenient short account of the trial appears in Richard Brandon Morris, *Fair Trial* (New York, 1953), Chap. V, on which this writer has leaned heavily. Albert J. Beveridge, *The Life of John Marshall* (4 vols., Boston, 1916–19), III, 274–364, describes the political climate; the trial is covered on pp. 274–529.

38 Quoted in Beveridge, *Marshall,* III, 376.

39 *Ibid.,* pp 125–127, 136–138, 454–456; Morris, *Fair Trial,* pp. 132–136. Beveridge, Marshall's principal and partisan biographer, thought Jefferson's rejoinder brilliant. Jefferson cited the independence of the three branches of government, as Washington had before him in an analogous circumstance. All Presidents have followed the precedent.

Jefferson more than Burr),[40] brought in an indictment charging several persons with treason, and describing Burr as "not having the fear of God before his eyes . . . but being moved and seduced by the instigation of the devil. . . ."[41] The court proceeded to empanel the petit jury, August 3–15, accepting any juror who was only a little prejudiced, and even taking one who publicly said Burr should hang. Burr knew he would win acquittal, if at all, not on the facts but on the law.[42]

The prosecution relied for law on a recent "tricky"[43] obiter dictum by Marshall in the hearing of Bollman's and Swartwout's successful petitions for writs of habeas corpus. Although Marshall said treason was assembly for war, not merely conspiracy, he had endorsed part of the old doctrine of constructive treason: no participants are accessories; all are principals. If the rule held up, the prosecutors had only to prove an assembly for war with which Burr was consciously associated. Otherwise, a man could organize a treason and remain an innocent bystander while other men executed the plot. According to the competent district attorney, George Hay, any other rule would delight traitors.[44]

For evidence the prosecutors—Hay, William Wirt, Alexander McRae—had their strutting, evasive star witness, Wilkinson, whose transparent pretense of violated innocence and whose meek submission to abuse in court or street soon showed him to be a cracked

40 Beveridge describes the witnesses and their impacts in *Marshall*, III, 456–491; William Cabell Bruce, *John Randolph of Roanoke, 1733–1833* (2 vols., New York, 1922) , I, 295–305, covers the trial as an episode of Randolph's life.

41 *ASP: Misc.,* I, 486–487.

42 Morris, *Fair Trial,* pp. 136–138. The trial opened on Aug. 3. A jury was chosen by Aug. 15. From Aug. 19 to 29, counsel argued on admissibility of evidence. Marshall ruled for the defense on Aug. 31, and the prosecution quit trying on Sept. 1.

43 Adrienne Koch, *Jefferson and Madison: The Great Collaboration* (New York, 1950) , p. 232, calls this "a tricky formulation of treason, providing the defendant the necessary loophole."

44 Carl Brent Swisher, *American Constitutional Development* (Boston, 1943) , pp. 126–131, and Andrew C. McLaughlin, *A Constitutional History of the United States* (New York, 1935) , pp. 324–330, give the essential constitutional background of the trial. See also *Ex Parte Bollman and Swartwout,* 4 Cranch 75 (1807) ; Associate Justice William Johnson dissented, but only to deny jurisdiction. Morris, *Fair Trial,* pp. 138–139, 146–152. Joseph Story, no incendiary, thought Marshall's dictum in the Bollman and Swartwout case was the best definition of treason, C. G. Haines and F. H. Sherwood, *The Role of the Supreme Court in American Government and Politics* (2 vols., Berkeley, 1944–57) , I, 285–286.

crutch. If Wilkinson's evidence proved a treason, the prosecution had diffuse corroborative evidence to link Burr with it, including William Eaton's signed avowal of the invitation to help capture Washington (weakened in skeptical minds by the very recent payment of his old claim for Tripolitan war expenses), rambling inanities from Blennerhassett's gardener, testimony of elderly Colonel George Morgan and bluff Captain Truxtun. Blennerhassett, a codefendant, was too myopic, literally, to be useful to either side.[45]

The learned, passionate, alcoholic Luther Martin, who wishfully thought Burr was victimized, and his five co-counsel for the defense, including two former Attorneys General of the United States, handled the prosecution witnesses skillfully, although not scrupulously. Assured of sympathetic press coverage by the presence of the youthful snob Washington Irving, they steered as near as they dared to incriminating Wilkinson equally, tacitly impeached the integrity of the theatrical Eaton, let Truxtun harmlessly talk of the glory of conquering Mexico at Burr's side, let Blennerhassett's gardener show his vacuity, and, rather nastily, had Colonel Morgan's son perjure himself by swearing to his father's senility. However, after a ten-day argument about the admissibility of evidence that Burr had caused the boatbuilding at Blennerhassett's island while absent, they won on the law, not the facts. Marshall, suspiciously partisan, reversed his Bollman-Swartwout dictum, construed the Constitution's treason clause as tightly as possible, and barred evidence of conspiracy until martial assembly was proved first. Marshall had checked prosecution. Hay had first to convict Blennerhassett and friends of treasonable boatbuilding assembly, and then get two witnesses to prove Burr caused it *in absentia*.[46] On the next day,

[45] Morris, *Fair Trial*, pp. 131–132, 136, 140–152; Francis F. Beirne, *Shout Treason: The Trial of Aaron Burr* (New York, 1959), p. 262; L. B. Wright and J. H. McLeod, "William Eaton's Relations with Aaron Burr," *Mississippi Valley Historical Review*, XXXI (1944–45), 523–536.

[46] T. C. Waters, "Luther Martin," American Bar Association, *Journal*, XIV (1928), 605–609, 674–677; J. Frederick Essary, *Maryland in National Politics* (Baltimore, 1932), pp. 59–78; Edward S. Delaplaine, "Luther Martin," *DAB*; Morris, *Fair Trial*, pp. 124–125, 140–152—Morgan's tipoff letter on the conspiracy was internally rational and lucid. Regarding Irving, despite his biographer's circumlocutions, the four-letter word must be applied to him at that age, Stanley T. Williams, *The Life of Washington Irving* (2 vols., New York, 1935). Haines and Sherwood, *Supreme Court*, I, 279–288; David G. Loth, *Chief Justice: John Marshall and the Growth of the Republic* (New York, 1949), pp. 242–247; Julius W. Pratt, "Aaron Burr and the Historians," *New-York History*, XXVI (1945), 461, 462.

September 1, the prosecution rested. The jury retired, deliberated, and brought in a "not proved" verdict, which Marshall entered as "not guilty."

There were two good lawyers on opposing sides who were not listed as counsel: Marshall for the defense and Jefferson for the prosecution. Neither was judicious, but only Marshall was sworn to be. As a great constitutional scholar has said, "the case is a blemish on Marshall's career."[47] His subpoena of the President, his acerbity about the government's eagerness to convict, his presence at a dinner which Burr attended, all allow one to think he let the trial become a party contest, and hint that he was grasping at judicial supremacy after the late victorious acquittal of Samuel Chase. Jefferson, too, was at his worst. Overwrought at the possibility of Federalist benefits, he published relevant affidavits and publicly prejudged Burr's guilt before trial, urged the prosecution to spend lavishly in investigation, promised pardons to any self-incriminators who might come forward to help to convict Burr, suggested indicting Luther Martin for the tone of his defense of Burr, and concealed his knowledge of a prior correspondence between Wilkinson and Burr.[48] One of Jefferson's most respectful biographers admitted that his practice, compared with his preaching, was "very illogical."[49] The President was more of a frontier vigilante than we usually remember.[50]

Like the echoes of a summer storm, Burr's cause was heard after it passed. Limited by Marshall's rule of law, Hay pressed the original Mexican filibuster charge, but lost again. He next moved to confine Burr for trial in Ohio for treason committed there after joining Blennerhassett. Instead, Marshall allowed bail and left town. Jefferson never forgave Marshall. He sent the record to the Congress,

47 A. C. McLaughlin, "The Life of John Marshall [review of Beveridge]," American Bar Association, *Journal*, VII (1921) , 233.
48 Morris, *Fair Trial*, pp. 129, 133, 134–135; Haines and Sherwood, *Supreme Court*, I, 283–284, 283 n.–284 n.; Nathan Schachner, *Thomas Jefferson, A Biography* (2 vols. in 1, New York, 1960) , II, 851–853.
49 Gilbert Chinard, *Thomas Jefferson, The Apostle of Americanism* (Boston, 1929) , p. 438.
50 *Ibid.*, pp. 434–439. For a documentation of Jefferson's vigilante instinct, and of what this writer thinks were his occasional and typically vindictive seventeenth-century Whiggery and tenth-century jurisprudential primitivism, see Leonard W. Levy, *Jefferson and Civil Liberties: The Darker Side* (Cambridge, Mass., 1963) . Levy showed an eagerness to convict, without which his study would have been even better than the skillfully constructed book he wrote.

hinting it might justify impeaching the Chief Justice. He unsuccessfully supported a constitutional amendment to weaken the tenure of judges. The Republican press took the cue and sounded off furioso, while a mob in Baltimore demonstrated against the court. Although Randolph tried hard to ruin Wilkinson, Agent Number 13 came out legally clean, perhaps because of culpable protections in high places. A Senate committee headed by John Quincy Adams recommended expelling Senator John Smith, a secretly sworn vassal of the King of Spain. It failed by one vote short of two-thirds, but Smith resigned on demand of the Ohio legislature. Jefferson fired the district attorney in Ohio for negligence. Luther Martin defended his own conduct in print and, pickled in whisky, was preserved another fifteen years.[51]

Burr, characteristically jumping bail, went to Europe, where he went hungry to rent streetwalkers, and tried to get an audience with Napoleon in order to interest him in making peace with Britain so that an Anglo-French force could conquer Mexico and the United States. This period of his life left us nothing but an unreserved diary of purple episodes. He died in New York in 1836 after a riotous old age in which he looted his second wife's ill-gotten estate, sired two children out of wedlock in his seventies, and won the crown of virility by being divorced for adultery at eighty. He had still one friend, who artlessly botched his biography so as to show him at his meanest. "Guilty" is a legal word. Whether Burr was guilty of treason has been moot since 1807, but he was surely the enemy of his country. Great as were his abilities, they were enfeebled by his even greater vices.[52]

51 Richardson, *Messages and Papers*, I, 417, 437–438; C. G. Haines, *The American Doctrine of Judicial Supremacy* (New York, 1959), pp. 250–253; Albany *Register*, Nov. 24, 1807. Republican anger glowed for a decade. Schachner, *Jefferson*, II, 856–858. Adams, "Jefferson's Military Policy," pp. 35–40; Miss Adams exculpated Jefferson on the question of improper protection of Wilkinson. M. Avis Pitcher, "John Smith, First Senator from Ohio and His Connections with Aaron Burr," *Ohio Archaeological and Historical Quarterly*, XLV (1936), 68–88; Burlington, Vermont, *Centinel*, Aug. 26, 1807. In 1822, when Martin was partially paralyzed and stony broke, Aaron Burr sheltered him until his death several years later. Delaplaine, "Luther Martin," *DAB*. This seems to have been Burr's only known selfless act.

52 The friend was Matthew L. Davis, who also edited *The Private Journal of Aaron Burr During His Residence of Four Years in Europe* (2 vols., New York, 1856–58). See also W. C. Ford (ed.), "Some Papers of Aaron Burr," American

Marshall's unwonted and un-Federalist strict construction of the treason clause had merit before the invention of the steam locomotive and the magnetic telegraph. Today it would not protect the people from a Caesar in the White House or an Alcibiades in the Department of Defense, who could subvert the nation by telephone or wireless. The Congress long ago evaded Marshall's rule by reestablishing the crime of constructive treason under other names, most recently by outlawing speech or print which advocates overthrowing the government by force.

Finally, just to complete the record, there *was* a judicially determined treason. A popular Hoosier politician named Davis Floyd, one of Burr's lesser codefendants, elected to be tried back home in Indiana Territory for treasonable acts alleged to have been committed there. He was convicted, fined $20, and sentenced to three hours in jail. A few days after his conviction, the Territorial House of Representatives elected him its Clerk, and he later became an Indiana state circuit judge.[53]

III

What lay beyond the swirling Mississippi? No tolerably accurate maps were available. Virginians of 1753 planned to seek the Pacific by way of the Missouri. As late as the 1790's, people thought it

---

Antiquarian Society, *Proceedings*, New Series, XXIX (1919), 43–53. To Burr's credit, he acknowledged every paternity claim presented to him.

Burr's propositions to Merry and Yrujo have been available since the 1880's (Pratt, "Burr and the Historians"), yet Nathan Schachner, *Aaron Burr* (New York, 1937) describes a monstrously animal and selfish protagonist and closed by asking, "Who in history has not similar smirches on his character?" (p. 517). The question is unanswerable, but only for lack of space to list all that fall between, say, "Arc, Joan of" and "Zoroaster." Charles A. Beard frivolously reviews Burr's life as a dramatic critic would see it, and concludes that he has been condemned for mistakes of dramaturgy, that republics can forgive mistakes but political parties never. Beard, Introduction to McCaleb, *Burr Conspiracy* (1936), pp. ix–xi. S. H. Wandell and Meade Minnigerode, *Aaron Burr* (2 vols., New York, 1925), II, 338–339, also evaluate him in theatrical language, concluding that he was harmless enough when he had a part that allowed panache, but dangerous when ad-libbing. Andrew Jackson took his true measure (Marquis James, *Andrew Jackson: The Border Captain,* Indianapolis, 1933, p. 124): "Burr is as far from a fool as any man I ever saw, and yet he is as easily fooled as any man I ever knew." Agent Number 13 would not have dissented from Jackson's opinion.

53 I. J. Cox, "The Burr Conspiracy in Indiana," *Indiana Magazine of History,* XXV (1929), 276–277, 280.

would be easy. Jefferson, in 1783, suggested to George Rogers Clark that he try it, and encouraged John Ledyard's frustrated tramp eastward across most of Siberia a few years later. When Jefferson had power to do more than merely to suggest, expeditions fanned out in several directions, usually led by young Army officers of a quality better than the public deserved. We credit Jefferson's scientific curiosity, but he was also explicit about the commercial benefits. (The incredulous Spaniards thought Jefferson was only meddling with the Indians.) [54] Obviously, his interest was a mirror of the sum of public interest: intellectual, economic, diplomatic.

The most stirring expedition went to the Pacific and back by way of the Missouri and Columbia rivers, 1804–6. Its leaders were both combat veterans of the Army: blue-eyed Meriwether Lewis, the born woodsman who served Jefferson as private secretary, and redheaded William Clark, the much younger brother of the famous George Rogers Clark.[55]

Jefferson, who had never been more than fifty miles west of Monticello, planned it, and easily got a secret appropriation even before he had any notion of buying Upper Louisiana. The initial planning was necessarily secret, and mostly oral, until the Louisiana Purchase was made, but we know the original purposes were to find a useful path to the Pacific, to learn geography, and to study Indian trade and diplomacy—all this on foreign soil. Development of the fur trade of Spanish Louisiana, Jefferson hoped, would lure private fur traders out of the United States, eliminating their influence over

54 Jefferson to G. Clark, Dec. 4, 1783, in Julian Boyd (ed.), *The Papers of Thomas Jefferson* (16 vols., Princeton, 1950–), VI, 371, and Clark to Jefferson, Feb. 8, 1784, in Donald Jackson (ed.), *Letters of the Lewis and Clark Expedition . . . 1783–1784* (Urbana, 1962), pp. 655–656. The Czarina refused permission to Ledyard (William J. Ghent, "John Ledyard," *DAB*), although in later years Jefferson confused the story by saying she had revoked permission. See also William J. Ghent, *The Early Far West . . . 1540–1850* (New York, 1936), pp. 82–83 n. Ledyard's march is briefly described in John Bartlett Brebner, *The Explorers of North America, 1492–1806* (London, 1933), pp. 458–463.

55 Ghent, *Early Far West*, pp. 83–100, 104–110; the best brief biography of Lewis is Jefferson's, written for inclusion in *History of the Expedition . . . to the Sources of the Missouri Thence Across the Rocky Mountains and Down the River Columbia to the Pacific . . .* (2 vols., Philadelphia, 1814). Lester J. Cappon considers the authorship of this text in *William and Mary Quarterly,* Third Series, XIX (1962), 257–268; see also John Bakeless, *Lewis and Clark, Partners in Discovery* (New York, 1947), pp. 2, 8–9, 37.

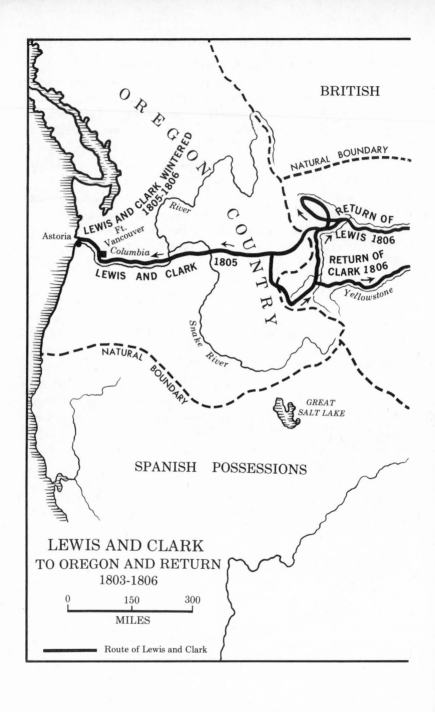

BRITISH

O R E G O N   C O U N T R Y

NATURAL BOUNDARY

LEWIS AND CLARK WINTERED 1805-1806

River

Astoria

LEWIS AND CLARK

Ft. Vancouver

Columbia

1805

RETURN OF LEWIS 1806

RETURN OF CLARK 1806

Yellowstone

Snake River

NATURAL BOUNDARY

GREAT SALT LAKE

SPANISH   POSSESSIONS

LEWIS AND CLARK
TO OREGON AND RETURN
1803-1806

0   150   300

MILES

Route of Lewis and Clark

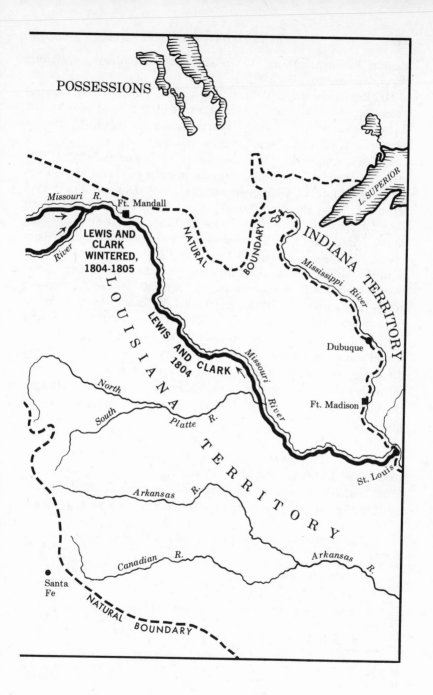

POSSESSIONS

Missouri R. ■ Ft. Mandall

LEWIS AND
CLARK
WINTERED,
1804-1805

River

NATURAL

BOUNDARY

INDIANA

L. SUPERIOR

Mississippi River

Dubuque

LEWIS AND CLARK 1804

L O U I S I A N A

Missouri River

Ft. Madison ■

North

South

Platte R.

T E R R I T O R Y

TERRITORY

St. Louis

Arkansas R.

Canadian R.

Arkansas R.

● Santa
Fe

NATURAL BOUNDARY

eastern Indians, making the Indians more submissive in signing away their hunting lands.[56]

Dr. Benjamin Rush planned the hygiene and the physiological research. His memoranda included a matchless rule of health: "10. Lying down when fatigued." Doubtless because of Rule 10, and because of the leaders' intelligence, only one of their men died.[57]

Embarking in May, 1804, the "Corps of Discovery," nearly fifty strong, worked its way in boats up the muddy, powerful Missouri as far as the Mandan villages in present North Dakota. There they wintered. So far they had discovered nothing. Frenchmen had been that far, perhaps a century earlier.[58] Lewis and Clark collected information, canoes, and a remarkable Shoshone girl named Sacajawea, "Canoe Launcher," usually miscalled "Bird Woman."

In the spring they plunged into the true unknown, living off the country, guided by Canoe Launcher, who also packed a papoose across the continental divide. Her French husband was supposed to be a guide, but he was worth little. Canoe Launcher, a true national heroine, was delighted to enlist in the Corps because Clark would not let her husband beat her. They crossed the continental divide in August. As they coursed down the foamy Snake and Columbia rivers, they lost personal elation while gaining coxswains' skills and becoming superb boatmen, doing a tough but routine job. They reached the Pacific Ocean in November, and Clark carved on a tree, "By Land from the U. States in 1804 & 5." After the winter they returned by nearly the same rugged route, completing the American epic of exploration at St. Louis in September, 1806. Unlike the wilderness sprints of the French or the gaudy cavalcades of the Spanish, the expedition had been well equipped,

56 The total cost, through Nov. 1806, was $22,393.51. Grace Lewis, "Financial Records, 'Expedition to the Pacific Ocean,' " Missouri Historical Society, Bulletin, X (1954), 465–489; Seymour Adelman, "Equipping the Lewis and Clark Expedition," American Philosophical Library, Bulletin 1945 (1946), pp. 39–44; Ralph B. Guinness, "The Purpose of the Lewis and Clark Expedition," Mississippi Valley Historical Review, XX (1933–34), 90–101.

57 George W. Corner (ed.), The Autobiography of Benjamin Rush (Princeton, 1948), pp. 265–267; Drake W. Will, "The Medical and Surgical Practice of the Lewis and Clark Expedition," Journal of the History of Medicine, XIV (1959), 273–297.

58 Abraham P. Nasatir (ed.), Before Lewis and Clark . . . 1785–1804 (2 vols., St. Louis, 1952), pp. 3–57. There was already a French trading station among the Mandans; A. H. Abel (ed.), Tabeau's Narrative of Loisel's Expedition to the Upper Missouri (Norman, 1939), p. 26 n.

coolly planned, minutely organized, and intelligently executed.[59] There was heroism, but no lost motion.

They brought news that the mountains were rich in furs (and grizzly bears) and they misinformed the world that their route was good for trade with Cathay. From 1806 until the War of 1812, the upper Missouri system was continuously searched by fur traders (and grizzly-dodgers). Next came a race to publish, but, partly because of Lewis's tragic suicide in 1809, only an enlisted man's journal (1807), a fake narrative (1809), and a synthetic journal (1814) appeared before the first accurate text of Lewis and Clark records came out in 1904. Charles Willson Peale's Museum got many Lewis and Clark exhibits, but the true scientific benefit was the appearance of their very influential map in 1814.[60]

While Lewis and Clark were out of ken, viewing white waters and *Ursus horribilis* with respect, Jefferson sent two expeditions to explore the Ouachita and Red rivers, both led by civilian scientists. They learned that such excursions needed lighter boats, found that only commissioned officers could keep enlisted men toiling, and no doubt discovered a great deal about chiggers and mosquitoes, but they added nothing to scientific geography.[61]

For reasons yet uncertain, Wilkinson also arranged a pair of

[59] Grace R. Hebard, *Sacajawea, A Guide and Interpreter of the Lewis and Clark Expedition* (Glendale, Cal., 1933), pp. 50–51, 89–93, 97, 235; Brebner, *Explorers,* pp. 458, 464–482.

[60] Bernard DeVoto, *The Course of Empire* (Boston, 1952), pp. 488 (on grizzlies), 519–520, 526–528. The fur traffic is described by Ghent, *Early Far West,* pp. 115–123. Beginning about thirty years after, people began to make a mystery of Lewis' death; there is no reason to doubt that it was suicide. Dawson A. Phelps, "The Tragic Death of Meriwether Lewis," *William and Mary Quarterly,* Third Series, XIII (1956), 305–318. Concerning the publication of the sources, see Cappon (cited in note 55) and Donald Jackson, "The Race to Publish Lewis and Clark," *Pennsylvania Magazine of History and Biography,* LXXXV (1961), 163–177. The definitive edition of Lewis and Clark is Reuben Gold Thwaites (ed.), *Original Journals of the Lewis and Clark Expedition, 1804–1806* (8 vols., New York, 1959); DeVoto abridged the journals for "the general reader" (Cambridge, Mass., 1963). On Peale's interest, see Charles Coleman Sellers, *Charles Willson Peale* (2 vols., Philadelphia, 1947), II, 232–233, 239–241. Carl I. Wheat, *Mapping the Trans-Mississippi West, 1540–1861* (5 vols., San Francisco, 1957–60), II, 31–60, gives the cartographical history and explains the magnitude of the achievement.

[61] Ghent, *Early Far West,* pp. 89–90, 102–104; Milford E. Allen, "Thomas Jefferson and the Louisiana-Arkansas Frontier," *Arkansas Historical Quarterly,* XX (1961), 39–64. Another expedition, under Colonel Constant Freeman, was turned back in 1806 by the growing Spanish military force on the border.

expeditions. He first ordered Lieutenant Pike to find the source of the Mississippi River (1805–6), and then sent him to reconnoiter the headwaters of the Arkansas (1806–7). Pike was not trained for scientific exploration. He picked the wrong fountain for the Mississippi, but his group showed the flag to Indians and British traders.[62]

Pike next ascended the Arkansas. Somebody alerted the Spanish to the approach of fourscore travelers. Pike had been ordered to report back only to Wilkinson. The party suffered severely in winter camp in the Rio Grande headwaters and was picked up by Spanish soldiery. The Spanish government later dunned the United States for the cost of hunting Pike—$22,000. The "captors" courteously escorted the Americans to Santa Fe, where half a dozen Americans and French creoles had been collected by Spanish patrols. Next they were conducted to Chihuahua for interrogation. Minus some of Pike's papers (rediscovered in 1910), the party was deported to Natchitoches, arriving there in July, 1807. The explorers were mistakenly credited with crossing the continental divide. Pike discovered Pike's Peak, but failed in a try at climbing it. Trade stepped on the heels of the flag bearers; sharp-dealing Jacques Clamorgan appeared in Santa Fe in 1807 with a pack train of St. Louis merchandise. Pike soon produced a southwestern map, cribbed from Alexander von Humboldt's unpublished work, and he contributed the myth that the most important western rivers all rise in one small area. Nevertheless, his description, which appeared before Lewis and Clark's, gave the nation its first panorama of the Great Plains and the Rockies.[63]

62 Pike made twenty errors of observation in eight successive days in the Arkansas watershed; Theodore H. Scheffer, "Following Pike's Expedition," *Kansas Historical Quarterly*, XV (1947), 240–247. He missed the altitude of Pike's Peak by 4,000 feet and, nearby, erred by about thirty-five miles in fixing his latitude. S. H. Hart and A. B. Hulbert (eds.), *Zebulon Pike's Arkansaw Journal* (Denver, 1932), p. lxxiii; Katherine Coman, *Economic Beginnings of the Far West* (2 vols., New York, 1912), I, 285–288.

63 Ghent, *Early Far West*, pp. 110–114; W. Eugene Hollon, "Zebulon Montgomery Pike and the Wilkinson-Burr Conspiracy," American Philosophical Society, *Proceedings*, XCI (1947), 447–456; Hollon, *Lost Pathfinder* (Norman, 1949), pp. 45, 126–127, 134–135; I. J. Cox, "Opening the Santa Fé Trail," *Missouri Historical Review*, XXV (1930–31), 30–66, establishes the economic frame into which the Pike episode fitted; Hart and Hulbert (eds.), *Arkansaw Journal*, pp. xlix–lvii, lxiii–lxxx; Joseph J. Hill (ed.), "An Unknown Expedition to Santa Fé in 1807," *Mississippi Valley Historical Review*, VI (1919–20), 560–562; Abel (ed.), *Tabeau's Narrative*, pp. 12–14. Pike's published account appeared in 1810; Elliott Coues (ed.), *The Expeditions of Zebulon Montgomery Pike* (3 vols., New

But the really interesting question about Pike's circular journey is, Why? No one really knows, but it is believed that Wilkinson plotted the capture of Pike's band. If true, Pike seems to have been an innocent pawn. Pike's ambition was not to be Agent Number 14 but to be appointed commissioner to trace the Louisiana Purchase boundaries. Surely he was no spy. His operation was too conspicuous. A sham trading expedition would have been more useful. John Hamilton Robinson, a civilian surgeon and Wilkinson crony, went along, apparently to tell the Captain General at Chihuahua that Wilkinson would try to prevent war. However, Pike moved so slowly that Wilkinson had prevented war by the neutral-ground agreement before the Captain General got the word.[64]

John Jacob Astor, a leading American enterpriser, reacted quickly to the findings of Lewis and Clark. Using his one-man American Fur Company, chartered in 1808, he projected a line of forts from the Missouri to the Pacific, politically protected by a deal with Alexander Baranov's almost autonomous Russian American Company to permit a post at the Columbia's mouth from which inland furs would go annually to China. The Russians clearly owned Alaska, and they claimed the coast down to California. Although Russia would not surrender jurisdiction, Baranov had no objection to the American exploitation of the inland beaver. Jefferson also approved; he had expected Oregon to become American even before he bought Louisiana. The project was bungled by Astor's energetic but vain and brutal subordinates. The coastal station, Astoria, was built, but by the time its first furs got to sea, the War of 1812 had started. In 1813, Astoria fell bloodlessly to the Northwest Company, its chief Canadian competitor.[65]

York, 1895), is the principal grand collation. Wheat, *Mapping*, I, 12–13; II, 18, 24–25.

Pike's evidence that he was not trespassing on Spanish soil was his rough map, on which he labeled the upper Rio Grande as the Red.

[64] Milo Quaife (ed.), *Southwestern Expedition of Zebulon M. Pike* (Chicago, 1925), pp. xv–xvii. A House committee reported no derogatory findings about the southwestern expedition, Mar. 10, 1808. Secretary of War Dearborn commended both Pike expeditions, Feb. 24, 1808 (*ASP: Misc.*, I, 719). But Pike gained no other kudos because Wilkinson, not Jefferson, was the promoter. Hart and Hulbert (eds.), *Arkansaw Journal*, pp. lxiii–lxxx, xcvi, 183. As for Robinson's presence, there were plenty of Army surgeons available. Robinson later served as brigadier general of Mexican revolutionaries.

[65] Kenneth W. Porter provides the best life of the single-minded immigrant who became the fur tycoon, *John Jacob Astor, Businessman* (2 vols., Cambridge,

The Astoria episode had as much diplomatic as economic potential. The British, too, had an interest in the region. The Columbia River was first noticed by a British naval officer a fortnight before Captain Robert Gray of Boston sailed into its mouth and named it, in 1792. David Thompson of the Northwest Company, when beginning to explore the Columbia system in 1807, was ordered out by a message from a still unknown "Lieutenant Jeremy Pinch," U.S.A., said to be nearby with forty-two men.[66] If there was a Lieutenant Pinch, his claim was the first explicit official American claim to the Oregon country. Otherwise, the planting of Astoria was the first overt act of the long Anglo-American rivalry.

IV

East of the Mississippi the country was booming. Only the Indians (and a few arch-Federalists) regretted it. About seventy thousand Indians lived there. They had known three sets of masters, French, British, and American, in forty years. Six-sevenths of them lived in the Old Southwest. They were debauched by private traders, peonized by government factories, policed by soldiers, and governed by incompetent agents and distracted, empty-handed territorial governors. Most palefaces thought they should go West or drop dead, but Jefferson feebly tried to teach them agriculture. Few citizens sympathized, and fewer helped. Instead the whites taught them property, and then how to convey it under the constitutional treaty clause. Presidents Jefferson and Madison negotiated fifty-three ces-

---

Mass., 1931), in which Chaps. VII–VIII tell the Astoria tale. Jeannette Mirsky, *The Westward Crossings: Balboa, Mackenzie, Lewis and Clark* (New York, 1946), pp. 352–355; M. Catherine White (ed.), *David Thompson's Journals Relating to Montana and Adjacent Regions, 1808–1812* (Missoula, 1950), pp. cvi n.–cvii n. Miss White gives all of the essential bibliography of her subject.

66 The Foreign Office in 1810 asked the British minister in Washington to learn of Astor's project. Frederick Merk, "The Genesis of the Oregon Question," *Mississippi Valley Historical Review*, XXXVI (1949–50), 583–586; George W. Fuller, *A History of the Pacific Northwest* (2nd ed. rev., New York, 1945), pp. 75–76, 78–83, 353 (note 31); "Pinch" to Thompson, Sept. 29, 1807 (said to be in Thompson's hand), R. C. Clark, *History of Willamette Valley, Oregon* (3 vols., Chicago, 1927), I, 839–841.

There was no Jeremy Pinch of any rank on the roster of either of Pike's expeditions, *ASP: Misc.*, I, 944. There was an early settler of Missouri named Jeremiah Painsch, but no connection has been established; Fuller, *Pacific Northwest*. Miss White thinks the man may have been an unscrupulous agent of Manuel Lisa of St. Louis who took a party up the Missouri that year, or a pseudonymous Wilkinson operative touring the Rockies for purposes unknown.

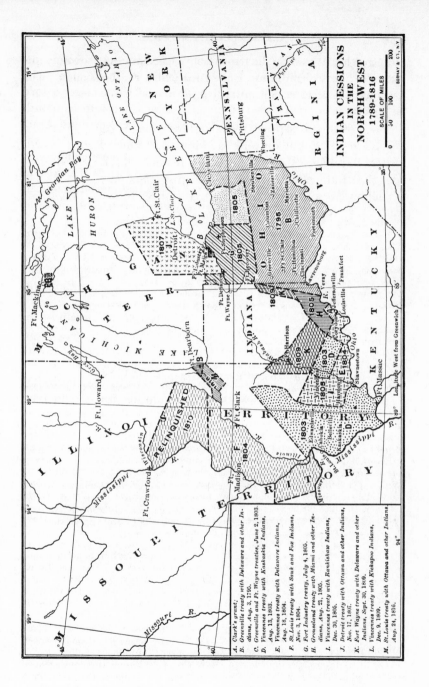

INDIAN CESSIONS
IN THE
NORTHWEST
1789-1816
SCALE OF MILES
0   50   100   200

A. Clark's grant.
B. Greenville treaty with Delaware and other In-
    diana, Aug. 3, 1795.
C. Greenville and Ft. Wayne treaties, June 2, 1803.
D. Vincennes treaty with Kaskaskia Indians,
    Aug. 13, 1803.
E. Vincennes treaty with Delaware Indians,
    Aug. 18, 1804.
F. St. Louis treaty with Sauk and Fox Indians,
    Nov. 3, 1804.
G. Fort Industry treaty, July 4, 1805.
H. Grouseland treaty with Miami and other In-
    dians, Aug. 21, 1805.
I. Vincennes treaty with Rankishaw Indians,
    Dec. 30, 1805.
J. Detroit treaty with Ottawa and other Indians,
    Nov. 17, 1807.
K. Fort Wayne treaty with Delaware and other
    Indians, Sept. 30, 1809.
L. Vincennes treaty with Kickapoo Indians,
    Dec. 9, 1809.
M. St. Louis treaty with Ottawa and other Indians,
    Aug. 24, 1816.

sion treaties, degrading the tribes from protectorates to wards, while acquiring tens of millions of acres for which the fictitiously sovereign nations received annuities to keep them in rags and drunken idleness.[67]

The land received from the states and Indians could produce a federal revenue, but only by favoring speculators with wholesale prices. Republicans opposed this for reasons of agrarian ideology and practical politics. By the agrarianist Land Act of 1800, half sections were sold on four years' credit at $2 an acre. This stimu-

[67] The Indian story was a story by whites, with little in the record by Indians. Clark Wissler, *Indians of the United States* (New York, 1954), pp. 73–80, 185–187; Ralph Hall Brown, *Mirror for Americans; Likeness of the Eastern Seaboard, 1810* (New York, 1943), pp. 25–28; one could calculate that in 1807 there were perhaps a third or a fourth as many Indians east of the Mississippi as there were in 1607. Jefferson's first and second annual messages reported total Indian peace. Francis Paul Prucha, *American Indian Policy in the Formative Years . . . 1790–1834* (Cambridge, Mass., 1962), pp. 102–108, summarizes the ineffectual efforts to dam the flood of alcohol flowing into the Indian country. Jefferson to Harrison, Feb. 27, 1803, in Clarence E. Carter (ed.), *The Territorial Papers of the United States* (24 vols., Washington, 1934–), VII, 91, suggested controlling the Indians by getting them into debt (for their own good, of course). R. S. Cotterill, "Federal Indian Management in the South, 1789–1825," *Mississippi Valley Historical Review*, XX (1933–34), 333–345, and Royal B. Way, "The United States Factory System for Trading with the Indians, 1796–1822," *Mississippi Valley Historical Review*, VI (1919–20), 220–235, evaluate the government factory system, as does Quaife, "An Experiment of the Fathers in State Socialism," *Wisconsin Magazine of History*, III (1919–20), 277–290. Ora Brooks Peake, *A History of the United States Indian Factory System, 1795–1822* (Denver, 1954), pp. 272–276, tots up the value of merchandise vended through the factories, 1808–11; the two largest were west of the Mississippi. Leonard D. White, *The Jeffersonians, A Study in Administrative History, 1801–1829* (New York, 1951), pp. 496–510, shows how much responsibility was placed on the military. Dorothy Burne Goebel, *William Henry Harrison, A Political Biography* (Indianapolis, 1926), pp. 89–91, explains the organization of Indian management.
Joseph A. Parsons, Jr., "Civilizing the Indians of the Old Northwest, 1800–1810," *Indiana Magazine of History*, LVI (1960), 195–216; Knox to Washington, July 7, 1789, *ASP: Indian Affairs*, I, 52–54, is the connecting link between federal and colonial Indian policy of "civilizing." Donald Jackson, "William Ewing, Agricultural Agent to the Indians," *Agricultural History*, XXXI (1957), 3–7. United States Bureau of Ethnology, *Eighteenth Annual Report* (Washington, 1899), II, 640–641, lists all Indian treaties. For details of a typical exercise in Indian diplomacy, see William T. Hagan, "The Sauk and Fox Treaty of 1804," *Missouri Historical Review*, LI (1956–57), 1–7. See also William Christie MacLeod, *The American Indian Frontier* (London, 1928), pp. 443–454, and Roy Marvin Robbins, *Our Landed Heritage* (Princeton, 1942), pp. 20–22.
The behavior of the Indians was irrelevant. Peaceable Indians received the same treatment as belligerent Indians.

lated a good many unsuccessful petty speculations, but the Congress eased matters after 1804 by selling quarter sections at $1.64 per acre and mitigating hardship cases by private laws. Pioneers thereafter pressed for lower prices and recognition of squatters' "rights."[68]

A gigantic fraud and its legal and political effects animate the frontier chronicle. In 1795 a corrupted Georgia legislature sold at least 35 million acres at less than two cents each to four "Yazoo Companies." James Jackson, later known as one of the loudest and least elegant men in congressional history, decided (for reasons quite apart from ethics) not to join the speculators, and carefully organized the indignation of Georgia. His work led to the formation of a legislative faction which repudiated the contract and sent Jackson to the gubernatorial chair and then to the United States Senate. Third parties, mostly New England voters, had already bought from the speculators, and to save their investments organized a power-interest group, inaccurately claiming to represent many widows and orphans, and set out to lobby for relief. A committee composed of Madison, Gallatin, and Levi Lincoln of Massachusetts advised the Congress to reserve 5 million acres to recoup these buyers. John Randolph and other Old Republican purists erupted molten vituperation, alleging a conspiracy to buy Republican votes in New England at the price of public probity. Their volubility blocked the relief measure for several years, but the Congress voted the compensation after the episode reached the Supreme Court as *Fletcher* v. *Peck,* in which the Court held that Georgia could not undo the sale because of the constitutional prohibition against the impairment of the obligation of a contract. This decision probably forestalled much later litigation hopefully founded on allegations of political corruption. The congressional relief of the losers showed that a strongly organized pressure group, aided by wise counsel and energetic lobbyists, could use politics to

---

[68] Alexander Balinky, *Albert Gallatin, Fiscal Theories and Policies* (New Brunswick, 1958) , pp. 49–51. Federal land law was loosely construed in favor of actual settlers; Robbins, *Landed Heritage,* pp. 18–27. A peculiar problem was the perfecting of titles derived from foreign governments, which was done laboriously but liberally; White, *Jeffersonians,* pp. 516–518. In 1804 Gallatin had more than a million dollars in accounts receivable for sections and half sections. At most, a fourth of this land was in production. State lands were going at from six to sixty cents an acre. See B. H. Hibbard, *A History of the Public Land Policies* (New York, 1939) , pp. 3, 73, 77–78.

gain a material benefit, a lesson obviously not lost on posterity even
unto the fifth generation. It may be added that, in the long run, no
one in the Yazoo affair lost a cent.[69]

The Americans hived out continuously, and the flag went up
wherever the swarms settled. The Congress admitted the states of
Ohio (1803) and Louisiana (1812), while creating the territories of
Indiana (1803), Illinois (1809), and Missouri (1812).[70]

Owing mainly to natural increase, the nation grew from 5.3 to 8.5
million between 1800 and 1815, with a tide setting westward. It was
hard to move across the land, so, in 1808, Gallatin proposed a
multimillion-dollar program to improve transportation. The War
of 1812 blocked it, but ten miles of the National Road westward
from Cumberland, Maryland (authorized in 1806), were complete
by 1813. Lacking safe roads, the way to go West was to take the
shortest trail to the nearest westering river. The Ohio floated most
of the westbound traffic. Many amateur rivermen sat with one hand
on the steering sweep, the other holding Zadok Cramer's *Pittsburgh
Navigator*. Migration filled in most of the blanks east of the Mississippi by 1812, except in the Old Northwest. Receipts of western
produce at New Orleans illustrated the economic growth: a rise
from $3.6 million to $5.4 million between 1801 and 1807. Back-

[69] C. Peter Magrath, *Yazoo, Law and Politics in the New Republic, The Case of
Fletcher* v. *Peck* (Providence, 1966), is definitive. See also Ellis Merton Coulter,
Georgia, A Short History (Chapel Hill, 1960), pp. 199–205. Irving Brant, *James
Madison, Secretary of State, 1800–1809* (Indianapolis, 1953), pp. 233–240, points
out that it was lucky the "dupes" agreed because by Fletcher v. Peck, 6 Cranch
87 (1810), they could have claimed an area equal to 125 per cent of Mississippi.
For a sample of Randolph's invective on the subject, see *Annals*, 9th Congress, 1st
Session, pp. 908–913, 916–919. Justice Johnson correctly thought Fletcher v. Peck
should not have been heard because it was a 'mere feigned case"; Donald G.
Morgan, "The Origin of Supreme Court Dissent," *William and Mary Quarterly*,
Third Series, X (1953), 364–365. The decision marked yet another departure
from the English legal tradition; Haines, *Judicial Supremacy*, pp. 269–270. Until
this case the contracts clause had not been given authoritative meaning; Haines
and Sherwood, *Supreme Court*, I, 323–326. See also Charles Warren, *The
Supreme Court in United States History* (Rev. ed., 2 vols., Boston, 1937), I,
392–399.

[70] Edward M. Douglas, "Boundaries, Areas, Geographic Centers and Altitudes
of the United States and the Several States," United States Geological Survey,
Bulletin No. 817 (2nd ed., Washington, 1930), pp. 167, 186–188, 192, 201. The
Constitution of Louisiana defined its much-disputed boundaries permanently,
and its admission as a state ended the argument about the constitutionality of
the Louisiana Purchase.

straining drudgery would often increase the value of wild lands eightfold in a few years.[71]

The typical white pioneer's first years on raw creation were brutish. Diet centered on corn—eaten, distilled, fed to porkers. The first shelter was the minimum needed to prevent death by exposure. Pioneers suffered from medical ignorance and quackery, from malaria, dysentery, from all those twinges lumped together as rheumatism, from exhaustion, and from endemic cultural regression. But if they chose land well, it catapulted them into relative affluence in a decade. Then, still fosterlings of the eagle, they could create a variant of the civilized life they remembered.[72]

[71] Curtis P. Nettels, *The Emergence of a National Economy, 1775–1815* (New York, 1962), pp. 131, 174, 177, 178, 307; Nettels exhaustively studies the integration of the economy and the polity. Carter Goodrich, *Government Promotion of American Canals and Railroads, 1800–1890* (New York, 1960), pp. 19–37; White, *Jeffersonians*, pp. 303, 474–478, 484–485; Balthasar Henry Meyer et al., *History of Transportation in the United States before 1860* (Washington, 1917), pp. 3–37. The booming impact of western trade on Pittsburgh is described in Solon J. and Elizabeth H. Buck, *The Planting of Civilization in Western Pennsylvania* (Pittsburgh, 1939), Chap. XIII. Zadok Cramer, *Pittsburgh Navigator and Almanac* (title varies) (Pittsburgh, 1801), met instant success and attracted many plagiarizers; the twelfth revised edition appeared in 1824, and the eighth edition is reproduced in Ethel C. Leahy, *Who's Who on the Ohio River* (Cincinnati, 1931), pp. 83–201. Percy Wells Bidwell and John I. Falconer, *History of Agriculture in the Northern United States* (Washington, 1925), pp. 69–83. Governor Claiborne asked that the Army escort travelers on the Natchez Trace, Claiborne to Madison, July 26, 1803, Madison Papers, Library of Congress. An index of growth was the increase in the number of post offices in the two decades after 1790, from 75 to 2,300.

[72] Marshall Smelser, "Material Customs in the Territory of Illinois," Illinois State Historical Society, *Journal*, XXIX (1936–37), 5–41, gives a fairly typical sampling of human development of raw creation.

CHAPTER 7

Tiger vs. *Shark*

THE Americans faced hard but understandable problems at home. Abroad, on the other hand, a long war between the two strongest powers of the globe, one peerless at sea, the other apparently invincible on land, presented nearly insoluble diplomatic perplexities. After the Royal Navy destroyed French naval power and limited continental Europe's ability to spread its own sails over the oceans, the persistent Americans were the only important neutral carriers. Their booming maritime enterprises stimulated British jealousy. The richly laden American merchant fleet was on a collision course with the proud Royal Navy.[1]

The West Indies was the danger zone. Shortsighted French politicians had inadvertently helped the Royal Navy before 1800 to ravage the French merchant marine. Americans rushed to replace it, to add the rich French West Indian trade to their already profitable North American commerce. Britain's reply was to invoke her unilateral Rule of 1756: a trade closed in peace may not be opened in war. No treaty ratified this rule. Furthermore, American shippers had legally traded with the French Antilles after 1783. Americans argued "the freedom of the seas," an indefinable concept based as much on economics as on ethics, a notion hard to discuss with detachment because its baptism in blood has infused it with na-

[1] John G. B. Hutchins, *The American Maritime Industries and Public Policy, 1789–1914* (Cambridge, Mass., 1941), pp. 170–177, analyzes American commerce after 1789, concluding that the British threw away an advantage when they denied themselves the purchase of American ships.

tionalistic spirit. If it meant "free ships make free goods," no big-navy nation has long accepted the doctrine.[2]

There was no Anglo-American rupture for some years because of a growing cordiality based on Jay's Treaty, on America's unde-clared war with France, and on the able diplomacy of Rufus King in London, where King was more competent than most of the men he dealt with. This minister, a Federalist holdover, achieved a settlement of the deadlocked money claims under Jay's Treaty (1802), and arranged for commissions to fix the Canadian bound-ary (1803), although the boundary convention failed of acceptance by the Senate because it was drafted before the great Louisiana bargain and its terms appeared to jeopardize the northern bound-ary of the Louisiana Purchase. Just before leaving for home (at his own request), King also proposed an agreement to prevent impress-ment of sailors on the high seas, but the British Admiralty insisted on impressment in the English Channel and the Irish Sea, a reservation unacceptable in America. He departed from Britain in May, 1803, at the zenith of Anglo-American amity, which owed much to his own amiability and intelligence.[3] Things went down-hill thereafter.

The American attitude toward France, then ruled by Napoleon Bonaparte as "First Consul," was reserved. Napoleon's *coup d'état* of 1800 convinced Jefferson and like-minded Republicans that enduring friendship with France was improbable; that French policy would necessarily be inconstant and, as we would say today, totalitarian. Jefferson now saw his friends among the French intel-lectuals as well-intentioned dupes of a despotism.[4]

[2] W. E. Lingelbach, "England and Neutral Trade," *Military Historian and Economist*, II (1917–18), 154–157; British West Indians often welcomed Ameri-can traders because of local shortages and high prices. Alice B. Keith, "Relaxa-tions in the British Restrictions on the American Trade with the British West Indies, 1783–1802," *Journal of Modern History*, XX (1948), 1–18; Benjamin H. Williams, *Economic Foreign Policy of the United States* (New York, 1929), pp. 338, 341–342.

[3] Bradford Perkins, *The First Rapprochement: England and the United States, 1795–1805* (Philadelphia, 1955), Chaps. I–X, covers the years 1795–1800, showing how the amity was achieved—see especially pp. 138–171; on the quality of British executives, pp. 15, 132–135, and D. M. Young, *The Colonial Office in the Early Nineteenth Century* (London, 1961), pp. 1–16; King to St. Vincent, May 15, 1803, to Madison, July, 1803, Charles R. King (ed.), *The Life and Correspondence of Rufus King* (6 vols., New York, 1894–1900), IV, 258, 259–261.

[4] Napoleon Bonaparte became First Consul Dec. 24, 1799, and Emperor Dec. 2, 1804. Jefferson to R. Livingston, Oct. 10, 1802, Paul Leicester Ford (ed.), *The*

The principal cause of Franco-American friction before 1806 was French privateering. French law on privateering had been fair enough—if one ignores administrative malfeasance. The Foreign Minister, Charles Maurice de Talleyrand-Périgord, opposed privateering because it provoked litigation and resentment out of proportion to its profits. The Franco-American Convention of 1800 intended to encourage neutral trade, but regrettably omitted a precise description of the ships' papers needed to protect a neutral carrier. This turned out to be a grave omission. Napoleon knew quite well that most American ships carried British commerce, but, during his Consulate, relations in France were not too prickly. He reorganized the Conseil de Prises, moderated the worst abuses, and complained mostly of Minister Robert R. Livingston's generosity in giving the protection of the Stars and Stripes to almost any shipowner who applied. Livingston, himself, thought prize cases were handled politically in France, corruptly in the French colonies, and wastefully (to American owners) everywhere, but he convinced no Frenchman (or Corsican). He soon asked to be recalled. His own choice of successor, John Armstrong, replaced him (1804).[5] Armstrong, an intellectual lightweight who knew too little French, was ultimately to earn the title *"imbécile"* from the Emperor.[6] France was represented in Washington by the observant but financially straitened and importunate Louis André Pichon, who was in turn replaced by the egregious Louis Marie Turreau (1804). Turreau outranked Pichon in the diplomatic service, but not in perspicacity nor *savoir-faire*.

The French privateering so much complained of was mostly

Writings of Thomas Jefferson (10 vols., New York, 1892–99), VIII, 173; Joseph I. Shulim, "Thomas Jefferson Views Napoleon," *Virginia Magazine of History,* LX (1952), 288–291, and *The Old Dominion and Napoleon Bonaparte: A Study in American Opinion* (New York, 1952); Lawrence S. Kaplan, "Jefferson's Foreign Policy and Napoleon's Idéologues," *William and Mary Quarterly,* Third Series, XIX (1962), 344–359; Gallatin to Jefferson, Sept. 7, 1801, Henry Adams (ed.), *The Writings of Albert Gallatin* (3 vols., Philadelphia, 1879), I, 46; Charles Francis Adams (ed.), *Memoirs of John Quincy Adams* (12 vols., Philadelphia, 1874–77), I, 316 (Nov. 23, 1804).

5 Ulane Bonnel, *La France, les États-Unis, et la Guerre de Course, 1797–1815* (Paris, 1961), pp. 44–47, 133–136, 141–151, 156–159, 173–177; unlike his brothers in London, Livingston had few problems of personal liberty to deal with, *ibid.*, p. 183, but see Lee to Madison, Jan. 20, 1802, Mary Lee Mann (ed.), *A Yankee Jeffersonian* (Cambridge, Mass., 1958), pp. 54–57.

6 Bonaparte to Cadore, Jan. 19, 1810, *Correspondance de Napoléon Ier* (32 vols., Paris, 1858–69), XX, 152–153.

reprisal for American relations with hungry colonists or with rebellious Negroes in the West Indies, especially in Saint-Domingue. Americans traded with them, sent agents to them, sold food cheaper to insurgents than to French, and sold weapons to rebel forces. There was no altruism in this conduct, but much profit. When the angry Napoleon took a sharp tone, the United States prohibited the trade by statute, partly because there was still hope of Napoleon's good offices in getting Florida, partly because the colored rebels set a scandalously successful example for American slaves.[7]

II

The Peace of Amiens, which had made possible the Louisiana coup, ended in 1803. American reaction to the renewal of war was cool— quite unlike the spirit of 1793. The new war was to make Jefferson's second term as stormy as the first had been tranquil, but it did not immediately portend vexations. Louisiana and Florida problems seemed foremost. While the tiger and the shark appeared equal, most Americans felt safe. Jefferson thought the combatants would compete for America's favor, and, until the spring of 1806, he and his colleagues made every possible erroneous judgment of the future of the war.[8]

British needs and attitudes took little account of the value of American good will. Severe naval discipline promoted a high rate of desertion, and the Royal Navy practiced impressment to recover (or replace) deserters. Thousands of seamen, deserters and civilians, shipped in the more attractive American merchant or naval services. The shorthanded Royal Navy resumed impressment in May, 1803. Naval vessels hovered off American harbors, impressing from British ships in American waters according to snap judgments of inter-

---

[7] Bonnel, *Guerre de Course*, pp. 154–155, 168–171; Irving Brant, *James Madison, Secretary of State, 1800–1809* (Indianapolis, 1953), pp. 270–279.

[8] Jefferson to Buchan, July 10, 1803, A. Lipscomb (ed.), *The Writings of Thomas Jefferson* (20 vols., Washington, 1903–4), X, 401; Jefferson, "Second Inaugural Address," Mar. 4, 1805, *Writings of Jefferson*, VIII, 343; Breckinridge to Clay, Mar. 22, 1806, James. F. Hopkins (ed.), *The Papers of Henry Clay* (3 vols., Lexington, 1959–), I, 232; Bradford Perkins, *Prologue to War: England and the United States, 1805–1812* (Berkeley, 1961), pp. 54–56. Perkins' study is intelligently constructed, although rather light on Spanish and French matters; it differs from most earlier treatments in that it gives less weight to tangible and rational causes, and more to pride, sensitivity, frustrations, to "emotion, chance, and half choices" (p. vii). The writer has the insights of a practiced politician, which are rare among academic historians.

national law by cocky lieutenants.[9] Excesses were dismissed by superiors as inevitable "irregularities."[10]

Thomas Barclay, an American loyalist once attainted by law, and now His Majesty's consul general in New York, inadvertently but rightly wrote of the port as under "blockade" in 1804.[11] Foreign ships could block New York only by entering American territorial waters, which the British captains did freely. Every British arrival, and some American, lost men by impressment. Barclay spied, suborned the press, suppressed public documents, and, with naval help, made New York a British outpost. Although the New York excesses stung both President and Secretary of State, Jefferson dreamed only of armed galleys, and James Madison thought only of closing American ports to British naval ships.[12] The only immediate congressional response was a new law to punish "treason, felony, misdemeanor, breach of the peace, or of the revenue laws," and to give the President authority to bar foreign public vessels at his discretion.[13] There was no feeling of crisis.

At sea there were annoying British seizures for unneutral conduct or for violation of the Rule of 1756. Even if the ships were freed by prize courts, the owners had to pay their own and the captors' costs, and sometimes the Navy kept the crews regardless. Madisons' staggeringly simple proposal that the flag protect all under it met only scorn in Britain.[14]

9 Allen Johnson, *Jefferson and His Colleagues* (New Haven, 1921), pp. 128–131; Perkins, *Prologue*, pp. 85–90; William Glenn Moore, "Economic Coercion as a Policy of the United States, 1794–1805," Ph.D. thesis, 1960, University of Alabama, University, Ala., pp. 298–302.

10 The word used by Harrowby to Merry, Nov. 7, 1804, *ibid.*, p. 300.

11 Barclay to Hammond, Nov. 9, 1804, George Lockhart Rives (ed.), *Selections from the Correspondence of Thomas Barclay* (New York, 1894), pp. 200–201.

12 Barclay to Merry, Aug. 14, 24, 1804, *ibid.*, pp. 185–189; Barclay's conduct of office in New York is covered, pp. 145–227; Jefferson to Madison, Aug. 15, 1804, *Writings of Jefferson*, XI, 46; to R. Smith, Sept. 6, 1804, Perkins, *First Rapprochement*, p. 177; to Lincoln, Sept. 16, 1804, *Writings of Jefferson*, VIII, 321–322.

13 *Debates and Proceedings in the Congress of the United States* (42 vols., Washington, 1834–56), 8th Congress, 2nd Session, Mar. 3, 1805, pp. 1694–1698. Often cited as *Annals*.

14 Whether a ship was "neutral" was for judicial determination; Charles Cheney Hyde, *International Law, Chiefly as Interpreted and Applied by the United States* (2nd ed. rev., 3 vols., Boston, 1945), has chapters on maritime war, contraband, blockade, and neutrality which are useful to the history student. Brant, *Madison*, pp. 254–258. Barclay had nerves of brass; he asked return of an

Today at least, impressment seems the most odious of British practices. Although taking ships and cargo was left to judicial process, taking men was not, because British courts saw impressment as a prerogative of the crown. The British ignored American naturalization, and naval officers, desperate for men, also took native Americans when they fancied. Every navy impressed at one time or other. The Royal Navy, being the largest, of course impressed the most. Having gotten his man, the captain would attempt to legalize the outrage by signing him on. If the pressed man refused, he might be treated with more than the usual brutality. It is hard to calculate how many were pressed. Both sides cooked the statistics. We do know there were about enough British subjects in American ships to keep the Royal Navy up to strength. J. F. Zimmerman's detailed study of the numbers of pressed Americans concluded that the closest possible estimate of those illegally conscripted for British naval service from 1793 through 1811 was 9,991. Most contemporary estimates were higher, although anti-Jeffersonians tended to fix the figure far lower.[15]

Perhaps the relative forbearance of Jefferson and Madison under these irritations was owing to their preoccupation with Florida. Meanwhile a million tons of American shipping paid handsome profits and taxes despite harassments, gaining more men from Britain by desertions than were lost by impressments. But human dignity was outraged and national sovereignty contemptuously

American ship, which, with its British prize crew, sought refuge from the weather in New London, Conn., where it was retaken by force. *Correspondence of Barclay,* pp. 183–187, 191.

[15] Barclay to Merry, April 16, 1805, *ibid.,* p. 219; no American federal officer formally denounced the idea of "indefeasible" nationality until 1848, no statute guaranteed to protect the naturalized until 1868, and Great Britain declined to recognize United States naturalization papers until 1870. Anthony Steel, "Anthony Merry and the Anglo-American Dispute about Impressment, 1803–1806," *Cambridge Historical Journal,* IX (1949), 331, 331 n.; see also I-Mien Tsiang, *The Question of Expatriation in America Prior to 1907* (Baltimore, 1942). Clement Cleveland Sawtell gives the details, with documents by men impressed and a bibliography of personal narratives, in "Impressment of American Seamen by the British," Essex Institute *Historical Collections,* LXXVI (1940), 314–344; other useful narratives are, "Epes Sargent's Account of a British Press Gang in 1803," *ibid.,* LXXXVIII (1952), 19–23, and "Letters of Samuel Dalton of Salem, an Impressed Seaman, 1803–1814," *ibid.,* LXVIII (1932), 321–329. James Fulton Zimmerman, *Impressment of American Seamen* (New York, 1925), has been adversely criticized only for using too few British sources.

flouted.[16] After ship seizures, owners might resort to courts, but in arbitrary executive impressment there was an issue that will stir free men forever.

British and American public opinion showed a warm reciprocal dislike. No British policy toward the United States went beyond British public tolerance. British behavior exasperated American Congressmen. American judges refused to deliver up deserters. Economics alone could almost explain the attitude of British leaders. American ship tonnage nearly tripled from 1790 to 1810. The American re-export trade of 1800–1812 was not to be equaled in dollar value until 1916, and probably not in real value until the late 1940's. The United States was becoming the first carrier of the Atlantic, the world's leading wholesaler of tropical produce. The British, isolated and feeling besieged, did not see that a prosperous America was a market for British manufactures. Instead they clung to outmoded mercantilism, and angrily noticed only specific breaches in the navigation system by a quasi enemy. It was particularly painful to British merchants, who had worked so long to crack the Spanish and Portuguese empires, to see Yankee shippers rush in to profit, even to sell food to hungry British West Indians. Some critics in England blamed a nonexistent Francophilia for the American behavior. When American-born painter Benjamin West naïvely likened Napoleon Bonaparte to George Washington, he was suspended from his presidency of the Royal Academy. Apparent favors shown to French merchants in America galled British residents, one of whom said Madison was physically afraid of the red-faced, fiery-eyed French Minister Turreau.[17]

16 James Truslow Adams, *New England in the Republic, 1776–1850* (Boston, 1926), pp. 239–248, covers maritime matters of 1801–7. Philadelphia insurance statistics showed ship seizures by the British were to seizures by the French and Spanish as ten to one. *American State Papers: Documents Legislative and Executive* (38 vols., Washington, 1832–61); *Foreign Relations*, II, 742–745.

17 Perkins, *Prologue*, pp. 1–31, well sketches the siege mentality of the British and its effects on polity; Moore, "Economic Coercion," pp. 291–295; United States Bureau of the Census, *Historical Statistics of the United States, Colonial Times to 1957* (Washington, 1960), pp. 537–538; G. G. Huebner, "The Foreign Trade of the United States Since 1789," in Emory R. Johnson *et al.* (eds.), *History of Domestic and Foreign Commerce of the United States* (2 vols., Washington, 1915), II, 20, Table 44; Arthur Preston Whitaker, *The United States and the Independence of Latin America, 1800–1830* (Baltimore, 1941), pp. 1–10, gives the background to 1808; Dorothy Burne Goebel, "British Trade to the Spanish Colonies, 1796–1823," *American Historical Review*, XLIII (1938), 288–297, shows why British jealousy flared; Moore, "Economic Coercion," pp. 282–291, tells how

William Pitt's return to power after the renewal of war (1804) was ominous, not for reasons of personality, but because of his determination to wage the war fiercely. His Foreign Secretary, Dudley Ryder, Lord Harrowby, was poorly informed, and his minister in Washington, Anthony Merry, was a bit of a dunce. James Monroe was less effective in London than predecessor Rufus King. The British friends of America, who saw value in American prosperity, were relatively helpless in opposition.[18]

Fuel for anti-American heat could be found in the enticement of British seamen by American shippers, in frauds against British underwriters, and in the ease and occasional chicanery of the issue of American citizenship papers. But there was another grievance far more important than those negotiable annoyances. That was the magnitude of American trade in enemy goods. The relative ease of North American–West Indian trade always made it difficult to prohibit. Much tropical produce went from the United States to Europe. When war brought its conflict of "military necessity" with "neutral rights," the British invoked their Rule of 1756. Re-export of Spanish and French produce from American ports to Europe, as "neutral" property, *could* be regarded as a fraudulent evasion. James Stephen, in *War in Disguise, or The Fraud of the Neutral Flags* (1805), said this neutral trade must be destroyed because it was fraud for the benefit of France and Spain, was contrary to the Rule of 1756, was ruinous to the British merchant fleet, and would pre-empt British continental markets. Stephen put in words what British conservatives were feeling. The book appeared on the day Horatio Nelson won Trafalgar, destroyed French sea power, and made it easier to control neutral carriers. The untimely expiration of the commercial articles of Jay's Treaty left Anglo-American maritime relations uncodified. Jefferson shortsightedly believed wartime a poor time to renegotiate the treaty. The British then decided they must revert to their pretreaty system of regulation by orders in council. Anglo-American relations had worsened steadily from 1803, and soon reached a new nadir.[19]

French merchants, trapped in American ports, were helped by fraudulent practices; Bonnel, *Guerre de Course,* p. 207 n., briefly sketches Turreau's career.

18 Perkins, *First Rapprochement,* pp. 172–175, and *Prologue,* pp. 16–20.

19 *Correspondence of Barclay,* pp. 153, 154, 179; Barclay to McKenzie, Apr. 2, 1805, *ibid.,* pp. 215–216; O. T. Howe, Introduction to *Autobiography of Capt. Zachary G. Lamson* (Boston, 1908?) , pp. 1–15; H. W. Briggs, *Doctrine of Continu-*

In the case of *The Polly* (1800), British Admiralty law admitted that enemy produce became neutral property upon import before re-export. In 1799 the Congress had legalized immediate re-export with a drawback of all but 3½ per cent of duties paid. Stephen made a point of the impolicy of *The Polly* case in his *War in Disguise*. Sugar, hides, coffee, indigo, and other products poured into Europe from Latin America, the East and West Indies, and the Philippines, via North American ports. Edward Channing, applying moral theology rather than the rule of *The Polly,* called this commerce "un-neutral."[20] Admiralty courts, in *The Essex* (1805), came to the same conclusion by refining their rule of *The Polly*. They now required the shipowner to prove that his importation of enemy goods into the United States had been in good faith, not merely to evade the Rule of 1756. If the Rule of 1756 was good law, a questionable point, most American transshippers *were* in the wrong. American feelings were not considered. No explanation was published for nearly a year, although prize-court lawyers got the word to the Royal Navy immediately. Seizures were quick. Americans, heedless of fine points of admiralty law, were angry. From this hour, the *rapprochement* of 1795–1805 was ended.[21]

III

Napoleon matched Trafalgar in the same year with Austerlitz, which made him as strong by land as Britain was by sea. Thereafter, the two powers warred by methods which mixed economic and military matters in a way unknown before. Britain intended to regulate French trade for British benefit, to force goods whether raw or finished, whether British or enemy, on the Continent. Its economic war was not carried forward in a flush of public fervor, as in more recent wars, but the steady legal and political power of the British

---

ous Voyage (Baltimore, 1926), pp. 11–12, 213–214 (his Chaps. I–II consider the subject to 1816); Moore, "Economic Coercion," pp. 295–298, 302–307. In 1801 Gallatin had told his collectors that ships should not be permitted to enter, pay duties, and clear again without unloading.

[20] Channing used the word in *A History of the United States* (6 vols., New York, 1905–25), IV, 353.

[21] Lingelbach, "England and Neutral Trade," pp. 156–165; Perkins, *First Rapprochement,* pp. 177–181; despite invective to the contrary, Sir William Scott, who handed down *The Essex* ruling, was an honest judge who did not degrade his court to make it a political and naval weapon. Perkins, "Sir William Scott and the *Essex,*" *William and Mary Quarterly,* Third Series, XXII (1956), 169–183; Perkins, *Prologue,* pp. 79–84.

crown—despite some opposition, more witty than obstructive—kept the screws turned tight. On his side, Napoleon's interest was two-sided, mostly continental but partly West Indian. In Europe he began a self-blockade to depress British business, even if it also hurt France. In the West Indies his hungry, isolated subjects tried to feed themselves from captured American cargoes. The international law of blockade is gaseous, with slogans substituting for ideas. Only neutrals with money at stake have pretended to scholarship in the subject. In the years from 1805 to 1812, the leading neutral carrier, the United States, was mortifyingly harried. The British did most of the harrying because they had command of the seas, but they did it with clear conscience, as incidental to the defense of the planet against the Corsican tyrant.[22]

The self-blockade of Europe by Napoleon may seem madness, but it had method and a prior history. If Britain could not sell to Europe, her gold must buy food instead of subsidizing continental allies. Physiocratic thought believed British prosperity, divorced as it was from agriculture, was fictitious. Napoleon's enormous power allowed him to apply the theory grandly. His first test of method was in the West Indies, where rebel islanders were placed under annoying paper blockades. Two hundred and seventeen American ships were seized by the French in Caribbean waters from 1800 to 1807. Napoleon did not see that a friendly neutral could be his most useful ally. His attitude toward the United States was openly derisory, and his aim was always to provoke the United States to defend its flag and pride against British abuse. The overture to his Continental System was a decree of June, 1803, confiscating all goods of British origin in French harbors, regardless of the nationality of the carriers.[23]

[22] Eli Filip Heckscher, *The Continental System, An Economic Interpretation* (Oxford, 1922), considers the subject as European history with admirable detachment; he presents a chronological table of the subject, and collects all of the relevant British documents; Bonnel, *Guerre de Course*, pp. 187–191, 198–205; James Madison and Noah Webster wrote the most logical exegeses in these years, although they made no converts among belligerents. See Harry R. Warfel, *Noah Webster, Schoolmaster to America* (New York, 1936), pp. 275–276, and Gaillard Hunt (ed.), *The Writings of James Madison*, (9 vols., New York, 1900–1910), VII, 204–375; Perkins, *Prologue*, pp. 3–5.

[23] Heckscher, *Continental System*, pp. 59–74, describes the illusory phantasm of the British economy as it existed in French imaginations; J. Steven Watson, *The Reign of George III, 1760–1815* (New York, 1960), pp. 406–407, 463–465; Bonnel, *Guerre de Course*, pp. 191–196, 207–212, 232, 373, 384; Perkins, *Prologue*, pp. 68–72.

William Pitt died early in 1806. The next government was the ministry of "All the Talents," including slovenly, magnetic Charles James Fox as Foreign Secretary. After Fox had verified that Napoleon would not make peace, he resolved to punish Prussia for siding with France and simultaneously to mollify the Americans by substituting a blockade for the abrasive rule of *The Essex* case. An order in council (May, 1806) proclaimed a blockade of Europe from the Elbe River to Brest, to be complete between Ostend and the River Seine. Other ports of the strip could be visited in certain circumstances. The Americans were not tranquilized; it seemed a paper blockade, and *The Essex* rule was not explicitly disavowed.[24]

Paper blockades is a game that any number can play. After defeating and appropriating Prussian force at Jena, Napoleon, fleetless but well supplied with parchment and sealing wax, flung down his Berlin Decree (November, 1806) verbally blockading the British Isles, declaring all cargoes from Britain to be good prizes, as were any ships which attempted to evade the decree by fraud. His accompanying tragicomic rationale was that Fox's blockade, being economic rather than military, subverted the rights of man. Alarmed Americans in France queried impassive French bureaucrats who concealed their ignorance while awaiting official interpretations. Napoleon imitated the sphinx until he had induced Czar Alexander, in July, 1807, to plug the last European outlet for grain, and until reasonably sure that Anglo-American co-operation was unlikely. Then, in September, he unleashed sleek French privateers to seize any ship carrying cargo of British origin. The Americans, as the chief neutral carriers, would obviously suffer most. When Armstrong expostulated, he was told that the Americans appeared to cooperate with Britain by tamely submitting to regulation, and would be exempted only when they made their flag respected. The Berlin Decree's self-blockade worked temporarily. Italy, France, and northern Europe were waterproofed enough by late 1807 to hurt British business seriously. But Napoleon hurt himself, too, by alienating neutrals, because, while Britannia ruled the waves, the neutral was the natural ally of Britain's enemy.[25]

24 Perkins, *Prologue,* pp. 101–106. The reader will understand that a legal blockade was thought to require the presence of men-of-war to make entry and clearance physically hazardous.

25 Bonnel, *Guerre de Course,* pp. 213–226; the *Chesapeake-Leopard* episode, which inflamed Anglo-American relations that year, will be a subject of Chapter 7, below.

The British government's response to the Berlin Decree was a shower of orders in council through 1807, prohibiting trade by neutrals between the ports of France or France's allies, under penalty of seizure and condemnation. The opposition called the policy contrary to international law, then attacked it because it was not severe enough.[26] It seemed harsh enough to American captains, who customarily shopped the Continent from port to port in search of new freight after discharging transatlantic cargoes.

At the end of March, the ministry of William Bentinck, Duke of Portland, succeeded "All the Talents," with the simple-minded Spencer Perceval in charge of economic warfare as Chancellor of the Exchequer. Quite willing to treat neutrals harshly, the ministry published a General Blockade Order (November, 1807), prohibiting trade with ports from which the Union Jack was barred, unless the ship first called at a British port, paid British customs dues, and received a fresh clearance. The object was plain. If France barred British trade, France could have *no* trade. If France had any trade, it would be an Anglicized trade, profitably directed and taxed by Britain. Subsequent implementing orders granted dispensations or set specific prohibitions.[27] Among the commodities which were absolutely prohibited to the enemy was "neutral salts," which stirred the Reverend Sydney Smith to write:

What a sublime thought, that no purge may be taken between the Weser and the Garonne . . . and the bowels of mankind locked up for fourteen degrees of latitude! . . . At what period was this great plan of conquest and constipation fully developed? . . . Depend upon it, the absence of the *materia medica* will soon bring them to their senses, and the cry of *Bourbon and Bolus* burst forth from the Baltic to the Mediterranean.[28]

No concession was ever made to sluggish continental peristalsis. As for the Americans, Minister Monroe was insulted by being kept wholly ignorant of the drafting of the General Blockade, and the government condescended to neutral sensitivity only to the extent

26 The principal order on the coasting trade appeared on Jan. 7, 1807. More detailed orders reinforced it on Feb. 7 and 18, and on Aug. 19; Heckscher, *Continental System*, pp. 390–393. *Cobbett's Parliamentary Debates*, VIII (1807), 620–633, report Perceval's speech for a more rigorous policy and, 633–640, the ministry's reply.

27 Perkins, *Prologue*, pp.12–13, 198–201; Heckscher, *Continental System*, gives the essential British documents, pp. 398–406.

28 Quoted at greater length in Hesketh Pearson, *The Smith of Smiths* (London, 1934), pp. 128–129. Smith despised Perceval for his smallness of mind on the Irish question.

of not officially interfering with direct American trade with the French West Indies.[29] The British were practically asking for a trial of strength.

Napoleon's answer was simple. In the Milan Decree (December, 1807) he said that any ship which submitted to British inspection, willingly or unwillingly, in British ports or on the high seas, would be seized if his minions could get their hands on it. If the Americans, the chief sufferers, would make the British respect their rights, he would revoke his decrees. Until then, he said, they were helping Britain. In short, if neutral trade allowed itself to be Anglicized, it lost its neutrality. This remained the French policy until 1812. The Emperor took personal charge of all American cases to make sure that *his* will reigned.[30]

[29] Perkins, *Prologue,* pp. 201–203.
[30] Bonnel, *Guerre de Course,* pp. 232–234.

CHAPTER 8

The American Terrapin

THE American response to the behavior of the European powers was governed by the hope of "making justice their interest. . . ."[1] Policy flowed from the executive because Federalist leadership was sterile and negative; narrower men had succeeded John Adams and Hamilton. Federalists were harsh when the administration did little; they became strident when it did much. The country was not uniformly isolationist, but isolationism governed foreign policy because of a simple-minded view of the balance of power. President Jefferson believed natural and international law would keep the peace, if rigorously upheld. In this conviction, he overrated reason and underestimated wartime passions. While fearing Napoleon, he thought Britain a greater danger.[2] America's oversimple approach to foreign problems confounded European diplomatists, who looked for subtleties where there were none. The American became the Inscrutable American to a series of British and French ministers.

[1] Jefferson to Gallatin, July 11, 1803, Henry Adams, *The Life of Albert Gallatin* (New York, 1943), p. 310.
[2] Bradford Perkins, *Prologue to War: England and the United States, 1805–1812* (Berkeley, 1961), pp. 33–36; Perkins has treated the embargo and related subjects very well, particularly in pp. 107–205. This chapter owes so much to his work that further citation, except to quotation, would be cumbersome. For Jefferson's application of rationalism to maritime rights, see Jefferson to R. R. Livingston, Sept. 9, 1801, Paul L. Ford (ed.), *The Writings of Thomas Jefferson* (10 vols., New York, 1892–99), VIII, 88–91; L. S. Kaplan, "Jefferson, the Napoleonic Wars, and the Balance of Power," *William and Mary Quarterly*, Third Series, XIV (1957), 196–217.

The first important reply to the European war of counterblockades was an essay by James Madison attacking the Rule of 1756 because it diverged so widely from the Golden Rule. Despite "massive unreadability,"[3] this 70,000-word document produced an anti-British bill in the Congress. With the understanding that the President would negotiate for a softening of the British position, the Congress passed a cataleptic Non-Importation Act, April 18, 1806, to sleep until the President awakened it and put it to work to prohibit the importation of certain products of the British Empire. The built-in delay let Federalists call it a cowardly and vacillating law. They read it as the portent of war, unsuccessfully urged fortifications, and complained of the money spent on quieting the Indians.[4] Administration senators, by one vote, defeated a simultaneous resolution that the President "demand" the restoration of property, a resolution attempting to usurp the presidential function of instructing negotiators.[5] Diplomatists work most effectively with armed forces in being behind them, but, lacking force, the United States had printed a statute and waved it menacingly.

Commercial coercion through self-denial was more than an economic weapon; it was self-therapy. The United States had been deeply hurt psychologically. Meek submission to foreign power was submission to colonial status. The history of the country from 1803 to 1812 is the story of attempts to keep both peace and dignity. Jefferson always sought a bloodless substitute for war.[6] He doubted that force was the best way to preserve neutrals' rights, preferring "peaceable coercions,"[7] and he showed this from the first by his indifference to a French plan for another league of armed neutrality. Discussing the Rule of 1756, he told the Congress of "reason,

3 Irving Brant, *James Madison, Secretary of State, 1800–1809* (Indianapolis, 1953), p. 297; Brant considers the essay, its circumstances, and its effects in pp. 297–301, 312, 314–315. The essence of Madison's view is the peroration, Gaillard Hunt (ed.), *The Writings of James Madison* (9 vols., New York, 1900–1901), VII, 373–375.

4 Edmund Quincy, *Life of Josiah Quincy of Massachusetts* (Boston, 1868), pp. 96–101.

5 Alfred Byron Sears, *Thomas Worthington: Father of Ohio Statehood* (Columbus, 1958), pp. 123–124.

6 Louis M. Sears, *Jefferson and the Embargo* (Durham, 1927), pp. 3–54, traces the clarification of Jefferson's idea of commercial coercion.

7 Jefferson to R. R. Livingston, Sept. 9, 1801, *Writings of Jefferson*, VIII, 91.

the only umpire between just nations. . . ."[8] Jefferson was probably influenced by Madison, who had advanced all the arguments in the Congress in 1794. To Madison, an embargo was a positive instrument of policy, not a backing down.[9]

There was empiric evidence to support commercial coercion. From 1794 to 1805 there had been many commercial self-restrictions for national ends, and they worked in the West Indies, where they had occasionally put the British on short rations and, regrettably, had weakened the Negro rebellion against France. Jacob Crowninshield, a successful Salem merchant, told the Congress British arrogance could be economically checked. Perhaps, as John Randolph said, Crowninshield only itched to go privateering, but where could the administration get better advice?[10] George Logan, the liberal Pennsylvania senator, thought commercial coercion practical enough to denounce it as "a cowardly sneaking attack on the domestic comforts of the poor"[11] British factory workers. The policy was not as witless as most critics have believed.[12]

But the price of peace and dignity was high. American shipping was prospering to a degree unknown again until the 1840's. The West Indies needed American produce to keep off starvation, but the British Isles were less dependent. Although half of British imports were American, other sources could be found, while Americans could find no equally valuable market. The Non-Importation Law (effective in 1807) initiated a policy painful to the United States, but which, with a few hiatuses, was to last until 1815.[13]

With the happy co-operation of Federalists, who hoped for a treaty as unpopular as Jay's, the Senate proposed negotiations.

[8] J. D. Richardson (ed.), *A Compilation of the Messages and Papers of the Presidents* (20 vols., Washington, 1897–1917), I, 372. There was no American judicial decision on the Rule of 1756, although John Marshall explained it in a few hundred of his crystalline words, *The Commercen. Lindgren Claimant*, 1 Wheaton 382, 396 (1816).

[9] Brant, *Madison*, pp. 392–403.

[10] William Glenn Moore, "Economic Coercion as a Policy of the United States, 1794–1805," Ph.D. thesis, University of Alabama, 1960, pp. 328–340; *Debates and Proceedings in the Congress* (42 vols., Washington, 1834–56) (hereafter cited as *Annals*), 9th Congress, 1st Session, pp. 552–555, 557.

[11] Frederick B. Tolles, *George Logan of Philadelphia* (New York, 1953), p. 284.

[12] This is the conclusion of Moore, "Economic Coercion."

[13] John G. B. Hutchins, *The American Maritime Industries and Public Policy, 1789–1914* (Cambridge, Mass., 1941), pp. 221–227.

Jefferson and Madison sent instructions to Monroe in London, based on earlier Madison drafts (and showing influences of Jefferson's remarkable notion that the Gulf Stream was America's eastern boundary). Primarily, Monroe was to seek the abolition of impressment and to properly define blockade. Monroe sourly thought his instructions were intended to ruin him politically, but his superiors wished sincerely for peace and for augmented trade. Most Republican leaders, whether regular or Quid, wished to avoid helping Napoleon, hoped for accommodation with Britain, and would even have aligned with Britain if alignment could be achieved without humiliation.[14]

Since the end of the Peace of Amiens, impressment seemed the chief inhibitor of harmony, but the abolition of impressment did not seem an impossible task. Successive ministers Rufus King and Monroe both reported optimistically on the prospect of coming to terms on the practice. The British would have been well advised to exploit American good will, but, after 1805, American feelings seemed of little consequence.[15]

Monroe was given help he did not wish. Senator Samuel Smith of Maryland thought Monroe incompetent, and successfully pressed Jefferson to send a mission. Smith wished to go himself, but the President appointed William Pinkney, the distinguished Federalist lawyer who had recently written an able attack on the Rule of 1756. Smith, much pained by the appointment, concluded that Madison was turning Federalist. Monroe suspected the appointment was intended to dilute whatever renown he might win, and thus frustrate his election to the Presidency in 1808. He had been overly optimistic about his progress in London before he learned that no American would be dealt with if he could be ignored. Madison told Pinkney to take a firm tone. Monroe thought Madison thus guaran-

14 Madison to Senate, Jan. 25, 1806, *American State Papers: Documents Legislative and Executive* (38 vols., Washington, 1842–61): *Foreign Relations*, II, 728 (hereafter, *ASP*); Jefferson to Monroe, May 4, 1806, Andrew Lipscomb *et al.* (eds.), *The Writings of Thomas Jefferson* (20 vols., Washington, 1903–4), XI, 111.

15 Bradford Perkins, *The First Rapprochement: England and the United States, 1795–1805* (Philadelphia, 1955), pp. 175, 182–186; Monroe to Jefferson, Nov. 16, 1803, S. M. Hamilton (ed.), *The Writings of James Monroe* (7 vols., New York, 1898–1903), IV, 97–98.

teed the failure of the mission, but he continued to work, and kept his pique private.[16]

At his first inauguration in 1801, Jefferson had proclaimed the continuity of foreign policy. The Monroe-Pinkney mission was an attempt to arrive at an agreement like the expired commercial articles of Jay's Treaty. Early in 1806 the death of William Pitt, and the appointment of Charles James Fox as Foreign Secretary, allowed hope. Certainly, Fox would have dropped *enforcement* of the Rule of 1756, although he would not have repudiated the Rule publicly, nor abolished impressment, nor paid indemnities for captured ships. However, his views became irrelevant with his death in September, 1806.

The relative priorities of the American demands will differ according to the temperament of the beholder. Monroe and Pinkney thought impressment and dignity less important than trade and prosperity. Many in America agreed. Monroe had offered to return deserters if impressment were abolished. He and Pinkney next promised a federal statute against harboring *any* British seamen. The Foreign Office cautiously agreed to exempt Americans carrying proofs of citizenship, but the Admiralty balked. The Navy appeared to doubt that the United States would keep an impressment bargain, hence negotiation on impressment was dropped.[17]

A treaty was signed on New Year's Eve, 1806. It went back to the rule of *The Polly* in allowing bona fide broken voyages, but banned American commercial restrictions for ten years, thus barring re-

[16] John S. Pancake, "The General from Baltimore: A Biography of Samuel Smith," Ph.D. thesis, University of Virginia, 1949, pp. 174–180; William P. Cresson, *James Monroe* (Chapel Hill, 1946), pp. 198–201, 222–227; Robert E. Spiller, *The American in England During the First Half Century of Independence* (New York, 1926), pp. 116–118.

[17] Edward Stanwood, "An Old Time Grievance," *Atlantic Monthly*, LVI (1885), 627–642, has a few impressment memoirs; James F. Zimmerman, *Impressment of American Seamen* (New York, 1925), pp. 116–124; Anthony Steel, "Anthony Merry and the Anglo-American Dispute about Impressment, 1803–1806," *Cambridge Historical Journal*, IX (1949), 331–351, and "Impressment in the Monroe-Pinkney Negotiations, 1806–1807," *American Historical Review*, LVII (1952), 352–359, sees American complaints as ignobly motivated. Steel suggests that the negotiators all knew impressment was necessary to Britain, that Jefferson denied it because of fanaticism, that Madison pressed the issue to win Napoleon's smile, that Monroe used it in hope of advancing his popularity, but that the American people themselves were indifferent. Such a view values men only as statistics.

prisals for any British abuses. Learning of the Berlin Decree, the British added a postscript requiring American disobedience of Napoleon's rule. Two authentic British concessions were, first, to give the United States a most-favored-nation clause, and, second, a promise not to stop unarmed ships within five miles of the American coast. Even so chilly a treaty might have raised an uproar in Britain, because any broken voyage weakened the Rule of 1756. And before the Americans could possibly react to the Berlin Decree, the British issued the double ban of coasting, a rule ruinous to American skippers who had to peddle from port to port to find cargo. The poles of world politics were obviously London and Paris. The Berlin Decree and the British counterresponse had made the Monroe-Pinkney Treaty immediately obsolete.[18]

The treaty bound Britain in no realistic way and was clearly inferior to the Jay Treaty. At best it would have established a nervous peace by reducing the country to a British satellite. Madison objected—partly because impressment was untouched, partly on other grounds. Crowninshield had told him it would kill the business of carrying to the Caribbean. When Madison suggested returning Britannia's runaway seamen, Gallatin hinted that the merchant fleet could not survive the return of deserters unless impressment ceased. The President, on his own responsibility, decided to bury the treaty, advising the Senate not to delay adjournment for a look at it. He had concluded that the price of amity was too high, and that commercial warfare against beleaguered Britain promised better results. Accordingly, Madison wrote to Monroe and Pinkney that the President preferred to rely on international law rather than to codify defective principles.[19]

Because Jefferson explained his reasons only in private and withheld the papers, Federalists suspected that he awaited a Napoleonic triumph. Actually, he would have reopened negotiations, but the intransigent British believed even the Monroe-Pinkney Treaty too generous. Napoleon began to enforce the Berlin Decree

18 For British justification of the appendix to the Monroe-Pinkney Treaty provoked by the Berlin Decree, see Howicke to Erskine, Jan. 8, 1807, Bernard Mayo (ed.), "Instructions to the British Ministers to the United States, 1791–1812," American Historical Association, *Report, 1936, III* (Washington, 1941), pp. 230 n., 230.
19 The text of the treaty, with Madison's objections point by point, may be found in *Writings of Madison,* VII, 408–445; Gallatin to Jefferson, April 16, 1807, Jefferson Papers, Library of Congress.

against America, and the British Navy was ordered to impress with diligence. Jefferson now invoked the dormant Non-Importation Act (December, 1807).

Dejected, Monroe returned; since time was America's "most precious" asset, Pinkney stayed and stalled.[20] In Richmond, Monroe found a refreshing Monroe-for-President boomlet, but received no invitation to the White House, which he interpreted as a snub for making the treaty. He concluded that the administration had depressed his reputation, and resolved to go it alone, standing aloof both from the government and from the Quids.[21]

To Jefferson the episode had proved the British did not value American friendship. The Americans had no bargaining power, no resource except economic coercion. By hindsight we can see that the failure of the Monroe-Pinkney negotiations elevated impressment to a major cause of war.

Regardless of disputes over impressment, few argued a right to impress from foreign navies, or to kill civilians while searching merchants, yet in 1798 and in 1805 British officers forcibly removed deserters from American warships. As for the safety of civilians, H.M.S. *Leander,* off New York in the spring of 1806, often simultaneously detained a score of ships, pending search, and in April she unluckily killed an American with a ball fired across the bow of another vessel. After a public funeral, indignation was high, New Yorkers rioted, and President Jefferson closed the port to *Leander* and her sister *Cambrian,* adding a futile order to arrest *Leander's* captain. In September, H.M.S. *Melampus* added insult by destroying a French warship within the Virginia Capes.[22] Such behavior helps to explain why Fox's blockade failed to have its intended conciliatory effect in America in 1806.

Worse was to follow in 1807. Vice-Admiral George C. Berkeley, commanding the Royal Navy on the American Station, chafed under audacious desertions. Berkeley and his brother were politically invulnerable because their parliamentary leverage was neces-

[20] Jefferson to Monroe, Mar. 21, 1807, Lipscomb (ed.), *Writings of Jefferson,* XI, 170. Pinkney remained as minister to London until 1811.
[21] The election of 1808 is a subject of Chapter 9. Monroe to Jefferson, Feb. 27, Mar. 22, 1808, to Tazewell, Oct. 30, 1808, *Writings of Monroe,* V, 25, 27–35, 70–71.
[22] The *Leander* and *Melampus* episodes may be studied in the correspondence printed in George L. Rives (ed.), *Selections from the Correspondence of Thomas Barclay* (New York, 1894), pp. 230–243, 248.

sary to the stability of the ministry. The admiral believed America was a paper panther which would collapse if cuffed. When he learned of deserters enlisted by the Frigate *Chesapeake* at Norfolk, and received no redress from the Navy Department, he unsheathed his claws. After *Chesapeake* left territorial waters with Commodore James Barron aboard, she was hailed by H.M.S. *Leopard,* which demanded to search for deserters. Barron temporized. *Leopard* opened fire (June 22, 1807). Unready, Barron surrendered, but the British took only four deserters. *Chesapeake,* splintered, bloody, hulled twenty-two times, suffering twenty-one casualties, had fired but one shot.

A ripple of anger pulsed across the country. Mass meetings truculently demanded reparation, editors declared war, and in Virginia, where feeling was hottest, militia were called, Royal Navy watering parties roughed up, and Royal Navy men taken into temporary custody. In Massachusetts only the arch-Federalists held aloof from popular demonstrations. Pacific Gallatin now thought war inevitable, and therefore immediately advisable. He spent July and August at the distasteful task of planning military finance.[23]

Jefferson might have had united support for war in June, but by late July the passion spent itself. Ten days after *Chesapeake's* humiliation the President closed all American ports to the Royal Navy, called a special session of the Congress for October 26, and sent coast surveyor William Tatham, commanding a sailing whaleboat, to keep observant eyes on British movements. Madison notified American representatives abroad, asking them to pass the word to American shipping, especially to the Navy. Jefferson did not forget that *Constitution, Hornet,* and *Enterprise* were in the Mediterranean, from which they could not possibly have escaped if war had been declared immediately.[24] The President probably hoped to keep the diplomatic kettle singing, just short of a boil, while

23 Edwin M. Gaines, "The *Chesapeake* Affair: Virginians Mobilize to Defend the National Honor," *Virginia Magazine of History and Biography,* LXIV (1956), 131–142; Raymond Walters, Jr., *Albert Gallatin: Jeffersonian Financier and Diplomat* (New York, 1957), pp. 195–197. Gallatin's intelligent plan to finance war was sketched in Gallatin to Jefferson, July 25, 1807, Henry Adams (ed.), *The Writings of Albert Gallatin* (3 vols., Philadelphia, 1879), I, 340–353.

24 *Messages and Papers,* I, 410–412; Elizabeth G. McPherson (ed.), "Letters of William Tatham," Second Installment, *William and Mary Quarterly,* Second Series, XVI (1936), 362–376; Madison to Monroe, July 6, to Armstrong and Bowdoin, July 15, to Monroe, to Bowdoin, July 17, 1807, *Writings of Madison,* VII, 454–466.

awaiting a British response. If Britain swaggered unabashed, the American case against her would be strengthened.

Like wolverines scenting blood, the British commanders in American waters gallingly tested Jefferson's restraint by anchoring in Chesapeake Bay, seizing ships, fulminating, impressing, and by shooting up the coast of Maine. In January, 1808, a competent court-martial suspended the irresolute Barron for five payless years, finding lack of foresight and premature surrender. It is hard to disagree with the court. Although he had time enough, he did not beat to quarters, even when *Leopard* demanded to search.[25]

Monroe learned of the episode from Foreign Minister George Canning, who denied any claim to search public ships and promised to chastise any officer *if* guilty. But Madison soon instructed Monroe to insist on the immediate renunciation of impressment. Canning said impressment was another question; he had now learned that three of the four deserters recovered were American volunteers in the Royal Navy. Only one had been impressed; that one, Jenkin Ratford, a British subject, was promptly hanged. Within a month of the Monroe-Canning exchanges, a royal proclamation recalled all British seamen to duty, explicitly repudiating naturalizations.

Although David Erskine had succeeded Merry in November, 1806, Canning sent George Rose to Washington, more to menace than to mollify. He was allowed to speak only of the *Chesapeake* matter, and insisted that, before talk began, Jefferson revoke his seaport cloture, denounce Barron for denying he carried deserters, and censure officers for harboring deserters. Madison, who wished first to take up reparation for the *Chesapeake* insult, could hardly see the *Leopard* through Rose's verbal fog, but suggested some disavowals due from Britain. Rose, in reality Canning's ventriloquist-dummy, could not speak by himself, and therefore discussions could not begin. The British could have made a case, since the port cloture came before reparation was asked. One Foreign Office counselor asserted that harboring deserters justified hostility, perhaps war. And it *was* unkind to make British captains go to Halifax for water and rations. But by March, 1808, Rose's limitations were apparent,

[25] *ASP: Foreign Relations*, III, 6–24; the Navy caused the publication of the bulky *Proceedings of the General Court Martial convened for the Trial of Commodore James Barron . . . 1808* (Washington, 1822), but the Judge Advocate's summary in *ASP* will suffice for most inquirers.

the Milan Decree had been received, and Rose went home, carrying only some near-seditious letters of applause from arch-Federalists.[26]

Britain made a short-term profit from the affair. Because the United States linked the questions of reparation and impressment, Canning could avoid war, negotiation, or apology; but Britain lost in the long run, because American resentment focused on Britain before the Americans learned the extent of Napoleon's excesses. Canning's admission that public ships were immune to search was a solid concession, well ahead of British opinion, but Jefferson's circumspection was interpreted abroad as pacifism. Domestic politics were envenomed: John Lowell, penman of arch-Federalism, produced acid pamphlets maligning the administration's position which still read as though written by a British agent.[27]

The derisory armed forces of the United States could make no strong reply to insult in 1807, for frugality had frustrated every plan of coast defense since 1789, and friendship with Britain—up to the diplomatic watershed of 1805—had dulled interest in military preparations. Jefferson's passion for peace and the nation's military weakness provoked contempt in Europe. When British friendship seemed unreliable after 1803, Jefferson had briefly reflected on building seagoing warships, but dismissed the notion, to the disgust of Navy Secretary Robert Smith. By 1807, Jefferson formulated a naval program comprising coastal fortifications, mobile land batteries, floating batteries, and gunboats, all to be manned by pickup crews when dangers loomed. The tactics anticipated were not those of the American eagle, but of the terrapin. The gunboats are the best remembered, usually with scorn. Fifty to seventy feet long, propelled by oars and sails, armed with one or two guns, they had served well in the Revolution and in the Tripolitan War. They were useful against single vessels in calms, shoals, or cramped channels, and could flee, close-hauled, from any square-rigger, but their only other virtue was cheapness. Gallatin opposed their construction, arguing that they could be built hastily when needed. Nevertheless, through 1807, the Congress authorized 263 gunboats;

26 Canning to Erskine, Jan. 23, 1809, "Instructions to Ministers," pp. 262–264; Brant, *Madison*, pp. 404–418.
27 Bradford Perkins, "George Canning, Great Britain, and the United States," *American Historical Review*, LXIII (1957), 4–8; John Lowell, *Peace Without Dishonor: War Without Hope* . . . (Boston, 1807), and *Thoughts upon the Conduct of Our Administration* . . . (Boston, 1808).

many were extravagantly built inland, partly for Gulf Coast defense, and partly for congressional-district political defense.[28]

When he heard the true voice of Britain bark through *Leopard*'s gunports, Jefferson reacted energetically, concealing his acts from view to gain time for Britain to make decent reparation, to leave options for the Congress when it met, and to bring American ships home. While he remained President, military preparations continued incessantly but silently. Jefferson recalled the Navy and the merchant fleet, ordered gunboats readied, armed seven coastal forts, spied on British shipping, sent field guns rolling to militia batteries, warned frontier posts, and notified the governors he might call a hundred thousand militia to form a screen behind which a regular army could be raised if wanted, and he took all these preliminary steps without money or congressional mandate. His policy may not have been the best, but he tried. He preferred to experiment with economic coercion before waging war, but he did about as much as possible to activate what was essentially a friendless third-rate military power in a world at war. And, not being clairvoyant, he could reasonably hope that peace would break out in Europe at any moment.[29]

Jefferson's second term had been disheartening: the Florida problem remained; *The Essex* case, the aborted treaty, and *Leopard*'s impudence worsened Anglo-American relations; Napoleon's decrees were bad news, but British indignities seemed worse. British policy, while less cynical than Napoleon's, hurt more because the two maritime nations collided more often. British contempt for the United States, naval hunger for prize money, the *de facto* blockade of America, and the arbitrary, costly procedures of British admiralty courts humiliated and shamed the United States. The younger

[28] For example, the Marine Corps numbered 726 officers and men. See also Harold and Margaret Sprout, *The Rise of American Naval Power, 1776–1918* (rev. ed., Princeton, 1942), pp. 58–61; *Messages and Papers*, I, 373; Jefferson to Crowninshield, May 13, 1806, Ford (ed.), *Writings of Jefferson*, VIII, 453.

These vessels were more properly galleys than gunboats, but the word gunboat is firmly embedded in our historical vocabulary. They are well illustrated and described in Howard I. Chapelle, *The History of the American Sailing Navy* (New York, 1949), pp. 179–241.

[29] Mary P. Adams, "Jefferson's Military Policy, With Special Reference to the Frontier, 1805–1809," Ph.D. thesis University of Virginia, 1958, has confounded the conventional wisdom on the subject by troubling to read military archives instead of drawing deductions from Jefferson's reputation for military idiocy.

Adams and Pinkney were not Francophiles; Britain's behavior, the younger Adams said, struck "at the root of our independence,"[30] and Pinkney wrote from London late in 1807 that "established principles of public law are sacrificed" and described Britain's conduct as "wanton & extravagant aggression. . . ."[31] Naval pressure was firm. H.M.S. *Columbine* searched a federal cutter within Sandy Hook; another warship held an impressed American lad prisoner while anchored in Hampton Roads. Orders were enforced at least as rigorously near American shores as in European waters. Of course, the French behaved as badly, when possible, but they had far fewer opportunities to dishonor American sovereignty. Only arch-Federalists—Fisher Ames, George Cabot, John Lowell—overtly justified British conduct.

Foreign trade seemed the country's only trump. That trade, described by John Randolph as "this fungus of war,"[32] was truly mushroomlike. The increase in tonnage and value of exports had no parallel in history. Grain and land prices rose similarly; sales to the West Indies built credits in Europe to pay for British manufactures; southern exports remained level, but the re-exporting maritime states almost quadrupled their shipments while domestic exports of the middle and northern states increased trivially in comparison. Shipping employed 65,000 seamen, and New York and New England together registered about half as much tonnage as the United Kingdom. Americans built about 70,000 tons and needed 4,200 new seamen yearly. Domestic manufactures increased steadily before 1808, but this growth owed as much to westward expansion and to the difficulties of internal transportation as to anything else. Foreign harassments did not cut seafaring profits, for higher risks were insurable and meant higher prices while broken voyages were longer voyages and increased the freight receipts. Canny merchants changed operations according to circumstances and enriched themselves by each change. To them, foreign interference, like foul

[30] J. Q. Adams to Otis, Mar. 31, 1808, W. C. Ford (ed.), *Writings of John Quincy Adams* (7 vols., New York, 1913–17), III, 200.
[31] Pinkney to Madison, Nov. 17, Dec. 7, 1807, Dorothy Brown (ed.), "Excerpts from Two Pinkney Letter Books," *Maryland Historical Magazine*, LV (1960), 361, 363.
[32] *Annals*, 9th Congress, 1st Session, p. 557.

weather, was just another hazard of trade and, so long as balance sheets were pleasing, they did not complain.[33]

The war of decrees between tiger and shark had not annihilated trade; it had merely ruined individuals and blighted public morals. Whether envious Britain or humiliated America had the better of the balance of trade is unknowable, but both made money. The British monopolized the trade of northwestern Europe, but their jealousy of America's other trade provoked them to annoy American commerce. Such a policy was obtuse; the United States absorbed a third of British manufactures, and Britain needed that market. Nevertheless, the order of November, 1807, taxing American goods bound for Europe, reduced the United States to a colony. Credulous Britain was trying to buy neutrality from an allegedly avaricious and craven republic in exchange for a degrading way to wealth.[34]

II

The Americans could fight Britain or France (or both), try to evade the rules, or stop exporting. Few south of Manhattan advocated submission. Jefferson thought war quite possible, but the United States was obviously unprepared, and, with his inclination to test economic coercion, he naturally leaned toward an embargo. It was at least a way of gaining time, which might end the dilemma by bringing peace to Europe. Jefferson's choice was not a symptom

[33] Timothy Pitkin, *A Statistical View of the Commerce of the United States of America* (New Haven, 1835), pp. 368–373; Anna C. Clauder, *American Commerce as Affected by the Wars of the French Revolution* (Philadelphia, 1932), pp. 71–75; Boston *Columbian Centinel*, Sept. 24, 1808; Gallatin to Jefferson, April 16, 1807, Jefferson Papers, Library of Congress; Rolla M. Tryon, *Household Manufactures in the United States, 1640–1860* (Chicago, 1917), pp. 143, 162–163; John H. Reinoehl (ed.), "Some Remarks on the American Trade: Jacob Crowninshield to James Madison, 1806," *William and Mary Quarterly*, Third Series, XVI (1959), 87–90; Stuart Bruchey, "Success and Failure Factors: American Merchants in Foreign Trade in the Eighteenth and Early Nineteenth Centuries," *Business History Review*, XXXII (1958), 272–292, gives little weight to warfare as compared with other hazards such as careless accountancy.

[34] O. T. Howe (ed.), *Autobiography of Capt. Zachary G. Lamson* (Boston, 1908?), pp. 25–26, 26 n.; Arthur P. Whitaker, *The United States and the Independence of Latin America, 1800–1830* (Baltimore, 1941), pp. 9–26, well describes Latin-American trade in this era.

of a near-psychotic compulsion to peace,[35] but his first opportunity to experiment with "the power of this great weapon, the embargo." If it succeeded, the American republic would have perfected "an effectual weapon" for use "in future as well as on this occasion."[36] Such an embargo differed from the old pre-Revolutionary boycotts, being a different kind of self-denial, nonexportation instead of non-importation, but both tried to manage commerce so as to make Europe respect American rights.

Jefferson's associates were not encouraging: Robert Smith objected, Monroe seems to have disapproved, Vice-President George Clinton was reported as adverse, Governor James Sullivan of Massachusetts thought it militarily enfeebling, and Gallatin wrote "I prefer war . . ."[37] but Jefferson's great influence in the Congress got it enacted.

A short presidential message on the "safety" of shipping[38] produced the Embargo Act (December 22, 1807), prohibiting clearance of any ships bound to foreign ports, with special safeguards to prevent violations by coasters and fishermen. Despite arch-Federalist opinion to the contrary, French arrogance, specifically the enforcement of the Berlin Decree against Americans, encouraged enactment of the embargo, but Jefferson probably knew it would help Napoleon while hurting the British. However, the Louisiana Purchase and the Battle of Trafalgar made French embroilments a tolerable nuisance compared with the near and present dangers from the British Navy. The embargo was supposed to put the British on short rations, and thereby make the British government sweetly reasonable, but, alas, nations inflamed by passion often ignore pure reason.[39]

In its conception the embargo was a simple thing: coasters

---

35 Leonard D. White, *The Jeffersonians, A Study in Administrative History, 1801–1829* (New York, 1951), on which the writer has drawn so heavily as to make detailed citation cumbersome. Adams, "Jefferson's Military Policy," pp. 225–230.

36 Jefferson to Gallatin, May 6, 15, 1808, *Writings of Jefferson*, XII, 52–53, 56.

37 Gallatin to Jefferson, Dec. 18, 1807, *Writings of Gallatin*, I, 368.

38 *Messages and Papers*, I, 421.

39 Ships might leave in ballast or if already laden. The fishermen's provision was slipped in as a bit of parliamentary legerdemain by Josiah Quincy. News of the order in council to impress from neutrals (Oct. 17) reached Washington on Dec. 16. News of the application of the Berlin Decree came on Dec. 17. The embargo message went to the Congress on Dec. 18. Kaplan, "Jefferson and the Balance of Power," pp. 196–204.

bonded, no clearances for foreign parts except that foreigners in
port might leave with what they had, special presidential permits
for American ships to go to foreign places, which, in practice, meant
departures only on public business. Samuel Smith, the Baltimore
merchant, saw the bill through the Senate easily, after answering a
few friendly questions from John Quincy Adams. The House was a
bit less decisive, but accepted the Senate's text with slight changes,
its vote proclaiming Jefferson was still the darling of the South.
Only a twentieth-century opinion analyst would have seen troubling portents in the defection of 20 per cent of the Republican
representatives. The bill became law after just four days' debate. It
passed partly because of the President's popularity, and partly
because the situation demanded that government do *something*.
Because of the reticence of the presidential message, which argued
safety, not coercion, debate was not really adequate; if there had
been more argument, there might have been less surprise at later
troubles unforeseen. Passage had been a personal triumph for the
President, but, by the same sign, a failure of his great experiment
could become a personal failure. The people at first generally
accepted the law, although the President never effectively tried to
rally public support, but a few Federalists saw it as a Francophile
stride toward war.[40]

While the general public approved in principle, merchants found
loopholes. They were plugged by supplementary laws. River and
harbor craft must post bonds, fishermen's bonds were sharply raised,
and penalties were increased to levels ruinous to convicted violators. The Congress next embargoed inland waters, controlled wagons and sleighs, and (allowing the statutory easing of a few
hardship cases) practically barred all export. Four million dollars
were voted for gunboats, forts, militia weapons, and eight regular
regiments, and the President simultaneously received discretion to
suspend the embargo during any congressional recess. Gallatin continuously implemented these acts with detailed customs circulars.
The Treasury was statutorily authorized to detain any vessel if the

40 Thomas P. Abernethy, *The South in the New Nation, 1789–1819* (Baton
Rouge, 1961), pp. 319–321; for a temperate man's belief in the Francophiliac
motivation, see King to Gore, Dec. 31, 1807 (and related letters of the next few
months), Charles R. King (ed.), *The Life and Correspondence of Rufus King* (6
vols., New York, 1894–1900), V, 42.

local collector believed its owner intended to violate the Embargo.[41]

Almost inevitably, some grumblers decided that what they disliked must be unconstitutional. The Massachusetts Chief Justice Theophilus Parsons could find no delegated embargo power; the New York *Post* said: No export tax, ergo no ban on exports. Young Daniel Webster, discovering his new clients of Portsmouth in pain, wrote a pamphlet to prove the embargo violated the Tenth Admendment and illegally stretched the commerce power by destroying commerce. The political Francophobia of his piece vitiated its strength. A brief skirmish between Jefferson and his first Supreme Court appointee, William Johnson, gave arch-Federalists glee but little profit. Jefferson, on his own, ordered that *all* provision cargoes be detained. Johnson, on plea of a shipowner, ordered the Charleston collector to grant clearance because the President had overstepped the statutes. Jefferson published a contrary opinion by Attorney General Caesar Rodney, and directed collectors to follow Rodney. He later got statutory authority for general detentions. Eventually, Judge John Davis of the Massachusetts District Court, a Federalist, ruled the embargo constitutional despite the plea that no embargo could be permanent. There was no appeal, probably because John Marshall would doubtless agree that the commerce power was fully delegated. (Joseph Story later disapproved, for reasons more political than legal.) [42]

The embargo was not un-Jeffersonian. As Secretary of State, Jefferson had believed the presidential power in foreign affairs to be

[41] The three main supplementary acts became laws on Jan. 9, Mar. 12, and April 25, 1808. The plaintive shipowner could not require the local collector's honest opinion to be also a correct opinion. Otis *v.* Watkins, 9 Cranch 339 (1815).

[42] Claude M. Fuess, *Daniel Webster* (2 vols., Boston, 1930), I, 97, 129–131; Daniel Webster, *The Writings and Speeches of Daniel Webster* (18 vols., Boston, 1903), XV, 564–574; Donald G. Morgan, *Justice William Johnson, the First Dissenter* (Columbia, S.C., 1934), pp. 55–74, describes the Charleston case and its effects; Charles Warren, *The Supreme Court in United States History* (rev. ed., 2 vols., Boston, 1937), I, 316–352, gives the constitutional history of the embargo; on Jefferson's rationale, see Caleb P. Patterson, *The Constitutional Principles of Thomas Jefferson* (Austin, 1953), pp. 146–149. Marshall's opinion in Gibbons *v.* Ogden, 9 Wheaton 1 (1824), appears to have settled the question permanently. In 1831, Story wrote that the embargo "went to the utmost limit of constructive power under the Constitution" and "stands on the extreme verge of the Constitution." Mortimer D. Schwartz and John C. Hogan (eds.), *Joseph Story* (New York, 1959), p. 35.

strong, and he was in character in purchasing Louisiana and promoting the embargo. Alexander Hamilton, knowing Jefferson's view of executive power, predicted his pattern of policy. The constitutional argument over the embargo teaches more about the slow growth of national patriotism than about law. The list of Massachusetts men who accepted its constitutionality is intellectually impressive, but the opposition now began its ideological drift to the adoption of a New England sectionalist position, similar to and more revolutionary than the execrated Kentucky and Virginia Resolutions of 1798. Not only can it be said that the embargo was not un-Jeffersonian; it may be added that opposition to it was un-Federalist. When the Federalists controlled the government, neither Federalist nor anti-Federalist questioned the legal authority of the United States to regulate or to prohibit international trade, but by 1808 the Federalists had reversed themselves and were calling the embargo not only imprudent but immoral. They did not put their new economics into the formal dress of a philosophical system, but they continually called for free trade and the right of businessmen to make their own judgments of risks.[43]

Although requested as a "safety" measure, the embargo was intended to test economic coercion as a substitute for war, regardless of injury to business. Success depended on American unity (and British necessity), but American merchants were unaccommodating and evasions were immediate. The physical burden of enforcement fell on Gallatin and his collectors.[44]

Evasions benefited Florida and Canada and all points overseas. Florida garrisons ate American food because General James Wilkinson never missed a chance to make a Spanish friend. The Middle States were not impeccable, but maritime New England bestrode the lawless world like a colossus. Federalist indignation, linked with the threat to shipping, provoked open defiance by shippers and

[43] Hamilton's opinion of Jefferson's strong nationalism in foreign affairs is printed in Henry Cabot Lodge (ed.), *The Works of Alexander Hamilton* (12 vols., New York, 1904), X, 413; Henry Adams (ed.), *Documents Relating to New-England Federalism, 1800–1815* (Boston, 1877), pp. 60, 79, 91, 223, 243–244, comprise the list of eminent Yankees who admitted the constitutionality; Homer C. Hockett, *The Constitutional History of the United States* (2 vols., New York, 1939), I, 328–331; see also J. Adams to Jefferson, May 3, 1812, Lester Cappon (ed.), *The Adams-Jefferson Letters* (2 vols., Chapel Hill, 1959), II, 303; D. H. Fischer, *The Revolution of American Conservatism: The Federalist Party in the Era of Jeffersonian Democracy* (New York, 1965), pp. 170–171.

[44] Walters, *Gallatin*, pp. 200–209.

spread epidemic pessimism among Treasury officers. Contrary to conventional lore, Bostonians entered the bonded and untaxed coastal trade and illicitly prospered by steering for foreign ports when out of sight of land. The embargo failed on the New England littoral for the same reason Napoleon's decrees failed: there was no consensus of support. Flour, the key commodity, had to move coastwise to feed Americans, yet was in great demand abroad. Jefferson let governors license flour shipments, a grave error because governors, unlike collectors, could not be disciplined. Until Governor Sullivan of Massachusetts died late in 1808, his licenses were traded like shares of stock. And every other conceivable variety of fraud was practiced, whether requiring hidden coves or forged papers.[45]

Solicitude for hardship cases encouraged profitable perjury. Merchants could export to pay for goods bought before December, 1807, and Jefferson gave hundreds of permits on dubious affidavits. According to legend, John Jacob Astor guilefully costumed a stray Chinese as a Mandarin, secured permission to return him to China, sent $200,000 to Canton for Oriental wares, and profited hugely. But finesse was unnecessary. One convicted violator forfeited his double bond after selling his illegal cargo for double the amount of the bond.[46]

American evasions encouraged the British to deprecate the embargo, and, after April, 1808, an order admitted provision vessels to British West Indian ports, even if without ship's papers. As Madison fumed, this made the ships "necessarily smugglers if not pirates. . . ."[47] Such quasi pirates were fair game for Napoleon, because authentic papers could not be had; hence they often carried American and British papers, both sets forged in Britain.

The Enforcement Act of April 25, 1808, did not make enforcement easy. Gallatin directed a river of letters and circulars to his collectors (most of whom behaved creditably). The Canadian and Floridian borders leaked badly and the coasting trade was so flagrantly abused that Jefferson allowed himself the ungenerous

45 Robin D. S. Higham, "The Port of Boston and the Embargo of 1807–1809," *American Neptune*, XVI (1956), 189–208, shows how historians sympathetic to Federalism have deprecated the ingenuity and enterprise of their ancestors; see also J. D. Forbes, "Boston Smuggling, 1807–1815," *ibid.*, X (1950), 144–149.

46 Vincent O. Nolte, *Fifty Years in Both Hemispheres* (New York, 1854), pp. 141–143, retails the Astor artifice; Higham, "Port of Boston and the Embargo," pp. 202–203.

47 Pinkney to Madison, Sept. 7, 1808, "Pinkney Letter Books," p. 367; Madison to Pinkney, July 18, 1808, *ASP: Foreign Relations*, III, 224.

reflection that the reputations of persons and ports should be criteria of enforcement. Meanwhile, exports by land had not been banned until March, 1808. Beef and flour seemed irresistibly drawn to Lakes Erie and Champlain, places very hard to police. In April, Jefferson proclaimed the region of the Canadian–New York border in insurrection and vainly invoked the civil officers to intervene. Most freights went through easily, some fought their way, and two collisions with federal force were almost large enough to be called battles. Furthermore, interference with the fur trade generated Indian and Canadian enmity. By October, Gallatin gloomily concluded that New England lacked virtue and enforcement was impossible, but, if the embargo were repealed, the country would have to submit to foreign maritime regulation or fight.[48]

So far, so bad. The embargo had merely made foreign trade inconvenient. Although harassed by hostility and litigation, its administrators had generally been diligent. What to do? Gallatin now promoted the most repressive measure enacted to that time. Perhaps he hoped to shock Jefferson into restraining foreign foes instead of American citizens. (The Treasury offered to finance a war for a year without loans or new taxes.) Nevertheless, Jefferson agreed to a new statute based on Gallatin's proposals which passed the Senate 3–1, the House 2–1 (January 9, 1809). Giles's Enforcement Act, as it was known, heaped up force to overcome defiance. Every screw was tightened. The President could use the militia freely. The Treasury received power to frustrate the most remotely suspected intention of exporting. Every shipmaster and wagoner was guilty until proved innocent. Militia commoners were pitted against the local elite. The law killed the coasting trade.[49]

III

If America was necessary to Europe, the embargo would have been disastrous to Europe, but it wounded only English workmen and

48 A. L. Burt, *The United States, Great Britain, and British North America, from the Revolution to the Establishment of Peace after the War of 1812* (New Haven, 1940), pp. 257–259; Gallatin to Nicholson, Oct. 18, 1808, Adams, *Life of Gallatin*, p. 375.
49 Gallatin to Jefferson, Nov. 15, 1808, *ibid.*, pp. 377–378; Gallatin to Giles, Nov. 24, 1808, *Writings of Gallatin*, I, 428–435, and "Campbell Report," 435–446. Rufus King, a relatively dispassionate Federalist, has left no opinion that the embargo was unconstitutional, but he believed Giles's Act was, King to Pickering, Jan. 15, 1809, *Rufus King*, V, 128.

French colonists, of little political influence, while gratifying the landed aristocrats by raising farm prices.[50]

At first news of the embargo, the British felt something like relief at the prospect of lessening the quarrels over neutral rights, and at the apparent gift of a monopoly of oceanic trade. Jefferson may have made a grave mistake in striking at British imports instead of at exports. Britain sold less to the United States because of the embargo (down 56 per cent in 1808), but the simultaneous Spanish rebellion and the unshackling of Latin America offered new markets. Those English manufacturers whose sales declined because of American policy were not directly influential in the Foreign Office since they usually sold to British merchant-exporters, not to foreign customers. There was cotton in British warehouses, more cotton on order from Turkey, and importers realistically relied on American evaders. When prices rose and employment declined, only the powerless poor were seriously hurt at first. The United Kingdom, through 1808 at least, seemed well able to ignore the embargo. True, by late 1808, Liverpool trade with the United States was gravely depressed, but the then teetering government, with all Europe watching, could not at that moment admit error. *If* the Americans had obeyed their own laws, *if* the Spaniards had not unexpectedly risen against Bonaparte, *if* the embargo had been maintained longer, the British might have decided to coddle their best customer, if only to discourage American manufactures.[51]

America had friends in Britain who were wiser and more generous than the Anglophiles in America. Jefferson had counted on their help, but they proved impotent, especially when the Spanish rebellion helped traders recover some of the embargo damage. These sympathizers understood that British orders provoked the embargo, and that no American need prove his Francophobia by favoring Great Britain. They failed to make these points well, al-

[50] Walter W. Jennings, *The American Embargo, 1807–1809, with Particular Reference to Its Effects on Industry* (Iowa City, 1921), pp. 70–93.
[51] Norman S. Buck, *The Development of the Organization of Anglo-American Trade, 1800–1850* (New Haven, 1925), pp. 98–120; Schuyler Dean Hoslett, "Jefferson and England: The Embargo as a Measure of Coercion," *Americana*, XXXIV (1940), 47–53; S. G. Checkland, "American versus West Indian Traders in Liverpool, 1793–1815," *Journal of Economic History*, XVIII (1958), 151–155; J. Steven Watson, *The Reign of George III* (New York, 1960), pp. 465–467; Sears, *Embargo*, pp. 253–301.

though the published American official documents spoke more harshly against France than Britain.[52] Perhaps they circulated the opposition speeches more effectively than they circulated imported American official documents.

The British official mind was nourished by Federalist correspondents and pamphlets. The popular economic theorist in England was old Lord Sheffield, who still persuasively argued that American commercial prosperity was a bad thing. Predictably ignoring the embargo, Minister David Erskine in Washington, early in 1808, said his government would continue to regulate commerce according to British interest. When Pinkney in London later offered to suspend the embargo against Britain but keep it on France, in exchange for withdrawal of the offensive orders, Canning valued the offer so little he almost forgot to write his routine rejection. He said he considered the embargo as merely a municipal regulation to conserve American shipping, and none of His Majesty's business, thus confirming Gallatin's prediction that the embargo would not change British policy. However, as the impact of the embargo began to be felt in 1809, the ministry would have acted if it could have saved face, but then came news of the impending repeal of the law, which might bring relief without the appearance of yielding to American pressure.[53]

Meanwhile, although still scornful of America, Napoleon, whose own oceanic trade had almost disappeared, rather liked the embargo, although he regretted it was less than war. The new American law certainly was injurious to the starving French West Indies, which one by one surrendered to British arms, but Napoleon cared little for his defenseless few remaining colonies. The embargo was scarcely felt in metropolitan France, and Napoleon would surely have endured ten times as much inconvenience if only his enemies had to suffer even more. Americans had thus far so eagerly flouted Napoleon's Continental System that he believed they were obeying the direction of the United States government rather than following

[52] Bradford Perkins, "George Joy, American Propagandist at London, 1805–1815," *New England Quarterly*, XXXIV (1961), 194–197.

[53] Perkins, "George Canning," pp. 11–13. Gallatin thought hope of changing British policy by an embargo "entirely groundless," Gallatin to Jefferson, Dec. 18, 1807, *Writings of Gallatin*, I, 368.

their own commercial instincts.[54] In America it was rumored that Napoleon, in consequence, said "he would have no neutrals."[55]

The rumor was correct. Napoleon's shortsighted program was to propel the United States into war against Great Britain. Neutrals were anathema to him, and the embargo gave him the opportunity to abolish the concept of neutrality. Minister John Armstrong in Paris had been attacking the Continental System, as set forth in Napoleon's decrees, because it was not in accord with the Convention of 1800, which had codified Franco-American commercial relations. Napoleon contemptuously responded with his Bayonne Decree (April 17, 1808), ordering that all American private ships arriving in Europe must now be considered as illicitly coming from British ports, in violation of the embargo and in Britain's service, and therefore good prizes. Any American freighters lucky enough to escape the patrols of the Royal Navy were now prey to France. By June, Napoleon's administrative rule of thumb had become: Let no American ship go, and give no reasons. This rule detained ships which had violated neither belligerent's regulations, because they had been seaborne before the war of paper blockades began. That October, Napoleon ordered his depleted Navy to take all ships flying the American flag. Fearing the hazards of carrying ships into port, the captors usually burned them, making it impossible for judicial process to right any wrongs. At long last, after much expostulation in Minister Armstrong's limited French, Bonaparte consented in February, 1809, to release ships not charged with any specific transgressions. This imperial generosity was little applauded by Americans bred in a different tradition of law.[56] Napoleon was not completely arbitrary. American Consul General William Lee reported from Bordeaux that many quasi-American ships never saw America, but carried papers ingeniously forged in England. On the

[54] The French islands all fell by 1810; Ulane Bonnel, *La France, les Etats-Unis, et la Guerre de Course, 1797–1815* (Paris, 1961), pp. 231–232, 260–261. The Spaniards of Texas found themselves denied access to their usual sources of Indian trade goods. The embargo was lifted before they moved, as planned, to build the first active Texan seaport. C. Norman Guice, "Trade Goods for Texas: An Incident in the History of the Jeffersonian Embargo," *Southwestern Historical Quarterly*, LX (1956–57), 507–519. Mme. Bonnel, pp. 238–249, describes the operations of Napoleon's System as recorded in port and naval records.

[55] Newton to Madison, June 23, 1808, James A. Padgett (ed.), "Letters from Thomas Newton," *William and Mary Quarterly*, Second Series, XVI (1936), 200.

[56] Bonnel, *Guerre de Course*, pp. 233–237, 252.

other hand, the United States had notice of the Bayonne Decree only in letters from Armstrong to Madison, containing information pieced together by Armstrong working on his own.[57]

America's basic industry, agriculture, was temporarily depressed. Farm prices went down, although cotton was firm until December, 1808. Land and slaves depreciated. Lenders foreclosed mortgages except where legislatures passed stay laws. Commodity speculators got rich, since staples could be stored awaiting rises. Agricultural distress was keenest in the South, which suffered quietly in contrast to New England.[58]

It is hard to know the effect on shipping, because shippers masked their doings very well, but *recorded* exports dropped 80 per cent in 1808. Rufus King pointed out lost opportunities for great profits, but these were paper losses. The unpredictable coincidence of the Spanish revolting against their unwanted Corsican monarch certainly put Britain ahead of the United States in developing the suddenly free trade of Latin America. Ports wholly dependent on seafaring and auxiliary industries, such as Norfolk and Salem, were nearly ruined, although diversified port cities survived. Unemployed seamen emigrated, possibly to find themselves soon pressed or enlisted in the Royal Navy. Curiously enough, British ships could bring in manufactures unlisted in the Non-Importation Act of 1806, and legally take out gold. The most reliable wholesale-price indexes for the years 1804 through 1808 show a drop of about 9 per cent, with Philadelphia's declining least and Charleston's most. Furs accumulated in the Indian trade and spoiled for lack of a market. The embargo promoted manufactures in the Middle States more than in New England, where John Lowell wrote that manufacturing must fail because New England lacked the necessary multitude of destitute workers. The South had high hope of industrializing. Perhaps the stimulus to Middle State manufacturing and the industrial optimism of the South explain why regions south of Connecticut more easily tolerated the law. Customs receipts were steady through 1808, but fell more than 55 per cent in 1809; as military spending increased, the operating revenue (exclusive of debt service) was $1.3 million short by December, 1809. All of these

57 Clauder, *American Commerce*, p. 142, quotes Consul Lee; Beckles Willson, *America's Ambassadors to France, 1777–1927* (London, 1928), p. 142.

58 Jennings, *Embargo*, pp. 182–203. Contemporary price quotations were alleged to vary with the politics of the quoters.

phenomena stimulated Republican conversion to the once-maligned belief that the United States must have a balance of farming, foreign trade, and manufactures.[59]

The economic effects of the Embargo have been summarized: it "stimulated manufactures, injured agriculture, and prostrated commerce."[60] Edward Channing went farther. He concluded that it put the southeastern planter on the road to everlasting ruin,[61] but it seems unlikely that an economic system 190 years old could have been so badly wounded so quickly; southeastern agriculture had been declining for fifty years. The government began the year 1808 with a great Treasury surplus, merchants who were damaged suffered but briefly, violators got rich, and the economy lived on "the fat of the good years. . . ."[62] True, the embargo was blockade without the compensations of military booty, but it made neither widows nor orphans.

Deferring a description of the presidential contest of 1808,[63] it is useful to look at political responses to the embargo. In assessing political effects, voting is the standard, not the press. The scolding press represented only the small commercial minority. Although some Republicans straddled, and Federalism gained, voting in lesser contests in 1808 reflected no national sense of outrage. According to some Federalists, the embargo was intended to buy Napoleon's necessary help in getting Florida. French complaints of

---

[59] King to Pickering, Jan. 24, 1808, *Rufus King*, V, 66; Whitaker, *Independence of Latin America*, pp. 49–52; Winifred J. Losse, "The Foreign Trade of Virginia, 1789–1809," *William and Mary Quarterly*, Third Series, I (1944), 161–178; James Duncan Phillips, "Jefferson's 'Wicked Tyrannical Embargo,'" *New England Quarterly*, XVIII (1945), 468–470, 472 (as strongly partisan as its title); United States Bureau of the Census, *Historical Statistics of the United States, Colonial Times to 1957* (Washington, 1960), pp. 116, 119, 120, 122; Jennings, *Embargo*, pp. 166–181. In 1808 and 1809, cotton mills increased from 15 to 87, spindles from 8,000 to 80,000, yarn from 300,000 pounds to 2,808,000; Gallatin, "Manufactures," April 17, 1809, *ASP: Finance*, II, 427. Sears, *Embargo*, pp. 197–252, describes the embargo's effect on the Middle States and South; Joseph J. Spengler, "The Political Economy of Jefferson, Madison, and Adams," David K. Jackson (ed.), *American Studies in Honor of William Kenneth Boyd* (Durham, N.C., 1940), pp. 12–14. The embargo hurt Jefferson as much as any farmer; Dumas Malone, "Thomas Jefferson," *DAB*, calls its effect on him "ruinous."

[60] Jennings, *Embargo*, p. 231.

[61] Edward Channing, *A History of the United States* (6 vols., New York, 1905–25), IV, 392–393.

[62] Curtis P. Nettels, *The Emergence of a National Economy, 1775–1815* (New York, 1962), p. 329.

[63] The election is a subject of the following chapter.

their embargo parity with Britain show that this view was absurd. Jefferson was on the worst of terms with France when the embargo was enacted.[64] The truth is, the strident elder Federalists of New England (but not their hard-working younger colleagues) abstained from constructive party work and became an Anglican band. Fisher Ames died in 1808, and the bitter John Lowell succeeded him as the most influential arch-Federalist pamphleteer of New England. Senator Timothy Pickering, the slow-witted but quick-tongued Federalist figurehead, was the voice of political paranoia, telling his constituents the embargo was designed only to excite war. For ideology Pickering had the advice (and ghost-writing) of Massachusetts financier Israel Thorndike. Intellectuals who joined the phalanx were Washington Irving, who satirized Jefferson as a bumbling governor of New Amsterdam, and William Cullen Bryant, aged thirteen, who wrote a widely read defamatory poem, *The Embargo*,[65] which he later called a "foolish thing."[66]

No local party could ignore the embargo. Republican organizations everywhere endorsed it, even in Essex County, Massachusetts, headquarters of the "British faction."[67]

New England had the hottest local rivalries. Massachusetts Federalists had been slightly in minority, and now gained a slight majority despite fervent Republican efforts, although Federalism made no eminent converts, and Marblehead and Salem stayed Republican. Nevertheless, the Federalist stirrings in New England encouraged British obstinacy. In Connecticut the national issue took the place of moribund local issues, with temporarily disastrous effects on the Republican vote, but it was a superficial change; only a handful of federal officeholders defected.[68]

[64] For examples of French complaint, see Madison to Armstrong, July 22, 1808, *Writings of Madison*, VIII, 38–40; Sears, *Embargo*, pp. 306–312.

[65] Timothy Pickering, *A Letter from the Hon. Timothy Pickering . . . to His Excellency James Sullivan* (Boston, 1808); J. D. Forbes, *Israel Thorndike, Federalist Financier* (New York, 1953), pp. 105–109; Washington Irving, *Knickerbocker's History of New York* (2 vols., New York, 1895), I, 327–329; a facsimile edition of William Cullen Bryant's *The Embargo*, both the 1808 and 1809 renderings, was printed at Gainesville, Fla., 1955.

[66] Herman E. Spivey (ed.), "William Cullen Bryant Changes His Mind: An Unpublished Letter about Thomas Jefferson," *New England Quarterly*, XXII (1949), 528 n.

[67] Noble E. Cunningham, Jr., *The Jeffersonian Republicans in Power, Party Operations, 1801–1809* (Chapel Hill, 1963), pp. 121, 135, 140, 166, 291–292.

[68] Thorp Lanier Wolford, "Democratic-Republican Reaction in Massachusetts to the Embargo of 1807," *New England Quarterly*, XV (1942), 35–61. In Connecticut, Hartford went Republican in 1807, Federalist in 1808.

The embargo animated politics in New York and Maryland. New York Federalists attacked it, posing as protectors of labor. Among Republicans, DeWitt Clinton was the paladin of the embargo. Because James Cheetham, his once-tame editor, was lukewarm, Clinton set up a rival newspaper, and then the legislature endorsed the embargo. Nevertheless, the Federalists captured the legislature in 1809, the first time in ten years. Maryland Federalists revived themselves, but failed to gain congressional seats and won only the state's lower house. Baltimore, despite its booming commercial interest, remained Maryland's strongest Republican citadel.[69]

South of the Potomac there was less excitement. Of course, John Randolph found contrary arguments, and Monroe, in temporary rustication, later grumbled of "pernicious experiment";[70] but southern legislatures supported Jefferson, and most leaders preferred embargo to war. New England sectionalism had provoked a southern nationalism. The relative stoicism of the South under its agricultural suffering suggests that opposition to Jefferson's policy, wherever found, reflected political enmity rather than economic interest.[71]

The elections of 1800–1806 might have destroyed Federalism, if it had not had the stimulus of the embargo issue to revive it in 1808. Facing denunciation and frustration, Jefferson and his followers showed self-denial in contrast to the opposition. Jefferson may have had an "excessive love of popularity," but in promoting the embargo he risked his popularity willingly.[72]

In estimating its political effects, attention turns toward New England, where opposition was shrill. Merchants had been excited by *The Essex* case, the Berlin Decree, and *Leopard*'s attack, but each time accounting principles prevailed over nationalism. They saw the embargo as an aid to France. Such polemics persuaded the New England commercial element that Jefferson was the public

69 Dixon Ryan Fox, *The Decline of Aristocracy in the Politics of New York* (New York, 1919), pp. 99–104; Dorothy M. Brown, "Embargo Politics in Maryland," *Maryland Historical Magazine*, LVIII (1963), 193–210.

70 Monroe to Brent, Feb. 25, 1810, *Writings of Monroe*, V, 115.

71 Delbert H. Gilpatrick, *Jeffersonian Democracy in North Carolina, 1789–1816* (New York, 1931), pp. 158–162; John Harold Wolfe, *Jeffersonian Democracy in South Carolina* (Chapel Hill, 1940), pp. 203–237. This writer's political generalization was drawn after reading Jennings, *Embargo*, Chap. 8.

72 Sears, *Embargo*, p. 318.

enemy. The section became complacent and self-centered,[73] and for years remembered the embargo as "treacherously"[74] enacted. Nevertheless, arch-Federalism paid a price in brains for its paranoia. It cast out John Quincy Adams; lost New England's largest shipowner, William Gray; and for a while suspected the moderate counsels of Harrison Gray Otis.

The question of New England's loyalty in 1808 and 1809 has been often raised. Much New England talk was anticonstitutional, but a political bond not strengthened by fear or love has rarely been felt as a heavy obligation. American nationality was yet a tender shoot. As early as May, 1808, Napoleon's Minister André Turreau in Washington believed an Anglo-American war would precipitate New England's secession. At the end of 1808, Massachusetts leaders drafted detailed tactics for New England's resistance to law, although Otis cautioned against secessionism.[75]

Then came Giles's Enforcement Act, the apocalyptic vision of hell. It excited town meetings, which in turn prodded their legislators. It was openly known that British and Federalist leaders were in sympathetic correspondence. The irrational conspiracy theories of the opponents had prevented even their valid reasoning from getting serious Republican attention, but, late in 1808, some influential Republicans decided that the choice was now between repeal or civil war. Privately, John Quincy Adams learned that a British agent, the Vermonter John Henry, was in New England early in 1809, conducting seditious conversations. As John Adams later told Jefferson, Henry said that in case of war Britain would ask of New England only neutrality in exchange for free trade.[76] (Repeal of the embargo dulled Federalist interest.)

Did Jefferson abdicate his leadership by taking no part in repealing the embargo? His temperament dictated his abstention

[73] James Truslow Adams, *New England in the Republic, 1776–1850* (Boston, 1926), pp. 241–244; Lowell, *Thoughts*, pp. 18–28; Timothy Pickering, *Interesting Correspondence Between . . . Governour [sic] Sullivan and Col. Pickering* (Boston, 1808).

[74] Samuel Eliot Morison, *The Life and Letters of Harrison Gray Otis* (2 vols., Boston, 1913), I, 298.

[75] Otis may have lost the nomination for governor in 1808 because he was descended from a revolutionary, *ibid.*, I, 327, 327 n.; see also II, 4–10; Sears, *Embargo*, pp. 143–196, exhaustively considers the effect on New England. Turreau is quoted in Bonnel, *Guerre de Course*, p. 230.

[76] Paul A. Varg, *Foreign Policies of the Founding Fathers* (East Lansing, Mich., 1963), pp. 199–202.

from the destruction of the cherished policy he alone had created. He had enforced it rigorously, and, when told he must accept civil war or repeal, said, "we [were] driven by treason . . . from the high and wise ground we had taken. . . ."[77] Paradoxically, Giles's Enforcement Act made enforcement possible, but enforcement made the embargo too obnoxious for congressional waverers. A young Republican from Massachusetts, Joseph Story (later of the Supreme Court), was elected to the Congress in 1808 to complete the term of the suddenly deceased Republican merchant-stalwart Jacob Crowninshield. By the time Story took the seat, in December, his successor had already been elected, and Story left in January, thus making himself but a thirty-day congressman. In his brief term he collaborated with a fellow Massachusetts Republican, Ezechiel Bacon, to promote the repeal of the embargo. If Jefferson's testimony may be trusted, the campaign against the embargo in the House of Representatives was chiefly Story's work, and was surprisingly successful. It is hard to believe that a known lame-duck first-and-last-termer could have that much influence. The fact is, Bacon had a letter from John Quincy Adams which argued against the embargo: it was unenforceable, it would be resisted with the help of state governments, juries would not convict violators, there would be much use of litigation as a delaying tactic, Republican popularity seekers were already wavering, and, finally, it would have no effect on Britain and France. It is certain that this letter circulated, because its gist appeared in the press within three weeks. Adams' views were probably more influential than those of young Mr. Story.[78]

With no help from the frigid President, who believed they were surrendering on the eve of victory, congressmen argued alternatives, beat down a Federalist move to discard all regulation as a prelude to negotiation, and, rather suddenly, turned to Giles's repealer in February, 1809. Jefferson had said that if Britain failed to withdraw her obnoxious orders, the embargo should be replaced only by war.

[77] Jefferson to Pinkney, July 15, 1810, Massachusetts Historical Society, *Proceedings,* Second Series, XII, 268.
[78] Gerald T. Dunne, "Joseph Story: The Germinal Years," *Harvard Law Review,* LXXV (1961–62), 707–754; J. Q. Adams to Bacon, Dec. 21, 1808, *Writings of J. Q. Adams,* III, 276–279, 280 n.–281 n. Story claimed less influence than Jefferson attributed to him; his account may be found in Schwartz and Hogan, *Joseph Story,* pp. 33–35.

Instead, the Congress sketched a smuggler's dream, a Non-Intercourse Act (March 1, 1809) which allowed exports to all except Britain and France, and allowed renewal of trade with whichever showed respect for neutral rights. It was a plain appeal to their cupidity. Stronger alternatives had been rejected: convoys, an ultimatum against ship seizures, and, strongest, a plague of privateering. Privateering failed 39–57, the 39 probably representing the war faction.[79] For the next several years, legislation tried to lure Britain to an accommodation, and tended to favor Britain over France.

Jefferson's search for a bloodless substitute for war had ended in an auctioneer's cry by the Congress, which asked Britain and France to bid against each other for American favor. It was claimed the embargo cost $10 million. We now know the War of 1812 cost $30 million annually, and near 6,000 casualties. Would 1807 have been a better year for war? One can argue that Britain was tougher in 1807 than in 1812. In 1811, John Quincy Adams believed the embargo had delayed war and was ready to approve another to delay it again.[80] The successes of violators, and the repeal, did not prove it unenforceable; a study of the movement of actual cargoes showed it "more of a success than a failure."[81] Jefferson's and Gallatin's executive problems were difficult; embargo evaders were scattered, rich, articulate, and numerous. Southerners accepted it more readily than New Englanders, because the orders in council, by reducing them to the Old Colonial status, had hurt the agrarians as much as the embargo hurt the merchants. In the agrarian attitude was a seed of the War of 1812. Authorities contradict each other on the embargo as a measure of Jefferson's capacities. Louis Martin Sears said it was "a plan which came near enough to success to vindicate its sponsor as a practical statesman."[82] Bradford Perkins replied, "The philosopher-king had asked too much of his people."[83] In any case, the embargo was tolerated too briefly to

[79] Morton Borden, *The Federalism of James A. Bayard* (New York, 1955), pp. 174–177; Sears, *Embargo*, pp. 140–141, 189–190.

[80] J. Q. Adams to T. B. Adams, July 31, 1811, *Writings of J. Q. Adams*, IV, 160–161.

[81] W. Freeman Galpin, "The American Grain Trade Under the Embargo of 1808," *Journal of Economic and Business History*, II (1929), 71–100, quotation at p. 100.

[82] Sears, *Embargo*, p. 320.

[83] Perkins, *Prologue*, p. 183.

answer Jefferson's question whether commercial coercion was a useful instrument of foreign policy.

Despite its few satisfactions and its many frustrations, continuous negotiation would probably have been better policy than war or commercial coercion. The embargo went against the grain by coercing Americans and demanding the subordination of grave economic interests to inglorious peace. Warfare requires active heroism and bestows glory. The embargo required the invisible heroism of self-denial. Jefferson probably overestimated the patience of his fellow citizens.

CHAPTER 9

A New Captain Conns the Ship

THE Republicans triumphantly gained three congressional seats in the off-year election of 1806. President Jefferson had appeased Maryland's influential Smiths by keeping their Robert as Secretary of the Navy. In Pennsylvania's 1805 gubernatorial election, moderate Republicans, with Federalist help, defeated truly radical Republicans.[1] New York's DeWitt Clinton spurned Burrite approaches, yet emerged the state's leader.

The façade of Republicanism showed no serious crack, but deep inside, away from the polling places, there were structural strains. The Samson pushing at the interior supports was John Randolph. Fuming over the Yazoo question, disappointed of getting a foreign legation, despising the tradesmanlike northern Republicans, he made his own principles the test of orthodoxy. Few met the test. Because Jefferson's reputation was invulnerable, Randolph clawed at Madison's jugular.[2] In "personal . . . coarse and vulgar"[3] speeches, he repeatedly attacked Madison's honesty in the Yazoo business; any issue would have served. The strategic objective, as Albert Gallatin saw, was the election of 1808.[4]

[1] Claude Milton Newlin, *The Life and Writings of Hugh Henry Brackenridge* (Princeton, 1932), pp. 267–270.

[2] William Cabell Bruce, *John Randolph of Roanoke, 1773–1833* (2 vols., New York, 1922), I, 180–200, 223–247, 265–281.

[3] William Plumer, quoted in Everett S. Brown, *The Territorial Delegate to Congress and Other Essays* (Ann Arbor, 1950), p. 79.

[4] Irving Brant, *James Madison, Secretary of State, 1800–1809* (Indianapolis, 1953), pp. 232–234; Gallatin to Jefferson, Oct. 13, 1806, Henry Adams (ed.), *The Writings of Albert Gallatin* (3 vols., Philadelphia, 1879), I, 310.

When Jefferson announced in November, 1807, that he would not run again, he occasioned the first presidential nominating contest. Madison, James Monroe, and George Clinton each had support. Unless the Republican congressional caucus decided, the election would end in the House of Representatives. The Monrovians and Clintonians objected, ostensibly to the caucus, but actually to its probable endorsement of Madison. A Monroe-Clinton alliance was impossible because each wished to be President. With the anti-Madisonians conspicuously absent, the congressional caucus approved Madison, 83–6, and generously renominated Clinton for Vice-President. John Quincy Adams boldly attended this Republican caucus, at the cost of his Senate seat.[5]

Republican opponents of Madison could rally only an unorganized genus of political leaders who called themselves the Tertium Quids—Quids for short. They were men dissatisfied with the local or national policies or leadership of the party, and their dissatisfactions varied from state to state and from year to year.[6] John Randolph was typical (but not suzerain), opposing the national administration from 1805 with what seems to have been neurotic frenzy. Because his scornful obstructionism provoked anger rather than agreement, he was not followed by a band of loving disciples, but was a solitary, towering nuisance to responsible officials. He put it plainly in April, 1806, "I found I might co-operate or be an honest man—I have therefore opposed, and will oppose them."[7] His acid was usually sprayed at Madison, but hurt the whole

[5] Robert Kent Gooch, "Jeffersonianism and the Third Term Issue: A Retrospect," *Southern Review,* V (1940–41) , 736–739, summarizes Jefferson's views on a possible third term through 1807. Regarding the caucus method of nomination, its most serious defect was that districts unrepresented by Republicans were unrepresented in the nominating contest. Alex B. Lacy, Jr., "Jefferson and Congress: Congressional Method and Politics, 1801–1809," Ph.D. thesis, University of Virginia, 1963, pp. 288–301; Brant, *Madison,* pp. 419–427. Adams' motive and the emotional reaction among Federalists to his attendance at the Republican caucus are reflected in J. Q. Adams to A. Adams, April 20, to Bacon, Nov. 17, 1808, W. C. Ford (ed.) , *Writings of John Quincy Adams* (7 vols., New York, 1913–17) , III, 232, 253; and Gardenier to King, Jan. 26, 1808, C. R. King (ed.) , *The Life and Correspondence of Rufus King* (6 vols., New York, 1894–1900) , V, 68–69.

[6] Noble E. Cunningham, Jr., "Who Were the Quids?" *Mississippi Valley Historical Review,* L (1963–64) , 252–263; a Quid could be a practical eclectic Jeffersonian (like Jefferson) who detested his state's Republican leaders for local reasons; see, Newlin, *Brackenridge,* pp. 267–270.

[7] *Debates and Proceedings in the Congress of the United States* (42 vols., Washington, 1834–56) , 9th Congress, 1st Session, p. 984 (hereafter cited as *Annals*) .

executive branch. With him was Nathaniel Macon, the great "no"-voter, who lost the title of Mr. Speaker in 1807 for temporary alignment with Randolph. John Taylor of Caroline had the only respectable mind among the Quids, but as an apologist for strict construction, his writings began to appear only when nationalism was too firmly founded to be shaken by pamphlets. Jefferson later called his notions "far-fetched, affected, mystical conciepts [sic], and flimsy theories . . ." too much trouble to study.[8] Monroe's was the only personality strong enough to endanger Madison's candidacy.[9] Jefferson wrote obliquely, and fruitlessly, to Monroe to withdraw.

Monroe's minor boom had illusory support in Virginia. What he gained from any pain caused by the embargo was canceled by distaste for Randolph. Administration congressmen kept Virginia Madisonian by superior politicking against the desperate attempt to blame Madison for the foreign imbroglio. Superannuated Clinton, claiming to be the healthier aspirant, campaigned vainly for President in New York—and for Vice-President elsewhere. The dissident Republicans of Pennsylvania wished they could support Monroe but, to avoid backing a loser, supported Madison. The Quid campaign defeated itself. Randolph's denunciations of the Yazoo settlement merely strengthened Madison among Yazoo claimants in New England; attacks on the caucus united those who attended. To say Madison was simultaneously inept and Machiavellian was nonsense. His public record being unblemished, his vices must be hidden in the executive files. Opponents therefore denounced him as an indecisive, wavering Secretary. Jefferson sent a bale of diplomatic papers to the Congress which took six days to read aloud, and Americans who heard them or who read the selections which appeared in the press rejoiced at the firmness Madison showed in dealing with all foreign governments.[10]

In the other party, some Federalists thought of approaching George Clinton, but previous flirtations with New York Republicans had ended painfully. So the Federalists went alone, convening

[8] Jefferson to J. Adams, Jan. 24, 1814, Lester J. Cappon (ed.) , *The Adams-Jefferson Letters* (2 vols., Chapel Hill, 1959) , II, 421.

[9] Eugene H. Roseboom, *A History of Presidential Elections* (New York, 1964) , pp. 57–60.

[10] Harry Ammon, "James Monroe and the Election of 1808 in Virginia," *William and Mary Quarterly*, Third Series, XX (1963) , 33–56; Brant, *Madison*, pp. 431, 436–445.

in secret at New York and naming Charles Cotesworth Pinckney
and Rufus King. The formality of a ticket may have helped congressional candidates, but it also promoted unity among Republicans. Federalist campaigners sketched Madison as both an impracti-
cal dreamer and an efficient Jacobin schemer. The embargo was
their liveliest issue, but, again, attacks only further cemented the
Republicans.[11]

The Federalists of 1808 were in a transitional stage, during which
the elders wasted their time in fruitless hectoring while the ambitious but still elitest younger Federalists began to work the
polling places seriously. These younger men still believed in government by the Best People, but the disaster of 1800 had proved
that to say it out loud was political suicide. While the elder
Federalists published angry pamphlets and wrote defeatist letters to
each other, proving their obsolescence, the younger men decided to
use the language of democracy to establish oligarchy. For this they
had to have a political party, and, for the first time, Federalists
became fervent for party discipline, which they righteously justified
in the manner of all men who think they are fighting a moral
battle. The elders had been long on political theory and short on
practice, but the younger men, busy on their moral battlefield,
found political theorizing distasteful. They despised the people but
respected their power, and hoped to direct popular power through
the channel of the Federalist party.[12]

Young Federalists took the efficient Democratic-Republican organizational methods as their models, simply because they were impressed by their enemies' successes. Beginning in 1801, they set up
state organizations patterned on the committees of correspondence
of earlier American history. By 1808, such state committees had
been founded in New York, Massachusetts, New Hampshire, Connecticut, Rhode Island, Pennsylvania, Maryland, and Virginia (in
that order). There was little to do in Delaware, where local
Federalists had skillfully organized themselves in the 1790's. The
leaders of these state organizations ran them with strong hands and

11 S. E. Morison, "The First National Nominating Convention, 1808," *American Historical Review*, XVII (1911–12), 744–763; Brant, *Madison*, pp. 433,
450–451, 456–459. On the Federalist interstate meeting of 1808, D. H. Fischer,
*The Revolution of American Conservatism: The Federalist Party in the Era of
Jeffersonian Democracy* (New York, 1965), pp. 84–87, is fresh and persuasive.

12 Fischer, *Revolution of American Conservatism*, pp. 33, 41.

firm wills; their correspondence—sometimes with almost the tone of military command—shows a steady growth of party spirit. The older and still better remembered Federalists were much less active, except for some transitional holdover figures, because they thought political suitoring a demeaning job. After all, they had succeeded in the past by exploiting the deference paid to them for decades, an experience which made it hard to pretend to love equalitarianism. As imitators of opposition successes, the new Federalist state organizations were not very inventive, and usually just copied whatever had worked for the other side.[13] About their only innovation was the secret meeting of state leaders in New York, 1808, called in the hope of concerting policy.

In early presidential elections, national issues absorbed less attention than local politics, and so it was in 1808. In Pennsylvania, although Gallatin doubted of Republican success, the battle was won when quarrelsome Republican factions reunited; Federalism was barely noticeable—but more than twice as many votes were cast for governor as for President. In Maryland, where Baltimore grew 244 per cent in twenty years, enfranchisement and apportionment were overriding questions, totally eclipsing national concerns. New York's DeWitt Clinton appears to have spent less energy on Uncle George's presidential campaign than on thrashing Livingstonian Republicans. South Carolina thought of rebuking Clinton, but decided it was unnecessary. New Jersey Republicans, a party of officeholders, practically ignored policy and ideology.[14] One pattern emerges from the jigsaw puzzle: where Republicans won, they won big; where Federalism conquered, it was close. A principal effect of Federalist partisan activity was the injection of the element of competition, which much increased the size of the vote.

It took a month after November 4 to choose electors. Their vote

13 *Ibid.*, pp. 59, 60–66, 74.
14 J. R. Pole, "Election Statistics in Pennsylvania, 1790–1840," *Pennsylvania Magazine of History and Biography*, LXXXII (1958), 217–219, and "Constitutional Reform and Election Statistics in Maryland, 1790–1812," *Maryland Historical Magazine*, LV (1960), 275–292; Gallatin to Jefferson, Sept. 14, 1808, *Writings of Gallatin*, I, 417; Sanford W. Higginbotham, *The Keystone in the Democratic Arch: Pennsylvania Politics, 1800–1816* (Harrisburg, 1952), pp. 174–176; John Harold Wolfe, *Jeffersonian Democracy in South Carolina* (Chapel Hill, 1940), pp. 227–231; Carl E. Prince, "Patronage and a Party Machine: New Jersey Democratic-Republican Activists, 1801–1816," *William and Mary Quarterly*, Third Series, XXI (1964), 571–578; J. Adams to Jefferson, Sept. 3, 1816, *Adams-Jefferson Letters*, II, 488.

was about what had been knowledgeably predicted in April: Madison 122, Pinckney 47. Electors chosen directly by the voters gave Madison 98, Pinckney 16. Federalists gained twenty-four congressional seats—a kind of victory, if holding 34 per cent of congressional votes represented party triumph.[15] The Republican success has been deprecated with the argument that embargo pains were felt too late to affect the election. Embargo had been law for nearly a year, and twice reinforced. With proof lacking, it is equally arguable that the embargo was felt, and the administration trusted.

The mode of Madison's election was portentous, for he was, in truth, made President by the Republican caucus. Jefferson made the Congress an instrument of the majority, and Congress ruled the caucus that created Madison. As the creation of the caucus, Madison could never dominate his makers.[16] When elevated to headship by a small band of associates, only a despot, a leader with much patronage to exchange for personal loyalties, or a man of enormous personal charm can thereafter bring that band of associates to heel, be he Archon of Athens, Doge of Venice, or chairman of the Grasslands County Central Party Committee. Madison's contemporary chief of state Napoleon Bonaparte achieved it by a *coup d'état*, but the mind boggles at thinking of Madison and despotism simultaneously.

Madison owed the caucus his Presidency, but needed no other prop. Educated in Princeton's class of 1771, he ranked socially near the top of the Virginia squirearchy. He had been close to President Washington when in the First Congress, but the frenzied speculation encouraged by Federalist policy shocked him into opposition against what he believed was a dangerous tendency toward financial oligarchy. He first won election to the Congress against the opposition of Patrick Henry and James Monroe, who thought him dangerously conservative, but he proceeded to found what were later called the Jeffersonian Republicans. He was constructive, patient, companionable, and learned. His self-restraint and his ability to carry motions without making enemies were external marks of a mildness much deprecated by writers who prefer fiery politicians

[15] United States Bureau of the Census, *Historical Statistics of the United States, Colonial Times to 1957* (Washington, 1960), pp. 681, 685, 691–692. The relative popularity of the candidates would be somewhat more accurately reflected by the votes of the electors chosen by direct popular vote.

[16] Lacy, "Jefferson and Congress," pp. 299–301.

and cutting epigrams. Because he once collaborated with Alexander Hamilton, then skilfully opposed him, Federalists said Lucifer Jefferson seduced Madison: thus, his reputation was that of a man irresolute and submissive. Outgeneraled Federalist foes knew better.[17]

The short and tidy Madison was no junior Jefferson, but loomed large to contemporaries. His early divergence from Federalism disappointed Hamilton, who concluded his coauthor was sentimentally but briefly attached to the Constitution. Taking the opposite view, John Taylor and other Quids theorized that Madison's divergence *to* Federalism malevolently Federalized Jefferson, although Jefferson later said his and Madison's principles were identical. Gallatin said Madison made decisions slowly, but firmly. Almost no one really thought him a nonentity. To Madison the Constitution established one republic, which the Federalists were preverting to government by bankers and stockjobbers, and his republicanism made him resist. He never wrote systematically on "Jeffersonian" Democracy, but penned pseudonymous polemics to affect events; by selection, he could be shown to be nearly as nationalistic in the 1780's as Hamilton.[18] His United States was to be "the workshop of liberty to the Civilized World." Individual liberty was not an absolute, because of human frailty, and government was to be the "least imperfect."[19] To summarize Madison's political philosophy would merely be to restate Jeffersonian-Madisonian Democracy. It may be noticed, however, that Madison was somewhat less optimistic about the perfectibility of the American democratic republic, probably because of the scars he bore from his longer experience in fiercely contentious deliberative assemblies. He

[17] Irving Brant, *James Madison, Father of the Constitution* (Indianapolis, 1950), pp. 236–242, 325, 341–343. Brant's *James Madison, the Nationalist, 1780–1787* (Indianapolis, 1948), gives the story of Madison's political apprenticeship; see also his "James Madison and His Times," *American Historical Review*, LVII (1952), 853–870.

[18] Alpheus T. Mason, "The Federalist—A Split Personality," *American Historical Review*, LVII (1952), 625–643; Brant, *Madison, Nationalist*, pp. 411–417; Arnold A. Rogow, "The Federal Convention: Madison and Yates," *American Historical Review*, LX (1955), 330–331, 334–335; George B. Dangerfield, *The Era of Good Feelings* (New York, 1952), pp. 17–20.

[19] Adrienne Koch, "James Madison and the Workshop of Liberty," *Review of Politics*, XVI (1954), 175–193 (the quotations are from pp. 177 and 185); also her "Toward an American Philosophy," *Virginia Quarterly Review*, XXIX (1953), 187–197.

was also more rigorous than Jefferson in the concrete application of general principles; no taint of vigilantism stains his record. Madison was the ablest American champion of constitutional republicanism.[20]

In symbolic homespun, Madison delivered an inaudible,[21] noncommittal inaugural address, with generous notice of Jefferson's "exalted talents."[22] At that night's reception the new President was bored, but Jefferson seized upon congenial John Quincy Adams to discuss Homer, Vergil, minor poets, and light verse before inconspicuously leaving to let Madison endure the evening's tedium. To Republican congratulations of the next few weeks, Madison replied: peace before war, war before submission. Dolley Madison and servants, soon established on muddy-dusty Pennsylvania Avenue, found the East Room *still* unfinished, but converted the dwelling from a widower's barracks to a presidential mansion.[23]

Madison was the first President to be denied a free hand in his cabinet choices. He lacked a widespread personal following, and the Congress which made him hobbled him. His prime frustration was his inability to have Gallatin as Secretary of State. Senator Samuel Smith, no ideologue, detested Gallatin because Gallatin questioned the propriety of the Smiths' business with the Navy. Gallatin was invulnerable in the Treasury, but his transfer could be blocked. William Branch Giles, an aspirant himself, told Madison that senators would not confirm Gallatin as Secretary of State. The golden apple then went to Robert Smith, while disappointed catspaw Giles fell into a permanent rage of isolated Quiddery. Although Smith had maintained the little Navy as a good one, Madison thought the President would have to run the Department of State. Madison never forgave the anti-Gallatins, and Gallatin thought of running for the House of Representatives, but was dissuaded. If he left, there would be no one of distinction in the

20 Ralph L. Ketcham, "James Madison and the Nature of Man," *Journal of Historical Ideas*, XIX (1958) , 62–76; Neal Riemer, "The Republicanism of James Madison," *Political Science Quarterly*, LXXIX (1954) , 45–64.

21 J. Q. Adams to L. Adams, Mar. 5, 1809, *Writings of J. Q. Adams*, III, 288–289.

22 J. D. Richardson (ed.) , *A Compilation of the Messages and Papers of the Presidents* (20 vols., Washington, 1897–1917) , I, 453.

23 J. Q. Adams to L. Adams, Mar. 5, 1809, *Writings of J. Q. Adams*, III, 289; the domestic life of the Madisons was sketched by Irving Brant, *James Madison, The President, 1809–1812* (Indianapolis, 1956) , pp. 31–33.

cabinet. Madison filled a Supreme Court vacancy in 1811 by the unexpected appointment of Joseph Story of Massachusetts, aged 32. Jefferson, who opposed the appointment of this pseudo Republican, was not influential in this administration. The Madison-Jefferson correspondence shows that Jefferson's suggestions were amicably disregarded many times, and that Jefferson felt no resentment.[24]

II

It took Jefferson a week to clear out of the White House and depart for Monticello. The departure has been thought of as a flight from failure by a man "discredited and disillusioned"[25] who suffered such a painful "loss of popularity"[26] that "he practically abdicated . . . and . . . fled. . . ."[27] One could make out a case, in the manner of a prosecutor, that Jefferson had discarded practically all of the important policies he had urged before he became President.[28] Such a case makes Jefferson an ambitious, unscrupulous demagogue (except that demagogues are supposed to be eloquent pleaders), or, more charitably, it describes a good dreamer but a poor executive.[29]

Did Jefferson reverse his position? Virginia, which shaped him before 1800, was not then a land which despised government; government often moved to modify vested rights. Jefferson's utopian agrarianism became eclectic in his responsible years, and was practically abandoned by 1815. This may be learning, instead of reversal. He falls into place more sensibly if we remember that he

24 Brant, Madison, President, pp. 22–25; Charles C. Tansill, "Robert Smith," in Samuel Flagg Bemis (ed.), The American Secretaries of State and Their Diplomacy (10 vols., New York, 1958), III, 151–156, does justice to Smith as Secretary of the Navy; George E. Woodbine, "Joseph Story," DAB; Charles Warren, The Supreme Court in United States History (rev. ed., 2 vols., Boston, 1926–37), I, 400–419, describes the circumstances of the Story appointment; Roy J. Honeywell, "President Jefferson and His Successor," American Historical Review, XLVI (1940–41), 64–75.

25 Dumas Malone, "Thomas Jefferson," DAB.

26 Henry Adams, History of the United States During the Administrations of Jefferson and Madison (9 vols., New York, 1889–91), IV, 454.

27 Edward Channing, A History of the United States (6 vols., New York, 1905–25), IV, 346.

28 Thomas A. Bailey, A Diplomatic History of the American People (6th ed., New York, 1958), p. 100.

29 Joseph Charles, The Origins of the American Party System: Three Essays (Williamsburg, 1956), pp. 74–77, sketches the puzzle of Jefferson.

did not know he was to be measured by the canons of Jeffersonian Democracy. He thought of himself as an American. He did not think his every act must conform to standards formulated by later generations. His deeds were public; his writings were mostly private. Most of his influence on the United States derives from the deeds. He often wrote generalities applicable in ideal circumstances, but rarely had the opportunity to act in ideal circumstances. To literal minds the disparity will ever seem hypocrisy.[30] A further example of his on-the-job training was his conclusion, after eight years as President, that men cannot be freed of "the floating lies of the day,"[31] hence informed and reasonable public stewards must govern, a view not very far from that of John Adams.

What of his popularity in 1809? He received enough congratulations on his Presidency to justify mentioning "consoling proofs of public approbation."[32] A reasonable man could conclude that Jefferson was beloved on the day he left the presidency.[33] Assuming Jefferson to have been a doctrinary, and analyzing his practices by the use of doctrinary formulae, his record can certainly be described

[30] Charles M. Wiltse, *The Jeffersonian Tradition in American Democracy* (Chapel Hill, 1935), pp. 112–119, collects Jefferson's chief observations on the Presidency; Wiley E. Hodges, "Pro-Governmentalism in Virginia, 1789–1836: A Pragmatic Liberal Pattern in the Political Heritage," *Journal of Politics*, XXV (1963), 333–360; A. Whitney Griswold, "The Agrarian Democracy of Thomas Jefferson," *American Political Science Review*, XL (1946), 657–681; Louis M. Sears, "Democracy as Understood by Thomas Jefferson," *Mid-America*, XXIV (1942), 85–93; L. K. Caldwell, *The Administrative Theories of Hamilton & Jefferson* (Chicago, 1944), pp. 234–236.

[31] Jefferson to Madison, Mar. 17, 1809, Andrew Lipscomb *et al.* (eds.), *The Writings of Thomas Jefferson* (20 vols., Washington, 1903–4), XII, 267.

[32] Jefferson to Du Pont de Nemours, Mar. 2, 1809, *Writings of Jefferson*, XII, 260.

[33] Henry Adams was chiefly responsible for the belief in Jefferson's low standing when he left office, but no reliable analysis of public opinion (except by counting votes) was possible. Anyone may analyze Adams' admirable rhetoric and discover that his work was eloquent, ironic, occasionally perspicacious, and often seductive; but if the reader remains detached, he will also notice that important parts dealing with the attitudes of Jefferson, and with opinions about Jefferson, rest as much on impression as fact. Adams, *United States*, IV, 454–474. The durability of Adams' interpretation is shown by its adoption by Nathan Schachner, *Thomas Jefferson, a Biography* (2 vols. in 1, New York, 1960), II, 885–887, to bring the second term to an end with a whimper. Adams' methodology is studied from internal evidence in Edmund Burke, III, "A Tarnished Image: The Historians' Jefferson," A.B. honors thesis, 1962, Notre Dame Collection, Memorial Library, Notre Dame, Indiana.

as inconsistent, yet a deviation from a stated principle may be an intelligent adaptation to unforeseen circumstances.[34]

What happened to the union while Jefferson presided from 1801 to 1809? The population increased by half, Ohio became a state, the trans-Allegheny grew by nearly 600,000 souls, the Mississippi trade more than doubled. The low capital investment in the Louisiana Purchase had brought inestimable profit. Manufactures were booming. Excise taxes no longer vexed an agricultural people. The administration reduced both public expenditures and debt—admittedly because of the lucky accident of a phenomenal foreign trade stimulated by foreign wars. It is easy to poke fun at Jefferson's initial hope of applying rationalism to diplomacy, at his gunboats, his embargo, but not easy to suggest alternatives to war or submission except these much-ridiculed experiments. All the while, clergymen campaigned against his character, and pamphleteers indicted him for malfeasance, misfeasance, and nonfeasance. He endured moral innuendo of a most venomous kind. But the contemporary evaluation of intelligent supporters has weight: he kept the devotion of Madison and Gallatin, and, perhaps more significant, converted John Adams and John Quincy Adams.[35] Such men outweigh many arch-Federalists and neurotic Quids.

Jefferson was the first President to lead the nation by leading an organized party which put his program through. He discarded theoretical Quiddery and took personal charge of public business in order to make government work. When the Congress became habit-

[34] Merrill D. Peterson, "Henry Adams on Jefferson the President," *Virginia Quarterly Review*, XXXIX (1963), 187–201; Lyman H. Butterfield, "The Dream of Benjamin Rush," *Yale Review*, XL (1950–51), 297–319, tells the story of the reconciliation of John Adams and Jefferson. Henry Adams' presidential ancestors had strikingly different views. Senator John Quincy Adams, no intellectual grasshopper, twice supported Jefferson by votes offensive to his most powerful constituents in Massachusetts. John Adams soon wrote newspaper pieces praising the sincerity of Jefferson's conduct of office. The Virginian would probably value the respect of the Presidents Adams more than that of their descendant.

[35] Sidney Ratner, *American Taxation: Its History as a Social Force in Democracy* (New York, 1942), pp. 31–33; Alexander Balinky, *Albert Gallatin, Fiscal Theories and Policies* (New Brunswick, 1958), pp. 89–127; Fred C. Luebke, "The Origins of Thomas Jefferson's Anti-Clericalism," *Church History*, XXXII (1963), 344–356; see the most effective anti-Jefferson pamphleteer at work in John Lowell, *The New England Patriot* (San Francisco, 1940); Lynn W. Turner, "Thomas Jefferson Through the Eyes of a New Hampshire Politician," *Mississippi Valley Historical Review*, XXX (1943–44), 205–214.

uated to acting as a disciplined body, there was no reason why it could not run itself. The nominating caucus of 1808 presaged the end of executive predominance, but only because Jefferson had made the Republican party the vehicle of the voters' consensus. He was as much the father of the effective party system as Madison was the father of the Constitution. The Constitution therefore survived the unforeseen rise of the party system. In eight years Jefferson's lieutenants marshaled a majority for every measure he deeply wished, and he never had to resort to the veto. Except for his effective leadership of the smoothly working congressional party organization, organized partisanship might have frustrated the democratic process and the federal government might have died of paralysis.[36] The Americans never had a Philosopher-King, but they once had a Scholar-Boss.

III

Madison's first quiet months in the Presidency promised well, but the promise was false. The Non-Intercourse Act which had succeeded the embargo allowed escape from economic impasse, and it growled in print for the honor of the flag, but its best friends rightly valued it little.[37] It barred French and British ships and imports, and embargoed trade to Britain and France; but once a ship left America, how could it be controlled? The law reversed the effect of the embargo, helping Britain while hurting France. The British could catch Americans steering for France, but France was helpless to retaliate—an annoyance which killed any hope of quickly tempering Napoleon's commercial policy.[38] Englishmen could complacently view the law as an American surrender. No one abroad seriously believed the United States would fight anybody.

The Portland ministry (1807–9), through its irritating Foreign Secretary, George Canning, mortifyingly initiated Madison into the

---

[36] Ralph Volney Harlow, *The History of Legislative Methods in the Period before 1825* (New Haven, 1917), pp. 165–193, describes presidential leadership of the Congress; Noble E. Cunningham, Jr., *The Jeffersonian Republicans in Power: Party Operations, 1801–1809* (Chapel Hill, 1963), pp. 302–305; Lacy, "Jefferson and Congress," pp. 302–314.

[37] Bradford Perkins, *Prologue to War: England and the United States, 1805–1812* (Berkeley, 1961), pp. 205–260, covers the diplomatic affairs of 1809–11. This chapter owes so much to his work that further citation would be superfluous.

[38] Ulane Bonnel, *La France, les États-Unis, et la Guerre de Course, 1797–1815* (Paris, 1961), pp. 253–285, drawn mostly from French archives.

fraternity of chiefs of state during Britain's economic boom year of 1809. Madison's foreign relations began favorably, if enigmatically, with a relaxation of British toughness. The ministry wished to find an excuse to recede somewhat, after beating back a parliamentary attack on its American policy. Using news of the new Non-Intercourse Act as a face-saver, Canning promoted an order in council (April 26) relaxing maritime regulation in details. But Minister David M. Erskine was simultaneously negotiating much easier terms in Washington, hence the London order puzzled Americans.[39] The puzzle was solved by autumn: Erskine was generously disobeying orders. Convinced that the Americans uncontrollably craved amity, Canning had told Erskine to settle the *Chesapeake* unpleasantness and promise the repeal of the odious orders if the Americans would admit the Royal Navy but not the French, if they would bow to the Rule of 1756, and if they would meekly authorize the British to enforce American maritime laws. In short, they were to wear the colonial collar again. Erskine took his own line to preserve peace. He ignored the proposal for British enforcement of anti-French embargoes, agreed that the United States need not accept the Rule of 1756, and ignored an infuriating clause in Smith's acceptance of the *Chesapeake-Leopard* reparation: punishment of the responsible admiral was "due from His Britannic Majesty to his own honor."[40] The Erskine agreement distilled to this: the orders would be inapplicable to the United States after June 10; thereafter, Anglo-American trade would be legal.[41]

On the day after Erskine reduced the understanding to a brief letter, Madison (April 19, 1809) proclaimed that trade with Britain would be open on June 10, because the abhorrent orders were no longer applicable against the United States. When Erskine's agreement reached Canning, the Foreign Secretary, overheated by the

39 *Cobbett's Parliamentary Debates* (London, 1809), XII, 1159–1210; Bradford Perkins, "George Canning, Great Britain, and the United States," *American Historical Review*, LXIII (1957), 12–16; Biddle to Monroe, June 21, Walsh to Biddle,- Aug. 1, 1809, Reginald C. McGrane (ed.), *The Correspondence of Nicholas Biddle, 1807–1844* (Boston, 1919), pp. 5–7.

40 Smith to Erskine, April 17, 1809, *American State Papers: Documents Legislative and Executive* (38 vols., Washington, 1832–61): *Foreign Relations*, III, 296 (hereafter cited as *ASP*).

41 Erskine to Smith, April 18, Madison's proclamation, April 19, 1809, Gaillard Hunt (ed.), *The Writings of James Madison* (9 vols., New York, 1900–10), VIII, 51 n., 50–52.

reference to the King's honor, wrote scorchingly in disavowal.[42] Erskine gratuitously believed friendship was his goal, but Canning wished only a workable prohibition of Franco-American trade so the United States could not dicker with France. In this war Britain could not even appear to make concessions. Unaware of Canning's repudiation, which Madison later called a "mixture of fraud and folly,"[43] six hundred American ships legally sailed for Britain on June 10. In August, the blameless Madison had to re-embargo British trade by a reversing proclamation. Anglo-American relations were more acid than ever, the *Chesapeake* matter remained unsettled, and the time bomb of impressment ticked on. Only Erskine's father defended him, while jingoes objected to letting bona fide American shipping depart from England unmolested. Curiously enough, the legal trade during the interval increased British exports to America by 30 per cent that year.

Some daring American skippers gambled that Napoleon would match the Erskine agreement with an equivalent relaxation. They bet wrong. True, there was a possibility that British searches of American ships would not alone be used to justify French confiscations, but, on the antineutral decrees, the French never thought of granting immunity except, perhaps, to the produce of American soil and to coffee and sugar. The admission of those products only would make certificates of origin unnecessary, and would remove temptations to visit Britain. The disavowal of Erskine was known in Paris by mid-June, and the Franco-American Convention of 1800 expired in July. Thereafter, Napoleon would take no initiative in conciliating America, because he wished to harass American shipping in whatever way would cause the most Anglo-American friction, and he advertised his onerous policy in February, 1810, when he ordered the seizure of American ships in Spanish ports in reprisal for the Non-Intercourse Act of March, 1809.[44]

Francis James Jackson succeeded Erskine in Washington. He had nothing to offer. He felt no pressure to get results, because the Erskine agreement had temporarily filled British warehouses. He superciliously remarked that Americans were free to choose to trade

[42] Canning to Erskine, May 22, 23, 30, 1809, Bernard Mayo (ed.), "Instructions to the British Ministers to the United States, 1791–1812," *American Historical Association Report 1936* (Washington, 1941), III, 270–276.

[43] Madison to Jefferson, Aug. 3, 1809, *Writings of Madison,* VIII, 64.

[44] Bonnel, *Guerre de Course,* pp. 254 n., 256, 258–265.

with Britain thriftily and directly, or expensively and deviously. Jackson was so arrogant the Americans would deal with him only in writing, and when he implied that they duped Erskine into exceeding instructions, he was peremptorily dismissed.[45] While Jackson blustered in America, his government at home, upon the death of Portland in October, dissolved. Canning left office, having proved his personality worse than his policy, which was milder than his colleagues wished. His order of April, 1809, moderated the order of November, 1807, a fact eclipsed by Erskine's misadventure. Canning's weakness was not malice but a misunderstanding of America, complicated by haughtiness.

From the new ministry, headed by Spencer Perceval, Madison anticipated "quackeries and corruptions . . ."[46] although Pinkney mistakenly thought it an improvement. Canning's successor, Richard Wellesley, Marquis Wellesley, was indolent and inefficient. The composition of the ministry convinced Madison there was no British reservoir of benevolence. George Logan confirmed the opinion by touring England, in defiance of the "Logan Act," talking of mankind, manure, ships, sheep, peace, and planets, to return home depressed by English narrowness.[47] From the administration's viewpoint, the only cheerful fact of 1810 was the folly of Federalists, who canceled their recent political gains by lionizing Jackson, thus helping numerous New England Republicans to regain office.

Bad news came from France. The French economy could have used American support, but it survived without it by tolerating legal loopholes which benefited an illegal market. Napoleon vacillated so unpredictably that reclusive Minister John Armstrong could not keep abreast of attitudes.[48] Foreign Minister the Duke of Cadore told Armstrong that American trade would be unmolested

[45] Tansill, "Smith," in *Secretaries of State*, III, 165–175. Madison wrote the notes; Smith signed them. The Erskine-Jackson dealings may be studied in *ASP: Foreign Relations*, III, 299–323; see especially Smith to Jackson, Nov. 8, to Pinkney, Nov. 23, 1809, III, 318–323.

[46] Madison to Jefferson, Nov. 6, 1809, *Writings of Madison*, VIII, 79.

[47] Smith to Pinkney, Jan. (4?), 1810, Bernard C. Steiner (ed.), "Some Papers of Robert Smith . . . 1801–1809, and . . . 1809–1811," *Maryland Historical Magazine*, XX (1925), 145; Frederick B. Tolles, *George Logan of Philadelphia* (New York, 1953), pp. 286–294.

[48] J. Steven Watson, *The Reign of George III, 1760–1815* (New York, 1960), pp. 466–468; Mary Lee Mann (ed.), *A Yankee Jeffersonian: Selections from the Diary and Letters of William Lee of Massachusetts . . . 1796 to 1840* (Cambridge, Mass., 1958), index: "Armstrong."

if the United States would make its flag respected by preventing British inspections of American ships. After sending this contemptuous precept to America, Armstrong proposed a renewal of the expired Convention of 1800. Napoleon would have been pleased to get a new treaty, if it committed the United States to resisting British orders and ignored reparations for past French seizures. To put those seizures on legal grounds, beyond discussion, he issued the Rambouillet Decree (March 23, 1810), ostensibly as reprisal for the Non-Intercourse Act, and retroactive to May, 1809. It barred all American shipping from any port controlled by France. From now on, apparently, there would be no neutrals. All prize-court proceedings stopped. The probable aim was to force the United States to take a stand against Britain in order to get access to the Continent again. The angry American reaction was intensified by the simultaneous arrival of the make-your-flag-respected message.[49] With Britain and the United States deadlocked, Napoleon might have made a diplomatic profit, but, instead, commanded retroactive confiscations in reprisal for a law a year old. Franco-American collaboration was now impossible.

The Congress which convened in November, 1809, faced deficits of money and defects of imagination. Secretary Gallatin suggested a way out, and Macon introduced it as Macon's Bill Number One: American ships might go anywhere; British and French imports could enter only in American bottoms. This old-fashioned Navigation Bill would increase revenue, and it was enforceable, but it met difficulties. Some said it was excessively Anglophobic; conversely, others thought it too submissive, as Senator Henry Clay argued in his maiden speech.[50] The House passed it, but Senator Samuel Smith and friends said it would anger Britain while weakening America. (Smith probably wrecked it because Gallatin initiated it.) Madison said, "the frustration of intermediate courses seems to have left scarce an escape. . . ."[51] So the bill became, by amendment, Macon's Bill Number Two, an impetuous offer of national favor to the higher bidder. The United States would trade with both Britain and France until one revoked its restrictions, whereupon the United States would cease trade with the other. Madison had no confidence

[49] Bonnel, *Guerre de Course*, pp. 264–267.

[50] James F. Hopkins (ed.), *The Papers of Henry Clay* (10 vols., Lexington, Ky., 1959–), I, 448–452, and Clay to Smith, Feb. 23, 1810, *ibid.*, I, 452.

[51] Madison to Pinkney, Jan. 20, 1810, *Writings of Madison*, VIII, 91.

in the policy, but hoped ship seizures might encourage the Congress to prepare for war. Protective convoys, and discriminatory duties against French and British goods, were proposed but killed. As the only compatible policy, the bill passed without a roll call. Josiah Quincy sardonically called it a compromise: the Senate refused to protect commerce; the House refused to tax. British businessmen were pleased, if scornful, because free trade was cheaper than cheating, and France seemed helpless. For ten months, trade again flowered as America absorbed British exports and fed the British colonies.[52] As for Napoleon, a wolfish grin must have flickered on his face when he read a copy of Macon's Bill Number Two.

Napoleon saw the opportunity for another swindle worthy of the man who had defrauded Spain of Louisiana. He had his Foreign Minister, the Duke of Cadore, hand a carefully ambiguous letter to Minister Armstrong (August 5, 1810) which alleged the revocation of the Berlin and Milan Decrees on November 1, as a consequence of the repeal of the Non-Intercourse Act, "it being understood" that the British would mend their ways or be made to reform by the Americans. Armstrong went home five weeks later, leaving Jonathan Russell as chargé.[53] Before Armstrong left, Cadore told him Napoleon's benevolence did not extend to reparations, because confiscations had been reprisals for past misconduct. Madison now showed himself a notable optimist, or, more likely, a desperately wishful thinker, although John Quincy Adams darkly advised that the French might be shamming. Fearing Napoleon might retract, Madison assumed French honesty and proclaimed nonintercourse against Great Britain (November 2). Only then did he write to tell the French he believed that they stated a policy, not a conditional offer. He was applying reason to diplomacy. If logic ruled, Britain would now seek advantages by concessions, and Napoleon would be sweetly moderate, to keep American friendship. But logic failed. Napoleon was contemptuous of America for selling

52 Wolfe, *Jeffersonian Democracy*, pp. 234–238, well illustrates the tension of a state vitally interested in both trade and agriculture; Josiah Quincy, *Annals*, 11th Congress 2nd Session, pp. 2051–2052 (May 1, 1810) ; Herbert Heaton, "Non-Importation, 1806–1812," *Journal of Economic History*, I (1941) , 194–196.

53 Napoleon probably was not enough at ease in French to work out his semantic stratagems by himself; see Ferdinand Brunot, *Histoire de la Langue Français des Origines à 1900* (13 vols. in 19, Paris, 1905–53) , X, 645–651. Louis-Barbé-Charles, Count Sérurier, appointed Sept. 11, 1810, presented his credentials in Washington as minister of France on Feb. 16, 1811.

itself so cheaply. He made no change of course; the United States had no success in getting neutral rights recognized. French conversations with Russell were as opaque as Cadore's letter was ambiguous.

In February, 1811, the Congress enacted a ratification of Madison's November nonintercourse proclamation. Now the British could import from America, in American bottoms, but could ship nothing to America. The law was to stand as long as the orders stood, and it worked pretty well. The Republican congressional majority had become wholly intransigent and was convinced that American withdrawal would be shameful. No matter how badly Napoleon behaved, his malevolence would be no reason to forgive Britain. By this time the United States would probably have settled for nothing less than a prohibition of trade to truly blockaded ports.[54] Madison has seemed a fool to some to have gotten into this vise, but it should be noticed that American blood was not flowing, and there was still hope of sudden peace in Europe.

Napoleon continued his sharp practices. On the day Cadore handed his letter to Armstrong (August 5), the new "Trianon tariff" duties rendered American trade unprofitable, and the secret Trianon Decree ordered all American ships sold which had arrived after early 1809. Russell, in 1811, complained of the lack of internationally credible evidence of French relaxations. In 1812 the French cited a decree of revocation, signed at Saint-Cloud, April 28, 1811. This mysterious decree certainly had no effect on the deeds and correspondence of French officials. Henry Adams said it was concocted in 1812, but Ulane Bonnel found it in its chronological order in the Foreign Ministry archives. It was probably an antedated fabrication, manufactured to embarrass the Americans. Madison had nominated the spotlessly democratic Joel Barlow, knowledgeable in French affairs and devoted to a dream of American greatness, to try to get a straight story from the French. The choice was excellent, but Samuel Smith tried to block Senate consent. Oddly enough, Timothy Pickering successfully led for confirmation, pointing out that Barlow's deism was a commonly respectable deism, and that the allegedly visionary poet had been practical enough to get

54 Heaton, "Non-Importation," p. 194; Carleton Savage (ed.), *Policy of the United States toward Maritime Commerce in War* (2 vols., Washington, 1934–36), I, 35, digests a projected Russo-American treaty which took this position on blockades (1811).

very rich. By this time Madison was suffering from a surfeit of Smiths. He fired Secretary of State Robert Smith and replaced him with James Monroe, thus healing an old fracture.[55] In France, Barlow, once famous for Francophilia, reflected with "horror"[56] on the possibility of a war with Great Britain when he saw for himself the bloodstained condition of the Continent and the megalomaniac character of its master. The Anglo-Franco-American triangular estrangement was complete.

[55] Adams, *United States*, VI, 254–258; Bonnel, *Guerre de Course*, pp. 297–299, 302 n.–303 n.; Joseph Dorfman, "Joel Barlow: Trafficker in Trade and Letters," *Political Science Quarterly*, LIX (1944), 83–100; James Woodress, *A Yankee's Odyssey: The Life of Joel Barlow* (Philadelphia, 1958), pp. 276–281.

[56] Irving Brant, "Joel Barlow, Madison's Stubborn Minister," *William and Mary Quarterly*, Third Series, XXV (1958), 439.

CHAPTER 10

Not Submission but War

THE United States, from 1806 to 1810, had tried every conceivable variety of commercial suasion, but American carrots were rejected and American sticks derided. The only choices left open were submission to British maritime rules, or persuasion of Britain that Napoleon had revoked his decrees and thereby removed the justification of unprecedented British regulations—or war. The London government was privately in disarray because King George III had lapsed into permanent illness which required the organization of a regency, and William Pinkney, the efficient United States minister to London, found the Foreign Secretary, Richard Wellesley, Marquess of Wellesley, indolent and unresponsive. The ministry seemed adamant against changing any policy, so Pinkney, pointedly observing that Britain was not represented in Washington by a minister, said he must depart, and had a farewell audience with the Prince Regent in February, 1811. Realizing that each nation would have but a chargé in the other's capital, the Foreign Office stirred itself to appoint Sir Augustus John Foster its minister to Washington,[1] but Wellesley told Pinkney that Foster's appointment meant no change of maritime policy. Pinkney took ship early in May.[2]

[1] Bradford Perkins, *Prologue to War: England and the United States, 1805–1812* (Berkeley, 1961), pp. 274–275, 307–312. This chapter is drawn so much from Perkins' work that complete citation would be unwieldy; his pp. 261–437 exhaustively treat its subject.

[2] *Niles' Weekly Register*, Nov. 16, 1811. Pinkney became Attorney General upon his return; John J. Dolan, "William Pinkney," *DAB*.

Young Foster had been in America as secretary to the self-important Anthony Merry. He thought of the United States as a clownish nation, crude but amusing, and his instructions were drafted by men contemptuous of America and convinced of American cowardice. The Prince Regent had friends who sympathized with American grievances, but they were few and he was too self-indulgent to be influential. Foster was to offer nothing concrete but reparation for the *Chesapeake* outrage, no longer a hot issue. He was to preach to the Americans that British trade regulation was the minimum needed for imperial security; neutrals might have been treated even less generously. The necessity was regrettable, but regulation of oceanic trade was the only defense against the complete destruction of British commerce by the Corsican enemy of civilization.[3]

The new Secretary of State, James Monroe, did not begin with anti-British prejudices. He had accepted office, vice the impolitic Robert Smith, with the hope of moderating what he believed was a dangerous tendency to Anglophobia in the administration. Perhaps he yet mourned his stillborn Treaty of 1806, but certainly his governing principle was that a fatal error by the Republicans would extinguish the world's solitary authentic republic. From April till November, 1811, Monroe thought republicide Napoleon the greater danger to republicanism, and hoped for amity with Britain. By autumn he reluctantly concluded the British were implacably hostile. This lean, quick-tempered, popular Virginian remembered the War for Independence approvingly. After months of Foster's patronizing little homilies, Monroe, in his mind, again declared war on the British Empire.[4]

If the extralegal orders in council were defenses against the Napoleonic decrees, and if the decrees were revoked, the orders should be canceled. But Britain denied the decrees were revoked. French policy *was* deliberately opaque, but Chargé Jonathan Russell reported from Paris that American ships in France were now inconvenienced only by "municipal" laws.[5] Monroe hinted

[3] Margaret K. Latimer (ed.), "Sir Augustus J. Foster in Maryland," *Maryland Hist. Mag.*, XLVII (1952), 283–296; Bernard Mayo (ed.), "Instructions to the British Ministers to the United States, 1791–1812," American Historical Association *Annual Report 1936* (3 vols., Washington, 1941), III, 310–319.

[4] William Penn Cresson, *James Monroe* (Chapel Hill, 1946), pp. 244–258.

[5] *Niles' Weekly Register*, Nov. 9, 1811.

that the orders could be withdrawn as ambiguously as Napoleon's revocation, and Madison added that Britain could preserve dignity by silently ceasing enforcement. Meanwhile the President released diplomatic correspondence selected to kindle congressional resentment. But Foster was deaf, except to Federalists who advised him to stand fast and expose administrative futility. In January, 1812, he still reported the United States as bluffing; the ministry should be firm. Nevertheless, an authentic concession was made by London in April, 1812. Britain would drop its monopolistic licensing of continental commerce if America would resume trade relations. It came too late.

In his attempts to fire up the Congress to vote military preparations, Madison blundered on stage into a true *opéra bouffe*. The British agent, John Henry, had toured New England seeking secessionists, his out-of-pocket expenses paid by the governor general of Lower Canada. His report was valueless to the British, who declined to pay his expected bonus. Henry, in revenge, had himself introduced around Washington by an adventurer calling himself the "Count de Crillon," and sold his report to the President for the whole secret-service fund—$50,000. Henry's papers, given to the Congress and the press, proved only that a British spy had been at work. Madison appears gullible, the implications were criminal, and enduring resentment among New England Federalists was predictable. The operetta had a jolly climax. After "Crillon" gratified Henry by deeding him a nonexistent château in France, the adventurer persuaded Monroe to give him a $5,000 draft on Joel Barlow in Paris. Next, a visiting foreigner exposed "Crillon" as a petty Gascon embezzler named Soubiran, who was wanted by the French police; when the bogus count challenged his discreditor to a duel, the challenge was declined because "Crillon" lacked enough rank to be shot at.[6]

Although the controlled French press insisted that France and the

---

[6] Chilton Williamson, *Vermont in Quandary, 1763–1825* (Montpelier, Vt., 1949), pp. 260–263, describes Henry's earlier activities as a secret agent; Samuel Eliot Morison, "The Henry-Crillon Affair of 1812," in his *By Land and by Sea* (New York, 1953), pp. 265–286, is the definitive account; the Henry letters and a brazen statement by "Crillon" were printed in *American State Papers: Documents Legislative and Executive* (38 vols., Washington, 1832–61): *Foreign Relations*, III, 545–557 (hereafter cited as *ASP*), and the letters and Foster's denial of any connection with them in *Niles' Weekly Register*, Mar. 14, 21, 1812.

United States were friends, and vigorously exploited Anglo-American frictions, Napoleon's policies were deliberately contradictory. It was awkward to be harsh with Britain and to ignore Napoleon's gall, but the United States told the French that America was dissatisfied with France's conduct, and told the British that Napoleon had behaved properly. The most conscientious of American editors got around the embarrassment by saying one could not learn the truth about French decrees *"while his majesty's ships captured all vessels bound to France. . . ."*[7] The pendulum of French maritime administration vibrated rapidly. In 1810 Napoleon had cashiered King Louis Bonaparte of Holland for admitting American flags to Dutch harbors. In 1811 the French chief admitted American merchants, but drafted prohibitorily detailed and rigorous rules about cargoes and required that every maritime case pass over his own desk. Napoleon's interest in these otherwise petty affairs reflected his concern with affairs in the Baltic, a concern which was to lead him to Moscow and to Waterloo.[8]

To keep the Baltic open, the Royal Navy had ruthlessly destroyed Danish sea power in 1807, but the Danes took to building gunboats in quantity. Their mosquitolike annoyance forced small British cruisers to hunt in pairs. Much worse than the Danes was the weather. The last convoys of 1811 lost more seamen from foul weather than were lost in any one sea battle of the wars from 1793 to 1815, but the fleet kept the trade moving. In 1809, 126 American carriers appeared in the Schleswig area, and later Americans found trade with Sweden and Russia practically free, if they could escape French and allied privateers. Because practically all ships in the trade used forged papers, openly hawked in London, Napoleon's privateers seized every merchant they could catch. Because every ship sailed under his enemy's control, Napoleon, for once, had international law on his side.[9]

The activity of Baltic maritime traffic was increasing in direct

<hr/>

[7] *Niles' Weekly Register,* Oct. 12, 1811.

[8] Ulane Bonnel, *La France, les États-Unis, et la Guerre de Course, 1797–1815* (Paris, 1961), pp. 283–286, 289–292.

[9] A. N. Ryan, "The Defence of British Trade with the Baltic, 1808–1813," *English Historical Review,* LXXIV (1959), 443–466, writes a useful correction of perspective for any who tend to think of the friction as only Anglo-Franco-American, and reinforces it with his "The Melancholy Fate of the Baltic Ships in 1811," *Mariner's Mirror,* L (1964), 123–124; Bonnel, *Guerre de Course,* pp. 289, 289 n.–290 n., 292–295; *Niles' Weekly Register,* Oct. 26, 1811.

proportion to the cooling of Czar Alexander's regard for Napoleon. The decision to cast off Napoleon's restraints was the Czar's own, for, from late 1809, the Czar opposed the Continental System and he persuaded Sweden to his views in 1810. Russia's principal exports were grain and naval stores, a trade necessary to the prosperity of the nobility, while French trade merely drained Russian gold for gewgaws. The Czar put domestic concerns first, a brave choice when Napoleon was at his zenith.

Meanwhile, Minister Joel Barlow arrived in Paris in September, 1811. Russell's optimistic report of the treatment of neutrals in French ports had given Madison his excuse to pretend the decrees had been repealed. Barlow was to get reparations for seizures, an end to paper blockades, and softer trade regulations. Sisyphus had no harder task. Almost immediately, the French sent raiders to sea to sink or burn any neutrals which had touched at enemy ports. Napoleon simultaneously suggested negotiating a commercial treaty, but when Barlow presented a prospectus for an ideal treaty it was ignored. His incoming diplomatic pouch was twice rifled; French officials politely suggested that his couriers smuggle his mail. Monroe finally told Barlow to see Napoleon personally. Thus far, Barlow's only accomplishment had been to elicit and to rush the dubious Saint-Cloud Decree to London.[10] His commercial proposals died because the parties could find no way around the fact that many British ships carried skillfully forged papers identifying them as American vessels, and because Napoleon knew American profits from French trade would go to pay British creditors.

The French permitted Barlow to travel to Napoleon, then in Russia. Off he went, jolting in a coach through starving, freezing country strewn with material and human wreckage, into the vortex of the Napoleonic death storm. He never met Napoleon, who was fleeing from his disaster, but wrote a swan song on the Emperor's enormities, and died of pleurisy near Cracow, in December, 1812. The Anglo-American war canceled any reason for France to negotiate; Barlow could not have succeeded.[11]

By spring, 1812, American leaders had formulated their view of

[10] Irving Brant, "Joel Barlow, Madison's Stubborn Minister," *William and Mary Quarterly*, Third Series, XV (1958), 441–443.
[11] *Ibid.*, XV, 443–451; James Woodress, *A Yankee's Odyssey: The Life of Joel Barlow* (Philadelphia, 1958), pp. 302–305, and Barlow, "Advice to a Raven in Russia," *ibid.*, pp. 338–339.

international relations: Britain's unilateral revision of international law permitted the policing of neutral ships, barred from France by paper blockades, *"in the Chesapeake bay,"*[12] and Royal Navy officers in American waters misbehaved with barely credible arrogance. The opposition press blamed the administration's Francophilia, but from 1807 to 1812 the French seized more American ships than the British did. From the first year of Napoleon's consulate through 1813, French privateers took exactly 600 ships legally flying the Stars and Stripes, of which 274 were judged to be wholly good prizes, but only 34 of them were taken in 1811 and 1812. The French could no longer lay hands on them because they were in the protective custody of the British Empire, and this state of protective custody is the important key to understanding American sensitivity. It was doubly objectionable. First, by a licensing system it allowed Britain to direct trade in the manner most profitable to Britain and least profitable to competitors; some Englishmen said the system damaged America more than it damaged France. Second, and perhaps more important psychologically, Britannia's rule over the waves reduced every neutral exporter to dependency, putting a vast, heterogeneous fleet at the disposal of British economic strategy and making all neutral exporting nations tributaries of Great Britain. Not seizures but the one-sided rewriting of law and the mercantile subordination to British interest were what hurt.[13]

Equally reprehended were the British searches of private ships to impress alleged Englishmen into the Royal Navy, although some apologists said the peddling of fake naturalization papers justified the British policy, and Rufus King wondered whether naturalization took priority over natal allegiance. Jefferson once meditated a deal with Britain: the United States to prohibit the employment of English seamen, Britain to give up impressing from American ships, but Gallatin dissuaded him. Contemporaries argued about the

---

[12] *Niles' Weekly Register*, April 25, 1812.

[13] J. E. Smith, *One Hundred Years of Hartford's Courant* (New Haven, 1949), pp. 89–94, summarizes the attitudes of a typical Federal organ; Bonnel, *Guerre de Course*, pp. 317–318, 373, 384–385, 391, 403–404, 407; British custodial care of the Baltic trade is described in Ryan, "Defence of British Trade," pp. 463–466; A. L. Burt, *The United States, Great Britain, and British North America from the Revolution to the Establishment of Peace after the War of 1812* (New Haven, 1940), pp. 207–224, well analyzes the demotion of the United States to a dependency.

number of Americans affected, as though the impressment of a handful would be tolerable, the impressment of a multitude intolerable. Madison claimed 6,057 cases. The Massachusetts Federalists, by the methodology of the dirigible political legislative inquiry, which, in political controversy, almost invariably finds what the majority wishes to find, annihilated his figures. But the minimum number *can* be calculated. The British government surrendered nearly 2,000 before the war, and released 1,800 after the war—therefore 3,800 is the lowest possible number. The law and equity of the matter seem clear enough. The British denied expatriation on the feudal principle that birth imposed an obligation to serve the Prince, while, at the same time, they inconsistently nullified their own principle by naturalizing aliens. Whether, as argued, naturalization was contractual, or expatriation was a natural right, the United States, despite its weakness, despite fluctuating interest, never compromised its view of the principle. John Quincy Adams would have liked to declare war on that issue alone, and believed the mere declaration would cause the abolition of the practice.[14]

The international turbulence of the twenty years before the War of 1812 refashioned the foreign trade of the United States. Combat and economic coercions closed some markets, while Latin American ports opened a precarious and relatively small trade. After 1809, the British Isles received a decreasing flow of American grain and flour, but Wellington's army depended almost entirely for its bread on great cargoes of American wheat, a change of the direction of trade rather than of its volume. The intermittent interruptions of imports and exports—imports declined about 52 per cent from 1801 to 1811—and the high prices of smuggled goods promoted industrialization of the Northeast and encouraged cottage industries everywhere. Many newly invented devices to manufacture goods in short

14 King to Porter, Dec. 10, 1811, Charles R. King (ed.), *The Life and Correspondence of Rufus King* (6 vols., New York, 1894–1900), V, 254; Gallatin to Jefferson, April 13, 1807, Henry Adams (ed.), *The Writings of Albert Gallatin* (3 vols., Philadelphia, 1879), I, 332–333; Jefferson to Maury, Aug. 25, 1812, Andrew Lipscomb *et al.* (eds.), *The Writings of Thomas Jefferson* (20 vols., Washington, 1903–4), XIII, 145; J. F. Zimmerman, *Impressment of American Seamen* (New York, 1925), pp. 156–186, gives an account of the controversy from 1807 to 1812, mostly from American sources. Zimmerman quotes John Quincy Adams, whose remarks may also be found in J. Q. Adams to Eustis, Oct. 26, 1811, W. C. Ford (ed.), *The Writings of John Quincy Adams* (7 vols., New York, 1913–17), IV, 262.

supply, particularly textiles, were priced within the reach of prosperous farmers or of neighborhood groups. Southerners showed their false hopes of industrialization by the organization of a South Carolina textile company and of a Virginia association to promote manufactures. The shortage and overpricing of imports had quickened interest in self-sufficiency.[15]

Some of those most heated against British maritime policy lived far from tidewater and knew little of seafaring, but to call this paradox ignores the fact that the owners of common carriers do not usually own their cargoes, and care little about their direction so long as they move. While the proportion of British-owned tonnage entering American ports from 1807 through 1811 declined from 77 per cent to 30 per cent, the beneficiaries were the grumbling congenitally anti-Republican shipowners of America. Under successive federal inhibitions the illegal trade of Boston became too large to extinguish, and Boston's registered tonnage in 1810 was its largest yet. Yankee skippers anchored in Black Sea ports, while others warmed their bones with Archangel vodka, perhaps toasting the decade's doubling of ocean freight rates. At home, farmers muttered. Although wheat exports were highest in 1811, farm prices had fallen 15 per cent since 1801. Raw materials were required to go to England, and demand depended on British ability (or willingness) to re-export. Napoleon had allegedly revoked his decrees; therefore Britain's management of the American economy seemed to be the sole remaining cause of rural depression. Mississippi Valley exports determined the margin between grubby subsistence and some degree of luxury. Southerners, more dependent on exports, felt sharper economic pangs. There now seemed a choice of but two remedies: manufacturing, or forcible assertion of independent access to markets. The happiness of the docile carriers was irrelevant to farmers.[16] Britain was believed to be "supplying her

[15] Harold F. Peterson, *Argentina and the United States, 1810–1860* (New York, 1964), pp. 13–21, 84; W. Freeman Galpin, "The American Grain Trade to the Spanish Peninsula, 1810–1814," *American Historical Review,* XXVIII (1922–23), 24–26; Rolla Milton Tryon, *Household Manufactures in the United States, 1640–1860* (Chicago, 1917), pp. 276–280.

[16] Benjamin W. Labaree, *Patriots and Partisans: The Merchants of Newburyport, 1764–1815* (Cambridge, Mass., 1962), pp. 168–180, inclines one to conclude that the uncertainties of the future annoyed the carriers more than the realities of the present; J. D. Forbes, "Boston Smuggling, 1807–1815," *American Neptune,* X (1950), 149–152; Samuel Eliot Morison, *The Maritime History of Massa-*

enemy with the very articles with which she refuses to permit
neutrals to supply."[17] There was no stark distress in America, but
foreign direction of American enterprise provoked jealousy and a
sense of outraged honor.[18]

II

The Eleventh Congress (1809–11) appears to have chosen deliberately to temporize, which gave it the superficial appearance of an
addled parliament. The Twelfth Congress, elected 1810, moved
slowly but decisively. In its proportion of new members, its average
age, its legislative experience, and the issues on which individual
members were elected, it differed little from the Eleventh. But the
House had an impatient element which caucused and elected ex-
Senator Henry Clay as the first Speaker to be masterful with rules,
gavel, and personality. Clay, who could be a friendly persuader or a
stump shouter, weighted key committees with his fellow antitemporizers. The Senate, although Federalists thought it superior, receded
in importance. In addition to Kentucky's superb political techni-
cian, Clay, the Twelfth Congress's antitemporizers included the
political metaphysician John Calhoun of South Carolina (who read
John Locke's psychology at age thirteen), the greatly promising,
impressive, and cultivated William Lowndes of Charleston, and
others who, in 1811 and 1812, became what were called "war hawks":
Langdon Cheves and David R. Williams of South Carolina, Felix
Grundy of Tennessee, Richard M. Johnson of Kentucky, and Peter
B. Porter of New York. Their collective mood was prophetically

---

chusetts, 1783–1860 (Boston, 1941), pp. 193–195; very useful economic tables are
printed in Curtis P. Nettels, The Emergence of a National Economy, 1775–1815
(New York, 1962), pp. 389–393; Burt, U.S., Great Britain, and British North
America, pp. 306–308; Reginald Horsman, The Causes of the War of 1812 (Philadelphia, 1962), pp. 175–177; Margaret K. Latimer, "South Carolina—A Protagonist of the War of 1812," American Historical Review, LXI (1955–56), 914–929
(South Carolina exported more of its own produce per capita than any other
state); George R. Taylor, "Agrarian Discontent in the Mississippi Valley Preced-
ing the War of 1812," Journal of Political Economy, XXXIX (1931), 471–505.

17 William Milnor of Pennsylvania, in Debates and Proceedings in the
Congress of the United States (42 vols., Washington, 1834–56), 11th Congress,
2nd Session, p. 906 (hereafter cited as Annals).

18 Edward Channing, A History of the United States (6 vols., New York,
1905–25), IV, 421–422, displays an unexpected insensitivity toward the majority
agrarian interest when he writes that "A shrewd ruler" would let the prosperity
of the shipping and industrial sectors of the economy outweigh "the niceties of
international law. . . ."

stated in 1810, when Clay indignantly complained of British naval arrogance.[19] Only a quarter of the Congress was Federalist. Honestly skeptical of the resolution of the dominant Republicans, the Federalists felt safe in going along with them, while waiting for Clay and company to expose themselves as mere gasbags. They did not correctly evaluate the strength of the feeling that Britain, with American collaborators, was sapping American agriculture and dishonoring American nationality.

Months before the Twelfth Congress met, British naval haughtiness outraged the country and American valor inspired the nation. After trade with France was reopened, the coast was again infested with British cruisers. Secretary of the Navy Paul Hamilton told his officers to endure no abuse. In the spring of 1811, Commodore John Rodgers, in *President,* fell in with His Majesty's sloop-of-war *Little Belt.* Except that there was a twilight exhibition of incredibly bad gunnery which allowed the far weaker British ship to survive, what happened is not very clear, because each commander's report essentially contradicted the other's, and each Navy's court applauded its own captain. But most Americans trusted Rodgers, added a tally against British infamy, thought *Chesapeake* avenged, and felt pleasantly stimulated.[20]

Soon after the convening of the Twelfth Congress came the Battle of Tippecanoe, in Indiana Territory, fought on November 7, 1811. Broadly viewed, it was one of the many clashes of irreconcilable cultures in which volatile braves and determined Long Knives sought one another's blood. The United States was tepidly committed to civilize the Indians, but its inept Indian program was stingily financed, and frontiersmen were callous and land hungry. East of the Mississippi there were about seventy thousand Indians, about ten thousand of them living in an inflexible and primitive society in the Old Northwest. Unprotected against criminals, dependent for weapons, debauched with alcohol, deprived of land by

[19] A. Bigelow to M. Bigelow, June 7, 1812, "Letters of Abijah Bigelow, Member of Congress, to His Wife, 1810–1815," American Antiquarian Society, *Proceedings,* New Series, XL (1930), 338; the whole collection, pp. 305–406, mirrors Federalist phantasms. Clay to Rodney, Aug. 6, 1810, James F. Hopkins (ed.), *The Papers of Henry Clay* (10 vols., Lexington, Ky., 1959–), I, 481.

[20] *Niles' Weekly Register,* Sept. 21, 28, 1811, reprints the U.S. Navy court findings and the British contradictions; the papers sent to the Congress, including the records of the Navy's inquiry, are printed in *ASP: Foreign Relations,* III, 471–499.

unfamiliar procedures, their sporadic reprisals usually failed because of hopeless disunion. A rankling grievance was the cession of land by sedentary village chiefs for gifts and pensions, although Indian concepts required unanimous consent of the tribes concerned. The whites said Indians could make binding treaties, but treated them as racially inferior and blamed Indian resentments on British provocateurs. Shortly after 1800 a remarkable leader emerged, the peerless Shawnee, Tecumseh, born in present Ohio. Tecumseh never accepted coexistence, but cultivated the warrior chiefs and denounced the village chiefs, whom he regarded with justification as corrupted Indian-land jobbers. About 1806 he decided to found a confederacy against further white expansion, and his half-brother, called the Prophet, began preaching an Indian Puritanism. Contemporaries unite in praise of Tecumseh's character, bravery, and intelligence, although it was his flashier brother who first captured the popular imagination. The Prophet preached divinely ordained separatism, asceticism, and independence. His disciples became militantly antiwhite, although less keen on the whiskyless, primeval life. Skeptical whites, including Governor William Henry Harrison of Indiana, thought him a British agent, and saw with foreboding the building of Prophet's Town, Indiana, in 1808, at the confluence of the Tippecanoe and Wabash rivers (hence the name given to the battle: Tippecanoe). Tecumseh and the Prophet were not British pawns; Fort Malden, across from Detroit, fed thousands of hungry Indian visitors but gave them neither ammunition nor promises.[21]

In 1810, at Vincennes, Tecumseh questioned Harrison about white men's land titles. Harrison threatened their enforcement by arms if necessary. Deadlock and alarms followed. Tecumseh's white-containment league was taking shape, and he went south to try to enlist new nations. Harrison expected war when Tecumseh returned from recruiting, and decided to disperse the concentration at Prophet's Town (Tippecanoe), by persuasion if possible. He

21 Practically everything needed for an understanding of the events leading to and following from the Battle of Tippecanoe is assembled in Carl F. Klinck (ed.), *Tecumseh, Fact and Fiction in Early Records* (Englewood Cliffs, N.J., 1961), the editorial notes of which constitute a bibliography of the Indian problems of the day; the standard biographies of the two principal antagonists of the Wabash Valley are Glenn Tucker, *Tecumseh, Vision of Glory* (Indianapolis, 1956), and Dorothy Burne Goebel, *William Henry Harrison, A Political Biography* (Indianapolis, 1926), and the same author, same subject, in *DAB*.

marched a mixed force up the Wabash to the village. About six hundred Indians attacked his camp in the night. Harrison's troops beat them off, inflicted about three dozen casualties, dispersed the survivors, burned the settlement, destroyed its food, and withdrew, claiming a victory.[22]

All through 1811, American patience ebbed. *Little Belt*, Foster's frustrating circumlocutions, the Battle of Tippecanoe—all made tempers fragile. Because of Napoleon's transparent equivocations, a readjustment of British policy would have restored amity, but the obtuse ministry made no overture. Instead, the British were blamed for the Tippecanoe episode, fatally timed to coincide with a meeting of the new Congress. Tippecanoe was widely accepted as proof of an Anglo-Indian conspiracy, much more dangerous than a mere Indian confederation. To editor Hezekiah Niles of the newly founded *Weekly Register,* "patience ceased to be a virtue."[23] On the assumption that the British had given all possible aid to the Indians, the affair nourished overconfidence and caused Americans to underrate the British.[24]

To be sure, the House Republicans were not yet united. There were half a dozen or so doctrinaire Quids who were convinced that a war would be but the application of the code duello to international relations. Uninformed on Foster's talks, they hoped for Madison's help in preventing war. Another small fraction was congenitally anti-British, with closed minds and negligible influence. There was also a group of medicine-men Republicans who hoped that vague menaces and Anglophobic incantations could be used to frighten Britain into good behavior without a showdown. About half of the representatives were still open to persuasion. Their persuasion was undertaken by the remainder, the so-called war hawks, not a monolithic body, although their divisions were generally on naval policy: whether the Navy was useless or should be strengthened. These antitemporizers numbered about sixty. Their private papers show no reckless bellicosity; rather, they were

[22] Gayle Thornbrough (ed.), *The Correspondence of John Badollet and Albert Gallatin* (Indianapolis, 1963), shows Harrison through the eyes of an enemy, Badollet; H. B. Cushman, *History of the Choctaw, Chickasaw, and Natchez Indians* (Stillwater, Okla., 1962), pp. 244–260; Hull to Secretary of War, June 15, 1811, H. A. Cruikshank (ed.), *Documents Relating to the Invasion of Canada and the Surrender of Detroit, 1812* (Ottawa, 1912), pp. 1–3.
[23] *Niles' Weekly Register,* Dec. 7, 1811, Mar. 7, 1812.
[24] Harrison to Scott, Dec. 2, 1811, *ibid.,* Dec. 28, 1811.

sensitive to the hazards of their policy. Perhaps they have received most attention from posterity because *Niles' Weekly Register,* already warlike, gave them most space. The few Federalists believed the Republicans would never declare war, and prepared to support war measures to show up Republican insincerity. When they learned the antitemporizers were in dead earnest, they recoiled so actively that they were suspect as a British party.[25]

The gamut of attitudes may be seen in the comments of respected contemporaries. Josiah Quincy regretted that his fellow Federalists gave little reason to be trusted. Democratic George Logan opposed the war, wrote of "demagogues," and praised Jay's Treaty, which he had formerly detested.[26] Jefferson reluctantly concluded that it was war or submission. Monroe wrote to an intimate friend that he had done all he could for peace, but the British were immovable. Of course, it was the President's opinion that mattered most; no Congress has ever declared war except on request of the President. Madison's message to the new Congress satisfied the antitemporizers that there would be action, but it was no rouser. Rather, in Bradford Perkins' words, it "fell upon the surface of a rising tide and was borne with it."[27] It has even been said that Madison bought re-election in 1812 by yielding to war-hawk extortion in the House[28] and to the anti-Madisonian Republicans of the Senate, led by Samuel Smith of Maryland and named the "Invisibles" by Nathaniel Macon.[29] The President, the story goes, was prodded into war by an anonymous piece in the *National Intelligencer,* attributed to Clay. But the essay was written by Monroe, quite possibly in collaboration with Madison.[30] Madison, on his own,

25 Wilfred E. Binkley, *American Political Parties, Their Natural History* (2nd ed., New York, 1951), pp. 91–93; Norman K. Risjord, "The War Hawks and the War of 1812," *Indiana Magazine of History,* LX (1964), 155–158; Reginald Horsman, "Who Were the War Hawks?" *ibid.,* pp. 121–136; Roger H. Brown, "The War Hawks of 1812: An Historical Myth," *ibid.,* pp. 137–151.

26 Frederick B. Tolles, *George Logan of Philadelphia* (New York, 1953), pp. 296–297.

27 Perkins, *Prologue,* p. 299.

28 Wilfred E. Binkley, *President and Congress* (New York, 1947), pp. 56–58, states this as fact.

29 John S. Pancake, "The 'Invisibles': A Chapter in the Opposition to President Madison," *Journal of Southern History,* XXI (1955), 17–37; Macon to Nicholson, Jan. 28, 1811, Nicholson Papers, Library of Congress.

30 Irving Brant, *James Madison: The President, 1809–1812* (Indianapolis, 1956), pp. 434–436.

decided for war not earlier than November, 1811, not later than April, 1812.[31]

Shortly after the Congress convened, Felix Grundy of the House Committee on Foreign Relations recorded that war would be recommended in good time and the military strengthened, all with executive approval.[32] Receiving House resolutions to invigorate the Army, the Senate proposed to raise the House figure of ten thousand new regular troops to twenty-five thousand. Some in the House were for trusting Canadians to rally to the United States flag, but Clay defended the larger figure, arguing that security could hardly rely "upon the treason of the Canadian people,"[33] and Madison signed the Army Bill, with the Senate's changes, in January, 1812. Despite—or because of?—the lustrous lessons of British sea power, when the administration asked for more ships in 1811, the Congress merely rejuvenated the old ones and stockpiled materials. Antinavalism was an established Republican principle, and, besides, a building program might invite a pre-emptive British attack. Federalists supported building, but unintelligently; they proposed only harbor defense and commerce destruction, while the Republicans in the Congress wished forces large enough to disturb Britain, small enough to cost nothing. Gallatin's cost projections almost killed preparations, but the Congress finally authorized borrowing $11 million and doubling the tariffs. Grundy wished war first, taxes second, fearing there would be taxes first, peace second. Studying the finance bill passed in March, one could believe the United States was blustering, and war improbable. The President's constitutional theory and his position as a creation of the caucus restrained him from putting pressure on the Congress. After a taciturn winter he suggested an embargo (signed April 4, 1812), to let American shipping get home and give time for the warship *Hornet* to bring the latest news from Europe—adding privately that war

[31] Madison's Third Annual Message, November 5, 1811, delivered to a Congress convened early for the purpose, reported the failure of diplomacy, urged further measures for military preparedness, and closed with a statement of his "deep sense of the crisis." The President's secret message of April 1, 1812, in a mere twoscore words asked for a sixty-day embargo immediately. Such an embargo would safeguard the merchant fleet on the eve of war. J. D. Richardson (ed.), *A Compilation of the Messages and Papers of the Presidents* (20 vols., Washington, 1897–1917), II, 476–481, 484.

[32] Grundy to Jackson, Nov. 28, 1811, John Spencer Bassett (ed.), *Correspondence of Andrew Jackson* (7 vols., Washington, 1926–35), I, 208.

[33] *Niles' Weekly Register*, Jan. 4, 1812.

would probably follow. The Senate extended the embargo's length, which seemed the usual temporizing, and neither the public nor the British were told the embargo was the tocsin of war.[34] Foster correctly believed Madison wished peace, but Foster underestimated its price. The Federalists, few and uninformed, had no policy. The nation was placid, with no noisy bellicosity or firm opposition.

Just as the English acted in ignorance of American domestic political reality, the Americans acted in ignorance of Britain's internal stresses, which had made the ministry behave emotionally, as if besieged. At the end of May, Foster still said British maritime policy was necessary,[35] but British conduct seemed intended "not to distress an enemy but to destroy a rival."[36] We know the wind was hauling around, but Hezekiah Niles called peacemaking "labor without hope."[37] From 1803 to 1812, the British Foreign Office showed contempt for the United States, most recklessly by sending second-rate diplomatists to Washington. Foster, who was one of them, did not notice the stiffened sullenness around him, and the American chargé in London, Jonathan Russell, could not read portents which might have been obvious to an Adams. On the basis of facts and surmises available in Washington, the prospect of Britannia backing water could not be imagined.

In January, Robert Stewart, Viscount Castlereagh, succeeded Wellesley in the Foreign Office, and, in May, a lunatic assassinated Spencer Perceval, leader of the ministry. In the reshuffle, American affairs were let slide for weeks. The new ministry, formed by Robert Jenkinson, Earl of Liverpool, had serious economic problems. Beginning late in 1810, a depression, accompanied by poor harvests, had brought unemployment, higher taxes, higher prices, bread riots, and riots against job-destroying machinery. The war effort did not falter, but there was acute discomfort. In fact, Britain suffered less from hunger than from swollen inventories. The Continental System had begun to be effective, and exports to the Continent fell a third from 1809 to 1811, while the policy of the

---

34 Harold and Margaret Sprout, *The Rise of American Naval Power, 1776–1918* (rev. ed., Princeton, 1944), pp. 62–72; Grundy to Jackson, Feb. 12, 1812, *Correspondence of Jackson*, I, 216; Brant, *Madison, President*, pp. 426–431.

35 Perkins, *Prologue*, pp. 1–31, ably summarizes the British siege psychosis; Foster to Monroe, May 30, 1812, *ASP: Foreign Relations*, III, 454–457.

36 Clay, *Annals*, 12th Congress, 1st Session, pp. 599–601.

37 *Niles' Weekly Register*, May 30, 1812.

United States reduced exports to America by seven-eighths. Old hands denied that the government's American policy hurt business, blaming instead the exportation of gold to buy things which could be made at home. Their trumpetings sounded like defenses of the Navigation Act of 1696. Against the doctrinal purity of West Indian nabobs, traders to Spain, superannuated theorists, and shipowners, the manufacturers began to entertain heretical doubts of the sacred Old Colonial System: better to move the merchandise than to preserve the economic dogmas. *The Edinburgh Review* of February, 1812, printed a political and legal attack saying the policy toward America was illegal, its goal worthless, and, by further shrinking the channels of trade, the results of a war with America would be baleful. There was nothing of love in all of this, but only rational self-interest. It was a controversy of shipowners and doctrinaire mercantilists versus distressed industrialists. The question was not of yielding to the United States; the industrialists were rallying against the common carriers and the squires, contesting the control of the country's economic policy. In the Parliament, all old abuses and shortcomings were well ventilated. Using the dubious Saint-Cloud Decree to save face, Castlereagh rose in June to say the orders would be suspended. They were lifted on June 23, a decision unknown in Washington until August. To anticipate, the Americans, by then at war, ignored the olive branch because it had a string attached: suspension was for one year only and, comically enough, continuance depended on Napoleon's good conduct. But happy, overoptimistic, unprophetic Britons immediately consigned nearly $20 million of cargoes to America, and oblivion.[38]

The awaited dispatches from Europe came in *Hornet* on May 22 in a badly composed statement which *meant* to blame the orders in council on French policy, and to give Napoleon a plausible reason to speak more clearly, but *said* that Napoleon gulled the Americans and the orders would stick. Madison concluded the orders were

[38] The Earl of Liverpool had been Baron Hawkesbury during Jefferson's first term, when the Anglo-American *rapprochement* had been in flower. Mancur Olson, Jr., *The Economics of the Wartime Shortage* (Durham, N.C., 1963), pp. 60–72; *Niles' Weekly Register*, Oct. 19, 1811; *Edinburgh Review*, XIX (1811–12), 290–317; Paul A. Varg, *Foreign Policies of the Founding Fathers* (East Lansing, Mich., 1963), pp. 293–297; *Cobbett's Parliamentary Debates*, XXI (1812), 1092–1164, XXIII (1812), 486–537; Castlereagh's part of the dialogue is printed, *ibid.*, pp. 537–548; Castlereagh to Foster, June 17, 1812, Mayo (ed.), "Instructions to Ministers," pp. 381–383.

perpetual and began to draft a war message. He believed American ships in France were treated better, but he knew Napoleon purposely gave Britain every provocation to enforce the orders. With cold calculation, Madison would have signed articles of partnership with either tiger or shark if either earned it. Neither did.[39] Randolph tried to forestall the President on May 29 with a resolution that war would be "inexpedient," but, harassed by Speaker Clay's rule that he speak to the point, lost, 37–72.[40] The war message of June 1 recited the grievances—impressment, Indian incitement, paper blockades, hovering in American waters, and rejection of overtures—and concluded that Britain was in "a state of war against the United States."[41] The message was wrong on the Indian question, but it was straightforward, and its errors were honest errors attributable to an American bias not especially reprehensible in a President of the United States. Impressment received first attention because it was most heinous. After Trafalgar, foreign sea power was no threat to British survival, and Britain could not even put forward what John Milton earlier called "necessity, the tyrant's plea." The Congress considered the message in executive session, but its decision was predictable. Randolph spoke most floridly against war, but offered only the alternative of endurance.[42] Monroe appears to have written the report[43] on which the House declared war, 79–49 (June 4), and the Senate concurred, 19–13 (June 17). Support was far from unanimous, but it was closer to unanimity than the measures of 1798, which may have been closer than those of 1776.

Analysts of the House vote have called it a western expansionists' war, but twenty-four aye voters lived on or very near tidewater. A scrutiny of eleven roll calls on war measures in the First Session of the Twelfth Congress provokes doubt that the declaration of war was expansionist or directed chiefly against the Indian menace. Pennsylvania and South Carolina had no wilderness or Indian

39 Madison to Jefferson, May 25, 1812, Gaillard Hunt (ed.), *The Writings of James Madison* (9 vols., New York, 1900–1910), VIII, 190; Brant, *Madison, President,* pp. 478–483.
40 *Papers of Clay,* I, 660–663.
41 *Messages and Papers,* II, 484–490.
42 William Cabell Bruce, *John Randolph of Roanoke, 1773–1833* (2 vols., New York, 1922), I, 370–385, summarizes Randolph's fancies and whims from November 1811 to June 1812, with rhetorical illustrations.
43 Dexter Perkins, "James Monroe," *DAB.*

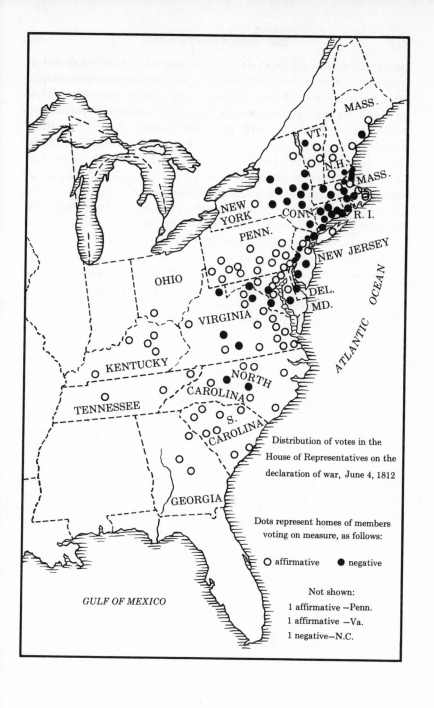

MASS.

VT.

N.H.

MASS.

NEW YORK

CONN.

R. I.

PENN.

NEW JERSEY

OHIO

DEL.

MD.

VIRGINIA

ATLANTIC OCEAN

KENTUCKY

NORTH

TENNESSEE

CAROLINA

S. CAROLINA

GEORGIA

Distribution of votes in the
House of Representatives on the
declaration of war, June 4, 1812

Dots represent homes of members
voting on measure, as follows:

○ affirmative ● negative

Not shown:
1 affirmative —Penn.
1 affirmative —Va.
1 negative—N.C.

GULF OF MEXICO

problems, yet, in support of war measures, they ranked fourth and fifth of the seventeen state delegations. Every western motive should have operated in Ohio, but it ranked only seventh in support of war measures, its lone representative three times voting no on important bills. The pattern seems more intelligible if basic material interests are weighed. Despite lack of district-by-district economic analyses, the states can nevertheless be roughly classed as more interested in farm production for export, or in the carrying trade. Of course, no state was interested in the one to the exclusion of the other. The House delegations representing producers (New Jersey, Delaware, Pennsylvania, Virginia, the Carolinas, Georgia, Ohio, Kentucky, and Tennessee) were 70 per cent for the eleven key war measures, while delegations from common-carrier states (Massachusetts, Rhode Island, Connecticut, New York, and Maryland) were but 46 per cent. On the declaration of war, producer states voted 64–18, freighting states 15–28.[44]

The Federalists now began to express themselves forcibly. Pickering had "no doubt" that Napoleon had bribed the majority, and Samuel Taggart of Massachusetts claimed his colleagues were terrorized into silence. Federalists could have argued that equality of power in Europe was America's best hope and that war was not the best means, but their extravagant rhetoric and their fatuous world views were self-defeating. While arch-Federalists foresaw only disaster, the national mood was not of celebration or mourning but of reserved acceptance. At the suggestion of Gallatin, a leader of the 1790's fight against founding the Navy, Madison sent Commodore Rodgers and Commodore Stephen Decatur to sea to protect homecoming American ships.[45] Ironically, among their first prizes were ships carrying news that Britain had suspended the orders in council.

[44] See map, p. 217, adapted from Warren H. Goodman, "The Origins of the War of 1812," A.M. thesis, Duke University, 1940, with the permission of the author and of the Duke University Department of History; the votes on eleven key issues were tabulated in Horsman, "Who Were the War Hawks?" The categorization of states is my own; Vermont and New Hampshire are omitted as inscrutable.

[45] Pickering to Pennington, July 12, 1812, Henry Adams (ed.), Documents Relating to New-England Federalism, 1800–1815 (Boston, 1877), p. 388; George Henry Haynes (ed.), "Letters of Samuel Taggart, Representative in Congress, 1803–1814," American Antiquarian Society, Proceedings, New Series, XXXIII (1923), p. 405; Gallatin to Madison, June 20 or 21, Hamilton to Rodgers, June 22, 1812, Henry Adams, The Life of Albert Gallatin (New York, 1943), p. 465.

III

The causes of the War of 1812 have been argued ever since late 1811. Contemporary explanations ranged from ultra-Federalist accusations of servility to Napoleon to infra-Republican jubilation at a divine mission to whack the British for their sins. No flaming incident stimulated national wrath on the eve of war. War was voted after seven months of talky domestic controversy. Life did not imitate art. How easy to understand, if *Leopard* had clawed *Chesapeake* in June, 1812—but that outrage had happened five years earlier to the week. Perhaps as many as fifty historians have offered original explanations of the war in the past seventy-five years, and more than a score of those studied its origins exhaustively.[46] The attempts of the United States at economic coercion have drawn economic historians as the magnetic pole draws the needle. Answers *why* have been found in international law, ethnology, geography, social psychology, economics, and in combinations of these sciences. Any definitive collection of alleged causes must include at least the following: violation of neutral seafaring rights, impressment of alien sailors, incitement of Indians, hunger for Florida—Canada, depressing effects of British policy on farm prices, competition for furs, anti-British propaganda by fugitives from British law, hope of promoting manufactures, endemic Anglophobia, national humiliation, and symptomatic Manifest Destiny. The list could be longer, and, by reversing the question to "Why was the War of 1812 not avoided?" one can collect mirror images of causes.

It would be conventional to assign quasi-arithmetical values to causes and to deterrents, name the weightiest ones as decisive, and get on to the war. But group decisions are not made so mechanically. One perceptive antimechanist has suggested, instead, the conceptual scheme of a ring of cause comprising indentifiable segments. When all segments fall into place to complete the ring, action follows.[47] After much experience of practical politics, one can, alternatively, advance the heap-of-motives theory—people deciding to act or not to act pile motives at random, and look at the heap for a kind of pattern which has the appearance of a defensible

46 The cause collector need begin no earlier than the excellent survey by Warren H. Goodman, "The Origins of the War of 1812, A Survey of Changing Interpretations," *Mississippi Valley Historical Review*, XXVIII (1941–42), 171–186.
47 Varg, *Foreign Policies*, p. 274.

reason for choice. The heap may be made of facts, prejudices, rumors, opinions, and feelings, and all of these are often mixed together.

The maritime grievances so heavily emphasized in President Madison's war message have been suspected as a false front by some, and it is true that public indignation at impressment was not outspoken immediately before the war, but there could have been no war without either the orders in council or impressment. The arguments of Madison's dry memoir of 1806 were just as sturdy in 1812. British courts followed the old sea law pretty well until after 1803, and then began to introduce more finely drawn distinctions. Practically every useful refinement was directed against the traffic of the United States. Apart from the prudence of declaring war, the legal position of the United States was unassailable, and it is certain that Great Britain would not have been easygoing if the situations were reversed.[48]

Using the President's indictment of the British for promoting Tecumseh's activities, and the unanimity of trans-Appalachian war votes in the House, theories developed from 1911 to 1925 that the war was naked aggression to get more land, or that southern and western congressmen united to quiet the Indians and to enlarge the nation in order to secure its boundaries; the ambitions of the "madmen of the West" were to increase the land area and to control the fur trade.[49] L. M. Hacker, who then thought John Randolph both wise and sane, said the Westerners were unaffected by oceanic concerns but needed more tillable land. Apparently he had not yet heard the corn rustle or smelled a pen of feeder hogs; the corn and hog belt was empty in 1812. Julius W. Pratt demolished his view with a survey of yet unbroken sod, a proper emphasis on the Indian terrors, and an evaluation of John Randolph's testimony. He suggested—with more restraint than some of his disciples—a bargain between West and South to annex Canada

---

[48] Alfred Thayer Mahan, *Sea Power in Its Relation to the War of 1812* (2 vols., Boston, 1905), I, 1–41, makes maritime grievances *the* causes of the war; Burt, *The U.S., Great Britain, and British North America*, pp. 225–316, restores maritime grievances as worthy of serious and more sophisticated consideration; Stuart Gerry Brown, *The First Republicans* (Syracuse, 1954), considers the international law of the situation.

[49] The pejorative description of the western politicos is that of Dice R. Anderson, "The Insurgents of 1811," American Historical Association, *Annual Report 1911* (2 vols., Washington, 1913), I, 167–176.

and Florida, but cautioned that he presented only one set of causes. A Canadian has theorized that the Americans went about acquiring Canada awkwardly, because Upper Canada was receiving a stream of United States citizens who might have brought Ontario into the union peaceably. The hypothesis of a union of West and South to get Canada and Florida is intriguing, but rests on equivocal evidence, such as a speech by Andrew Jackson's reckless friend Felix Grundy of Tennessee, who would have set out to conquer Canada with a handful of switches. In December, 1811, he spoke in the House on the advantages of annexing both Florida and Canada, but he referred to the settlement of Louisiana in such a way that he seemed to be declaiming to the sullen New England opponents of Louisiana statehood, offering Canada as bait to New England, not to frontiersmen for plow, trap line, or Indian peace. Expansionism was surely a craze in the lower Mississippi Valley, but the historian of the West Florida controversy did not find it necessary to blend his subject into the stream of affairs leading to the War of 1812.[50]

A referendum would be needed to find a true sectional pattern, if one existed. Nearest to a referendum was the House vote for war, which showed many anomalies. Massachusetts voted 6–8; five of the six were coastal votes. Vermont's solitary nay came from its most remote district. Half of Pennsylvania *might* be called West; Pennsylvania voted 16–2, and Maryland, hardly western, voted 6–3. All coastal Republicans of Virginia and North Carolina voted aye; their nays were central inland votes. If all Mississippi and St. Lawrence watershed ayes were switched to nays, the House would have been approximately tied, which shows how strongly the eastern seaboard supported the war. The districts south of the Potomac and Ohio rivers provided less than half of the ayes. West and South needed many other votes, and their power, at most, lay in energy and eloquence. One student attributed the war to the agitation of the "Ohio Valley," thus introducing the enigma of Ohio voting. Its House member voted for war; its only senator present voted nay

[50] Louis M. Hacker, "Western Land Hunger and the War of 1812," *Mississippi Valley Historical Review*, X (1923–24), 379–395; Julius W. Pratt, "Western Aims in the War of 1812," *ibid.*, XII (1925–26), 36–50, and *The Expansionists of 1812* (New York, 1925), especially pp. 12–14; C. P. Stacey, "The War of 1812 in Canadian History," *Ontario History*, L (1958), 158; Grundy, *Annals*, 12th Congress, 1st Session, pp. 426–427; I. J. Cox, *The West Florida Controversy, 1798–1813* (Baltimore, 1918).

because he feared for the safety of his frontier constituents, a position wholly out of conventional western political character.[51] On the eleven key war measures, its House member was much cooler than his Kentucky colleagues of the same Ohio drainage system, and cooler than the delegations of half a dozen states, including littoral New Hampshire and South Carolina.

In the House debates of 1811–12, John Randolph canvassed all unworthy motives of the majority, but spoke most mockingly and memorably of the lust for Canada. Certainly, ever since the *Chesapeake* trouble, American congressmen had been speaking of reprisal against Canada. Where could the nearly fleetless nation most hurt the ruler of the waves? Hezekiah Niles, Calhoun, and others answered: conquest of Canada would cut off naval stores and food from the British sugar islands, it would close a vent of manufactures, it would neutralize bases from which royal ships vexed the coast, it would demolish a nest of spies, and it would quiet the Indians.[52] Americans, ignoring their own criminally provocative behavior toward Indians, believed that Britain, using Canadian posts as advanced bases, was wholly to blame for Indian malevolence.

Pain no doubt stimulates to action at least as strongly as hope. George R. Taylor, in 1931, stepped beyond Pratt's position, adding that the West was economically overstretched, had been in depression since 1808, blamed its condition on foreign regulation of its exports, and urged war as the remedy. Taylor corrected narrower views that the Westerners knew nothing of the significance of oceans, and his theory has been nationalized, so to speak, by a finding that South Carolina was suffering commercially and blamed the same causes.[53]

Two questions present themselves: the quality of leadership and the immunity of France. British leaders were assertively self-righteous about their battle against the Enemy of Mankind. The Republicans relied too much on the logic of affairs; they talked loud

---

[51] Goodman, "Origins," pp. 176–177; Christopher B. Coleman, "The Ohio Valley in the Preliminaries of the War of 1812," *Mississippi Valley Historical Review*, VII (1920–21), 39–50; Alfred B. Sears, *Thomas Worthington: Father of Ohio Statehood* (Columbus, 1958), pp. 160–170.

[52] *Niles' Weekly Register*, May 30, 1812; Calhoun on Canada, Dec. 12, 1811, Mar. 10, May 6, 1812, Robert L. Meriwether (ed.), *The Papers of John Calhoun* (3 vols., Columbia, S.C., 1959–), I, 82, 92–93, 104–105.

[53] Taylor, "Agrarian Discontent"; Latimer, "South Carolina."

and carried twigs. Madison did not take the public into his confidence, and lost the publicity which would have killed the domestic theory of Francophiliac servility and the British view that America was all bluster and no blows. A foreign chancellery could reasonably doubt the resolve of the Americans to enforce a treaty, distrust their police of their own trade, and question their ability to keep a contract on impressment. Shortsighted British officials, encouraged by Federalist polemics, believed the United States would never act vigorously, and overestimated the price the Americans would pay for peace.[54] Why not a war with France? A triangular war would be patently absurd; France could not be attacked except in unthinkable alliance with Britain. France appeared to have abandoned its maritime abuses. Clay wrote, "As to France we have no complaint . . . but of the past. Of England we have to complain in all the tenses."[55] British behavior had been arrogant but overt; France's had been evasive, dishonest, but never arrogant.[56] Britain commanded the Americans as one commands lackeys. Napoleon appeared to treat the Americans as sovereign peers—while picking their pockets on the sly.

Lastly, to the heap of motives must be added the honest convictions of Republicans that Federalism was an infection of the body politic, and that further humiliation of the United States would discredit the grand concept of republicanism which had been in peril since their fathers rejected George III. Some erroneously believed monarchism a danger at home. Others, more realistic, saw the contradictory possibilities of the creation of a centralized oligarchy of merchants and financiers.[57] They cherished the United States as the only true republic in a world of warring kings and tyrants.

Diplomacy had failed. The Americans decided it was useless, and the British never really tried. The mediocre British ministers in Washington misunderstood the American toughening, partly because the inexperienced congressional leadership prepared for war

[54] Brant, *James Madison, Commander in Chief* (Indianapolis, 1961), pp. 13–21; "The Causes of the War of 1812," *Canadian Defence Quarterly,* X (1933), 462–464.

[55] *Papers of Clay,* I, 674.

[56] "Causes of the War."

[57] Roger H. Brown, *The Republic in Peril: 1812* (New York, 1964), gives a very satisfying appraisal of subjective causes, focusing on the strong emotional attachment to republicanism.

so ineffectively, and partly because they took Federalist opinion seriously. Madison was too laconic and too confident of the self-enforcing logic of principles, and he was unaware of the growing influence of Englishmen who believed mercantilist dogma a nuisance. Britain slighted American concerns to concentrate on fighting Napoleon.[58] Senior British officials were complacent; their juniors too often were cocky bullies. No nation mindful of its diplomatic fences would have kidnaped 3,800 neutral aliens of one nationality.

The Americans became edgy and irascible. Believing they had earned sovereign standing in the 1780's, they found themselves compelled to cringe under Britannia's menacing trident. They were reluctant to show fight, and wished they could forget the whole business, but the choice seemed only between submission or war. France was no present danger; therefore it was unnecessary to be meek at sea in order to avoid French conquest by land. War came after seven months of big talk and small plans. The obvious theater of operations would be Canada, because it was the accessible target and the base for British subversion of the Indians.[59] On the preposterous assumption that Tippecanoe represented the best the British could do on the frontier, false optimism flourished. Madison decided to ask for war if Britain's intransigence lasted through the First Session of the Twelfth Congress. The Congress came to the same view, not because the election of 1810 showed a war fever, but because men had been changing their minds, helped by the persuasion of antitemporizers who took charge of the House of Representatives in order to stop the degradation which might change the national character. The finally decisive influence in the minds of many congressmen was not where they lived, but what occupation interested their constituents more: production for export, or carrying freight. Soaring ideals and earthy concerns interlocked.

Thus Americans undertook to avoid permanent reduction of their country to the status of a protectorate. The British system made the United States the economic dependent of an imperious patron which even had the effrontery to suggest that the Royal Navy would be pleased to enforce American sea law. Britain's policy made money for American shipowners, but the economically

58 Horsman, *Causes of the War of 1812,* correctly reminds us that the Anglo-American quarrel was but a side effect of the great Anglo-French war.
59 Horsman, "Western War Aims," *Indiana Magazine of History,* LIII (1957), 9–18.

depressed cultivators blamed their troubles on foreign management of trade. Impoverishing republican pockets, shaming republican spirits, British policy revived the Old Colonial System again, without its reciprocity and preferential monopolies. Brooding in Russia, John Quincy Adams put it well: "in this question something besides dollars and cents is concerned . . . and no alternative left but war or the abandonment of our right as an independent nation."[60]

60 J. Q. Adams to A. Adams, Aug. 10, to J. Adams, July 13, 1812, *Writings of J. Q. Adams*, IV, 372, 388.

CHAPTER 11

The War of 1812: The Beginning

THE United States went to war in June, 1812, with long anticipation but much miscalculation.[1] It was the first time the federal government tried to organize for war. The militant Republican leadership was neither frivolous nor reckless, but it was unskilled and inexperienced. Lacking useful experience or wisely guiding allies, the young nation's preparations were poor, but not for lack of serious effort. The goals of the war were not extravagant; indeed to overly optimistic nationalists they seemed easily attainable. Considering population, geography, and Britain's European distractions, one can understand why Hezekiah Niles wrote, "The odds are greatly in our favor."[2] The First Session of the Twelfth Congress (November, 1811, to July, 1812) was busy with war measures. With variable majorities, the Congress passed 109 bills, of which more than thirty were directly military, producing a reassuring bustle of energetic military activity, all reported favorably in the prowar press.[3]

[1] Among the most recent military histories are Francis F. Beirne, *The War of 1812* (New York, 1949); J. Mackay Hitsman, *The Incredible War of 1812* (Toronto, 1965); Patrick C. T. White, *A Nation on Trial: America and the War of 1812* (New York, 1965); Harry L. Coles, *The War of 1812* (Chicago, 1965) the briefest and the best. All military histories of the war seem to lean heavily on Henry Adams, A. T. Mahan, and Theodore Roosevelt.

[2] *Niles' Weekly Register,* April 4, 1812.

[3] *Debates and Proceedings in the Congress of the United States* (42 vols., Washington, 1834–56), 12th Congress, 1st Session, II, 2225–2363 (hereafter cited as *Annals*); for examples of inspiring military miscellanea, the issues of *Niles' Weekly Register* for July, 1812.

The voices of trumpets and drillmasters distracted attention from weaknesses of the Army, which had twenty-four paper regiments, but which enrolled, in reality, fewer than seven thousand men. Most were scattered in petty garrisons, inspected occasionally by the unreliable Brigadier General James Wilkinson. The garrisons were immobilized by Indian hazards and by the shortage of men for the badly designed harbor defenses. Artillery was dispersed, and the sole regiment of dragoons was dismounted. There were half a dozen potential major generals, aged twenty-six to forty-five, but maturity seemed more identifiable than dash, so seven political major generals, aged fifty-five to sixty-two, headed this disarray, of whom but one had commanded a regiment under fire. Recruiting was slow, which may have been a blessing, since the few overworked and underpaid regular field and company officers could not adequately train the four thousand recruits received in 1812. The United States Military Academy had produced a few score engineers, all good, but few had remained in the Army. Britain's Canadian garrison mustered almost five thousand professionals. When the war started, there were several roving companies of mounted United States Rangers screening the frontier against attack from Canada.[4] That was all. This circumstance makes it seem that the Republicans feared their own army more than the enemy's.

The militia was the national reserve. Of a possible 1,200,000 men the militia enrolled 690,000—but the ablest part lived in sulky New England. Some leaders loved the militia because of antimilitarism, others because it was cheap. The militia was praised for republican purity, with little regard for logic or history, but the western militiamen were not soldiers. Undependable and individualistic, they were united in love of country and fear of Indians, but were headed by officers chosen mainly for popularity.[5] They met infrequently, for worthless training, and depended for efficiency on state supervision. Governors, finding units too numerous to inspect, commissioned hosts of bucolic colonels to muster inadequately

---

[4] I am indebted to Bernard Donahoe for the use of a manuscript history of military legislation, 1801–12; Norman W. Caldwell, "The Frontier Army Officer, 1794–1814," *Mid-America*, XXVI (1955), 101–128; Julius W. Pratt, "Fur Trade Strategy and the American Left Flank in the War of 1812." *American Historical Review*, XL (1934–35), 246–254.

[5] Perry LeRoy, *The Weakness of Discipline and Its Consequent Results in the Northwest During the War of 1812* (Columbus, 1958).

armed men who "hollered for water half the time, and whiskey the other. . . ."[6] If laws could do it, the reserve would have been respectable, but laxity, unnoticed in Washington, prevailed.[7] Any squad might provide good companions for hunting deer, but not for stalking animals which could shoot back.

There was not an American in authority who was qualified to evaluate strategy, nor a regular soldier over forty-five who could meet European standards for general officers, as such standards had developed during the Napoleonic Wars. Nobody could identify the able juniors, nobody could create armies, so the country marched to war behind incompetents. Since soldiers fight rarely but hope to eat daily, amateurishness showed up first in supply. The federal Army had never been large enough to need a supply service, hence all was inexpert improvisation. No officers were trained in transportation or purchasing, and civilian agents did the work, always tempted to get much for little, disregarding quality. It has been well said that the Army's price and value were the same—both low. Northwestern armies suffered most, but operations were everywhere handicapped by the hit-or-miss, hand-to-mouth supply method, which cannot be called a system.[8]

As for the Navy, it survived Albert Gallatin's economy drives because of the Barbary Wars. New building appropriations, 1803–7, added but five brigs, four bombs, three schooners, one blockship, and 158 gunboats. The same men who voted for war in June had voted against ten frigates in January. If not prudentially burned on their stocks by British amphibious raiders, these frigates might have been launched into the claws of the British blockading squadrons as early as the last months of 1814, and would surely have been

[6] James Ripley Jacobs, *The Beginnings of the U.S. Army, 1783–1812* (Princeton, 1947), p. 382, quoting C. H. Smith, *Bill Arp's Scrap Book*, p. 236.

[7] James T. Doyle, *The Organizational and Operational Administration of the Ohio Militia in the War of 1812* (Columbus, 1958).

[8] Jacobs, *U.S. Army*, pp. 278–279, 369–386; if James Wilkinson had been disinterested, intelligent, and honest, it should have been possible to find and promote immediately at least several of the following: Jacob Brown, Edmund Pendleton Gaines, William Henry Harrison, Andrew Jackson, Zebulon Montgomery Pike, Winfield Scott, and Zachary Taylor, all born between 1767 and 1786; on logistic methods, see Erna Risch, *Quartermaster Support of the Army: A History of the Corps, 1775–1939* (Washington, 1962), pp. 115–180, and Marguerite M. McKee, "Service of Supply in the War of 1812," *Quartermaster Review*, VI (Jan., 1927), 6–19; (Mar., 1927), 45–55; (May, 1927), 27–39; VII (Sept., 1927), 23–32.

corked-up, captured, or sunk. Jefferson saw it correctly: when all other navies together equaled the Royal Navy, a new American fleet could tip the balance. After Trafalgar, a lonely, microscopic American fleet would have been gold cast into the sea and might have suffered a Trafalgarlike catastrophe with fatal consequences to morale, even to survival as a republic. To lose the whole basket of eggs in a few hours could have had effects quite different from the hit-and-run raids that were to annoy the Atlantic coast. Commerce-raiding brigs might have been useful until exterminated in about a year, but commerce raiding has been tested in the laboratory. Civil War Confederate chasers probably diverted ten times their tonnage of men-of-war, but, if they achieved anything tactically, did no more than prolong their war a little by delaying some amphibious operations. The strategic place to spend treasure was the Great Lakes.[9] If the talent dissipated on the high seas had been diverted to the Great Lakes, the War of 1812 might be remembered as glorious.

Unlike the Army, the Navy had found good officers. They learned the best naval practices during the war with France, and tasted combat with the Barbary pirates. Thus the nation entered war with men qualified for admirals' flags but no fleet, and men for armies but incapable generals.

The apologists for James Madison, Commander in Chief, usually indict the major generals, but he nominated them. He had the advice of Dr. William Eustis of Massachusetts, his Secretary of War, whose horizon was limited to practical precinct politics. Eustis' successor, John Armstrong of New York, was equally narrow and added qualities of deceit and intrigue, but it really made little difference. The Secretary of War had but a handful of clerks and no single commander of the troops. This structure[10] reflected the anti-militarist ethic of a people who dreamed of virtuous Cincinnati

---

9 K. Jack Bauer, "Naval Shipbuilding Programs, 1794–1860," *Military Affairs,* XXIX (1965) , 29–33; Harold and Margaret Sprout, *The Rise of American Naval Power, 1776–1918* (Princeton, 1944) , pp. 62–72, who view this generation's naval theories with horror; Jefferson to John Adams, May 27, 1813, Lester Cappon (ed.) , *The Adams-Jefferson Letters* (2 vols., Chapel Hill, 1959) , II, 324; Coles, *War of 1812,* pp. 99–106, plumps for raider brigs as the correct alternative; Adams to Jefferson, June 11, 1813, *Adams-Jefferson Letters,* II, 329, wrote of the importance of the Lakes long before Perry's victory.

10 Leonard D. White, *The Jeffersonians, A Study in Administrative History, 1801–1829* (New York, 1951) , pp. 211–237, analyzes the administrative structure carefully.

repelling corrupt foreign mercenaries and their savage native auxiliaries. The nation, not the administration, set the tone.

In war, of course, money is the public muscle. Unhappily, the
Treasury's muscle tone was poor. Gallatin, Secretary of the Treasury from 1801 to 1813, a man of many virtues, had cut spending,
reduced the debt, lightened the tax load, balanced the budget, and
by such homely cracker-barrel economics nearly destroyed the country by leaving its financial system unprepared for the crucible of
war. When Madison took the oath of office in 1809, he had a
Treasury surplus of $9.5 million, and, by 1810, Gallatin had paid
for Louisiana and had reduced the national debt by $27.5 million.
As a matter of pious agrarian doctrine, the country relied only on
the tariff and on public-land sales for revenue. By pure coincidence
the Napoleonic Wars made foreign trade boom, and the public
income swell, thus making Gallatin's policy work. If war could be
avoided the debt could soon be paid, and if there ever was a war it
could then be financed without great pain, but the several statutory
stoppages of foreign commerce were hard on public finance. As long
as peace was official, Gallatin persisted in his single-minded policy,
with the result that when war came he had a theory ready, but no
system.[11]

Worse, the country went to war without a central bank, although
that was not Gallatin's fault. Recharter of the Bank of the United
States was proposed in 1809, and Gallatin argued for the Bank as a
safe public depository, a clearinghouse, a tax collector, and a
potentially generous lender to the government. Recharter died
without a vote in the Senate, in 1810, which gave opponents of the
Bank time to rally. The Bank had been technically efficient, but
had let its political fences decay. It was aloof, it neglected to
cultivate Westerners, and it had an imbalance of Federalists in its
employ. Businessmen who later felt its loss keenly did not exert
themselves vigorously to defend the Bank. Besides the doctrinaire
opposition, poor public relations, and tactless lobbying, new motives for contention appeared: allegations of British dominance
(although no foreign shareowner could vote his stock), hunger to
get into state banking, envy of the state governments' bonuses from
state-bank charters, and mortal enmity toward Gallatin in the

[11] Alexander Balinky, *Albert Gallatin: Fiscal Theories and Policies* (New
Brunswick, 1958), pp. 128–163.

hearts of the men in the Senate called the "Invisibles," led by Samuel Smith, who had Maryland banking ambitions.[12] In January, 1811, the House voted to postpone recharter indefinitely, 65–64; the Senate vote to recharter was 17–17. Disgruntled Vice-President George Clinton, reflecting on the low party status of Clintons, voted nay.

The prospects of unhampered state banking probably weighed heavily in the decision. State banks numbered three in 1790 and 117 in 1811, capitalized at $42.6 million. When the Bank of the United States died, twenty-one state banks received its federal patronage, mostly at ports of entry, handy to the collectors' offices.[13] The death of the Bank was seen by myopic Republicans as a defeat of the British interest, and Nathaniel Macon, whose chief delight was opposition, said the supporters of the Bank had been ". . . on the federal side of the question."[14] It was hardly the interest of the United States to export $7 million in gold to liquidate the shares of foreign stockholders, thus losing a massive sum of specie on the eve of war. The number of state banks jumped to 143 in 1812, including South Carolina's and Virginia's wholly owned central banks, capitalized with state assets. State-bank reserves might be thought adequate today, but they were not proportionately distributed among banks or regions.[15] The system was too cumbersome for normal finance, and was a frail mechanism for public borrowing.

Gallatin, his influence much diminished, asked the Congress to pay the reckoning, and found many warlike members angered and dismayed by his cost estimates. Gallatin thought war expenses should be met by loans and regular expenses by imposts, but war

[12] James O. Wettereau, "New Light on the First Bank of the United States," *Pennsylvania Magazine of History and Biography,* LXI (1937), 263–285; Philip J. Green, "William H. Crawford and the Bank of the United States," *Georgia Historical Quarterly,* XXIII (1939), 337–350; Raymond Walters, Jr., *Albert Gallatin: Jeffersonian Financier and Diplomat* (New York, 1957), pp. 237–240.

[13] J. Van Fenstermaker, "The Statistics of American Commercial Banking, 1782–1818," *Journal of Economic History,* XXV (1965), 400–413; Davis Rich Dewey, *Financial History of the United States* (12th ed., New York, 1936), pp. 126–128.

[14] Macon to Nicholson, Jan. 28, 1811, Joseph Hopper Nicholson Papers, Library of Congress, in which Macon appears to be the first to use the word "Invisibles" to describe the impalpable faction of Republican Gallatin-haters in the Senate, led by Samuel Smith of Maryland and Michael Leib of Pennsylvania.

[15] Van Fernstermaker, "American Commercial Banking."

reduced the imposts so much that excises were needed. Men moved only by logic would have enacted excises, but the True Republican Faith excluded excise taxation. Instead, the Secretary had authority in 1811 to borrow $11 million, but received only $6 million, of which opulent New England contributed less than a million. The issue of notes in smaller denominations and at higher yields in 1812 helped little, and the Congress ignored other and more detailed advice from Gallatin.[16] There was even a spirited attempt to reopen trade with Britain for sake of the customs duties, which lost only by Speaker Henry Clay's casting vote. Hezekiah Niles, estimating Britain's public expenditures at $25 per capita, wrote that American reluctance to pay $2 per capita was "contemptible."[17] Truly, talent for leadership was scarce, but the predilections of the American people would have made leadership difficult for philosopher-kings.

In Canada the war was instantly a matter of the gravest concern, but overseas the British did not immediately take the new American war seriously. *The Gentleman's Magazine* tucked the first news into a column of miscellaneous paragraphs from small or remote places. The following month it printed the opposition invective of John Randolph, and suggested that New England would not be dangerous.[18] Months later, the Prince Regent perfunctorily denounced the "abetter of French tyranny,"[19] but the perseverance of America, some humiliating naval defeats, and American threats to Canada gradually swung British opinion (excepting *The Edinburgh Review*) behind the ministry.

Except for merchants in Montreal who saw possible expansion of the fur trade,[20] the news of war chilled the Canadians, and, as Major General Isaac Brock wrote, "Most of the people here lost all confidence."[21] In print and in legislative assemblies there had been much talk of loyalty, but within weeks regular troops shot down

16 Balinky, *Gallatin*, pp. 164–212, well describes the dilemma and the efforts to avoid it; Walters, *Gallatin*, pp. 246–250, 254–256; Balinky, "Gallatin's Theory of War Finance," *William and Mary Quarterly*, Third Series, XVI (1959) , 73–82.

17 *Niles' Weekly Register,* June 27, 1812.

18 *The Gentleman's Magazine*, CXII (July, 1812) , 77; (Aug. 1812) , 179–180) .

19 *Ibid.*, CXIII (Jan., 1813) , 71.

20 Fred Landon, *Western Ontario and the American Frontier* (Toronto, 1941) , pp. 26–28.

21 Quoted in C. P. Stacey, "The War of 1812 in Canadian History," *Ontario History*, L. (1958) , 156.

insurrectionaries who were actively resisting the levy of militia in the neighborhood of Montreal. In Upper Canada, civil government had to be subordinated to the military by repeated proclamations of martial law, because of civilian demoralization and because of the grave shortage of every military supply.[22] On the face of it, the Canadians had reason for defeatism. In population they were outnumbered 25:1, in militia 9:1, in regulars 7:5. Britain was almost wholly preoccupied with Napoleon and, except for cultivating the western Indians, had made no special Canadian preparations. Canada's survival depended on the exertions of officers already on the ground.

The battle of Tippecanoe (1811) had proved the fallibility of the Prophet and had destroyed Tecumseh's hope of building a strong antiwhite confederacy which could operate independently. Now the Indians could be no more than second-class barbarian auxiliaries of the British Empire. Before Tippecanoe, British officers discouraged Indian hostilities toward the United States. After Tippecanoe, they recommended more partisanship by Indian agents and the issue of ammunition. In the spring of 1812, Tecumseh had a growing number of hungry followers, who converged on Fort Malden for rations. In sum, Governor William Henry Harrison had driven the Indians to King George's side, in an almost inevitable alliance, but not because Tecumseh loved Englishmen; of the two white groups, he simply detested the Americans more. British tact and food had preserved the Indians for British use, and, by June, 1812, there were hundreds of Indians at Fort Malden, ready to fight but needing British aid.[23]

The British would have to take Detroit and Michilimackinac to keep the respect of the Indians. Otherwise, Canadian strategy must be defensive. Any offensive operations would fall to the Royal Navy, which hoped to block the Mississippi River and to relieve

22 Lawrence A. H. Smith, "*Le Canadien* and the British Constitution, 1806–1810," *Canadian Historical Review*, XXXVIII (1957), 93–108; William M. Weekes, "The War of 1812: Civil Authority and Martial Law in Upper Canada," *Ontario History*, XLVIII (1956), 147–161.

23 Moses Dawson, *Historical Narrative of the Civil and Military Services of Major-General William Henry Harrison* (Cincinnati, 1824), pp. 266–269; Brock to Taylor, Mar. 4, 1811, to Prevost, Dec. 2, 1811, in Carl F. Klinck (ed.), *Tecumseh: Fact and Fiction in Early Records* (Englewood Cliffs, N.J., 1961), pp. 112–113, 116–120; J. C. Dent, *Canadian Portrait Gallery* (Toronto, 1880), *ibid.*, p. 139; Reginald Horsman, "British Indian Policy in the Northwest, 1807–1812," *Mississippi Valley Historical Review*, XLV (1958), 63–66.

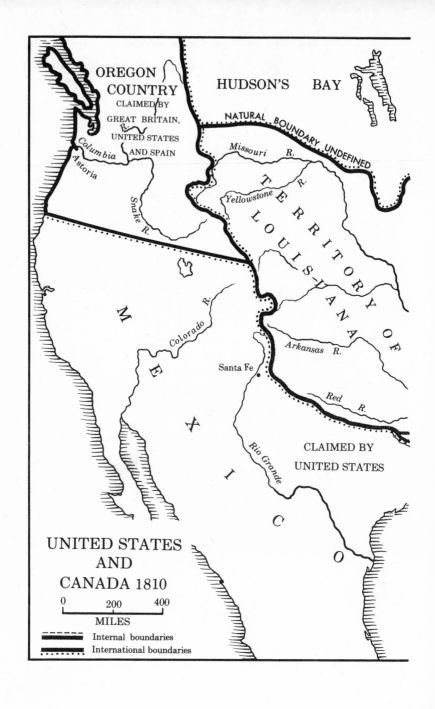

OREGON
COUNTRY
CLAIMED BY
GREAT BRITAIN,
UNITED STATES
AND SPAIN

HUDSON'S   BAY

NATURAL   BOUNDARY   UNDEFINED

Columbia

Astoria

Snake R.

Missouri   R.

Yellowstone   R.

T
E
R
R
I
T
O
R
Y

O
F

L
O
U
I
S
I
A
N
A

Arkansas   R.

Santa Fe

Red   R.

M
E
X
I
C
O

Colorado   R.

Rio Grande

CLAIMED BY
UNITED STATES

UNITED STATES
AND
CANADA 1810

0   200   400
MILES

- - - - -   Internal boundaries
· · · · ·   International boundaries

COMPANY

BOUNDARY NOT MARKED

L. SUPERIOR

MICH.

ILLINOIS TERRITORY

Mississippi R.

TERRITORY OF LOUISIANA

L. MICHIGAN

MICH. TERR.

L. HURON

Michillimackinac

Detroit

L. ERIE

Ottawa R.

UPPER CANADA

York

Toronto

ONTARIO L.

Cleveland

Wheeling

Dayton

Cincinnati

INDIANA TERRITORY

Fort Wayne

St. Louis

Lexington

KENTUCKY

TENNESSEE

Nashville

MISSISSIPPI TERRITORY

SEIZED BY U.S. 1810

Mobile

TERR. OF ORLEANS

Sabine R.

New Orleans

W. FLA.

GEORGIA

SOUTH CAROLINA

Columbia

Savannah

EAST FLORIDA

GULF OF MEXICO

St. Lawrence R.

Gulf of St. Lawr.

AMER. CLAIM

NEW BRUNSWICK

Quebec

LOWER CANADA

Montreal

Plattsburg

Sacketts Harbor

Oswego

NEW YORK

Buffalo

Albany

Erie

PENN.

Pittsburgh

Cumberland

Baltimore

Annapolis

Washington

DEL.

MD.

VIRGINIA

Richmond

Raleigh

NORTH CAROLINA

Wilmington

Cape Fear

Charleston

BRITISH CLAIM

PART OF MASS.

NOVA SCOTIA

N.H.

Vt.

MASS.

Portland

Portsmouth

Boston

Providence

Newport

R.I.

Conn. R.

New York

Philadelphia

NEW JERSEY

ATLANTIC OCEAN

Amelia Is.

St. Augustine

pressure on Canada by diversionary raids on the Atlantic coast. All other resources were needed to defend the jugular vein from Newfoundland to Lake Superior, with but five thousand regulars, unproved militia, and Indian allies.[24]

II

Geography dictated that the natural military theaters be the Lake Erie, Niagara, and Lake Ontario regions, and the Lake Champlain trough. (Something might have been done by the United States farther east, except for New England noncompliance.) The British needed control of the Lakes as much as the Americans, because if the water route were blocked, everything west of that point would be inaccessible. Defense was the job of Governor General Sir George Prevost, who could expect no reinforcements because of British Army commitments against Napoleon in Europe, and Major General Isaac Brock, commander in Upper Canada—Canada west of the Ottawa River—who began early in 1812 to stiffen his militia.[25] Brock was right. The Americans were looking in his direction.

Canada was the place to hurt Britain, but it has been thought the blow should have been against Montreal. However, there were inducements for starting in the West. A victory anywhere on the water line would probably isolate the Indians, thus reducing the Canadian strength to regulars and doubtful militia. The Americans expected help from recent expatriates, and most of them lived in Upper Canada.[26] The apathy of New England and the nationalistic ardor of the West made it preferable to use the western militia where possible. Therefore the prospectus called for Major General William Hull to make a triumphal progress from Detroit to Niagara, overawing the Indians and recruiting from the Upper Canada militia.

The western force of Ohio militia and dragoons, strengthened by the Fourth Infantry Regiment of the regular Army, assembled at

24 St. George to Brock, July 8, 1812, Elliott to Claus, July 15, 1812, in Klinck (ed.), *Tecumseh*, pp. 128–130; Richard K. Murdoch (ed.), "A British Report on West Florida and Louisiana, November, 1812," *Florida Historical Quarterly*, XLIII (1964), 36–51; John K. Mahon, "British Command Decisions in the Northern Campaigns of the War of 1812," *Canadian Historical Review*, XLVI (1965), 219–223, 227.

25 Brock to Upper Canada Legislative Council, Feb. 3, 1812, *Niles' Weekly Register*, Mar. 7, 1812.

26 *Ibid.*, Oct. 5, 1811.

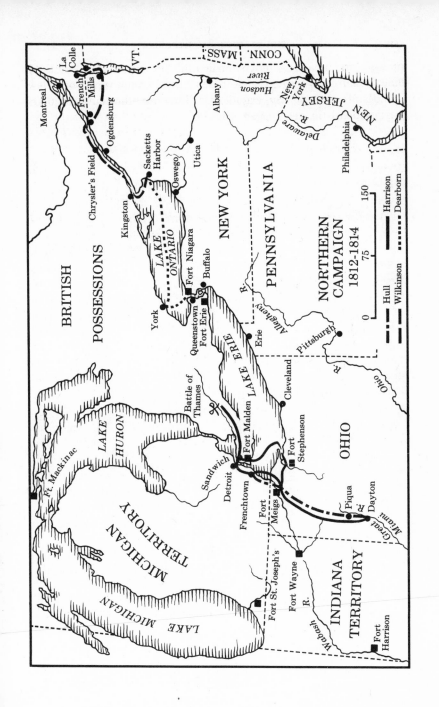

NORTHERN CAMPAIGN
1812-1814

0   75   150

Hull — · — · —
Wilkinson — — —
Harrison ————
Dearborn · · · · · ·

Dayton, 1,600 strong. Hull, although nearing sixty and rusty, showed energy in his early operations. Jumping off for Detroit early in June before the war was declared, his men made good speed despite unceasing rains, mud, and the need to build a road through Black Swamp to the Maumee River. The British in Canada learned of the declaration of war before Hull did, from a routine letter of John Jacob Astor to Canadian business associates. Hull, still in ignorance, sent a schooner with his baggage and papers to Detroit, and the alerted British captured it below Detroit and learned everything necessary. Once arrived at Detroit, Hull crossed to Canada on July 12, proclaiming mercy or calamity according to the inhabitants' behavior, and enlisted some defecting Canadians, but someone bungled the artillery movement so that the British Fort Malden was left to menace the Americans.

General Brock, on the Niagara frontier, scraped together what force he could and went by water along the north shore of Lake Erie to the Detroit River. Meanwhile Hull had recrossed to Detroit to try to re-establish his untenable line of communications. Brock crossed the river and demanded Hull's surrender, with a hint that his Indians could not be restrained if Detroit were stormed. When Brock moved to attack on August 16, Hull sent out the white flag of surrender and the British had a firm footing in Michigan Territory. Far to the north, Fort Mackinac had been taken by Captain Charles Roberts on July 17, with four or five hundred red and white men from the Saint Joseph Islands below Sault Sainte Marie. Roberts' and Brock's successes convinced the Indians that the British would win.[27]

It would be over simple to say that the intervention of the Indians had been decisive at Detroit, but that was the way it seemed to Hull. Although the small British garrison strengthened the physical defenses of Fort Malden, there were few white Canadians to draw on for man power, and the local officers cosseted the Indians and deferred to Tecumseh. When Hull announced that Canadians fighting alongside Indians would not be allowed to surrender, Tecumseh had sent west for more Indians. Early in August he had persuaded the prestigious Wyandots to rally to the Union Jack, and showed his political acumen by letting himself appear

27 A. L. Burt, The United States, Great Britain, and British North America from the Revolution to the Establishment of Peace after the War of 1812 (New Haven, 1940), pp. 329–331.

subordinate to their warrior chief, Round Head. Tecumseh personally had led the band of braves who proved that Hull's communications could be cut at will (casualties: one Indian, fifty Long Knives), and skirmished in the forests southwest of Detroit in a manner that the redcoats were unable to imitate. He held a thousand or more warriors steady, stopped them from wasting munitions, and kept them sober. His pesky redskins were the first to pursue the harassed Hull when he withdrew from Canadian soil, and Hull blamed their envelopment and rapid increase in numbers for making his situation hopeless and compelling his surrender. The northwestern auxiliaries came at Tecumseh's call, and British control of them relied on Tecumseh's magnetism, perseverance, and intelligence. It is worth adding, parenthetically, that his triumphant braves paddled back to Fort Malden under good discipline when Detroit fell; although Colonel Richard Procter, the local commandant at Fort Malden, and Tecumseh's bronze peers tolerated savage atrocities by excited Indian victors in other places, there was never any barbaric behavior in the presence of either Brock or Tecumseh. Of course we know that even small naval strength could have prevented the Detroit disaster, but the neglect of naval power let the Indians play a very large part.[28]

The bad news from Michigan was compounded by word of massacre near Fort Dearborn on the day before Hull surrendered. Beyond armed help, the garrison evacuated the fort and left its supplies. When the party of soldiers and dependents marched out, the neighboring Indians found the powder and rum destroyed, which may have provoked them to kill about 85 of the 130 whites. Indian Agent William Wells had recently come from Fort Wayne with Indian friends. Wells's head ornamented a pole, while the chiefs divided his heart and ate it raw.[29]

Published clamor against Hull arose immediately, amplified by

28 Procter to Brock, Aug. 11, 1812, in Klinck (ed.), *Tecumseh*, pp. 150–151; William James, *A Full and Correct Account of the Late War between Great Britain and the United States of America* (London, 1818), cited *ibid.*, pp. 158–159; John Richardson, *War of 1812* (Brockville, 1842), quoted *ibid.*, pp. 155–157; Hull to Eustis, Aug. 26, 1812, *ibid.*, pp. 160–161; William Stanley Hatch, *A Chapter of the History of the War of 1812 in the Northwest* (Cincinnati, 1872), quoted *ibid.*, pp. 163–164.

29 Mentor L. Williams (ed.), "John Kinzie's Narrative of the Fort Dearborn Massacre," *Journal of the Illinois State Historical Society*, XLVI (1953), 343–362; John D. Barnhart (ed.), "A New Letter about the Massacre at Fort Dearborn," *Indiana Magazine of History*, XLI (1945), 187–199.

his subordinates, who fed the press invidious commentary: "Eternal infamy," "deplorable and disgraceful,"[30] and verse: "Curst be this wretch—forever curst,/Who has his country's trust betrayed. . . ."[31] Hezekiah Niles linked his name with Benedict Arnold's; the administration was blameless; the fault must be Hull's. Hull *was* guilty of vacillation. He first said he would need naval support, but later believed a strong land force at Detroit would cause the fleeing British to abandon their shipping.[32] Madison accepted his second estimate. But Madison was no Bourbon; he remembered, he learned. Thereafter he understood that "The command of the Lakes . . . ought to have been a fundamental point. . . ."[33] Lacking naval power, Hull could only have reached Niagara from his almost inaccessible base by a lightning dash of the kind best executed by cavalry or modern armor. Moving with conventional sluggishness, he was easily frustrated by the genius of Brock and Tecumseh. Furthermore, the operation was made absolutely impossible by a truce (August 10, 1812) between Prevost and Dearborn, whose job was to attack Montreal. A stroke at Montreal would have required the concentration of all British power in the East. Madison canceled the armistice a fortnight later, but Hull, in effect, had been abandoned by his senior.[34]

Hull arranged the parole of his subordinates, who gratefully began to whip up public feeling against him and showed zeal to get him hanged. Hull's defense was that he was cornered, that is, the Indians were the key. When he was exchanged, a court-martial condemned him to death for cowardice, but Madison pardoned him for his bravery in the previous war. Only biographers of his juniors

---

[30] A Scioto editor and Colonel Lewis Cass in *The National Intelligencer,* Richard C. Knopf (ed.) , *The National Intelligencer Reports the War of 1812 in the Northwest* (Columbus, 1958) , Part One, pp. 160, 161.

[31] Milo M. Quaife (ed.) , *War on the Detroit; the Chronicles of Thomas Verchères de Bourcherville, and, The Capitulation, by an Ohio Volunteer* [James Foster?] (Chicago, 1940) , p. 309.

[32] *Niles' Weekly Register,* Sept. 19, 1812; Hull to Eustis, June 15, 1811, E. A. Cruikshank (ed.) , *Documents Relating to the Invasion of Canada and the Surrender of Detroit, 1812* (Ottawa, 1912) , 1–3; Hull to Eustis, Mar. 6, 1812. *ibid.,* 19–23.

[33] Madison to Dearborn, Oct. 7, 1812, Gaillard Hunt (ed.) , *The Writings of James Madison* (9 vols., New York, 1900–1910) , VIII, 217.

[34] Burt, *The U.S., Great Britain, and British North America,* pp. 325–328; William Wood (ed.) , *Select Documents of the Canadian War of 1812* (4 vols., Toronto, 1920–28) , I, 580–582; White, *Nation on Trial,* pp. 134–137.

now seem to think him guilty of more than mistakes, and the errors of seniors Eustis and Dearborn were grave. The best that can be said for Dearborn's lackluster operations was that the militia of the East had not risen, and he was short of men. Incongruously, Dearborn, whose armistice ignored Hull, presided over Hull's court.[35]

When Hull first marched toward Detroit, Governor Harrison was made a general; and when Hull surrendered, Harrison was told to retake Detroit. However, Fort Wayne's tiny garrison was besieged by Indians waiting for 1,150 redcoats, militia, and Indians who cockily "went off in great style" from Detroit to help.[36] Harrison relieved Fort Wayne, scared off the reinforcements, destroyed neighboring Indian towns, and sent out raiding detachments through December with uniform success. A flag-waving force of four thousand Kentucky militia marched up the Wabash Valley past Fort Harrison (Terre Haute), and then went home because of hardships and self-pity; meanwhile, regular Colonel William Russell dispersed a band of hostiles near present Peoria with professional skill. All Indians farther north sided with Britain and regained control of the Mississippi River above the confluence of the Des Moines. Harrison then settled for a fortified frontier in northern Ohio. An American station at Green Bay was abandoned, but Captain Zachary Taylor beat off an attack on Fort Harrison. At the end of 1812, the left flank ran from St. Louis to Vincennes to Fort Wayne to Sandusky. Nearly half of the Old Northwest was again British.[37]

[35] John G. Van Deusen, "Detroit Campaign of Gen. William Hull," *Michigan Historical Magazine*, XII (1928), 568–583; Hull to Eustis, Aug. 26, 1812, Klinck (ed.), *Tecumseh*, pp. 160–161; Quaife, "General William Hull and His Critics," *Ohio Archaeological and Historical Quarterly*, XLVII (1938), 168–182, makes a convincing case for Hull, as did Van Deusen, "Court Martial of Gen. William Hull," *Michigan Historical Magazine*, XII (1928), 668–694; Madison to Dearborn, Aug. 9, 1812, *Writings of Madison*, VIII, 205–208, shows that Dearborn's thrust at Montreal was to have been synchronized with Hull's operation.

[36] Quaife (ed.), *The John Askin Papers* (2 vols., Detroit, 1928–31), II, 728.

[37] Edgar B. Wesley (ed.), "A Letter from Colonel John Allen," *Ohio Archaeological and Historical Quarterly*, XXXVI (1927), 332–339, and Ashley Brown (ed.), "The Expedition of Colonel John B. Campbell of the 19th U.S. Infantry . . ." Northwest Ohio Historical Society, *Quarterly Bulletin*, VIII (1936), No. 1, pp. 1–6, sample this essentially defensive war of raids by detachments; "The Expeditions of Major General Samuel Hopkins up the Wabash, 1812: The Letters of Captain Robert Hamilton," *Indiana Magazine of History*, XLIII (1947), 393–402; William T. Hagan, *The Sac and Fox Indians* (Norman, Okla.,

It had been much like chess. Brock's move to the stockade at Detroit changed the balance everywhere West, and gave a year's time to build a Canadian defense. Hull's surrender was grand news in the British Foreign Office. Yet—a schooner off Fort Dearborn, a brig at Mackinac, a sloop of war in the Detroit River, and the West could have been held in silent subjection. The United States had the potential advantage on the Great Lakes because thousands of shipwrights were idled by war, and the Lakes were more accessible to the Americans than to the British. Lieutenant Jesse D. Elliott demonstrated how the defense of Canada could be hurt when, early in October, 1812, at Fort Erie, opposite Buffalo, he cut out the brigs *Caledonia* and *Detroit,* irreparably weakening the British. On Lake Ontario, in November, the American commander Isaac Chauncey overestimated inferior British strength and was bluffed out of shooting his way into Kingston Harbor and possibly winning the war, or at least making it possible to overrun everything west of Quebec citadel. The contest for Lake Ontario then degenerated into a shipbuilding race.[38]

A land operation had been planned to secure the Niagara peninsula to make William Hull's work easy. During the summer two American forces gathered on the river, one under Brigadier General Alexander Smyth of the regular Army, the other under Major General Stephen Van Rensselaer, whose commission was of the New York Militia. The concentration was slow because of lack of help from New England. In August, General Dearborn made the armistice with the British which gained him time, but Dearborn's profit was Hull's loss. By the end of the truce, Hull had surrendered and Brock was back at Niagara. When Hull was vanquished, the Niagara operation lost its sole purpose, but Van Rensselaer sent

---

1958), pp. 37–81, well summarizes the war along the upper Mississippi; Louise Phelps Kellogg, *The British Regime in Wisconsin and the Northwest* (Madison, Wis., 1935), pp. 283–292; Pratt, "Fur Trade Strategy," pp. 254–260.

38 W. Kaye Lamb, "Sir Isaac Brock: The Hero of Queenston Heights," in Philip P. Mason, *After Tippecanoe: Some Aspects of the War of 1812* (East Lansing, Mich., 1963), pp. 21–27; the difficulties of keeping track of British vessels on Lake Ontario are explained and remedied by C. P. Stacey, "The Ships of the British Squadron on Lake Ontario, 1812–1814," *Canadian Historical Review*, XXXIV (1953), 311–323; J. Mackay Hitsman, "Alarum on Lake Ontario, Winter, 1812–1813," in Morris Zaslow and Wesley B. Turner (eds.), *The Defended Border: Upper Canada and the War of 1812* (Toronto, 1964), pp. 45–55.

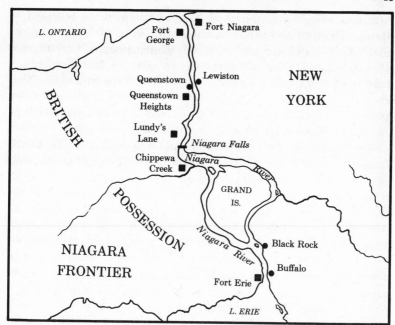

such regulars as he had across the Niagara to Queenston (October 13). During the Battle of Queenston, Smyth, upstream, remained inert, nor would the New York Militia cross their state boundary, but instead watched their Regular Army comrades crushed and captured. Van Rensselaer resigned, to be succeeded by nerveless but bombastic Smyth, who tried an invasion late in November which only added to the British bag of prisoners. He was removed, and thus ended a completely sterile campaign for the United States. From the enemy point of view it was a grand victory which saved Upper Canada, and it added a grace note to the flourish by giving Canada a martyr-hero when victorious Brock fell at Queenston.[39]

Because Montreal was essential to British defense of everything west of there, Dearborn was to have moved into Canada via Lake Champlain, but he spent midsummer fruitlessly recruiting in Mas-

---

[39] Brock to Van Rensselaer, Aug. 25, 1812, in Klinck (ed.), *Tecumseh*, p. 166; Stacey, "The Defence of Upper Canada," in Zaslow and Turner (eds.), *The Defended Border*, pp. 11–20; Brock's successor was Sir Gordon Drummond, whose career is well sketched in Cruikshank, "Sir Gordon Drummond," *ibid.*, pp. 315–320.

sachusetts. Finally organized in November, Dearborn marched to the border, learned his militia would not leave the state, counter-marched to Plattsburg, and went into winter quarters. Gallatin said Dearborn had "done all that was in his power,"[40] which, on reflection, seems rather equivocal. John C. Calhoun thought, "Our executive officers are most incompetent,"[41] but Hezekiah Niles pointed out that almost no American soldiers had seen combat; the Army merely needed experience.[42]

Britain was almost wholly successful in the West, as far as the Pacific. In the Oregon Country, where Spain, Britain, Russia, and the United States competed, John Jacob Astor's post, Astoria, built in 1811, was untenable when war came. Astor's local associates sold it to agents of the North West Company of Canada, arousing the outspoken anger of the company of the British sloop of war *Racoon*, which arrived too late to capture it and thus lost the prize money. As a business venture Astoria was a fiasco, costing sixty lives, two ships, and much money; Astor was unable to get United States naval help to retake it in 1813. In Wisconsin, where British interest was keen, a garrison of sixty United States regulars at Fort Shelby, Prairie du Chien, surrendered to ten times that many attackers in July, 1813, and British artillery kept away vengeful keelboaters thereafter. Fort Madison, more warehouse than citadel, was abandoned in September, 1813. An American expedition destroyed most British property in the Lake Huron region west of the shores of Georgian Bay in 1814, but failed at Fort Mackinac, which remained a threatening outpost for the rest of the war.[43] The fur trade of the Far West was completely demoralized, and the western Indians, understandably, were contemptuous of the Long Knives who could not enforce their claims to suzerainty over vast hunting grounds.

[40] Gallatin to Jefferson, Dec. 18, 1812, Henry Adams, *The Life of Albert Gallatin* (Philadelphia, 1879) , p. 470.

[41] Calhoun to Macbride, Dec. 25, 1812, Robert L. Meriwether (ed.) , *The Papers of John Calhoun* (2 vols., Columbia, S.C., 1959–) , I, 146.

[42] *Niles' Weekly Register*, Feb. 27, 1813.

[43] George Taylor, "Spanish-Russian Rivalry in the Pacific, 1769–1820," *The Americas*, XV (1958–59) , 109–121; Vernon D. Tate (ed.) , "Spanish Documents Relating to the Voyage of the *Racoon* to Astoria and San Francisco," *Hispanic American Historical Review*, XVIII (1938) , 183–191; Stanley T. Williams, *The Life of Washington Irving* (2 vols., New York, 1935) , II, 72–91, explains why parts of Irving's *Astoria* (many editions) are still useful; Horsman, "Wisconsin and the War of 1812," *Wisconsin Magazine of History*, XLVI (1962–63) , 3–6; Alec Richard Gilpin, *The War of 1812 in the Old Northwest* (East Lansing, Mich., 1958) , pp. 242–251.

intervals of one to three minutes, until damage, casualties, and the fatigue of handling the guns caused the enemy to surrender. Shares of the value of prizes stimulated the fighting men: 50 per cent to the government for naval pensions, 32.5 per cent to officers and petty officers, 17.5 per cent to lower enlisted men. In the summer of 1812, about 185 privateers also fitted out. The opening naval operation was a transatlantic sweep by senior Captain John Rodgers, with five ships, which netted eight merchantmen.[51]

In August the superfrigate *Constitution,* Captain Isaac Hull (nephew of the unhappy William), fell in with *Guerrière* about 450 miles southeast of Halifax and took her in a shattering thirty minutes, losing seven killed and seven wounded to the British fifteen killed and sixty-three wounded. The American ship had more guns, and handled them better; she also had about double the crew. Hull sank the splintered *Guerrière.* In October the brig *Wasp* took the evenly matched brig *Frolic* (although a British frigate recaptured *Frolic* and took *Wasp* shortly after); gunnery did it: ten American casualties, ninety British. A week later, off the coast of Africa, superfrigate *United States,* Captain Stephen Decatur, took the frigate *Macedonian* and brought her to New London; gunnery again: American losses a dozen, British more than a hundred. Off Brazil, in December, *Constitution,* Captain William Bainbridge, met the frigate *Java* and battered her so badly she had to be burned; casualties: 34 Americans, 122 British. At the end of 1812 the British had three victories over sloops and brigs in addition to the capture of *Wasp,* but in each case the winner had at least twice as many guns as the loser.

Since Trafalgar the defeat of a British ship had seemed contrary to the laws of nature. News of American sea triumphs brought rapture to Americans and angry surprise to Britons. An American balladeer sang, "We dare their whole navy to come to our coast,"[52] and Hezekiah Niles trumpeted immediate enlargement of the Navy, predicting "IMPRESSMENT WILL CEASE."[53] But *The Gentleman's Magazine* printed the loss of *Macedonian* with accounts of the captures of forty-nine French and American privateers, and tucked

---

[51] *Niles' Weekly Register,* Jan. 9, 1813, Aug. 15, 1812; Charles O. Paullin, "John Rodgers," *DAB.*

[52] George Cary Eggleston (ed.), *American War Ballads and Lyrics* (2 vols., New York, 1889), I, 124.

[53] *Niles' Weekly Register,* Nov. 7, Dec. 12, 1812.

Java's destruction into an account of American troubles, from secession rumors to possible slave insurrections.[54] The British even seemed annoyed at the superdimensions of American frigates, and one suggested that it would be "no disgrace" to avoid combat.[55] As morale building, the American hunts succeeded, but their strategic benefits were trivial. They cost the Royal Navy less than 1 per cent of its strength, while losing 20 per cent of America's, and the shocked Admiralty soon shifted vessels to interdict the American bases of these humiliating adversaries.[56]

54 *The Gentleman's Magazine,* CXIII (Supplement, 1813), 651–654; CXIII (March, 1813), 277–278.
55 Quoted in *Niles' Weekly Register,* Mar. 6, 1813.
56 Howard I. Chapelle, *The History of the American Sailing Navy* (New York, 1949), Chap. IV, gives all the known details of the naval architecture.

CHAPTER 12

The War of 1812: Combat, 1813-15

E NOUGH naval victories were won in 1812 to flame in glory and keep national pride heated amidst the general gloom of disaster. The Second Session of the Twelfth Congress, sobered by the otherwise dismal record, raised the soldiers' pay, enlarged the Regular Army, voted ten vessels for the oceans, and, in March, 1813, created nine military districts as a gesture against Army chaos. John Armstrong, who had become Secretary of War in February, had sense enough to move some sedentary generals to quiet commands. The question of the generals was the most vexing. As Jefferson wrote, "so wretched a succession of generals never before destroyed the fairest expectations of a nation. . . ."[1]

Governor William Henry Harrison of Indiana had become senior officer in the Northwest. He had not waited for the command to seek the man, but sent an intelligent operational plan to Secretary William Eustis while William Hull was failing at Detroit. Kentucky made Harrison a major general of militia, and, with Speaker Henry Clay's help, he soon became major general, U.S.A.[2] One of his juniors said that his "darling passion, next to victory, was the safety

[1] Jefferson to Rush, Mar. 6, 1813, Andrew Lipscomb *et al.* (eds.) , *The Writings of Thomas Jefferson* (20 vols., Washington, 1903–4) , XIII, 226.
[2] W. M. Hoffnagel, *The Road to Fame—W. H. Harrison and National Policy in the Northwest* . . . (Columbus, Ohio, 1959) , pp. 26–31, describes Harrison's self-advancement; Harrison to Eustis, Aug. 10, 1812, Carl F. Klinck (ed.) , *Tecumseh: Fact and Fiction in Early Records* (Englewood Cliffs, N.J., 1961) , pp. 168–170; Clay to Monroe, July 29, 1812, James F. Hopkins (ed.) , *The Papers of Henry Clay* (10 vols., Lexington, Ky., 1959—) , I, 699.

of his men . . . he was naturally very passionate, & sometimes profane. . . ."[3]

Harrison had superseded Brigadier General James Winchester, a Tennessean who was given the left-flank troops, mostly Kentuckians. Late in 1812, Harrison ordered Winchester forward to the Maumee to await reinforcements. His men were underfed, short of whisky, inadequately clothed, and declining toward defeatism. By the first of the year, few thought Detroit could be retaken. Contempt for Winchester was obvious: "At one encampment, they killed a porcupine and skined [sic] it and stretched the Skin over a pole that he used for a particular purpose in the night, and he went and sat down on it, and it like to have ruined him."[4]

Kentucky officers persuaded Winchester that the troops should be used, and suggested rescuing the Americans in Frenchtown on the Raisin River. Winchester, perhaps seeking instant glory, agreed. But British Brigadier Henry Procter with about nine hundred men, half whites, half Indians, surprised Winchester at Frenchtown (January 22, 1813), killed four hundred, and took five hundred prisoners, including Winchester. Only twoscore escaped back to the Maumee. Procter prudently withdrew for fear of Harrison, taking the unwounded prisoners to Detroit, but the wounded left at Frenchtown were massacred or taken in charge by rum-soaked Indians (Tecumseh was absent). Procter became infamous, but has been excused by the Canadian historian Victor Lauriston because this was his first experience as commander of Indian allies.[5]

After the Frenchtown tragedy, Harrison moved to Winchester's

3 Colonel Alexander Bourne characterized Harrison in Neil E. Salsich (ed.), "The Siege of Fort Meigs, Year 1813: An Eye-Witness Account . . ." *Northwest Ohio Quarterly,* XVII (1945), 147, 150.

4 Quoted by Thomas D. Clark, "Kentucky in the Northwest Campaign," Philip P. Mason (ed.), *After Tippecanoe: Some Aspects of the War of 1812* (East Lansing, Mich. 1963), p. 88.

5 Perkins to Meigs, Jan. 28, 1813, Richard C. Knopf (ed.), *Return Jonathan Meigs, Jr., and the War of 1812* (Columbus, Ohio, 1957), p. 225; Procter to Sheaffe, Jan. 26, 1813, Klinck (ed.), *Tecumseh,* pp. 170–171; Vernon L. Beal, "John McDonnell and the Ransoming of American Prisoners after the River Raisin Massacre," *Michigan History,* XXXV (1951), 331–351; a Kentucky soldier wrote that the British knew the prisoners would be massacred, Elias Darnell, ". . . Brigadier General Winchester's Campaign Against the British and Indians and His Defeat at Frenchtown . . ." Historical Society of Northwestern Ohio, *Quarterly Bulletin,* III, No. 1 (1931); Victor Lauriston, "The Case for General Procter," Morris Zaslow and Wesley B. Turner (eds.) *The Defended Border: Upper Canada and the War of 1812* (Toronto, 1964), pp. 123–124.

assigned position at the Maumee rapids in February and built Fort Meigs, garrisoned by about twelve hundred men. Twice it endured siege by Procter, April 27–May 9, and July 21–28. The darkest hour came in May, when Colonel William Dudley brought 866 Kentuckians to break the British lines but was ambushed by Tecumseh's Indians. Of the relievers, 630 were killed, wounded, or captured. About thirty of the prisoners were murdered seriatim by Indians until Tecumseh intervened (Procter was present). A British witness saw the Indian camp decorated with drying human skin, while dogs gorged on human flesh.[6] Fort Meigs survived because Indians disliked sieges; as Tecumseh said, "It is hard to fight people who live like ground-hogs."[7] In the garrison, 270 were casualties. Although the British lost only a few, their campaign failed. Meanwhile, Fort Stephenson had been built at the head of the Sandusky River. United States ships were abuilding at Presque Isle (Erie, Pennsylvania), and the British needed to eliminate Fort Stephenson to get at the shipyards. Early in August they attacked the small garrison of green regulars under youthful Major George Croghan. When the Indians became bored, the British had to quit or assault. They chose to assault and were shot down (August 3). Croghan became the first authentic land-fighting hero of the war.[8]

The difficulties at Detroit, Frenchtown, Fort Meigs, and Fort Stephenson showed that the Lake Erie shores were barely tenable as long as the British moved freely by water. Not only supply but even survival was problematical. Harrison advised static land defense and vigorous naval offense. Commodore Isaac Chauncey properly selected Presque Isle as the base—there was a road from Pittsburgh —and Master Commandant Oliver Hazard Perry superseded Lieutenant Jesse D. Elliott as senior officer on Lake Erie. Although chronically short of veteran seamen, Perry, with constructor Noah Brown, began to build vessels (of which, unluckily, no plans have

[6] Glenn D. Bradley, "Fort Meigs in the War of 1812," Historical Society of Northwestern Ohio, *Bulletin No. 1* (1930), explains the topographical and meteorological circumstances of the campaign; Wilfred Hibbert, "The Recently Discovered Pictorial Map of Fort Meigs and Environs," *ibid.*, VI (1934), 1–4; Major John Richardson in Klinck (ed.), *Tecumseh,* p. 178.

[7] As reported by Richardson, Klinck (ed.), *Tecumseh,* p. 184.

[8] Emmanuel Hallaman, *The British Invasions of Ohio—1813* (Columbus, Ohio, 1958), pp. 1–17; David D. Anderson, "The Battle of Fort Stephenson: The Beginning of the End of the War of 1812 in the Northwest," *Northwest Ohio Quarterly,* XXXII (1961), 81–90.

survived). Perry's opponent was able Captain Robert H. Barclay, who at all costs had to keep the water route open to supply the British western forces. Unlike Perry, Barclay had no road. Barclay's superiors rightly regarded Lake Ontario as strategically more important and gave him a minimum of material help.[9]

Barclay blockaded Perry at Presque Isle but was called away briefly, and Perry steered to Put-in-Bay, where Barclay had to fight to clear the lake so Army supplies could move. They met off Put-in-Bay (September 10) in light airs, with a maximum wind velocity of about three knots. Perry directed his flagship *Lawrence* into a melee, where she took and gave almost incredible punishment, suffering 85 serious casualties of 103 aboard.[10] Perry shifted his flag to the tardy Elliott's ship *Niagara,* and crippled the remainder of Barclay's squadron. He then sent a lapidary signal to Harrison, "We have met the enemy and they are ours. . . ."[11] Perry had won by smashing at close range, because his close-range broadside outweighed the British broadside 900 pounds to 460. He outgunned the British because the Royal Navy could not risk Lake Ontario guns to secure Lake Erie. He had outbuilt an older enemy squadron because the United States could supply materials overland with less difficulty.[12]

Elliott had some explaining to do. In a three-knot breeze, while *Lawrence* became a slaughterhouse, *Niagara* kept her distance for two hours, and there was murmuring in the fleet which led to an inconclusive inquiry in 1815. Elliott tried to destroy Perry's reputation for years thereafter. The boastful and contentious Elliott has never been venerated. It is possible that he delayed closing with the enemy at Put-in-Bay until he thought Perry was dead and the command had devolved on him. As for poor blameless Barclay, who could not have won unless Perry had bungled, he was cleared by an

[9] Robert J. Dodge, "The Struggle for Control of Lake Erie," *ibid.,* XXXVI (1964), 10–30, compares the manning, ships, and armament; John K. Mahon, "British Command Decisions in the Northern Campaigns of the War of 1812," *Canadian Historical Review,* XLVI (1965), 219–237, a very useful study.

[10] Barclay to Yeo, Sept. 6, 1813, Knopf (ed.), *Anecdotes of the Lake Erie Area, War of 1812* (Columbus, Ohio, 1957), p. 37; Charles J. Dutton, *Oliver Hazard Perry* (New York, 1935), pp. 144–170, a vigorous but undocumented narrative.

[11] Quoted in every account, including the standard collection of documents by Charles O. Paullin (ed.), *The Battle of Lake Erie* (Cleveland, 1918), of which pp. 17–37 are especially useful.

[12] C. P. Stacey, "Another Look at the Battle of Lake Erie," *Canadian Historical Review,* XXXIX (1958), 41–51.

inquiry, but the ministry withheld publication to deprive the opposition of evidence of its miscalculations. This hushing-up unintentionally clouded Barclay's record and he died in oblivion.[13]

Perry's victory was deserved and rousing, but not really necessary. If the United States Navy had been strong and pugnacious on Lake Ontario, Erie could have been disregarded. Command of Lake Ontario was within American grasp if all naval energy of the Great Lakes region were spent there, particularly since the British had divided themselves to try to control both lakes in order to support their western Indians.

As soon as Harrison received Perry's laconic signal, he moved against Fort Malden at top speed, carrying his men from Ohio in forty-five-foot landing craft, previously built at Cleveland. Procter's position was indefensible. Tecumseh balked at Procter's proposal to withdraw, but when he had the map explained to him he understood that Harrison could easily land to the eastward and cut them off entirely. So the British shipped their baggage east in small Lake St. Clair vessels which evaded Perry's chase, and the forces withdrew rapidly toward Niagara. The pursuing Americans, many of them mounted, caught Procter at Moraviantown on the Thames River (October 5). Procter had a battalion of regulars, a few horses, some Canadian militia, and perhaps as many as 1,500 impatient Indians under Tecumseh and Indian Agent Matthew Elliott. Harrison had 2,700, of whom about 2,500 were grudge-bearing, ferocious, leather-clad Kentucky militia under their Governor Isaac Shelby. Procter formed his whites in line between a river and a swamp, his Indians in brushy ground to the left. The line was hastily formed, and all of Procter's reserve ammunition had been captured. Harrison showed the audacity which is praised as brilliant when it succeeds—he sent a detachment to skirmish with the Indians while his mounted riflemen dashed into the British front, which collapsed and surrendered in a minute. The Indians spied and sniped for half an hour before melting away.[14]

---

13 *Niles' Weekly Register,* June 3, 1815; Ralph J. Roske and Richard W. Donlevy, "The Perry-Elliott Controversy—A Bitter Footnote to the Battle of Lake Erie," *Northwest Ohio Quarterly,* XXXIV (1962), 111–124; Allan Westcott, "Commodore Jesse D. Elliott: A Stormy Petrel of the Navy," United States Naval Institute, *Proceedings,* LIV (1928), 773–778; Howard H. Peckham, "Commodore Perry's Captive," *Ohio History,* LXXII (1963), 220–227.

14 Howard S. Miller and Jack Alden Clarke, "Ships in the Wilderness: A Note on the Invasion of Canada, 1813," *Ohio History,* LXXI (1962), 124–128; Procter

Harrison had won a great tactical victory. At a cost of twelve dead and nineteen wounded, his men killed and wounded forty-eight uniformed whites and captured 601. Thirty-three dead Indians were found in the bushes. Procter escaped indecorously at a gallop. After a bitter apprenticeship, the American western militia differed from the Indians mostly in complexion and the possession of horses, while the British regulars and Canadian militia lacked skill in forest warfare. Tecumseh met his end, although his body was never found or his slayer positively identified. Politicians muddled the tale in the 1830's, when Colonel Richard Johnson was a rising political moon shining in reflected light from the Battle of the Thames. Friends manufactured a literature to prove he shot Tecumseh; enemies produced contradictory memoirs. No coroner could have certified the cause, place, or time of death, but Johnson's claim elected him Vice-President of the United States. Harrison quit the Army in 1814 because Secretary Armstrong issued orders to officers Harrison thought were his subordinates, and because his relaxed but not dishonest method of acquiring Army supplies was criticized. He received a congressional medal in 1826.[15]

It has often been said that the northwestern campaigns achieved nothing, but they had considerable effects. In sixteen months after the declaration of war, Perry and Harrison had disorganized the principal Indians, making the Northwest safe for agriculture. No Indian buffer state could be erected; the British fur men were to find such dreams illusory. The later clear marking of the international boundary was the final fruit of the northwestern war.

---

took down Tecumseh's vehement argument to show the strong pressure of the Indians to affect his tactical decisions, Benjamin Drake, *Life of Tecumseh* (Cincinnati, 1847), pp. 189–190—Drake interviewed many witnesses and, incidentally, came to the dubious conclusion that a Harrison landing could have been repelled; *Lucubrations of Humphrey Ravelin*, in Klinck (ed.), *Tecumseh*, p. 186; Bullock to Friend, Dec. 6, 1813, *ibid.*, pp. 190–193; Richardson's version of Tecumseh's argument to Procter, *ibid.*, p. 184–185; for the Lake St. Clair chase, Richard P. Joy, "A Bit of Naval History of the Great Lakes," *Michigan History*, XIV (1930), 651–654; the protagonist of Reginald Horsman, *Matthew Elliott, British Indian Agent* (Detroit, 1964), went through the war, pp. 192–219, as an officer of the important Indian Department.

15 Klinck (ed.), *Tecumseh*, collects the necessary documents and early secondary accounts of the battle, pp. 189–199, and the conflicting texts on Tecumseh's death, pp. 200–231; Dorothy Burne Goebel, *William Henry Harrison: A Political Biography* (Indianapolis, 1926), pp. 191–203, and in brief, "William Henry Harrison," *DAB*.

East of the Thames true strategic concepts were not formulated until the summer of 1813, after several scattershot, scatterbrain operations. The opposing naval commanders were Commodore Issac Chauncey, U.S.N., and Commodore Sir James Yeo, R.N. Chauncey chose Sackett's Harbor for his base, while Yeo based his ships on strategically important Kingston, a key bastion since the 1670's. Chauncey had an overland supply route to near Oswego, but from there his materials came by water along the shore of Lake Ontario. Yeo's had to be manhandled up Lachine Rapids. But both were richly supplied in comparison with the forces afloat on Lake Erie.[16] Yeo was particularly overstocked with "bald and Grey" midshipmen and let them seek fame by raiding Chauncey's supply shuttle in small boats—a constant nuisance to Chauncey.[17]

Chauncey found petty schemes attractive. Instead of attacking Kingston, he accepted Dearborn's suggestion to raid York (Toronto) in the opposite direction. In April a strong force sailed to York, carrying troops under Dearborn and Brigadier Zebulon Montgomery Pike. Pike commanded the landing. York, the capital of Upper Canada, held supplies and two incomplete ships. The handful of British regulars offered unintelligent resistance and the York militia did almost nothing, but the promising Pike was killed when the garrison blew up its magazine. The incomplete ships were burned, and the loss of naval stores was one reason why Barclay lost on Lake Erie. The raiders burned the public buildings, and did enough looting to provoke twenty-two damage claims by civilians. The looters worked closely with local collaborators (who also guided a smaller raid in July). The force then took Fort George on the Niagara River (May 27). Meanwhile, Yeo and Sir George Prevost landed at Sackett's Harbor (May 28–29), burned an incomplete ship, and withdrew under fire of some regulars and the spirited local militia commanded by the remarkable Jacob Brown, brigadier of militia. The Sackett's raid recalled Chauncey from his dreamy, idle wandering.[18]

[16] George F. G. Stanley, "Historic Kingston and Its Defence," *Ontario History*, XLVI (1954), 21–29.

[17] M. K. and C. I. A. Ritchie, "A Laker's Log," *American Neptune*, XVII (1957), 203–211, reprint the narrative of one of the competing midshipmen, who made lieutenant.

[18] Charles W. Humphries, "The Capture of York," *Ontario History*, LI (1959), 1–21; Edith G. Firth (ed.), *The Town of York, 1793–1815: A Collection of Documents of Early Toronto* (Toronto, 1962), pp. 315–320.

Leaving Sackett's Harbor exposed was but one of several follies of the eastern theater. Dearborn, in poor health since April, was unstuck by Secretary Armstrong in July. Boston was scandalized that Republican Dearborn was courting a widow Bowdoin, no less, but no one seemed alarmed when the egregious Wilkinson succeeded Dearborn as senior officer in the Northeast. Wilkinson would have to co-operate with Major General Wade Hampton, and each despised the other. Worse, Wilkinson was physically ill and his mind was confused, perhaps manic-depressive; he probably kept going on opium. Giving them adequate man power, Armstrong set Wilkinson and Hampton in motion against Montreal, down the St. Lawrence and the Lake Champlain trough respectively. Wilkinson's sluggish force was roughly treated on a flat plain at Chrysler's Farm (November 11), where the thin red line handled its opponents easily. On the next day Wilkinson learned that Hampton, alarmed by a pickup enemy army, had turned back from Chateaugay (October 26).[19] It had all been an aimless chess opening played by witlings. These unimaginative leaders were to be gone by mid-1814. The only constructive action below Niagara Falls had been the capture of Fort George in May, and its benefits had been indirect. British distractions allowed American vessels above the Falls to join Perry and aid his victory. As for Fort George, the British took it back in December, took Fort Niagara, and burned Buffalo for good measure.

Below Niagara Falls, the British survived the campaign of 1813; survival was itself a victory. Chauncey had not brought the question of the command of Lake Ontario to a determination, although that was the supreme issue of the theater.[20] Wilkinson, long the senior American officer, was nothing if not a soldier; 1813 proved him no soldier. Fortunately, better commanders were rising to the top.

For 1814, Secretary Armstrong decided to use Lake Erie as a secure highway to invade the Niagara peninsula. This would

19 John Adams to Jefferson, Dec. 19, 1813, Lester J. Cappon (ed.), *The Adams-Jefferson Letters* . . . (2 vols., Chapel Hill, 1959), II, 406–409; Thomas Robson Hay, "Some Reflections on the Career of General James Wilkinson," *Mississippi Valley Historical Review*, XXI (1934–35), 487–489; R. L. Way, "The Day at Crysler's [sic] Farm," in Zaslow and Turner (eds.), *Defended Border*, pp. 61–83.
20 A. L. Burt, *The United States, Great Britain, and British North America from the Revolution to the Establishment of Peace After the War of 1812* (New Haven, 1940), pp. 332–339, does a workmanlike autopsy on the campaigns of 1813.

weaken Canada by drawing redcoats westward, so that Americans at
Sackett's Harbor and Plattsburg could move toward Montreal.
Wilkinson acted first, and played in character. With 4,000 men he
was unable to dislodge a garrison of 332 in a stone mill at Lacolle
(March 30). He retreated to Lake Champlain, demanded a trial,
was acquitted, and never commanded again. The western campaign
began reprehensibly in May with the inexcusable looting and
burning of Dover, on Lake Erie, by the United States Nineteenth
Infantry. (The Canadians were having domestic troubles as well.
Many gave aid and comfort to United States invaders, and, at about
the same time that American troops sacked Dover, a Canadian court
found sixty-nine bills of high treason, for which eight were hanged
and—at least sentenced to be—drawn and quartered.) [21] While
Americans bungled (and Canadians betrayed), in the United States
Army leadership had arisen: Jacob Brown, Winfield Scott, and
Edmund Pendleton Gaines—three men of steel.

Brown's orders were to sweep down the Niagara River and
then—covered by the Navy—to loop westward around Lake Ontario to York. He cockily challenged Chauncey to meet him at Fort
George on the Lake on July 10. The British might thus be drawn
to leave open the door to Montreal. Brown campaigned with skill
and pugnacity. Crossing the Niagara, he took Fort Erie (July 3)
and moved northward until he met a British force of about equal
size at Chippawa (July 5). His sturdy gray-clad regulars took four
British volleys without flinching, smashed the British line, inflicted
515 casualties, and suffered 297. Physical courage, discipline, rapid
musketry, and superior artillery had won. British Major General
Phineas Riall abandoned the whole peninsula except Fort George,
and Brown pressed on to Lake Ontario. But the horizon was
empty—no Chauncey. Without cautious Chauncey's collaboration,
Brown could not attack the garrison of Fort George, four thousand
strong. The fuming Brown marched back to Chippawa, followed in
a fortnight by the somewhat more numerous British. They clashed

[21] Armstrong to Madison, April 30, 1814, in E. A. Cruikshank (ed.), *Docu-
ments Relating to the Invasion of the Niagara Peninsula by the United States
Army Commanded by General Jacob Brown in July and August 1814* (Niagara,
Ont., 1921), pp. 15–16; Wilkinson's defense is in *Daily National Intelligencer*,
July 30, Aug. 3, 4, 1814; Cruikshank, "The County of Norfolk in the War of
1812," in Zaslow and Turner (eds.), *Defended Border*, pp. 232–235; W. R.
Riddell, "The Ancaster 'Bloody Assize' of 1814," *ibid.*, pp. 241–250.

at Lundy's Lane (July 25), in a battle which raged until midnight. The Americans took a 42 per cent casualty rate, the British endured 29 per cent; but the Americans, with Brown wounded, got off in good order to Fort Erie. Chauncey finally arrived off Fort George on August 5 and ungraciously twitted America's roughest, toughest general on his absence.[22]

The British assaulted Fort Erie (August 15), but Edmund Pendleton Gaines, a new-breed general acting for Brown, repulsed them with 905 casualties while suffering only 84. A British field officer carrying a copy of orders, ". . . The Lieut.-General *most strongly recommends a free use of the bayonet,*" died of a bayonet thrust.[23] When Brown returned to duty, he sallied against superior numbers (September 17), inflicted 609 casualties, suffered 511. The British commander proclaimed a victory and quickly departed, leaving terrier Brown alone, and the Americans themselves dismantled Fort Erie in November. The bravely and skillfully fought Niagara peninsula campaign of 1814 had been a strategic failure. The American soldiery had found their tactical leaders, and it is not too much to say that the northern army was a collection of magnificent regiments, but their skill and gallantry were wasted. The military situation at the end of the war was much the same as it had been in the beginning, so far as the Niagara peninsula entered into military thinking. This strategic nullity was partly because of somewhat unimaginative thinking at the highest levels. But even the most creative military mind would have been puzzled to solve the problem of mounting decisive land operations in the North with the handicap of the passive disobedience of the rulers of New England.

Throughout 1814, Yeo and Chauncey contested the table of weights and measures. Instead of fighting, each strove to build a fleet of crushing superiority. Yeo commissioned *St. Lawrence,* 112 guns—one of the largest in the world—in October, and corked Chauncey in Sackett's Harbor, where Chauncey laid down *New*

22 John T. Horton (ed.), "An Original Narrative of the Niagara Campaign of 1814," *Niagara Frontier,* XI (1964), 9, quotes British admiration of United States troops; these splendid, forgotten regular regiments are connected to the American national tradition only in that the dress uniforms of the United States Military Academy resemble theirs.

23 James W. Silver, *Edmund Pendleton Gaines: Frontier General* (Baton Rouge, 1949), pp. 41–49.

Orleans and *Chippewa,* which would have been *the* largest in the world if ever finished.[24] This naval ticktacktoe continued while the Niagara peninsula was wastefully irrigated with the blood of the best American Army yet seen, a force which never again yielded easy victory.

II

Britain of course had not forgotten America. Napoleon abdicated in April, 1814, freeing veteran British forces for use in America. A Halifax editor prophesied that his government might keep some of the former colonies for the kindly purpose of giving them government—Hezekiah Niles replied, "GOODY, GRACIOUS!"[25] The ministry aimed to avenge the defeat of Indian allies, repay the stab in the back, and revise the boundaries of 1783. It promised Governor General Sir George Prevost an excellent army and three of Wellington's best brigadiers. He was told to take over the lakes (including Champlain), the Niagara region, and Michigan (for the Indians), and get enough of Maine to cut a road from Halifax to Quebec. These achievements would secure Canada.

Taking a bit of Maine—then a district of Massachusetts—was easy. The British occupied a hundred miles of coast east of the Penobscot River with little difficulty (July–September), while twelve thousand males of military age acquiesced, and were even said to have cheered the arrival of royal power. The loss of the United States ship *Adams,* trapped in a river, caused no regrets. After all, it was easier to trade with the British in Maine than to go to Halifax.[26] The Halifax-Quebec road seemed assured.

The Maine occupation climaxed coastal operations begun in 1812, clamping a blockade progressively from south to north. By spring, 1813, Chesapeake Bay was hazardous to shipping, and Captain Stephen Decatur's force was permanently locked in New London, Connecticut. In London, the opposition grumbled that the Navy used too many ships and behaved very badly, but the block-

24 C. Winton-Clare, "A Shipbuilder's War," in Zaslow and Turner (eds.), *Defended Border,* pp. 165–173; C. P. Stacey, "The Ships of the British Squadron on Lake Ontario, 1812–1814," *Canadian Historical Review,* XXXIV (1953), 311–323.

25 *Niles' Weekly Register,* Feb. 5, 1814.

26 New England trade with the enemy, and giving of hindrance and discomfort to friends, are major topics of Chapter 13.

ade was efficient. New England was exempted at first, because it
was a difficult winter station, and because neutral provinces should
be coddled. Merchants carrying foodstuffs for British troops received passes, and the British consul in Boston licensed cargoes for
two months after war began. In December, 1813, the Congress
responded with an embargo, by straight party vote. Not until April,
1814, did Vice-Admiral Alexander Cochrane extend his blockade to
New England, mostly because warships were under construction
there. Even so, the New England blockade was strongly protested by
Nova Scotian merchants, although, among American citizens who
lived west of the Hudson the tendency was to snicker at Yankee
sufferings. American privateers and coasters had a meteorological
advantage in that the prevailing westerlies south of Cape Cod
helped schooners dart out with wind abaft. Off New England,
howling nor'easters made blockaders withdraw for safety. Nearly half
of American wartime trade—such as it was—traveled in Baltimore
schooner-rigged clippers. Long Island Sound was a favorite exit for
New York privateers until blocked in December, 1813. The Navy's
much-derided gunboats guarded many shoal-water coastal convoys.[27] In 1813, a Mr. E. Mix "of the Navy" alarmed the British by
exploding a drifting mine near a Chesapeake blockader and slightly
damaging its hull.[28] The British called it "dishonourable" and
distributed American prisoners through the blockading squadron as
hostages.[29]

The British raided the coast at will. Almost all raids were tactical
successes, and each was a strategic blunder, because nothing in the
war so stiffened resistance. Typical raids would be carried out by
landing parties of about 150, which would ingloriously destroy or
steal private property, leaving behind an enraged populace. Some
Englishmen appeared to believe they created "alarm" and "con-
sternation,"[30] but legislative votes, private letters, and the press

27 *Niles' Weekly Register,* January–April, 1813, describes the steady tightening
of the Chesapeake blockade; for other specific incidents herein, see Mar. 13, June
12, Sept. 4, Nov. 6, 1813, Jan. 8, May 14, 1814; for the safe conduct of ninety
coasting vessels in two convoys protected by gunboats, including one three-hour
stern-chase battle (and a solitary casualty), June 4, 1814, Jan. 7, 1815; for
opposition grumbling about overelaborate blockading operations by the Royal
Navy, see *Cobbett's Parliamentary Debates,* XXVII (1813–14), 70–75.

28 *Niles' Weekly Register,* Aug. 7, 1813.

29 *The Gentlemen's Magazine,* CXIV (Oct. 1813), 388–389.

30 *Ibid.,* CXIII (June, 1813), 581.

prove they created anger and indignation. The most sensible raid was an unsuccessful attempt to destroy blockaded *Constellation* at Norfolk. The most fatuous was the loosing of two organized companies of French deserters on Hampton, Virginia, where they were guilty of revolting atrocities. Even the citizens of Orleans, Massachusetts, resisted a British landing. The Norfolk *Herald* printed a satire on the work of British Marines surprising henhouses, storming pigpens, sacking smoke houses and dairies, and then withdrawing without loss when counterattacked by turkeys.[31] But the blockade, as blockade, worked. In 1814, American legal trade was 11 per cent of the trade of 1811, the last full peacetime year.

By August, 1814, Prevost, when ten thousand veterans from Europe joined his force, could begin aggressive operations to make Canada secure. In 1813, he had paid a brief unfriendly visit to Plattsburg, New York; now he would go to stay longer. He had to thread the Lake Champlain corridor because only there could he get enough food, since most of his beef came from Vermont. Major General George Izard, U.S.A., Wilkinson's successor, had 7,300 men east of the Niagara to face Prevost. On Armstrong's feeble-minded orders, he took most of them west to Sackett's Harbor, leaving Major General Alexander Macomb at Plattsburg with 1,500 effectives. In the end, no harm was done by ordering the troops elsewhere, but Armstrong deserves no credit. Captain Thomas Macdonough was there with Perry's efficient constructor Noah Brown. They built sapwood ships on Vermont's shore with marvelous speed: twenty to forty days to convert trees to warships, leaving Macdonough only leisure enough to spend about ten minutes daily with his family. Delayed by the need to finish *Confiance,* flagship of the naval force under Captain George Downie, Prevost marched in September, coming down the west side while the Green Mountain cowboys herded his beef north on the other. Macomb fortified the hills near Plattsburg.[32]

---

31 D. H. Gilpatrick, *Jeffersonian Democracy in North Carolina* (New York, 1931), pp. 204–208, for a legislature's refusal to complain to Washington of the defenseless condition of its ravaged coast; J. M. Hitsman and Alice Sorby, "Independent Foreigners or Canadian Chasseurs," *Military Affairs*, XXV (1961), 11–17, on the French deserters; Richard K. Murdoch, "The Battle of Orleans, Massachusetts (1814), and Associated Events," *American Neptune*, XXIV (1964), 172–182; Norfolk *Herald,* reprinted in *Niles' Weekly Register,* Apr. 3, 1813.

32 Waldo H. Heinrichs, Jr., "The Battle of Plattsburgh, 1814—the Losers," *American Neptune*, XXI (1961), 42–56, a good account.

Meantime Downie weighed anchor to seek Macdonough, who anchored at Plattsburg in such a way that his opponent had to fight as Macdonough wished him to fight (September 11). Four British warships and twelve gunboats (ninety guns, 736 pounds of short-range broadside) opposed four American warships and ten gunboats (eighty-six guns, 1,274 pounds of short-range broadside). Macdonough, thirty years old and Tripoli-schooled, laid his first gun himself and ordered a signal, "Impressed seamen call on every man to do his duty." The close-on fight was hot, Downie perished early, and Macdonough was twice knocked unconscious, once by flying gear and once by the head of a decapitated seaman. When his flagship *Saratoga*'s broadside was knocked out, he smartly wound ship on springs[33] and presented a fresh battery. When rising water in the British flagship *Confiance* threatened to drown her wounded, her captain struck. Excepting the gunboats, Macdonough took or destroyed all of the enemy. Considering the light construction of the closely aligned vessels, the casualty figures (American 110, British 129) were small.

Prevost called off his dogs and went back to Canada quickly. He said the roads were becoming impassable, and it *is* hard to see how he could have been supplied. Yeo blamed Prevost for rushing Downie into battle prematurely, writing that Macdonough would have had no base if Prevost had overrun Macomb's defenses. The ministry called Prevost home and accepted his explanations, but a Navy court then blamed him for defeat. Before he could respond, he died, his reputation stained by the Navy and by Canadian pamphleteering. He had done pretty well.[34] Yeo was preoccupied with evading a Lake Ontario decision, and Prevost's supply problem was grave. His best defense came from Wellington, who declined the command in North America, writing in December," . . . a naval superiority on the lake is a *sine quâ non* of success. . . ."[35] After Plattsburg there was some indecisive fighting on the Niagara peninsula, but General Izard, seeing no profit in driving redcoats to

---

[33] See diagram among illustrations, "Winding Ship."

[34] Yeo to Croker, Sept. 24, 1814, *The Annual Register*, LVI (1814), 215; *The Gentleman's Magazine*, CXVI (Nov., 1814), 490; J. Mackay Hitsman, *The Incredible War of 1812* (Toronto, 1965), chiefly novel for a vindication of Prevost.

[35] Wellington to Murray, Dec. 22, 1814, quoted ubiquitously, perhaps most accessibly, in Edward Channing, *A History of the United States* (6 vols., New York, 1905–25), IV, 506 n.

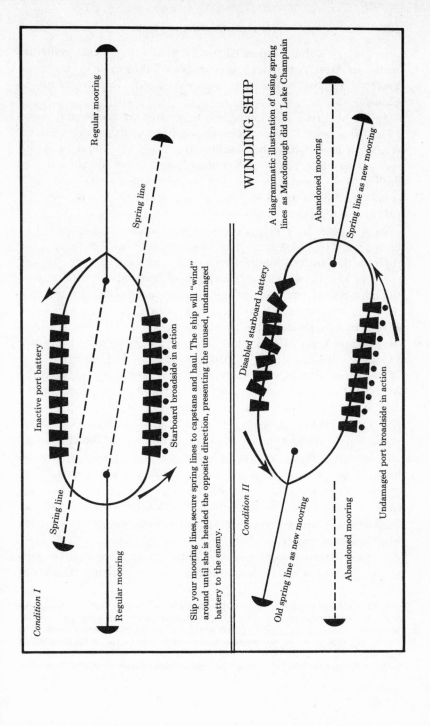

WINDING SHIP

A diagrammatic illustration of using spring lines as Macdonough did on Lake Champlain

Condition I

Regular mooring

Spring line

Inactive port battery

Spring line

Regular mooring

Starboard broadside in action

Slip your mooring lines, secure spring lines to capstans and haul. The ship will "wind" around until she is headed the opposite direction, presenting the unused, undamaged battery to the enemy.

Condition II

Disabled starboard battery

Abandoned mooring

Spring line as new mooring

Old spring line as new mooring

Abandoned mooring

Undamaged port broadside in action

blue Ontario's shore unless Chauncey would trap them, went into winter quarters. American leaders expected 1815 to be grim around Sackett's Harbor when they counted 27,000 British troops in Canada.

In the long run, Macdonough's victory was the northern decision which dissipated British hopes of acquiring territory in that area. American leaders have been so heavily coated with mud by American writers that one might profitably reflect on the difficulty of finding any American commander with such relatively great strength who so quickly suffered an irretrievable and decisive calamity as did poor Prevost.

As a diversion to help Prevost, a substantial British force had been sent into Chesapeake Bay; it occupied Washington and unsuccessfully attacked Baltimore. British parties had been stealing chickens and burning barns in the neighborhood for so long that the inhabitants were used to their comings and goings, and preparations against larger targets were not noticed. In fact, when the British had demonstrated against Washington in 1813, the residents showed more fear of their slaves than of the enemy. In late June, 1814, the President began to think about preparing the defenses of Washington, although Secretary Armstrong was still convinced the British would choose to loot Baltimore instead of the "sheep walk" on the Potomac. No serious fortification had been attempted, and this very weakness probably drew attack. Madison trusted Armstrong's judgment too much. Finally, on July 2, the Tenth Military District was created, comprising Maryland, the District of Columbia, and Virginia north of the Rappahannock, under command of regular Brigadier General William H. Winder (rhymes with finder), who spent the next six weeks studying the terrain and unsuccessfully calling for militia. Armstrong left the defense to Madison and Winder.[36]

Major General Robert Ross brought an army of combat veterans to join Vice-Admiral Cochrane at Bermuda in July. Cochrane was

[36] The American habituation to Royal Navy operations against Chesapeake hens and smokehouses seems plain from a reading of *Niles' Weekly Register* for 1814; Constance McLaughlin Green, *Washington, Village and Capital, 1800–1878* (Princeton, 1962), pp. 58–60; *American State Papers: Documents Legislative and Executive* (38 vols., Washington, 1832–61); *Military Affairs*, I, 524–599, has the relevant documents collected by the Congress (hereafter cited as *ASP*).

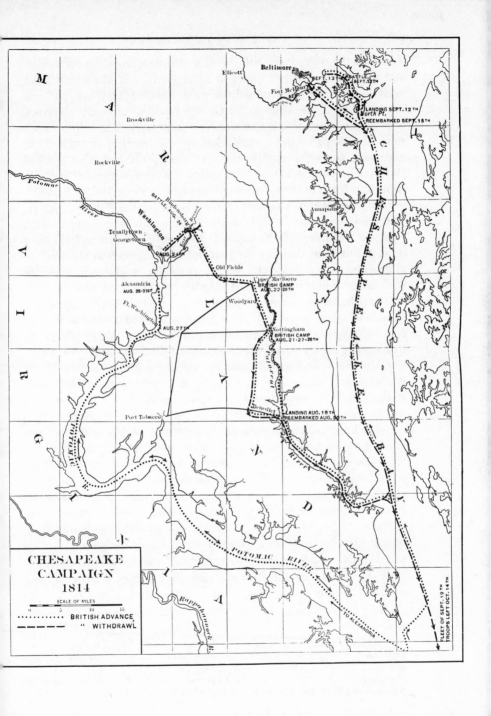

M
A
R
Y
L
A
N
D

V
I
R
G
I
N
I
A

Baltimore
Ellicott
Fort McHenry
SEPT.
Patapsco R.
SEPT. 13
BATTLE
SEPT. 12TH
LANDING SEPT. 12TH
North Pt.
REEMBARKED SEPT. 15TH

Brookville

Rockville

Potomac River

Washington
BATTLE, AUG. 24
Bladensburg
AUG. 24TH
Tenallytown
Georgetown

Annapolis

Old Fields

Alexandria
AUG. 28-31ST
Ft. Washington
AUG. 27TH

Upper Marlboro
BRITISH CAMP
AUG. 22-26TH
Woodyard

Nottingham
BRITISH CAMP
AUG. 21-27-28TH

Patuxent River

Port Tobacco

Benedict
LANDING AUG. 19TH
REEMBARKED AUG. 30TH

POTOMAC

RIVER

POTOMAC   RIVER

TO ALEXANDRIA

Rappahannock R.

FLEET OF SEPT. 19TH
TROOPS LEFT OCT. 14TH

CHESAPEAKE
CAMPAIGN
1814

SCALE OF MILES
0   5   10   15
············· BRITISH ADVANCE
------- " WITHDRAWL

to choose the objectives, with the aim of distracting the government and exacting vengeance, short of killing civilians. He would have preferred the well-provisioned shores of Rhode Island, but, perhaps impressed by Rear Admiral Sir George Cockburn's cheap successes, ordered the force to the Chesapeake. Contrary to the conventional story, the British sought no reprisal for the burning of York. That had been revenged amply, but the Americans had since sacked Dover, Upper Canada, which called for retribution. The only American force in the Chesapeake was Commodore Joshua Barney's flotilla of gunboats. Cochrane chased them up the Patuxent River, where Barney salvaged his guns and blew up his boats (August 22). Now—to Washington? Annapolis? Baltimore? Cochrane had some doubts, but Ross thought the road to Washington was the road to glory. The redcoat force of 4,500 moved off for Washington, meeting with no great difficulty than the deep soft sand underfoot.[37]

When news of Barney's frustration reached Washington, the President called more militia, Winder wrote orders furiously, and citizens began to dig along lines staked out at Bladensburg by Engineer Colonel Decius Wadsworth. Winder could not know whether the British would come by way of the Navy Yard bridge or Bladensburg, where the Eastern Branch (the present Anacostia River) was but a sedgy brook, so he rode to watch the invaders from the bushes. Barney's four hundred seamen and their guns arrived while Winder was concentrating force at the bridge to contest any crossing there. Before his plans were complete, Winder learned that Ross was obviously coming by way of Bladensburg. Henry Adams wrote of Winder in a manner at once patronizing and excoriating.[38] In combat Winder showed no competence, but it was unfair to ridicule him for thinking the British flotilla might come up the Potomac to help Ross cross the Eastern Branch. Winder was duty-bound to reflect on the possibility until the threat passed. Adams said Winder could not have done anything there, but Barney's guns could have wrecked a British squadron which tried to cover a river crossing. Winder should receive some slight credit.

Once Bladensburg was the known field, the motley Americans

[37] Mahon, "British Command Decisions," pp. 234–235; Ralph Robinson, "New Light on Three Episodes of the British Invasion of Maryland in 1814," *Maryland Historical Magazine*, XXXVII (1942), 277–279.

[38] Henry Adams, *History of the United States During the Administrations of Jefferson and Madison* (9 vols., New York, 1888–91), VIII, 152–155.

streamed there to form before the British arrived. The militia of Maryland and the District of Columbia, a low-trained lot, occupied one hillside and Barney emplaced his batteries on another. Madison and Monroe were briefly on the field, and Monroe even altered some militia dispositions. Only Barney and his men fought well. The battle—facetiously called the Bladensburg Races—was hardly worth describing, since the Americans quickly ran. Barney was wounded and outflanked when the militia evaporated, but fired while he had ammunition, and ordered the guns spiked and their crews to retreat. He himself, having lost too much blood to withdraw, was taken prisoner by the British and treated well. Ross reported the British losses as 249 killed and wounded, most of them probably hit by Barney's gunners. The sprinting Americans lost but seventy-seven in all.[39]

The Capitol might have been defended and sold dearly, but what was left of the force was somewhere west of Georgetown. The residents of the Executive Mansion left dinner on the table and fled westward, the gardener and the doorkeeper saving the Stuart portrait of Washington before local looters temporarily took charge. The President crossed the river in a boat and took a carriage to the west, in Dolley Madison's wake. Monroe rejoined Winder upstream and acted as Secretary of War, although Armstrong still held the title. The British entered the outskirts of Washington on the evening of August 24 and set the Capitol afire. Ross and Cockburn ate Dolley Madison's dinner and with their own hands set the presidential palace ablaze. Meanwhile the Americans burned the Navy Yard and its vessels. William Thornton saved the Patent Office by arguing that its destruction would hurt humanity in general more than the United States in particular. Except for the office of the *National Intelligencer,* private property was respected by the British. August 25 brought a rainstorm which extinguished the fires, and the British marched to their ships without hindrance. Cochrane wrote to Monroe that reprisals would continue until the Canadians were compensated for American pillaging. The tiny

39 Hulbert Footner, *Sailor of Fortune: The Life and Adventures of Commodore Barney, U.S.N.* (New York, 1940), pp. 280–285, the standard life, although inadequately documented; Frederick P. Todd, "The Militia and Volunteers of the District of Columbia, 1783–1820," Columbia Historical Society, *Records,* L (1952), 379–439, exhaustively, lovingly, and extenuatingly describes this neglected mendicant corps.

American administration reorganized itself in makeshift quarters on the night of August 27.[40]

After Ross's men left, a small British naval force worked up the Potomac to Alexandria, loaded everything from the town's warehouses, and got away safely on August 31 despite hastily erected shore batteries. Success made the raiders careless, and they mounted a poorly planned small landing up the Bay on August 30 which cost the life of Captain Sir Peter Parker and forty casualties besides. The Washington episode refreshed the English press by allowing a tinsel contrast with the catastrophic news of Plattsburg. Ross proudly reported his achievement, magnifying the resistance, in three columns of London print, but editor Niles, taken by surprise, published the news as something like a stop-press story.[41] Secretary Armstrong disappeared into private life as Madison let Monroe carry on as Secretary of State and of War; Armstrong resigned early in September with an attack on Madison's administration.

The people of Washington feared the Congress would leave. Graffiti appeared on walls: "The capital and the Union lost by cowardice" and "A ——— sold the city for 5,000 dollars." The House soon voted to stay, 83–54, but the Senate argued for months, with Senator Rufus King helping to win the vote to stay.[42] With permanence assured, Benjamin Henry Latrobe repaired and finished the Capitol—except for the dome—in two years.[43] Workmen slapped white paint over the smoke-stained presidential residence, and it has been the White House ever since.

If the British had wished to hold Washington, the only power which could have prevented it would have been naval power—

[40] Ray W. Irwin (ed.), "The Capture of Washington in 1814, as Described by Mordecai Booth," *Americana*, XXVIII (1934), 7–27—Booth was a civilian Navy clerk who stayed at his job; Paul Jennings, *A Colored Man's Reminiscences of James Madison* (Brooklyn, 1865), pp. 8–13; S. A. Wallace (ed.), "Georgetown Is Saved from the British!" *Social Studies*, XLIII (1952), 233–237, excerpts from the diary of Anna Marie Brodeau Thornton (Mrs. William Thornton); Cochrane to Monroe, Sept. 19, 1814, *ASP: Foreign Relations*, III, 694.

[41] *The Annual Register*, LVI (1814), 218–229, sandwiches the Washington report between the Plattsburg disaster and the Baltimore fiasco; *The Gentleman's Magazine*, CXVI (Oct., 1814), 372–373; *Niles' Weekly Register*, Aug. 27, 1814.

[42] Green, *Washington*, pp. 62–66.

[43] Claude M. Fuess, "Rufus King," *DAB;* Talbot Hamlin, "Benjamin Henry Latrobe: The Man and the Architect," *Maryland Historical Magazine*, XXXVII (1942), 352–358.

which did not exist. The administration had only political reasons for defending Washington, which had no tactical value, and it might have been strategically wiser to evacuate the city, leaving Britain to bear the odium of wanton destruction. Evacuation would have been humiliating, but no more humiliating than the Bladensburg Races. However, it seems that no one seriously proposed abandoning the "sheep walk" to the avengers of Dover.

To tally reprisals at this point, the Americans had unnecessarily damaged York, Newark, and Dover, and the British responded by burning Lewiston, Buffalo, Havre de Grace, and Washington. Now, after eight days of vacillation, Ross and Cockburn turned Cochrane's mind toward Baltimore, a delay which gave Baltimore time to prepare. Baltimore had a well-organized civic committee which took care of internal policing and fortification. General Winder came to command, but Senator Samuel Smith, major general of militia, brushed him off and took command himself, although defeat seemed more probable than glory. Smith entrenched the obvious waterside approaches. Four thousand overconfident redcoats advanced up Long Point on September 13, where 1,545 militia in ditches stood them off for an hour, inflicting two-to-one casualties, and killing General Ross. To give naval support Cochrane sent 1,200 men forward in barges and rocket boats, but Forts Covington and McHenry drove them away. The forts, especially the stronger Fort McHenry, would have to be silenced, so Cochrane rained bombs, case-shot rockets (like shrapnel shells), and red-glaring incendiary rockets on the garrisons. The powerful but inaccurate rockets had scared the daylights out of American troops in earlier engagements.[44]

The bombardment failed. That night the fleet threw nearly 1,800 missiles at Fort McHenry, of which 400 fell inside or fragmented

44 Mahon, "British Command Decisions," pp. 236–237; William D. Hoyt, Jr. (ed.), "Civilian Defense in Baltimore, 1814–1815: Minutes of the Committee of Vigilance," *Maryland Historical Magazine*, XXXIX (1944), 199–224, 293–309, XL (1945), 7–23, 137–153; Franklin R. Mullally, "Ft. McHenry, 1814: Part I, The Battle of Baltimore," *ibid.*, LIV (1959), 61–91; John L. Sanford, "The Battle of North Point," *ibid.*, XXIV (1929), 356–365; Fort McHenry, erected in 1794, was well modernized in 1813–14, and rebuilt to its present appearance between 1824 and 1837, Richard Walsh, "The Star Fort: 1814," *ibid*, LIV (1959), 296–309, and S. S. Bradford, "Fort McHenry: The Outworks in 1814," *ibid.*, LIV (1959), 188–209; Ralph Robinson, "The Use of Rockets by the British in the War of 1812," *ibid.*, XL (1945), 1–6.

above, but only thirty of the garrison were casualties, because the gun crews, unable to reach the British vessels with their weapons, took cover and sweated it out. Two-thirds of Cochrane's siege power could bear on the fort—all but his ships of the line—but he hurt it very little. The British report falsely said that blockships kept them from getting up the channel to Fort McHenry, and that has become the conventional story. The report showed considerable pride in having at least made the Baltimoreans jumpy. The British departed, and Winder's friends censured Smith for letting them escape. The militia went home, properly pleased with themselves, and Francis Scott Key, who saw the night explosions reflected in water, wrote "The Star Spangled Banner." And Monroe profited. The Washington campaign was the last sensational triumph of British arms in America. After Bladensburg, Monroe was Secretary of War and received enough credit for Baltimore and later events to make him Madison's heir apparent.[45]

III

Sea fighting was high in public interest and low in achievement. The tardy and probably misguided naval enthusiasm of the Congress led to appropriations in 1813 for eleven ships and frigates and for twelve sloops of war for the high seas.[46] Some of the new sloops were launched before the war ended, but as of March, 1814, only ten public vessels were at sea.[47]

Early in 1813, *Hornet,* Captain James Lawrence, riddled His Majesty's sloop of war *Peacock,* which sank shortly after.[48] The

---

[45] Mullaly, "Ft. McHenry, 1814," pp. 91–103; John S. Pancake, "The General From Baltimore: A Biography of Samuel Smith," Ph.D. thesis, University of Virginia, 1949, pp. 227–286, restudies the campaign and demolishes Cochrane's alibis; *The Gentleman's Magazine,* CXVI (1814), 581–585, prints the commanders' dispatches, in which too much trust has been placed; J. S. Skinner, "Incidents of the War of 1812. From the *Baltimore Patriot,*" *Maryland Historical Magazine,* XXXII (1937), 340–347.

[46] A sloop of war was a ship-rigged vessel (square sails on three masts) with one tier of guns, which cost a fifth as much to build as the two-tiered superfrigate and could be built much more quickly.

[47] K. Jack Bauer, "Naval Shipbuilding Programs, 1794–1860," *Military Affairs,* XXIX (1965), 29–33; *Niles' Weekly Register,* Apr. 2, 1814.

[48] Hardin Craig, Jr. (ed.), "Notes on the Action between *Hornet* and *Peacock,*" *American Neptune,* XI (1951), 73–77, reprints marginalia on a copy of Lawrence's report by Purser's Steward Joshua Keene, R.N.

Massachusetts Senate refused congratulations to fellow-citizen Lawrence because such "approbation" would demean "a moral and religious people. . . ."[49] This seemed to hex the Navy. Captain Lawrence received command of hard-luck *Chesapeake* at Boston, where he was blockaded by *Shannon*, Captain Philip Broke. Lawrence took a raw crew out to fight, but the duel lasted only nine minutes before *Chesapeake* was taken by boarders while her dying captain was carried below murmuring, "Don't give up the ship; blow her up"—from which the United States Navy took its motto.[50] When Lawrence's body was interred at Salem, his funeral was boycotted by the North Meeting House congregation, by a local militia company, and by the government of Massachusetts. The brig *Argus,* Captain William Allen, carried Minister W. H. Crawford to France and then raided in English waters. She took at least twenty prizes in three weeks before meeting the royal brig *Pelican.* Allen would not run from any brig, and lost his ship and life in a short engagement. Contrary accounts notwithstanding, his crew was *not* drunk on captured wine.[51]

Captain David Porter with his frigate *Essex* went raiding in the Pacific in 1813, but was trapped by two Britishers at Valparaiso, Chile, in March, 1814. When a squall damaged his top hamper, his attackers disregarded international law and took him in Chilean waters, bagging, among other prisoners, Midshipman David G. Farragut, aged twelve years. The United States sloops *Wasp* and *Peacock* cheered Americans in 1814 by capturing prizes in the Irish Sea,[52] as an officer noted, *"in smelling distance of coal fires,"*[53] but Decatur sneaked *President* out in January, 1815, during foul weather, only to be "completely mobbed" by four blockaders.[54]

---

[49] Quoted in Samuel Eliot Morison, *The Maritime History of Massachusetts* (new printing, Boston, 1941) , p. 198.

[50] A variant report of the second phrase was ". . . sink her first."

[51] Wilbur E. Apgar, "The Last Cruise of the U.S. Brig 'Argus,'" United States Naval Institute, *Proceedings,* LXV (1939) , 653–660; Victor H. Paltsits (ed.) , "Cruise of the U.S. Brig Argus in 1813; Journal of Surgeon James Inderwick," New York Public Library, *Bulletin,* XXI (June, 1917) , also published separately, 1917.

[52] The British dispatch about *Essex,* dated Mar. 30, 1814, noticed no legal question, *The Gentleman's Magazine,* CXVI (Aug., 1814) , 171–172; *Niles' Weekly Register,* Oct. 15, 1814, on raiding in British home waters.

[53] R. W. Mindte, "Another Navy Rodgers," *American Neptune,* XIX (1959) , 217.

[54] Admiral Cochrane's words, Allan Westcott, "Stephen Decatur," *DAB.*

Peacock got as far as Sunda Strait, where she took a brig in June, 1815, in the last fight of the war.[55]

The successful naval duels helped to keep up public spirits, and the defeats could be endured because none was disgraceful. American design theories were fully vindicated. Comparisons of operational efficiency[56] and the records of courts support the notion that the miniature United States Navy was intrinsically the better—but the power ratio favored Britain 500:3. The single indisputable strategic gain for the Americans was the withdrawal of British blockaders in order to chase American commerce raiders late in 1812, making it easier for the merchant fleet to get home safely. The other gain was a pantheon of heroes, helpful in creating a sense of nationality in a loosely united people.

The United States had a privateer navy vastly larger than the public fleet, comprising publicly licensed, privately owned men-of-war which hunted prizes for profit. Enemy officers gratuitously admitted Britain's inability to build their equals. Most sailed from ports south of New England, including a few of dubious legality in Louisiana waters. The owners split the profits with the crews (in proportion to rank). Although owners sometimes gambled by using small crews, if a captain handled his crew as skillfully as a good ocean-racing yacht skipper the life was not particularly hazardous, unless avarice led to attacking a powerful ship. Some privateers had spectacular success. *Yankee,* of Bristol, Rhode Island, netted a million dollars from prizes which included a six-hundred-ton East Indiaman thrice her size. *America,* of Salem, stronger than most merchantmen afloat, made a profit of a million in sixteen months. *Comet,* of Baltimore, commanded by audacious Thomas Boyle, who once proclaimed Great Britain blockaded, took more than forty prizes in two cruises, two of them by defeating a Portuguese Navy brig. Of course, others failed completely.[57]

[55] T. Frederick Davis, "U.S.S. Peacock in the War of 1812 . . ." *Florida Historical Society, Quarterly,* XVI (1938), 231–241.

[56] Channing, *United States,* IV, 545–546, tabulates sixteen naval battles, giving variant figures from his sources and considering duration of fighting, weight of metal thrown, sizes of crews, and casualties. Henry Adams first popularized the technique of quantitative comparison of naval power, ship by ship, even gun by gun, taking into account the weight of metal thrown.

[57] Stanley Faye, "Privateersmen of the Gulf and Their Prizes," *Louisiana Historical Quarterly,* XXII (1939), 1012–1094, begins his story before 1812 and carries it into the period of Latin-American wars of independence; the typical

The estimated 526 American privateers had no decisive effect, but provoked zealous countermeasures, raised insurance rates, and required the Royal Navy to convoy all trade in the Western Hemisphere. Hovering off the British Isles, these maritime predators hurt some British businessmen seriously and caused acid complaints to the Admiralty about the hazards of coastal waters. The privateers of this war were the most successful of all time, starting out with any available vessels and ending with ships equal to royal sloops of war. Probably 1,408 prizes were taken, and, although recaptures by both sides made statistics unreliable, British commerce suffered a net loss. In the privateering ventures of Baltimore, a leading and typical center, some made money and some lost, but more was made than lost. The apparent success of commerce raiding inspired the Congress to authorize twenty Navy-manned raiders late in 1814, but few got to sea before the peace. The Navy Department also arranged to certify pensions for wounded and disabled privateersmen, and their widows and orphans, good evidence of popular esteem.[58]

IV

West Florida had been on the agenda since the Louisiana Purchase.[59] The Congress had given the land between the Pearl and Perdido rivers to the Territory of Mississippi in April, 1812. Governor David Holmes defined the region as a county in the following summer, although Spaniards still garrisoned Mobile. Gallatin opposed occupation and taxation by force because it might prejudice future negotiations, and Holmes feared the Spaniards would rally

---

disciplinary troubles of some privateer captains are illustrated in Wilfred H. Munro (ed.), "Extracts from the Log Book of the Private Armed Schooner Blockade, Manly Sweet, Commander," Rhode Island Historical Society, *Collections*, XIII (1920), 131–139; Kenneth Scott, "The Privateer *Yankee* in the War of 1812," *American Neptune*, XXI (1961), 16–22; Munro, "The Last Cruise of the Privateer Yankee," Rhode Island Historical Society, *Collections*, XIII, 66–68; Frank F. White, Jr., "The *Comet* Harasses the British," *Maryland Historical Magazine*, LIII (1958), 295–315; the sorry voyage of an unsuccessful privateer is described in Harold A. Mouzon, "The Unlucky *General Armstrong*," *American Neptune*, XV (1955), 59–80.

[58] Channing, *United States*, IV, 527 and n., gives the total of captures as 1,344, although *Niles' Weekly Register*, Jan. 7, 1815, gives the figure of 1,408 in an admittedly incomplete calculation, the last published before it had certain news of peace; for Baltimore, see John Philips Cranwell and William Bowers Crane, *Men of Marque; A History of Private Armed Vessels Out of Baltimore During the War of 1812* (New York, 1940); *Niles' Weekly Register*, June 26, 1813.

[59] See above, Chapter 5.

powerful Indian allies, but General Wilkinson, by a mere show of force, persuaded Mobile to surrender in April, 1813.[60] Now the Indians must be brought to heel.

The principal crime of the southwestern Indians was that they existed. About twenty thousand pacific Choctaw and Chickasaw lived in Mississippi. A third of the Creek Confederation Indians lived in Georgia and Alabama, mastering the agricultural life. Two-thirds of them lived farther north, restless against the trespasses of white neighbors. They numbered not more than four thousand and were poorly armed. When six Creeks killed two white families in January, 1813, their tribes executed them, but reprisal led to reprisal and finally to the massacre of more than 250 whites at Fort Mims (August, 1813), where security had been so amateurish that the gate was open to the Indians. Although Indian Agent Benjamin Hawkins had a useful influence on peace-minded Creeks, four indecisive expeditions marched against the Indians in the winter of 1813–14. Major General Andrew Jackson, Tennessee Militia, ended the Creek War in the Battle of Horseshoe Bend (March, 1814) by killing nearly nine hundred warriors at slight cost. The Creeks ceded two-thirds of their land as indemnity. Jackson got a reputation for skill and ferocity, and a commission as major general, U.S.A.[61]

Jackson was soon to win greater fame at New Orleans. British officers had long hoped to plug the Mississippi.[62] At first they planned a frugal Louisiana campaign, basing the fleet on Pensacola, marching inland from Mobile, and taking New Orleans from above,

[60] I. J. Cox, *The West Florida Controversy, 1798–1813* (Baltimore, 1918), pp. 604–618; Julius W. Pratt, *The Expansionists of 1812* (New York, 1925), pp. 235–237.

[61] James F. Doster (ed.), "Letters Relating to the Tragedy of Fort Mims: August–September, 1813," *Alabama Review*, XIV (1961), 269–285; Merritt B. Pound, *Benjamin Hawkins: Indian Agent* (Athens, Ga., 1951), pp. 223–232; Albert Somit, "Andrew Jackson: Legend and Reality," *Tennessee Historical Quarterly*, VII (1948), 291–313.

[62] Practically all of the *Louisiana Historical Quarterly*, XLIV (1961), is devoted to hitherto little-used British documents, edited by Carson I. A. Ritchie, which demand a restudy of the tactical history of the Louisiana campaign of 1814–15. Ritchie adds his own ninety-page perspicacious introduction to these materials. What follows here on the subject owes so much to Ritchie and his texts that further citation would be unmanageable. The most important are the journals of the chief artillery officer and the assistant quartermaster general, whose difficulties were the most important within the power of the British to overcome.

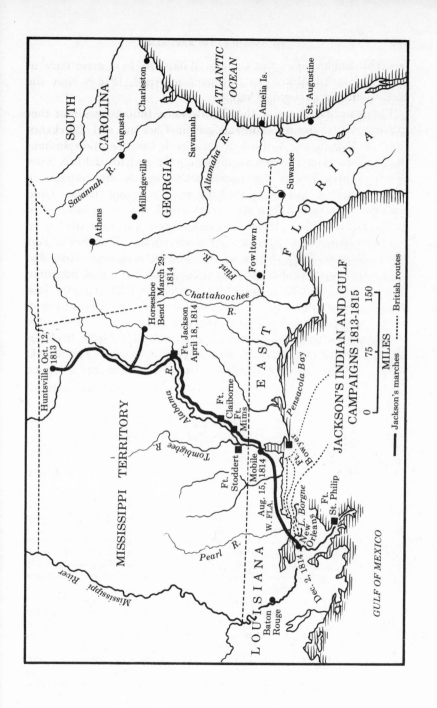

JACKSON'S INDIAN AND GULF
CAMPAIGNS 1813-1815

— Jackson's marches   ······· British routes

MILES

0   75   150

GULF OF MEXICO

Huntsville Oct. 12, 1813

Horseshoe Bend March 29, 1814

Ft. Jackson April 18, 1814

Alabama R.

Ft. Claiborne
Ft. Mims

Tombigbee R.

Ft. Stoddert

Mobile Aug. 15, 1814

W. FLA.

Pearl R.

Dec. 2, 1814

Baton Rouge

LOUISIANA

MISSISSIPPI TERRITORY

Mississippi River

Chattahoochee R.

Flint R.

Fowltown

Suwanee

E A S T   F L O R I D A

Pensacola Bay

Bowyer

L. Borgne

New Orleans

Ft. St. Philip

SOUTH CAROLINA

Augusta

Charleston

Savannah R.

Milledgeville

GEORGIA

Athens

Savannah

Altamaha R.

ATLANTIC OCEAN

Amelia Is.

St. Augustine

but they changed the plans when a large army became available in 1814. An invasion is usually launched against weakness, or against a point so valuable that great efforts are worth while. New Orleans was valuable because it offered much plunder and possibilities of economic development. Wellington later privately accused Cochrane of gambling an army against loot. Certainly the operation Cochrane helped to organize was beyond the capacity of the Navy.[63]

With Indians inland and the Royal Navy omnipotent, the people of Louisiana had reason for anxiety. Regular troops in the region were few, and the federal government drained a thousand militia for service elsewhere. A rich store of commodities accumulated in warehouses. Until 1814, the principal local warlike acts were covert filibustering expeditions against the Spanish neighbors, none successful. In April, 1814, rumors of invasion circulated, but Jackson was free to attend to defense and, when the British moved into Pensacola, decided Mobile was the gate to guard. To make invasion harder, he seized Pensacola himself in November.[64]

The British mounted their attack on Louisiana from Jamaica. Because of the adverse Mississippi current, Cochrane and General Sir Edward Pakenham decided to come in by way of Lake Borgne's connecting bayous, which required an eighty-mile movement in boats after brushing aside five well-commanded United States gunboats.[65] Jackson expected attack by an easier route, and 1,600 unexpected redcoats reached the Mississippi on December 23, only seven miles below New Orleans. The city was momentarily vulnerable, but Pakenham waited for more men. (Jackson might best

---

63 Yeo to Melville, Feb. 19, 1813, unreservedly states Pensacola's "vast importance to us . . . as an excellent port" in Edward A. Parsons (ed.) , "Jean Lafitte in the War of 1812: A Narrative Based on Original Documents," American Antiquarian Society, *Proceedings*, LV (Part 2), 206; Reed McC. B. Adams usefully relates city to campaign, "New Orleans and the War of 1812," *Louisiana Historical Quarterly*, XVI (1933) , 221–234; Mahon, "British Command Decisions Relative to the Battle of New Orleans," *Louisiana History*, VI (1965) , 64–66, uses inference to contradict Wellington's categorical accusation against Cochrane and, in the larger picture, ignores Ritchie's work, published four years earlier; E. O. Rowland, *Andrew Jackson's Campaign Against the British, or the Mississippi Territory in the War of 1812* (New York, 1926) , pp. 219–254, readably describes the preliminary sparring in a work scented with magnolia blossoms.

64 Adams, "New Orleans," pp. 479–503, 681–865; Harris Gaylord Warren, "Southern Filibusters in the War of 1812," *Louisiana Historical Quarterly*, XXV (1942) , 295–297.

65 *Niles' Weekly Register*, Feb. 4, 1815, exultantly estimates British casualties in the gunboat action as "perhaps" five hundred.

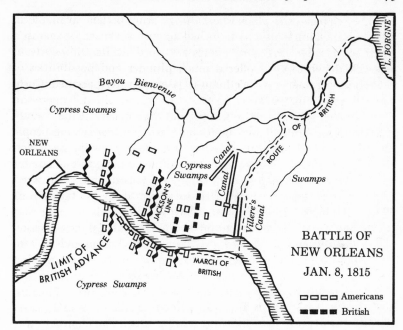

Bayou Bienvenue

Cypress Swamps

NEW
ORLEANS

Cypress
Swamps

Canal

Canal

JACKSON'S LINE

Villere's
Canal

ROUTE OF BRITISH

Swamps

LIMIT OF
BRITISH ADVANCE

MARCH OF
BRITISH

Cypress Swamps

L. BORGNE

BATTLE OF
NEW ORLEANS
JAN. 8, 1815

□ □ □ □ Americans
■ ■ ■ ■ British

have cut the levee and flooded all approaches.) During twilight
skirmishes the schooner *Carolina* dropped downstream and drove
the British behind the levee with grapeshot at close range. Contrary
to the myth of later sniper-fire demoralization, the invaders remained confident.

Jackson fixed his defense behind a canal, flooded with six feet of
water, across the only firm approach. For the next ten days the
invaders laboriously brought guns from the fleet; this artillery was
poorly supplied and, of necessity, inadequately emplaced, as proved
in a gunners' duel on New Year's Day, 1815. The British burned
Carolina with red-hot shot, but neglected an opportunity to cross to
the right bank to enfilade Jackson's lines. By this time Jackson had
plenty of man power, including Jean Lafitte's pirates, who had
Jackson's personal "protection from Injury and Insult,"[66] and a
separate but superior Jim Crow militia unit.[67] He could now afford

[66] Jackson to Reynolds, Dec. 22, 1814, Parsons (ed.), "Jean Lafitte in the War
of 1812."

[67] Donald E. Everett, "Emigrés and Militiamen: Free Persons of Color,
1803–1815," *Journal of Negro History*, XXVIII (1953), 377–402.

to send a detachment across the river to erect a battery to sweep his front. Pakenham tardily saw the advantage of the left bank, and easily overran Jackson's ground there on January 7 as the Kentuckians "ingloriously fled."[68]

On January 8, Pakenham assaulted Jackson's defenses. It was not a battle but a massacre. Shooting went on for about seventy-five minutes, but the decisive fire fight lasted five minutes as twenty converging cannon, aided somewhat by small arms, inflicted 2,036 casualties. (American casualties were twenty-one.) Pakenham and another general were killed, another badly wounded, and command fell to the fourth-ranking general. While Jackson warily awaited firm assurance of victory, the British re-embarked on January 27 and steered to attack Fort Bowyer, below Mobile.[69]

Jackson's topographical engineer and a French-speaking company officer credited the gunners for the triumph, but legend has attributed victory to crashing volleys fired by hawk-eyed frontier riflemen. The British knew the artillery had done them in,[70] and history does not know the militia unit which could *quickly* fire a second true volley with the muzzle-loading rifle. No eyewitness claimed victory for the rifles until 1874, which, incidentally, was after the general adoption of the breech-loading rifle.

The British seem to have lost the Louisiana campaign because of overconfidence which led to logistical errors. The supply line was too long to provide enough ammunition for the artillery to fire for more than sixty minutes. This was supposed to be an amphibious operation; *The Gentleman's Magazine* inadvertently gave Cochrane away when it said, "The Navy had no share in the action."[71] It was Cochrane's job to plant the army *firmly* on land. The chief artillery

68 Jackson to Monroe, Jan. 9, 1815, John Spencer Bassett (ed.) , *Correspondence of Andrew Jackson* (7 vols., Washington, 1926–35) , II, 137.

69 In Jackson's nine pitched battles, his average total of casualties suffered was fewer than sixty men killed and wounded; *Correspondence of Andrew Jackson,* II, 136–152, shows the slow growth of Jackson's conviction that he was, indeed, victorious.

70 Bassett (ed.) , *Major Howell Tatum's Journal While Acting Topographical Engineer (1814) to General Jackson* (Northampton, Mass., 1922) , pp. 125–127, and Dagmar R. LeBreton, "The Man Who Won the Battle of New Orleans," *Louisiana Historical Quarterly,* XXXVIII (1955) , 26–30; the decisiveness of artillery is a particular conclusion of Ritchie (see note 62) , and Henry Adams surmises it, *United States,* IX, 231–232, but, despite the fact that most recent writing on the period has been merely dehydrated Henry Adams, it sometimes seems that the riflemen conquered the American imagination if not Pakenham's unfortunate army.

71 *The Gentleman's Magazine,* CXVII (Mar., 1815) , 271.

officer, Major General Alexander Dickson, knowing his fire-power inferiority, made the crucial decision when he advised abandoning the battery on the right bank. That decision ended the campaign.[72]

On the American side, it should be noted that Louisiana was saved by its native inhabitants. The New Orleans French outnumbered more recently arrived residents about seven to one, and practically all Creole eligibles bore arms. They provided about 40 per cent of all man power and practically all of those cannoneers who so intimidated General Dickson. Jackson at first lacked confidence in the inhabitants, because conscription met resistance. Although Edward Livingston formed an unofficial loyalist committee, mostly French, which maintained high morale, Jackson declared martial law. A local writer denounced Jackson after the battle, and, before the quarrel ended, Jackson jailed both the federal district judge and district attorney—for which imprudence he later paid a thousand-dollar fine.[73]

Although it is universally admitted that Jackson's victory intensified American patriotism,[74] its strategic importance has often been disregarded. True, a peace had been negotiated earlier, but the British did not need to exchange ratifications if Cochrane and Pakenham succeeded. Pakenham and Cochrane brought out officers for a complete British civil government, and a governor's commission stating the fraudulence of the Louisiana Purchase. Had not the United States crushed the Creeks, defended Mobile, seized Pensacola, and held New Orleans, all of the Louisiana Purchase could have been lost and part, perhaps, given to Spain at the Congress of Vienna.[75]

[72] A scapegoat was found in the person of an obscure captain, holding brevet rank of lieutenant colonel. See "General Court Martial Held at the Royal Barracks, Dublin, for the Trial of Brevet Lieutenant-Colonel Hon. Thomas Mullins . . . 1815," *Louisiana Historical Quarterly*, IX (1926), 34–110.

[73] Bernard Marigny, "Reflections on the Campaign of General Jackson in Louisiana in 1814 and '15," trans. by Grace King, *ibid.*, VI (1923), 61–85— Marigny's defense of creole conduct originally appeared in 1848; the documents on Jackson's Caesarian behavior in New Orleans are collected in James A. Padgett (ed.), "The Difficulties of Andrew Jackson in New Orleans . . ." *ibid.*, XXI (1938), 367–399; W. B. Hatcher, *Edward Livingston, Jeffersonian Republican and Jacksonian Democrat* (University, La., 1940), pp. 198–212; Adams, "New Orleans and the War of 1812," pp. 505–509.

[74] For examples of the literary effect of patriotic inebriation, see the editorial rhetoric of *Niles' Weekly Register*, Feb. 11, 18, 1815.

[75] For speculations on the future of the trans-Mississippi if New Orleans had fallen, Thomas P. Abernethy, *The South in the New Nation, 1789–1815* (Baton Rouge, 1961), pp. 400–402; Philip C. Brooks, "Spain's Farewell to Louisiana,

There was more fighting before peace was assured. Cochrane took Mobile (which had repulsed him in September, 1814) because his opponents laxly assumed the cool British veterans were too shaken to fight again. It offered pleasant refreshment to seamen and soldiers, and won the distinction of being the first place in the United States where a man ate a meal from a can (a British officer on Dauphin Island). There were four frontier skirmishes with inland Georgia Indians, and Indians were hostile along the upper Mississippi River for months. Monroe planned the first really promising Canadian campaign—forty thousand men in the Saint Lawrence Valley, under bellicose Jacob Brown—but peace was soon certain, and when the news reached the farthest ships there was an end to bloodshed.[76]

V

In the conventional view, an incapable President mismanaged an unnecessary war. New England leaders popularized that interpretation, but New England leaders were equally vulnerable to *ad hominem* argument, withholding money, militia, and brains, betraying their sons who formed more regular regiments than the youth of any other section. Madison did not find his generals until two years elapsed; it took Lincoln about as long.[77]

Army engineering and artillery were good when available, and, in victory or defeat, the British usually suffered a greater proportion of casualties. The best generals were unknown at first, and competent company-grade officers were always scarce. Of the land heroes, only Jackson equaled naval victors in public esteem.[78] As Wellington remarked, the weakness of the United States was "the inexperience of its officers."[79] In ocean duels the Navy won thirteen of twenty-five, a better score than any other navy which ever fought

---

1803–1821," *Mississippi Valley Historical Review*, XXVII (1940–41), 33–35; and H. L. Coles, *The War of 1812* (Chicago, 1965), pp. 233–235.

[76] Kate L. Gregg, "The War of 1812 on the Missouri Frontier," *Missouri Historical Review*, XXXIII (1939), 342–348; Monroe to Brown, Feb. 1815, C. P. Stacey (ed.), "An American Plan for a Canadian Campaign . . ." *American Historical Review*, XLVI (1940–41), 348–358.

[77] Irving Brant, *James Madison, Commander-in-Chief, 1812–1836* (Indianapolis, 1961), revises the traditional out-of-character image, carefully scrutinizing Henry Adams' tendentious selections, omissions, and ellipses.

[78] *Niles' Weekly Register*, Mar. 19, 1814, complains of the "odious and unwarrantable distinctions" between land and sea heroes.

[79] Quoted in Hitsman, *Incredible War*, p. 240.

the British. American naval gunnery generally excelled. American officers were keyed-up, and the enlisted men were incomparable with their leavening of enthusiastic citizen volunteers. The Navy could not have affected the war on the oceans, but a victory by Chauncey on Lake Ontario could have won the war. However, Chauncey was the least truculent man on the Navy List, and one may only speculate on what a Decatur might have accomplished against the hesitant Yeo in that decisive theater where no decision was attempted.

How each side tried to attract Indians, and how they used them, have been much studied, but whether they were worth the trouble has not been much considered. Indians had important roles, especially on the British northwest front, but they were no bargain. They were in council infuriating, in victory inhumane, in defeat invisible. A British general believed they were "only to be found useful in proportion as we are independent" of them.[80] Field commanders sometimes made tactical decisions contrary to good military judgment in order to keep Indians' favor. After any slight success they were apt to go home to brag and to show scalps, loot, and prisoners.[81] To praise Indians as allies, one must have a high regard for terrorism, their principal contribution.

Civilian morale held up well because there never was a period in which the press could not celebrate some recent victory,[82] execrate a British atrocity, or report a hero's welcome, complete with gift of plate and sword. The public had a much higher opinion of the conduct of the war than posterity has held.

The War of 1812 is usually scored as a military stalemate. Canadians, outnumbered fourteen to one, created a myth of a sturdy militia winning a glorious moral victory, although Canada was actually saved by the British regulars.[83] Sir John Fortescue

[80] From a bitter letter of Procter to Prevost, Aug. 9, 1813, Klinck (ed.), *Tecumseh*, p. 181.

[81] For examples, *ibid.*, pp. 180–182, and Brock to Prevost, Sept. 18, 1812, *ibid.*, p. 167.

[82] *Niles' Weekly Register*, Sept. 10, 24, 1814, in two successive issues (there was no issue on Sept. 17 because everybody in the plant except the office boy was bearing arms) could report the destruction of Washington, the defense of Baltimore, Macdonough's Lake Champlain triumph, and Prevost's withdrawal to Canada.

[83] Stanley, "The Contribution of the Canadian Militia During the War," in Mason (ed.), *After Tippecanoe*, pp. 28–48.

made wonderful nonsense when he wrote of the effect of the blockade on the American people, "They were in fact utterly exhausted."[84] Except for the bloodshed, Britain and the United States did not hurt each other very much. In the one permanent military result of the war, the United States outpointed Great Britain, although it may depend on one's complexion whether it should be called a gain: The military power of the Indians east of the ninety-fifth meridian was broken forever.[85]

[84] John W. Fortescue, *History of the British Army* (13 vols., London, 1910–35) , X, 181.

[85] The diplomatic consequence of the Indian campaigns is a subject of Chapter 14.

CHAPTER 13

Hindrance and Discomfort

A S in all wars there were derangements of the economy and of public spirit. The economic trauma is more easily described than the civic psychoses.

Madison denied the legality of the blockade and encouraged neutral shipping, but oceanic commerce withered. The peak year of foreign trade had been 1807, when imports and exports totaled nearly a quarter of a billion dollars. By 1814 the figure had fallen 90 per cent and the Latin American, Caribbean, and Oriental trades were practically dead. The decline of shipbuilding by 80 per cent in the years 1811–14 was a predictable result. An ingenious people responded to the challenge by going into manufacturing, especially textiles—particularly in New England and in previously depressed Delaware. Manufactures provided a market for blockaded cotton and drained a river of gold into New England banks. As Thomas Jefferson put it, Britain resembled Satan, leading people from the paradise of peace and agriculture to war and manufactures. Wholesale prices rose remarkably. Formerly the rise was attributed to the rise in overland freight costs, as compared with waterborne freights, but the Ohio Valley, which was served by inland navigation, paid about the same prices, indicating that demand exceeded supply everywhere. In the Indian country the frontier stood still or receded and the government frontier posts went out of business. The private traders saw their market for fur disappear and their risks increase as the Missouri Valley Indians became contemptuous of American military power.[1]

The public finance of the republic was successful, but it reeled and staggered through the war in a manner horrifying to tidy people and to check-stub economists of later generations. The doctrine of dependence on tariffs—more theology than statecraft—proved false. A doubling of duties in 1812 was followed by a halving of revenue in 1813, so the war engine was mostly fueled by loans and Treasury notes. The necessary reliance on state banks made it hard to borrow and inconvenient to transfer money, and provided chaotic media of exchange. Some excises and constitutionally apportioned direct taxes were levied, but most of the revenue came from $37 million in Treasury notes and by borrowing $80 million in paper equaling $34 million in gold. Of the loans, less than $3 million came from rich but tightfisted New England. All loans after early 1813 sold below par, although United States bonds were alleged to stand at par in London in 1814.[2]

In the darkest hours of 1813, four foreign-born citizens combined to do what Yankees would not. British A. J. Dallas arranged for French Stephen Girard and Germans John Jacob Astor and David Parish to take $9 million in bonds at 88. Dallas, quite logically, became Secretary of the Treasury several months after Albert Gallatin went abroad in diplomacy. On the eve of peace the imaginative Dallas was even planning inheritance and income taxes. The debt in 1815 was $127.3 million. Annual expenditures had tripled since 1811, yet the Treasury began the year 1816 with the largest credit balance to that time, having received $13 million

[1] Carleton Savage (ed.), *Policy of the United States Toward Maritime Commerce in War* (2 vols., Washington, 1934–36), I, 38–39, 287–288; John H. Frederick, *The Development of American Commerce* (New York, 1932), pp. 50–53; Samuel Eliot Morison, *The Maritime History of Massachusetts, 1783–1860* (Boston, 1921), pp. 203–205; Curtis P. Nettels, *The Emergence of a National Economy, 1775–1815* (New York, 1962), pp. 242, 335–338; Jefferson to Short, Nov. 28, 1814, Andrew Lipscomb et al. (eds.), *The Writings of Thomas Jefferson* (20 vols., Washington, 1904–14), XIV, 214; United States Bureau of the Census, *Historical Statistics of the United States, Colonial Times to 1957* (Washington, 1960), pp. 115, 119–121; Ora Brooks Peake, *A History of the United States Indian Factory System, 1795–1822* (Denver, 1954), pp. 153–165.

[2] Davis Rich Dewey, *Financial History of the United States* (New York, 1924), pp. 132–134; *Niles' Weekly Register,* June 4, 1814, quoting the antiadministration Baltimore *Federal Republican;* Sidney Ratner, *American Taxation, Its History as a Social Force in Democracy* (New York, 1942), pp. 33–35.

more than it needed.[3] Being "crudely self-sufficient," the country could produce its own war materials independent of foreign help,[4] and a good thing too, because it has never been so cramped and isolated before or since.[5] A generation earlier its fathers had financed a war with a currency based on rag paper and by panhandling occasional handouts from barely solvent kings. It is not too absurd to think that the more intricate, weary, and nervous British public finance might have cracked as soon.

II

The change of political mood was most noticeable in New England, where the Federalist elders intensified their hatred of everything Republican, but there were republican intransigents as well. Kindly George Logan, for example, reflecting on the "mutual acts of irritation" by the United States and Britain, found "both in the wrong."[6] The North Carolina legislature felt it necessary to censure one of its United States senators, quondam Republican David Stone, for obstructionist voting on war measures. John Randolph, out of Congress and temporarily out of favor, wrote many private letters against the war, loaded with sectionalism, devoid of patriotism, and revealing no generous impulse or sentiment of any kind. Doubts of Republican orthodoxy in the Senate may have motivated Vice-President Elbridge Gerry to break precedent in 1813 by presiding continuously over the Senate so that no president *pro tempore* was elected. If both he and Madison had died, Speaker Henry Clay would have become President of the United States, and he was probably as warm for administration policy as any senator. (Madison was seriously ill in June and July of 1813, and Gerry died in

[3] Raymond Walters, Jr., *Albert Gallatin: Jeffersonian Financier and Diplomat* (New York, 1957), pp. 254–258, and *Alexander James Dallas: Lawyer-Politician-Financier, 1759–1817* (Philadelphia, 1943), pp. 175–188; for the details and a description of Girard's banking business, see John Bach McMaster, *Life and Times of Stephen Girard* (2 vols., Philadelphia, 1918), II, 239–269; Dewey, *Financial History*, pp. 135–142; the War of 1812 was written off the books with the payment of the last pension installment of $500 in 1946, *Historical Statistics*, p. 739.

[4] Nettels, *National Economy*, p. 335.

[5] Robert G. Albion and Jennie Barnes Pope, *Sea Lanes in Wartime, The American Experience* (New York, 1942), pp. 109–125; George Dangerfield, *The Era of Good Feelings* (New York, 1952), pp. 81–83.

[6] Logan to Jefferson, Dec. 9, 1813, Deborah Logan (ed.), *Memoir of Dr. George Logan of Stenton* (Philadelphia, 1899), p. 141.

1814.) For the record, it should be noted that New York's Mayor DeWitt Clinton, rump Republican candidate for President in 1812, incurred no reproach although disappointed of a general's commission. On balance, antiwar feeling was not as much of a problem among Republicans as was apathy. Measured by recruiting figures, patriotism was about 10 per cent as hot as during the Civil War.[7]

Federalist strength was greatest in New England, but there were pockets of Federalism elsewhere. Widely scattered Federalist countries in the South accepted the administration policy, but the war killed Federalism in South Carolina and in Georgia. Some western Virginians agreed with John Randolph, but Federalists were nearly extinct in Kentucky. The elections of 1814 gave the Federalists about the same proportion of congressional seats and clear majorities in New England, Delaware, and Maryland. Federalism did better than in 1812, but it was nationally weak. More ominous for the future of Federalism was the defection to Republicanism of former leaders, in the years 1807–15, including the Adamses; Samuel Dexter; William Plumer; Attorney General William Pinkney, who defended the administration in pseudonymous pamphlets; and James A. Bayard, who helped to negotiate the peace treaty.[8]

The Federalist doctrine was that the Republicans were Bonaparte's auxiliaries for ideological reasons and because a French victory would erase American debts to British creditors. This was ludicrously irrational. Napoleon's attitude toward America was now overtly arrogant, and Jefferson spoke for his fellows when he described him as "the greatest of the destroyers of the human

[7] Dorothie Bobbé, *DeWitt Clinton* (New York, 1933), pp. 188–202; D. H. Gilpatrick, *Jeffersonian Democracy in North Carolina, 1789–1816* (New York, 1931), pp. 208–211; William Cabell Bruce, *John Randolph of Roanoke, 1773–1833* (2 vols., New York, 1922), I, 386–416; Henry Barrett Learned, "Gerry and the Presidential Succession in 1813," *American Historical Review*, XXII (1915–16), 94–97; Irving Brant, *James Madison, Commander-in-Chief* (Indianapolis, 1961), pp. 184–188; A. L. Burt, *The United States, Great Britain, and British North America from the Revolution to the Establishment of Peace after the War of 1812* (New Haven, 1940), pp. 323–325.

[8] J. H. Wolfe, *Jeffersonian Democracy in South Carolina* (Chapel Hill, 1940), pp. 254–286; John E. Talmadge, "Georgia's Federalist Press and the War of 1812," *Journal of Southern History*, XIX (1953), 488–500; Thomas P. Abernethy, *The South in the New Nation, 1789–1819* (Baton Rouge, 1961), pp. 405–410; Shaw Livermore, Jr., *The Twilight of Federalism: The Disintegration of the Federalist Party, 1815–1830* (Princeton, 1962), pp. 3–15, gives a good psychological analysis of the decay of Federalism.

race. . . ."⁹ An occasional Napoleonic success was welcome and
administration denunciations of France were rather perfunctory,
but Madison would have preferred to settle with Britain peaceably,
and more directly, than by collaboration with France. The tone of
Federalist philippics was that of the late 1790's. Stoutly nationalist
Hezekiah Niles satirized the opposition in alleged quotations from
hostile newspapers, e.g., Madison had promised New England to
Bonaparte and William Hull's orders were written in Paris.¹⁰

The Republican rebuttals ranged from political theorizing to
lynching. Mathew Carey, Philadelphia publicist, wrote a mediating
pamphlet which went to nine printings, and John Quincy Adams
thought the pseudo debate was a naked contest for power.¹¹ John
Calhoun promised to stand against every "threat of disunion," and
identified the congressional minority as insurrectionaries.¹² A Baltimore mob attacked the house of A. C. Hanson, publisher of the
antiwar *Federal Republican*. When Hanson and Revolutionary
Generals Henry Lee and James Lingan accepted sanctuary in jail,
they were dragged out and beaten so savagely that Light-Horse
Harry was crippled and Lingan died. There seem to have been
instances of Federalist mob terrorism in New Haven, Milford,
Litchfield, Boston, Plymouth, Newburyport, and the towns of
Rhode Island, but the Baltimore lynching received all the pub-
licity.¹³

⁹ Jefferson to Mme. de Staël-Holstein, May 28, 1813, Marie G. Kimball (ed.),
"Unpublished Correspondence of Mme. de Staël with Thomas Jefferson," *North
American Review*, CCVIII (1918), 67.

¹⁰ Lawrence S. Kaplan, "France and Madison's Decision for War in 1812,"
Mississippi Valley Historical Review, L (1963–64), 652–671; Bradford Perkins,
Prologue to War: England and the United States, 1805–1812 (Berkeley, 1961),
pp. 61–64; *Niles' Weekly Register*, Aug. 15, 1812.

¹¹ E. F. J. Maier, "Mathew Carey, Publicist and Politician," American Catholic
Historical Society of Philadelphia, *Records*, XXXIX (1928), 121–125; Charles M.
Wiltse, "John Quincy Adams and the Party System: A Review Article," *Journal
of Politics*, IV (1942), 407–414.

¹² Calhoun to Macbride, June 23, 1813, Robert L. Meriwether (ed.), *The
Papers of John Calhoun* (3 vols., Columbia, S.C., 1959–), I, 177; *Debates and
Proceedings in the Congress of the United States* (42 vols., Washington, 1834–56),
13th Congress, 2nd Session, pp. 994–1002 (hereafter cited as *Annals*).

¹³ The lynching occurred on June 22, 1812. *Niles' Weekly Register*, Aug. 8,
1812, collects the available documents and reprints the essay in Hanson's
newspaper, which was said to have provoked the mob. D. H. Fischer, *The
Revolution of American Conservatism: The Federalist Party in the Era of
Jeffersonian Democracy* (New York, 1965), p. 157, 157 n., mentions reports of
Federalist mobs in the press.

The reading of Federalist journalism convinced British leaders that the Americans were only junior partners of Bonaparte and that prolonging the war would lead to the secession of New England. The Lingan murder seemed evidence of the gravest dissensions,[14] and early in 1814 the editor of *The Gentleman's Magazine* could believe that the course of events had brought American leadership to "the agonies of despair."[15]

Despair was not characteristic of the Republican administration, but exasperation at northeastern Federalists would have been understandable. Northeastern businessmen and clergy were sometimes incredibly provincial, seeing their region as a kind of New World Denmark. In those parts Federalism was a way of life which placed high values on the Congregational and Presbyterian churches, on a hierarchical society, and on the superior wisdom and virtue of the section. Some Baptist and Methodist clergy supported the war, but of Congregational and Presbyterian clergy only Alexander McLeod of New York and William Bentley of Salem were outspoken in support. The suspension of the new British-assisted American programs of missionary work in India and Burma because of the war may have been a cause of clerical resentment. Less rational were the accusations that weakling Madison chose war as a way to re-election, or because of subservience to Bonaparte, or to impoverish the maritime states and divert commerce to the western waters. Timothy Pickering gave out inside reports that both Jefferson and Madison wished war regardless of circumstances. The arguments of Republican villainy had antecedents in 1794, 1798, 1804, and 1808, and repetition began to make them popularly credible in New England, despite the sterling character of some nonpolitical Yankee Republicans, such as William Gray, the leading merchant of the section. The moral level of the administration was shown by the alleged daily drunkenness of Navy Secretary Paul Hamilton, and the Battle of the Thames was deprecated falsely as bloodless. New Bedford discouraged privateering to prevent the introduction of disease. And so on. Federalist politicians were knowledgeable

---

14 Gallatin to Crawford, April 21, 1814, Henry Adams (ed.) , *The Writings of Albert Gallatin* (3 vols., Philadelphia, 1879) , I, 602–603; *The Gentleman's Magazine,* CXII (Sept. 1812) , 283.
15 *Ibid.,* CXV (Supplement, 1814) , 683.

enough to weigh these things. If they were sincere, they had become captives of their dialectic.[16]

New England enthusiasm was not really necessary, but soldiers were indispensable. New England youth disregarded the old men and enlisted in the federal forces in a satisfactory proportion, but the best militia were unavailable because the governors of Massachusetts and Connecticut declined to put their militia at federal disposal. The militia system of New York weighed lightly on the gentry, and the poor were unenthusiastic about the service until a reorganization in 1814 equalized the burden on rich and poor. Twelve thousand New Yorkers would have been available in 1815. Very likely the New England governors were looking for constitutional quibbles to justify political predilections. The Massachusetts legislature supported Governor Caleb Strong by a pronouncement on states' rights—the union was a union of states as well as of people. As chief of a sovereign state, the governor was to decide whether an emergency was grave enough to justify a presidential call for the militia, and this view was supported by the Governor's Council and by the Massachusetts Supreme Judicial Court. Daniel Webster preached defiance of the United States on the narrow ground that the Constitution was chiefly intended to protect commerce, taking a position he would have denied to others fifteen years later. Honest men *could* differ on the President's authority over militia. Rufus King believed it was limited to instances of invasion, that militia organization must be preserved, and that no regular officer could be detached to command them. The officers of a Pennsylvania regiment submitted to arrest rather than accept the United States Army table of organization.[17]

[16] Morison, *Maritime History*, p. 211; John R. Bodo, *The Protestant Clergy and Public Issues, 1812–1848* (Princeton, 1954), pp. 198–202; Theodore Clarke Smith, "War Guilt in 1812," Massachusetts Historical Society, *Proceedings*, LXIV (1932), 319–345; Morison, *The Life and Letters of Harrison Gray Otis* (2 vols., Boston, 1913), II, 41–42; *The Gentleman's Magazine*, CXIII (May, 1813), 478; *Niles' Weekly Register*, Dec. 4, 1813, quoting a Rhode Island paper, and also Aug. 6, 1814; James Truslow Adams, *New England in the Republic, 1776–1850* Boston, 1926), pp. 290–295.

[17] John T. Horton, *James Kent, A Study in Conservatism, 1763–1847* (New York, 1939), pp. 237–241; the Supreme Court defined the law of the domestic use of militia only in 1827, and the question of the use of militia abroad was not settled until 1898 and after, as explained in Homer C. Hockett, *The Constitutional History of the United States* (2 vols., New York, 1939), I, 333–336; Rufus

The Northeast refused to lend much money to the United States, except for a few men who may have done so secretly. It was not for lack of money. By trading with the enemy, speculating in British treasury notes, and manufacturing, the section made money from both sides. From June, 1810, to January, 1814, the deposits in thirty-three Massachusetts banks tripled, and their gold quadrupled, despite allegations that the Americans were dying under the weight of taxes, especially of taxes on tea and coffee.[18] Refusal to take United States bonds had been advised as a matter of honor by a New York paper and a Boston paper weeks before the declaration of war; one put it this way: *"Let every highwayman find his own pistols."*[19] New England expected the loans of 1814 to fail. In that year the Treasury borrowed about $10.9 million, of which $377,000 came from the six lonely lenders in Massachusetts, which held the largest hoard of gold.[20]

The inhibitors were not overtly and extravagantly pro-British except when Bonaparte fell in 1814, upon which there was a public thanksgiving ceremonial in Boston at which the Czar was praised as "dear to every lover of national freedom."[21] A private portent was the knowledgeable Christopher Gore's report in 1813 of a proposal to declare the dissolution of the United States.[22]

Republicans were not shaken by northeastern intransigence. When the Boston *Repertory* called for *"physical force"* to oppose the war, Henry Clay, in *The National Intelligencer,* said the people of Massachusetts would put down treason and their militia would resist any foreign power called in by their leaders.[23] Jefferson

---

King, memorandum of June 27, 1812, Charles R. King (ed.) , *The Life and Correspondence of Rufus King* (6 vols., New York, 1894–1900) , V, 625; James Gore King, Jr., "Caleb Strong," *DAB;* Claude M. Fuess, *Daniel Webster* (2 vols., Boston, 1930) , I, 136–139. The final adjudication was Martin v. Mott, 12 Wheaton 19 (1827) .

18 *Niles' Weekly Register,* Dec. 3, 1814; Dec. 11, 1813.

19 *Ibid.,* May 2, 1812.

20 Charles Warren, *Jacobin and Junto; or, Early American Politics as Viewed in the Diary of Dr. Nathaniel Ames, 1758–1822* (Cambridge, Mass., 1931) , pp. 266–268, 267 n.

21 *Ibid.,* pp. 270–273.

22 Gore to King, Sept. 13, 1813, *Rufus King,* V, 345; Henry Adams (ed.) , *Documents Relating to New-England Federalism, 1800–1815* (Boston, 1877) , the indispensable collection.

23 Boston *Repertory* (summarized) , June 26, 1812, and Clay's reply, both in James F. Hopkins (ed.) , *The Papers of Henry Clay* (10 vols., Lexington, Ky., 1959–) , I, 692–694.

thought it would be easier to raise an army to fight against rebellion in Massachusetts than against a foreign foe in Canada, while Madison believed the true object of northeastern opposition was self-aggrandizement, as did John Adams, and only regretted that the intransigence protected and encouraged Britain.[24] Adams the Younger was incensed, describing New England's behavior as "whining hypocrisy" and "prostitution."[25] The Boston *Patriot* noted that an independent New England would have a restricted industrial market; separation would serve only those who thought it "Better to reign in hell than serve in Heaven."[26] Niles invoked the name of Washington against those who used it as an anti-Republican scourge, and dwelt on Washington's persistent nationalism. He also calculated the combined populations of Massachusetts towns which adopted remonstrances against the war as less than 10 per cent of the Massachusetts population.[27]

The numerical strength of the northeastern opposition can be sampled. In Army enlistments, New England's share was satisfactory. In votes, the Massachusetts Federalists received 57 per cent in 1813 and 55.5 per cent in 1814. In New Hampshire, although Governor William Plumer lost in 1813, the Republicans captured the Executive Council. The New York election of 1814 was a Federalist catastrophe; the Republicans won the Assembly, 74–38, and reversed the congressional delegation from 6–20 to 21–6. Republicans fared worst in Connecticut, where the Federalists received 80.5 per cent of the gubernatorial vote in 1812 and 78.5 per cent in 1814. The war obviously eroded Republican strength in New England, but it was still a force that required the attention of its opponents. Only in Connecticut, where the Young Federalists had organized so effectively, did Federalism approach unanimity. As for the nation at large, that pendulum of feeling, the House of Representatives, was remarkably free of vibration. The House elected in

[24] Jefferson to Short, Nov. 28, 1814, *Writings of Jefferson*, XIV, 217–218; John Adams to Jefferson, June 30, 1813, Lester Cappon (ed.), *The Adams-Jefferson Letters* (2 vols., Chapel Hill, 1959), II, 348; Madison to Nicholas, Nov. 26, 1814, Gaillard Hunt (ed.), *The Writings of James Madison* (9 vols., New York, 1900–1910), VIII, 319.
[25] John Quincy Adams to Eustis, July 25, 1815, Worthington C. Ford (ed.), *Writings of John Quincy Adams* (7 vols., New York, 1913–17), V, 329.
[26] Boston *Patriot*, Jan. 21, 1815, reported in *Niles' Weekly Register*, Feb. 11, 1815.
[27] *Ibid.*, Mar. 5, 1814.

1812 was Republican by 112 to 68, and the one elected in 1814 was 117 to 65.[28]

Northeastern sectionalism was a strategic and psychological handicap from the start. In his farewell conversation with Secretary of State James Monroe, British Minister Augustus J. Foster included New England sedition among American liabilities. The western campaigns have been called stupid, but more promising eastern theaters of operation were practically interdicted. The Royal Navy guarded Nova Scotia, but Massachusetts shielded New Brunswick. The whole of Lower Canada was insecure except for the protection given by the buffer province of New England. The conquest of Lower Canada would have been victory; Massachusetts (and Connecticut) said nay. Furthermore, the vituperation, invective, and abuse from Federalists, mostly New Englanders, prolonged the war, if not by aid and comfort to the enemy, at least by hindrance and discomfort to the United States as specifically shown in extreme British demands in the Ghent negotiations.[29] The only stated mitigation of the New England military position has been the citation of its good record in Army enlistments, but this is indirectly damning because it means that the sour elders watched their bravest youngsters go to battle unsupported in flesh or spirit.

One way to frustrate the war was to trade with the enemy, but some of this was legal, tolerable, even beneficial. Cargoes shipped from Britain before the declaration of war was known abroad were accepted until the end of 1812. Direct trade with British ports via Georgia was winked at in order to establish balances to pay British bondholders their interest on United States bonds. Nor were the British intolerant of Americans who fed the West Indies.[30]

However, most Anglo-American trade was blatantly detrimental to the United States. Shippers rallied enough support from grain growers late in 1812 to defeat an embargo on provisions, and British diplomatists generously distributed passes through the Royal Navy blockade before departing. The Royal Navy and the British armies needed American supplies. Hundreds of commercial licenses—called "Sidmouths" after Henry Addington, Viscount Sidmouth, the minister who instituted them—were hawked and traded in

28 *Historical Statistics*, pp. 691–692.
29 Burt, *U.S., Great Britain, and British North America*, pp. 319–322. The Treaty of Ghent is the major subject of Chapter 14.
30 Dangerfield, *Era of Good Fellings*, pp. 80–82; Albion and Pope, *Sea Lanes in Wartime*, pp. 116–118.

American ports at prices up to a thousand dollars each. Grain exports for the British armies in Spain and Portugal totaled 835,000 bushels in 1811 and rose to a peak of 973,000 bushels in 1813, although the number of American-flag ships declined sharply, possibly because denaturalization as Swedish, Spanish, or Portuguese was cheaper than buying Sidmouths. New England shipping was little disturbed through 1813, partly because the British needed provisions and, partly, it was thought, for political reasons. Nova Scotian authorities treated American skippers generously, and the home government made Halifax a depot of the Old Colonial System by drafting an old-fashioned enumerated-products list of the acceptable produce of the United States. Nova Scotian merchants protested the blockading of New England by the Royal Navy late in 1813, when Wellington no longer needed American rations, but the trade shifted inland by way of conquered Maine and all were happy again. Block Islanders supplied the blockading ships by conspicuously spending British guineas to buy foods they formerly exported to the mainland.[31]

The traders of a navyless nation, dealing with an enemy who could absorb almost everything offered for sale, needed no very sophisticated techniques. Notarized audits are wholly lacking in such a business, but one may guess that only one in five smugglers was caught. They surely had nothing to fear from Massachusetts, which scornfully refused to help the federal government reclaim the lost District of Maine, even with all expenses paid. Governor William Plumer of New Hampshire plugged the leaks in his Canadian boundary, but failed of re-election in 1813.[32]

After the rejection of an embargo in 1812, the administration continued to press the subject. The Congress, in July, 1813, prohibited any use of a British permit under penalty of condemnation as an enemy ship. The President also wished to prevent exports in

31 A. Bigelow to H. Bigelow, Nov. 8, 1812, "Letters of Abijah Bigelow, Member of Congress, to His Wife, 1810–1815," American Antiquarian Society, *Proceedings,* New Series, XL (1930), 341–342; Bradford Perkins, *Castlereagh and Adams, England and America, 1812–1823* (Berkeley, 1964), pp. 7–11, describes the trade; W. Freeman Galpin, "The American Grain Trade to the Spanish Peninsula, 1810–1814," *American Historical Review,* XXVIII (1922–23), 25 n., 44 n., 39–44; Gerald S. Graham, *Sea Power and British North America, 1783–1820, A Study in British Colonial Policy* (Cambridge, Mass., 1941), pp. 211–215; Walter Ronald Copp, "Nova Scotian Trade During the War of 1812," *Canadian Historical Review,* XVII (1937), 141–155; *Niles' Weekly Register,* May 29, 1813.
32 Burt, *U.S., Great Britain, and British North America,* pp. 341–344; Lynn W. Turner, *William Plumer of New Hampshire* (Chapel Hill, 1962), pp. 210–213.

foreign-flag ships (mostly denatured Americans). Finally, in December, 1813, when the British market had shrunk, he got his wish in a Force Act which killed maritime commerce except for the illicit trade of Maine and Georgia, although General Henry Dearborn did not realize his hope of extinguishing lighthouses. By 1814 the Supreme Court had twenty maritime cases on its docket. They were legally important but their outcomes could not affect the war, because the British had already immobilized both the United States Navy and the merchant fleet.[33]

It is practically impossible to measure the economic effect of trade with the enemy because the surviving price records are unrelated to the volume of goods. But we do know that New England became richer through the war, and, as New England became richer, New England became raspier. Swollen gold reserves certainly did not buy happiness.

III

New England antipathy toward the rest of the union increased from the election of Jefferson to 1814, when it reached the ignition point. The profits of illegal trade had soothing effects, but when the trade became hazardous the benefits of union seemed even less valuable. The power of the West increased in direct proportion to the decay of New England influence, and Yankees scanned all federal measures with the eyes of paranoia. In the fall of 1814, Massachusetts circularized the New England states to meet and consider remedies for their ills. There had been agitation for action since early 1813, and the idea of a convention of dissenters had ancient patriotic precedents. Massachusetts suggested Hartford as the site, and Federalists in the legislature chose George Cabot to lead their delegation.

Expectations varied. Some men seemed to anticipate separate peace with Britain or the ejection of the West from the union. In Newburyport, press and pulpit strongly urged secession. Timothy Pickering privately anticipated temporary secession and later reunion under a revised constitution. Pacific intentions have been read into Governor Caleb Strong's return of borrowed federal stores and arms, but his motives remain obscure inasmuch as he sent a secret agent to Halifax to learn the British attitude toward a

---

[33] Galpin, "Grain Trade," pp. 39–41; Charles Warren, *The Supreme Court in United States History* (rev. ed., 2 vols., Boston, 1926–37), I, 426–432.

separate peace. He received a promise of materials and naval help, but not of troops.[34] In a lower economic stratum there was a federal-license-fee strike in Hampshire County, pending the word from Hartford.[35] John Lowell, the most vitriolic Federalist pamphleteer, was downcast after he read the list of delegates, too many of whom were, as he described one delegate, "extremely prudent."[36]

The Massachusetts, Connecticut, and Rhode Island state legislatures sent delegations, but only three counties of New Hampshire and one county of Vermont were represented. The Connecticut delegation represented a near-totalitarian legislative machine, checked only by an intimidated electorate which had to vote orally and publicly. Rhode Island Federals showed their temper by refusing to enter the protest of the minority in their journal. (The vote to send delegates was 39–23).[37] The leadership of New England was paradoxically scatterbrained and narrow-minded, with the persecution and conspiracy view of the world of the radical right. What can be made of a sober politician-delegate who wrote that "Catiline, Cromwell and Jefferson were very similar characters"?[38] John Quincy Adams called it a secessionist meeting which intended to demand the impossible and then reconvene to secede, but it has been said that Strong's gesture of returning the federal arms proved Adams wrong. However, Strong's embassy to Halifax fits Adams' pattern. Perhaps the best explanation was that the leaders were attempting to practice limited treason, which could be as hard to keep in check as a limited war.[39]

[34] J. S. Martell, "A Side Light on Federalist Strategy," *American Historical Review*, XLIII (1937–38), 553–566, tells the story and publishes the documents.

[35] Benjamin W. Labaree, *Patriots and Partisans: The Merchants of Newburyport, 1764–1815* (Cambridge, Mass., 1962), pp. 196–199; Pickering to Gouverneur Morris, Oct. 21, 1814, Adams (ed.), *New-England Federalism*, p. 401; *Niles' Weekly Register*, Jan. 7, 1815. Governor Strong was one of the authors of the United States Constitution, although he left before it was completed.

[36] Lowell to Pickering, Dec. 3, 1814, Adams (ed.), *New-England Federalism*, p. 412.

[37] Adams, *New England in the Republic*, pp. 290–292; Richard J. Purcell, *Connecticut in Transition, 1775–1818* (Washington, 1918), pp. 174–216, 299–330, well describes the remarkable Connecticut theoplutocracy. (The second printing differs in pagination from the 1918 printing.)

[38] The radical right, to use an anachronistic term, exhibits itself well in William E. Buckley (ed.), "Letters of Connecticut Federalists, 1814–1815," *New England Quarterly*, III, 316–331.

[39] Morison, "The Massachusetts Embassy to Washington," Massachusetts Historical Society, *Proceedings*, XLVIII (1915), 343–351, is illuminating and, in editorial comment, makes the best brief for the moderation theory.

So far as the Hartford Convention movement had a popular base, it was grounded on the economic reaction against Democratic-Republican policies among—of all people—Jefferson's beloved yeomanry, in this instance the farmers of the Connecticut Valley. As early as 1808, Harrison Gray Otis thought it might be a good idea to have a meeting to seek relief, although he specifically opposed disunion and proposed only an appeal to sectional pride to gain a political profit. He and like-minded men never lost control of the movement, but their attitude was not universally approved among supporters of the Hartford idea. The coming of peace may have saved Otis and friends from having to undertake the nearly impossible job of restraining secessionist passion.[40]

The Hartford Convention, whatever its plans for 1815 may have been, was not ruled by advocates of Secession Now. The report of the convention said that unconstitutional federal acts should be countered by the states to shield their citizens. Defense should be left to the states, which should retain a part of their federal taxes. The convention proposed to amend the Constitution as follows: to apportion taxes and representation in proportion to the number of *free* persons; to prohibit embargoes of more than sixty days; to require a two-thirds vote of the Congress to declare war, restrict foreign trade, or admit new states; to bar naturalized citizens from federal office; and to limit the Presidency to one term. A committee of three carried the news from Hartford to Washington.[41]

The convention never received any official scrutiny, but there were some interesting private reactions. The Raleigh *Register* calculated that New England was 2 per cent underrepresented in the House and 14 per cent overrepresented in the Senate, hence had no apportionment misery.[42] John Adams said George Cabot "wants to be President of New England, sir."[43] John Randolph was shocked; not because provocation for secession was absent, but because secession would be unseemly until peace came. These several comments

40 Fischer, *Revolution of American Conservatism,* pp. 176–178, 178 n.

41 The convention is described, with documents supplementary to the author's text, in Morison, *Otis,* II, 78–199; the report of the Hartford Convention, dated Dec. 15, 1814, is printed in *Niles' Weekly Register,* Jan. 14, 1815, and is also available in the much more widely accessible Henry Steele Commager (ed.), *Documents of American History* (7th ed., New York, 1963).

42 Cited by Abernethy, *South in the New Nation,* p. 423.

43 Adams' oral remark is quoted in Cappon, *The Adams-Jefferson Letters,* II, 416 and n.

were weighted with the knowledge that the delegates ominously planned to reassemble in 1815 to evaluate the reception of their propositions. What they did not know was that Britain authorized negotiations for a separate peace with New England if useful. But the upshot was wholly anticlimactic. The arrival of news of Jackson's victory and of the Peace of Ghent made the veiled threat and its authors ridiculous and tainted them with suspicions of sedition which never died.[44]

Modern palliators of the Hartford Convention have said it was called by popular demand, it merely adopted the Republicans' theory underlying the Virginia and Kentucky Resolutions of 1798 (which, incidentally, were approved by legislative resolution nowhere outside of Virginia and Kentucky), and it observed the constitutional proprieties by offering its proposals as the work of states, not of autonomous sovereignties. But the convention had nothing like unanimous support, active Federalist leaders included many who had denounced the Resolutions of 1798, and the Supreme Court *after* 1798, under Federalist guidance, had become the judge of federal constitutionality. As for a comparison with the Kentucky and Virginia Resolutions of 1798, Kentucky and Virginia had published eloquent pleas for freedom as it was then defined, while the Hartford Convention argued for parochialism and privilege. It is also remarked that moderates carefully steered the convention away from extremism. The fact that New England manufactures had become worth $20 million annually in the American common market suggests that economic interest, not a philosophy of political moderation, probably reigned; plainly, national policy had not bankrupted New England. And there was always the military consideration: the unity necessary for successful secession was lacking, and the need of foreign help had already occurred to Governor Strong. As for the temperance and moderation of the men who kept the convention in bounds, George Dangerfield put it well: they only threatened civil war if they did not get their way.[45]

44 Abernethy, *South in the New Nation*, pp. 422–423; Martell, "Sidelight on Federalist Strategy."

45 Robert A. East, "Economic Development and New England Federalism, 1803–1814," *New England Quarterly*, X (1937), 430–446; Dangerfield, *Era of Good Feelings*, p. 88.

CHAPTER 14

The Corroboration of Nationality

ATTEMPTS at making peace began simultaneously with making war.[1] When the British ministry revoked the orders in council (June 23, 1812), the Foreign Secretary, Robert Stewart, Viscount Castlereagh, expected the revocation to relax American hostility. But impressment stuck in the throat. Jonathan Russell, the American chargé in London, on orders from Secretary of State James Monroe, had twice tried to discuss the Royal Navy's kidnaping practice and had twice been rebuffed. In mid-June, Castlereagh sent word of the revocation of the orders to Anthony St. John Baker, left behind in Washington by Minister Augustus John Foster. Both Baker's manner and his message raised the hair on American necks. His manner was blunt, and the message he bore was an ultimatum to rescind limits on trade with Britain in a fortnight or suffer the consequences of a revival of the orders. Someone in Britain had a second thought, and another message came a week later to cancel the repellent time limit, but it was too late to repair the damage. Baker and his instructions had no effect on the policy of the United States. However, the Admiralty was sending out a fresh commander, Admiral Sir John Borlase Warren. Castlereagh told him his first

[1] This chapter has drawn much from a manuscript entitled "The Indecisive Peace" by Joseph B. Starshak of Magdalen College, Oxford, a copy of which has been deposited in the Notre Dame Collection of the Memorial Library, Notre Dame, Indiana, and from Bradford Perkins, *Castlereagh and Adams, England and the United States, 1812–1823* (Berkeley, 1964), Chaps. i–ix. To avoid repetition, these materials are not hereafter credited except in cases of quotation. In fairness to the writers, it should be added that the author has not assimilated their views of the fiscal and strategic situation of the United States in 1814.

duty was "to endeavour to re-establish . . . Peace & Amity."[2] Unlike Baker, he was not mandated to threaten but only to request the dropping of restrictions on Anglo-American trade. By the time his proposition arrived in Washington, the war was known to both sides. Monroe made it clear that it must be agreed before any negotiation that Britain would resepct the persons of seafaring American citizens in return for a promise to bar His Majesty's subjects from American ships[3] (which prohibition was fruitlessly enacted into law in 1813). Warren had no such powers, and hope for a quick peace burned away in the fires of war.

Paradoxically, the road to negotiations was found after a preliminary exploration of a blind alley in St. Petersburg. Nicholas, Count Rumiantzov, the Russian Foreign Minister, unexpectedly offered his court's mediation to John Quincy Adams, who cautiously encouraged him. Russian overtures to the British received a polite rejection from Castlereagh, but the Russians pressed the point and sent the offer to Washington, where the Russian chargé, who had already suggested the same thing, transmitted it to the United States in March, 1813. Napoleon's disaster of 1812 may have influenced President James Madison to accept. Despite British chilliness, he appointed moderate Federalist James A. Bayard, Treasury Secretary Albert Gallatin, and Adams to assemble in St. Petersburg to do what they could. But the British chill seemed permanent. British recruiting practices did not seem debatable while Napoleon remained uncaged, and the British seemed indisposed to debate international law under the auspices of Russia, which had a history of inclining toward neutrals in their disputes with belligerents. The British blunted several probes from St. Petersburg with the argument that the Anglo-American war concerned only its combatants and finally told their minister to consult the Czar at army headquarters, where he believed he persuaded the Czar to withdraw the offer of mediation.[4]

<hr/>

2 Quoted in Perkins, *Castlereagh and Adams*, p. 13.

3 Monroe to Warren, Oct. 27, 1812, *American State Papers: Documents Legislative and Executive of the Congress of the United States* (38 vols., Washington, 1832–61): *Foreign Relations*, III, 596–597.

4 Charles Francis Adams (ed.), *Memoirs of John Quincy Adams* (12 vols., Philadelphia, 1874–77), II, 401–404; Adams to Monroe, Sept. 30, 1812, Worthington C. Ford (ed.), *The Writings of John Quincy Adams* (7 vols., New York, 1913–17), IV, 389–391; Castlereagh to Cathcart, July 14, 1813, and Cathcart's No. 79 to Castlereagh, Aug. 5, 1813, C. K. Webster (ed.), *British Diplomacy, 1813–1815* (London, 1921), pp. 14–16.

The British told the Czar they were willing to negotiate with the United States directly, but neither they nor the Russians bothered officially to tell the American guests. Instead, the Russian Foreign Office continued to press the mediation idea. It always received the same answer, but only told Adams that the British were hesitant. Adams characteristically doubted that the British would ever accept Russian mediation, because their case was too weak to lay on a foreign mediator's table, and because they seemed to believe the quarrel was a domestic affair of the British Empire. Adams and his colleagues had nothing to do except to look forward to a Russian winter, to collate rumors of British attitudes, and to endure the temporary refusal of the Senate to consent to Gallatin's membership in their mission. Getting nowhere, Bayard and Gallatin departed for London to try to lobby against kidnaping aliens for Royal Naval service. Gallatin had a promising lead. The banker Alexander Baring, bursar for the United States Treasury payments to British bondholders, had told him in the summer of 1813 that the British would at least talk. In the following winter Castlereagh came to the point, and in January, 1814, Madison agreed to Anglo-American negotiations apart from any would-be conciliator.[5]

There were advantages to Britain in making the suggestion. It removed the embarrassing pressure of the Russian Foreign Ministry, while leaving Castlereagh uncommitted either to terms of an American peace or a date on which to start talking. The Americans, after Bonaparte's Russian catastrophe and his defeat at Leipzig (October, 1813), could hardly decline, because peace in Europe would allow Britain to bring great power to focus in the New World. After Madison accepted, he added Russell and Speaker Henry Clay to the mission, and a few weeks later, on another try, the Senate consented also to the appointment of Gallatin. Little happened early in 1814, *outside* of the United States, to make it seem a good year for the Americans to play a hand. The Navy, a nuisance to Britain at best, had declined to impotence. The allies occupied Paris. Bonaparte became the petty potentate of Elba. Wellington's great army was free to seek laurels in another continent. English public opinion, apparently more intoxicated with martial glory than at any time

5 Castlereagh to Cathcart, *ibid.*, pp. 14–15; Adams to Monroe, June 26, July 14, Nov. 22, 1813, *Writings of J. Q. Adams*, IV, 491–492, 494–495, 532–533; *Memoirs of Adams*, II, 548–549.

since 1759, made "the punishment of America"[6] a national purpose, and the Marquis de Lafayette thought the very independence of the United States was in the balance.[7]

The first instructions drafted for the American mission reflected no anxiety. As in the abortive Russian mediation, Madison and Monroe insisted on their view of neutral rights and the personal security of American citizens. Gallatin believed the maritime grievances could be postponed, since the problems of neutrals were not especially urgent when Europe was at peace, and he thought the best object of negotiation would be the *status quo*. Britain would thus have no necessary military objective and peace would come when the British "tired of a war without object. . . ."[8] On the other side, the first British demands had a scope so extravagant as to show that the passion of revenge had governed their framing. Revenge was certainly the theme of most of the press, and Gallatin had everywhere heard grandiose strategic suggestions and excessive optimism. Actually, Castlereagh's files contained an agreement of the cabinet to accept as little as the *status quo*.[9] But it did not bar him from asking more.

Castlereagh had plenty of time. He put off appointing negotiators in the hope of finding Britain in a stronger position when the results of the year's operations in America could be learned. Crushing British victories would solve the American puzzle.[10] At his leisure he composed time-wasting instructions, for example, the Indians to be guaranteed certain boundaries as a mutually beneficial buffer between Canada and the United States. His schemes were the diplomatic equivalent of a "reconnaissance in force,"[11] not intended to commit the Foreign Office to battle.

The Americans accepted a suggestion that Ghent—noticeably remote from Russia—would be a good meeting place. Accordingly, the two delegations met there for the first time on August 8, 1814. The composition of the British mission, made up of an easygoing

[6] Gallatin to Crawford, April 21, 1814, Henry Adams (ed.) , *The Writings of Albert Gallatin* (3 vols., Philadelphia, 1879) , I, 602.

[7] Lafayette to Gallatin, May 25, 1814, *ibid.*, I, 620.

[8] Gallatin to Monroe, June 13, 1814, *ibid.*, I, 629.

[9] Gallatin and Bayard to Monroe, June 13, 1814, *ibid.*, I, 628; "Memorandum of Cabinet," Dec. 26, 1813, Webster (ed.) , *British Diplomacy*, p. 126.

[10] See Chapter 12 for military operations in America in 1814.

[11] Perkins, *Castlereagh and Adams*, p. 92.

admiral, James, Baron Gambier,[12] an Admiralty lawyer named William Adams, and a quick-tempered, fidgety young member of Parliament, Henry Goulburn, Undersecretary for War and Colonies, suggests correctly that the first team was preoccupied with remodeling Europe, leaving the American issue to a hastily improvised second-rate mission. Goulburn, distracted by family difficulties and functioning more as a good, if irascible, diplomatic transmitter than as a negotiator, did most of the drudgework. Thinking was done in London. John Quincy Adams disliked his opposite numbers, especially William Adams and Goulburn, finding both Adams and Goulburn those rare but egregious Englishmen who seem to take personal affront at everything not English.[13] Although John Quincy Adams was privately critical of nearly everyone, including himself, the British negotiators were much inferior in quality to the Americans—but it hardly mattered, since the British ministry guided every British decision.

Adams' standoffishness and introversion kept him from friendly intimacy outside his immediate family all of his life. Gallatin's personality and his knowledge of European thinking made him the actual leader of the Americans. Henry Clay's ill-humor in Ghent hints that he would have preferred to be in Kentucky, swapping cigars, swigs of bourbon, and poker bluffs with his constituents. Bayard's presence was valuable in America because of his Federalist alliances, but he and Russell were minor figures on the scene. The combined talents of Adams, Gallatin, and Clay hardly needed personal reinforcement. The only thing they needed to get a decisively favorable settlement was a big Navy, which, of course, was out of the question in that generation. The Americans fell out occasionally, but never on major issues.[14]

II

The light of 1814 shone on Vienna, where surviving notables gathered to reconstruct post-Bonapartist Europe. Whatever hap-

[12] Bayard described Gambier as "wellbred, affable and amiable . . ." J. Bayard to R. Bayard, Oct. 27, 1814, Elizabeth Donnan (ed.), "The Papers of James A. Bayard, 1796–1815," American Historical Association, *Annual Report 1913* (2 vols., Washington, 1915), II, 350.
[13] J. Q. Adams to L. Adams, Oct. 28, 1814, *Writings of J. Q. Adams*, V, 174–175.
[14] George Dangerfield, *The Era of Good Feelings* (New York, 1952), pp. 4–14, provides a satisfying group of sketches of the Americans who comprised the

pened at Ghent happened in the shadows. Castlereagh left most of his routine business to his colleague, Goulburn's superior, Henry, Earl of Bathurst, Secretary for War and Colonies, who had help when needed from Robert Jenkinson, Earl of Liverpool, leader of the ministry. To Liverpool, Castlereagh, and Bathurst the American issue was a side issue, to be dealt with during intermissions between more serious stretches of thought. To the Americans, of course, it was the matter of first importance.

From the beginning the British in Ghent took the hard line, harder than their superiors'. It is often forgotten that they made much more extreme demands than the Americans did at any time, such demands as to tempt speculation on what a treaty of peace of, say, May, 1815, might have been if Prevost and Pakenham had been wholly successful. Goulburn put the ball in play by proposing to discuss impressment, the necessity of a *quid pro quo* in the matter of permitting Americans to fish in Canadian waters, a proper boundary for the northern Indians, and vague shifts of the southern boundary of Canada. The Americans withdrew to caucus.

That very evening they received revised instructions from Madison and Monroe which, by a complete reversal of stance, freed them from making an issue of impressment. This has been thought of as whimsy or as truckling. But there was no way by which the United States could force Britain to disavow the practice, even though it was a humiliation of such magnitude as to require a declaration of war merely to prove the independence of the United States. Monroe had declared the war would continue until Britain renounced the policy, but, as Bayard believed, the contest would probably go on and on and on if that were its goal.[15] The change of instructions was a realistic move to keep the negotiations within the realm of practical diplomacy. It can hardly be called a surrender. It is inconceivable that the United States would have dropped the issue if it were still alive. Impressment was no longer a real day-to-day problem, although before the fall of Napoleon literally thousands of Americans had been forcibly and openly abducted for combat service against an officially friendly nation, an affront about as great

Ghent mission; J. Q. Adams to L. Adams, Dec. 16, 1814, *Writings of J. Q. Adams,* V, 239.

15 Monroe to Taylor, Nov. 30, 1813, W. C. Ford (ed.), Massachusetts Historical Society *Proceedings,* Third Series, XLII, Part II (May, 1909), 331; J. Bayard to A. Bayard, Feb. 14, 1813, "Papers of Bayard," p. 203.

as could be committed short of unilaterally abrogating the treaty of 1783 by which Britain recognized the United States as a sovereign nation. In retrospect it seems plain that when Horatio, Baron Nelson, destroyed the French naval menace at Trafalgar in 1805, the defense that necessity knows no law could hardly have been a good plea. But in 1814 to have required British negotiators to give up the now-hypothetical principle would have preserved an unnecessary obstacle to any settlement. The American mission was not dealing with a defeated foe—the Americans were, and always had been, on the defensive themselves, merely by relative weight of power available. When the administration dropped the demand for the abolition of impressment, and published its change of heart in America, it unified the country against what could thereafter only be a war to diminish or to destroy the United States.

On the next day Adams, for the Americans, replied that they could only discuss impressment and the national boundary. The British pushed the Indian question and finally admitted their wish to erect an Indian buffer territory north of the Ohio River, which, it may be added, had been on their minds since the 1770's at the latest. This nearly wrecked the conference. Not only would a wedge of Indian territory deform the map of the United States but it would also devalue the Louisiana Purchase, farther west. Adams blamed British jealousy of the expansion of the United States for an attempt "to stunt their growth."[16] The British were not merely jealous; they had fur-trading interests at stake, and seemed to feel guilty about abandoning the Indians who had been active friends since the 1770's. While it was true that no United States citizen could safely venture north of a line from the mouth of the Des Moines River to Saginaw Bay, the Americans at Ghent denied there could possibly be any precedent for treating *their* Indians, living in the United States, as independent, and affirmed that the only acceptable basis of conversation was the *status quo ante bellum*. As the Indian argument continued through September, the American missions had put the British in the position of seeking territory. This became a matter for the ministry to consider.

Goulburn, thinking small, believed it best to break off the negotiations, but his superiors examined the situation in the broadest possible framework. Castlereagh had already laid out the prob-

16 Adams to Monroe, Sept. 5, 1814, *Writings of J. Q. Adams*, V, 119–120.

lem for Liverpool: whether to go on fighting for territory; if not, whether this was the opportune moment to make peace, reserving all British rights and making claim to the fisheries, or to gamble on the military operations of 1814 and then, as it would be put today, playing by ear.[17] Liverpool and Bathurst wrote to their commissioners to ask for an American proposal on the Great Lakes and Canadian boundaries, and told them not to be too unyielding on the matter of the Indians. In due time the Americans gave the British a choice: forget the Indians or forget the negotiations. American campaigns had already eliminated the Indians as a force in the places where they had been most dangerous, and some had turned against the British. Fortunately for British pride and face, they learned that the Indian power was hopelessly declining at about the same time as they learned of the ignominious failure of the United States to defend the city of Washington. They allowed the Indian issue to wither. Hindsight sees that the Indian question had been more a test of American resolution than anything else. Goulburn had pushed it more forcibly than his government felt necessary, and it was dropped as gracefully as possible.

The British envoys next brought forward the question of the Canadian boundary. John Quincy Adams quivered with attention and realized that concessions could leave the United States with "nothing . . . worth defending."[18] The British hope was to redraw the boundary for the sake of the military security of Canada, and they made an offer of *uti possidetis*, or keep what you have, although they had much less than they had expected to win. They would have liked to keep part of Maine, and fervently wished for Forts Niagara and Michilimackinac. The Americans did not try to bargain for the whole of Canada, but did seek to arrange the restoration of occupied areas on both sides. Rejecting the *uti possidetis* proposition, they suggested trading outlines of a treaty. The British said their most recent note was such a project, so the Americans began to write a counterproposal.

While the Americans talked, scribbled, and blotted, their opposite numbers re-examined their own situation. The Washington

---

[17] Castlereagh to Liverpool, Aug. 28, 1814, Charles Vane (ed.), *Memoirs and Correspondence of Viscount Castlereagh, Second Marquess of Londonderry* (12 vols., London, 1848–53), X, 101–102.

[18] Adams to Crawford, Aug. 29, 1814, *Writings of J. Q. Adams*, V, 105.

episode had brought no military gain, Baltimore had defended itself and killed the British commander, and Macdonough had inflicted blue ruin on the invasion mounted from Canada. Only the incomplete Louisiana campaign could yet show a profit. Early in November the ministry talked about the American question. Castlereagh's letters from Vienna were pessimistic. Russia was being very Russian about unhanding Poland, and the Congress of Vienna might fall apart on that issue. The dispatches of Arthur Wellesley, Duke of Wellington, ambassador to Paris, reported that the French were restless under their restored anointed Bourbons. The Treasury thought another year of war might add £10 million to the national debt. Soon Parliament would meet, and the opposition would be able to pose difficult fiscal questions for Lord Liverpool.

The American delegates in Ghent were better off. They could see that the British were uncertain and stalling; Adams thought they formed their American attitudes according to the news from Vienna, and Bayard was quite right in his opinion that Britain would "hasten to make peace with us" if continental war threatened.[19] Unless bad news came from the Gulf coast, the military situation of the United States on land was the best ever, and a campaign in 1815 might bring rich fruit, despite the secret negotiations of Massachusetts at Halifax.[20] The United States was rich, even though the Treasury had to pursue a permanent policy of jumbled improvisation to get the money out of private pockets into the public purse, and even though Gallatin had done the apparently impossible in collecting hard money to send to the Barings in London for disbursement for prisoners of war and to British bondholders. In fact, the War of 1812 underscores the point that nations at war do not surrender merely because of problems resulting from balance of payments.

The events at Ghent were but a subplot in the world's political drama. The subplot moved again toward climax when the Duke of Wellington received a choice of going to Vienna or to America. He was quite pointed on the subject of America: Great Britain could not make good a claim to American territory except by trading some other advantage, insistence on the *uti possidetis* principle would give the Americans a plausible reason for breaking off the

19 J. Bayard to A. Bayard, Oct. 26, 1814, "Papers of Bayard," pp. 348–349.
20 See Chapter 13.

negotiations, and no military victory in America could be expected until the Royal Navy could guarantee control of the Great Lakes.[21] By coincidence, the Americans gave their proposals to the British delegation at Ghent the day after Wellington had so perceptively described the situation. Goulburn disparagingly transmitted the document to Liverpool, who studied it carefully with the ministry and decided not to prolong the American war for territory if all other matters could be arranged satisfactorily. Britain needed a free hand in Europe, and Liverpool valued Wellington's advice on American difficulties. Liverpool also needed to quiet the opposition clamor against a war of aggression. Immediate peace with America was desirable.

In less than a fortnight after Wellington's blunt note arrived, the ministry abandoned *uti possidetis* and agreed to get down to work on the basis of the American suggestion—to the pain of Goulburn. Adams read the omens correctly: "We have everything but peace in our hands."[22] Henceforward there was more argument among the Americans than with their British opposites, chiefly on how hard to push for continuation of the Newfoundland fishery privileges and on the question of British navigation of the Mississippi River. Since nobody really thought these matters, and the islands of Passama-quoddy Bay, worth a war, a few more days brought agreement to postpone the discussion of these points until later, when they would be arbitrated by mixed commissions (one American, one Britisher, and a neutral party if agreement could not be reached). On Christmas Eve, 1814, signatures to a simple statement called the Treaty of Ghent made a peace.

The United States gained no compensation for losses, nor an indisputable statement on fisheries. The policy of abducting aliens for combat service was neither approved by the Americans nor disavowed by the British. No bar was placed on American Oriental trade, nor did the British gain the navigation of the Mississippi, as they would have liked. All such questions were referred to future discussions. American students have thought the treaty weak, but it surrendered nothing except the right to shoot Englishmen, and the United States was once again free of the degrading status of membership in the Old Colonial System. The War of 1812 had

[21] Wellington to Liverpool, Nov. 9, 1814, *Memoirs of Castlereagh*, X, 187–189.
[22] J. Q. Adams to L. Adams, Nov. 29, 1814, *Writings of J. Q. Adams*, V, 219.

become obsolete rather than decisive. Most of the frictions of the prewar decade had been caused by relics of a policy more akin to the spirit of the Navigation Act of 1651 than to the economic realities of the early nineteenth century, as shown by the support of the peace in the British business community. The businessmen had good foresight, as was proved by the extraordinary rise of the value of exports from £8,000 to £13,000,000 in the years 1814–15. Thus the Treaty of Ghent may be called the last treaty of the mercantile age.[23] For the British it marked the rise of industrialists to power and the beginning of the end of the long reign of the alliance of squires and shipowners. For the Americans it left open the way West.

Gallatin, Adams, and Clay went to London to negotiate the commercial matters omitted from the treaty. Castlereagh appointed Goulburn, Dr. Adams, and Frederick J. Robinson of the Board of Trade to talk with the Americans. The six men wrote a very simple reciprocal trade agreement and confirmed for four years the freedom of American trade in Asia. This commercial convention was obscured by the Treaty of Ghent, and even more by the excitement of Bonaparte's return from Elba. If Liverpool's government had lost any popularity, Wellington surely recovered it at Waterloo.

The news from Ghent and New Orleans arrived at Washington closely enough to reinforce each other, to the great pleasure of most of the citizenry. The bearer of the British ratifications, Anthony St. John Baker, carried instructions to exchange ratifications immediately; but if he had appeared in Washington at the same time as news from the West that Governor Pakenham of His Majesty's Province of Louisiana, having crushed Jackson's force, had arrived in St. Louis to shake hands with the redcoated commandant of Fort Michilimackinac, he could have been excused for sewing his papers in his shirttail and waiting for later advice from London. As it was, the Senate consented to the Treaty of Ghent 35–0, Madison signed quickly, and ratifications were exchanged as soon as possible. Federalists could only grumble that success came in spite of Madison, but, of course, the good news from Baltimore, Plattsburg, New

---

23 David C. Douglas (ed.), *English Historical Documents* (12 vols., New York, 1953–), XI, A. Aspinwall and E. A. Smith (eds.), 551; Stephen R. Graubard, "Castlereagh and the Peace of Europe," *Journal of British Studies*, III (1963–64), 79–87, gives a favorable critique of Castlereagh's use of diplomatic techniques and his balance-of-power concept.

Orleans, and Ghent came in such rhythmic waves that it raised esteem for Republicanism and depressed Federalism in the same proportion. John Quincy Adams thought he and his colleagues had the privilege of "redeeming our union," and Bayard reported a higher regard for America in European eyes. Gallatin saw the strengthening of nationalism as the principal effect of the war.[24]

Who "won" the War of 1812 is often argued. Some American Westerners have thought the guarantee of continued western expansion was worth the trouble. Cis-Appalachians have claimed it a tie. Canada survived, and Canadians see survival as victory. Britain, as Britain, got nothing at all. Whoever "won," there was a group which lost the war, and that was the Federalist party. The emissaries from the Hartford Convention unluckily rode into Washington on a tide of good news from all fronts, and were annoyingly mocked by the press. Monroe and Alexander James Dallas, the Secretary of the Treasury, received them with courtesy, but Madison ignored them. One complained, "We have recd no invitation from Madison. What a mean and contemptible little blackguard."[25] A bit of homespun satire left at the headquarters of the Washington Benevolent Society in Philadelphia obliquely defended the contemptible little blackguard:

> *James Madison,* my Jo, Jim
> We wonder what you mean,
> You've disconcerted all our plans,
> They vanish like a dream;
> You've disconcerted all our plots,
> And this the world will know,
> Since *Peace* has come we are undone
> James Madison, my Jo.[26]

III

Before the United States could relax into peace, the Barbary pirates again required attention. As the United States became more deeply

[24] J. Q. Adams to L. Adams, Dec. 23, 1814, *Writings of J. Q. Adams,* V, 246; J. Bayard to R. Bayard, Dec. 26, 1814, "Papers of Bayard," p. 366; Gallatin to Lyon, May 7, 1816, *Writings of Gallatin,* I, 700.

[25] H. Otis to S. Otis, Feb. 23, 1815, Samuel Eliot Morison, *The Life and Letters of Harrison Gray Otis* (2 vols., Boston, 1913), II, 168.

[26] George L. Roth, "Verse Satire on 'Faction,' 1790–1815," *William and Mary Quarterly,* Third Series, XVII (1960), 473.

involved with British difficulties after 1806, the African corsairs went back to their old ways, plundering American ships and enslaving their crews. The Dey of Algiers was the most hostile of the Mediterranean potentates, although Tunis and Tripoli were unfriendly, too. The Dey's pretext was that the United States paid too little tribute; he preferred gold to goods, and he wished a higher cash value to be placed on his abstention from piracy. Algiers took three ships in 1807, and the Bey of Tunis bought one from French privateers in 1810. When the War of 1812 began, the Dey of Algiers demanded cash in lieu of the ship's stores of prior agreement. Consul General Tobias Lear borrowed the money at the painful rate of 25 per cent and skipped out late in July, leaving American affairs to be handled by the capable John Norderling, Swedish consul. A month later the Algerines took a Salem ship and enslaved its people. In 1813—after British intervention—they freed six, but ten were slaves until the war ended.

The Algerine timing was bad. The United States was elsewhere at peace, but Algiers, with only a dozen medium-sized ships, was officially at war with Spain, the Netherlands, Prussia, Denmark, Russia, and the Italian maritime states.[27] On March 2, 1815, the Congress authorized naval action against the Barbary powers and the redoubtable Captain Stephen Decatur, unleashed at last, departed New York Harbor on May 20 as commodore of a squadron of ten vessels, which, for once, were going to pick on somebody their own size. The objective was to end the payment of extortion. Decatur made a quick passage, took a forty-four-gun Algerine frigate in June, and captured a brig a few days later. William Shaler, the waspish secretary to the commissioners at Ghent, had come along to represent the State Department. Decatur, Shaler, and the Dey were three notes of a discord, none getting along with the other two, but Shaler did his share of the work well,[28] helped by a memorandum of orientation from the refugee Consul General Lear[29] and by the accommodating Swede Norderling.

27 Ray W. Irwin, *The Diplomatic Relations of the United States with the Barbary Powers, 1776–1816* (Chapel Hill, 1931), pp. 176–186, covers the subject more than adequately.

28 Roy F. Nichols, *Advance Agents of American Destiny* (Philadelphia, 1956), pp. 106–124, tells the story of Shaler's life.

29 Lear to Shaler, April 29, 1815, "Mission to Algiers—1815," *Foreign Service Journal*, XXVIII, No. 3 (March, 1951), 15–17.

The Americans sailed boldly into the harbor of Algiers. Decatur, his gold lace and tassels giving the African sun an object worthy of its glare, cowed the Dey and, with Shaler, made a favorable treaty, dated June 30, just forty-one days after leaving New York. The Dey promised to stop interfering with American trade and to forgo tribute. He released all prisoners without ransom—a thing unheard-of before. In exchange he was to get his ships back. Shaler settled in as consul general at Algiers and the satisfied Decatur laid his course for Tunis. The Spaniards had one of the Dey's captured ships and delayed its return so that the Dey began to be his old rancorous self again until Edward Pellew, Viscount Exmouth, commanding an Anglo-Dutch fleet, dropped in and shot up Algiers, destroying its sea power (and any hope of peaceful British economic penetration in North Africa). The Dey, a morally flexible man, reformed his character yet again, made a second treaty with the United States (December, 1816), and became a friend to all.

Meanwhile Decatur had made similar treaties with Tunis and Tripoli (July and August, 1815), each of which compensated the United States for ships taken by the British with piratical connivance. Earlier American diplomacy has been described as militia diplomacy; by analogy, this was commando diplomacy. There were no more serious difficulties with the scourges of the Middle Sea. Although the treaty with Algiers, by oversight, was not ratified until 1822, Christian slavery in North Africa ended with the American treaties and the last echo of Exmouth's guns. The human cost to the United States was one seaman killed by the corsairs in the taking of their frigate, three killed by the explosion of an American gun, and the crew of the sloop of war *Épervier*, which was sent to the United States with diplomatic papers but which foundered in the Atlantic in the late summer of 1815.

Decatur was praised and honored on his return. It was at a public dinner in Norfolk that he responded to a toast with the hyper-nationalist aphorism, "Our country! In her intercourse with foreign nations may she always be in the right; but our country, right or wrong."[30] His ethical position may have been debatable, but his country's sovereignty was unquestionable, and the gamecock spirit of his response was the spirit of the nation.

[30] Decatur's response is most easily found in Allan Westcott, "Stephen Decatur," *DAB*.

CHAPTER 15

The Democratic-Republicans on Balance

THE Republicans inherited and improved upon a good administrative system, but the acquisition of power did not Federalize them, even though the Quids and others have charged apostasy. For one example, in flat contradiction of Federalism, Thomas Jefferson held the most generous attitude toward immigrants and he never wavered. The Federalization argument stands on a selective comparison of Republican preaching in the 1790's and Republican practice thereafter: they talked peace but declared war; they opposed the national debt but increased it; they fought the Bank of the United States and proposed its recharter; they asserted only enumerated powers but purchased Louisiana, seized West Florida, and recommended internal improvements with federal funds. Such a comparison forgets the ticking of clocks. The Republicans adopted new positions to meet newly discovered circumstances. Debt declined until world politics took priority. Without a Bank, the more rapidly expanding nation could be at the grace and favor of provincial capitalists. An empire for liberty needed better communications. And, of course, they trusted their self-restraint more than that of their enemies. The important fact is that they neither repudiated nor repealed their original principles.

That the Republicans switched from strict construction of the Constitution to loose construction may well be true, but the phrases describe only political tactics. Generous construers often trade attitudes with rigorous construers when they trade places as ins and outs, and many former Hamiltonians became rigorists when out.

The more important difference was that the Republicans emphasized congressional responsibility and valued public opinion more
highly.[1] On the other hand, Whiggish-minded Americans tend to
fall into the fallacy that what was past was better. The years after
1801 were no golden age from which the country has steadily
declined. To illustrate, Americans of African descent received not
one benefit in those years. What happened was that liberals—such
as they then were—kept the republic alive while preserving both
their abstract principles and the world's least imperfect government.

In routine operations the administrations of the Republicans
were practically indistinguishable from their Federalist predeces-
sors. Both were in the hands of gentlemen, as the word might have
been used by Shakespeare, the only real difference being that
Federalists tried to select administrators according to prestige and
money while Jefferson hoped to appoint men of plainly apparent
superior intelligence and virtue. The Republicans and Federalists
had equal intelligence and talents, although the Republicans
boasted of them less. Having taken over a working government,
they would have preferred to be static rather than dynamic, but
change inevitably raised questions which required positive answers.
By 1815, affirmative federal activity was accepted by a generation
which knew nothing else. Within the limits of normal deviation the
official behavior of responsible Republicans was impeccable. Co-
operation and legislation were persuaded rather than bought. The
Chase impeachment and the prejudgment of Aaron Burr seem the
only possible exceptions to the general conclusion that passion was
kept within acceptable bounds.[2]

From 1789 to 1815, the United States was ruled by the generation
that declared independence, won the war, and framed the Constitution. The Federalists inclined to be more doctrinaire, the Republicans more traditionalist. Every responsible leader (excepting
Alexander Hamilton, who poorly understood America) wished to
preserve the United States and its character. The Republicans were
more maintenance men than philosophers—patching and repairing as
needs arose. Among their principles, none seemed more important
than preservation. Their unconscious conservatism worked so well

---

[1] Leonard White, *The Jeffersonians: A Study in Administrative History* (New
York, 1951), pp. 550–553, is most useful, although White may have placed too
high a value on the use of the concepts of strict and loose construction.

[2] White, *Jeffersonians*, pp. 43, 43 n., 412, 546–550, 553–559.

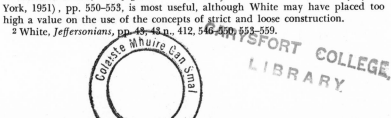

that it made the Federalist brand of conservatism, in a manner of speaking, unnecessary.

The tendency to describe so-called Jeffersonian Democracy, which would be really as much Madisonian, as a systematic moral philosophy, and then to excommunicate Jefferson and Madison for heresy, owes something to the tortuous writing of the political precisian John Taylor of Caroline. Few in his time paid attention to him, and his reflections were printed only after the important decisions had been irrevocably made. He has been the delight of those who like political theory in a vacuum, but he had almost no philosophical influence on his contemporaries.[3] He has been sketched in a tableau with John Adams, the authors of *The Federalist Papers*, and John Calhoun, comprising "the greatest of American political thinkers."[4] Definitions of greatness admittedly differ, but it is difficult to see greatness in an unread philosopher and equally hard to accept his system as the deposit of faith.

II

Jefferson's standing as a folk hero has been unstable. He has been continuously remembered and quoted on both sides of many questions. Because he became a great democratic symbol, the traditionalist bent of American politics encouraged political leaders to make generous use of his aphorisms for their own purposes. As an image rather than a person he has attracted and repelled men ever since.[5]

The squire of Monticello used gentlemen instead of commoners for the higher public service because the only men with political experience were men of property. But the workings of the Democratic-Republican spirit made the commoner eligible for public office, and later generations were to be moved by that same spirit to let him get the training needed to hold the office.[6]

[3] Benjamin F. Wright, Jr., "The Philosopher of Jeffersonian Democracy," *American Political Science Review*, XXII (1928), 870–892, a good brief survey; the standard life of Taylor is H. H. Simms, *Life of John Taylor* (Richmond, 1932).

[4] Grant McConnell, "John Taylor and the Democratic Tradition," *Western Political Quarterly*, IV (1951), 17–31, quoted from p. 31.

[5] The changes in Jefferson's reputation are well described in Merrill Peterson, *The Jefferson Image in the American Mind* (New York, 1960), summarized in pp. 443–458.

[6] Sidney H. Aronson, *Status and Kinship in the Higher Civil Service* (Cambridge, Mass., 1964), pp. 194–196, 199.

Although Jefferson rather ostentatiously stayed at home to over-see brickmaking during the election of 1800, it is notable that the leaders of the new Seventh Congress were all acceptable to Jefferson, indeed, can almost be styled Jeffersonian lieutenants. And for eight years, despite small mutinies, the President covertly but skillfully managed the legislature.[7] This perceptive leader was a shrewd politician who saw so many sides to every question that he occasionally luxuriated in inconsistency. His was no single-track mind like Washington's; rather, it "was a whole switchyard."[8] Anachronistic admirers have let themselves be saddened by blank spots in his libertarianism: his assumption of white superiority, his vigilante spirit, his not inventing feminism. His views on human pigmentation, his vigilantism, were very American for his time, but a man who diligently read the history of law, as he did, might better have avoided adopting the view that impeachment was a good means to the good end of destroying the independence of the judiciary. It was the Congress which surrendered on that point, never Jefferson. However, few such voluminous writers have had such a small proportion of their writings exhaustively studied, and the attempt, if any, to systematize his philosophy should wait until his writings have been properly assembled. Until then, no doubt, the profession of Jeffersonian exegesis will continue to produce widely varying declarations of democratic faith to support states' rights and nationalism, racial discrimination and perfect equality.[9] He might better be remembered as the President who enlarged an empire for liberty in which his abstract democratic principles could later be concretely applied, and who energetically sought every bloodless substitute for war.

While Jefferson quietly preserved the Federalist conception of presi-

---

[7] White, *Jeffersonians*, pp. 45–51.

[8] Quotation from Dixon Wecter, *The Hero in America* (New York, 1941), p. 171.

[9] Clement Eaton, "The Jeffersonian Tradition of Liberalism in America," *South Atlantic Quarterly*, XLIII (1944), 1–10, which collects in a short space the seemingly most influential characteristics of the political school which can be called Jeffersonian; Charles G. Haines, *The American Doctrine of Judicial Supremacy* (2nd ed., rev., New York, 1959), pp. 241–253; Carl Becker, "What Is Still Living in the Political Philosophy of Thomas Jefferson," *American Historical Review*, XLIII (1942–43), 706, writes a democratic creed phrased along the lines of the Declaration of Independence, beginning with Jeffersonian language and ending with Lincoln's rhetoric, to show the flexibility of Jeffersonian doctrine.

dential power, during Madison's terms the Presidency yielded much to the Congress and became decidedly weaker. The rise of the congressional nominating caucus was a principal cause of the decline of presidential power and made the President, in a sense, the creation of the Congress. The two-term precedent meant that every second term must be like a chess game, with the White House as the prize. Congressional leaders thus grew in political stature at the expense of the President. The character of the Presidency during Madison's tenure depended more on personality and circumstances than on positive ideologies, a situation tacitly acceptable to Madison. The growth of congressional power, exerted through Speaker, caucuses, and standing committees, was well illustrated by Madison's inability to have Albert Gallatin as his Secretary of State. The Congress did not attack the constitutional position of the President, but it took more initiative in policy and spoke more loudly in the matter of appointments. This was not an ideological victory but the annexation of a larger share of existing power. Madison never took a policy case to the people. It would have been difficult, physically, and it would have been out of character. The result of letting policy take its course was that the Presidency was weaker in 1815 than at any earlier time. The Congress made policy and, to some extent, influenced administrative detail.[10]

Madison's conduct has brought him condemnation as a weakling. Actually, the father of the Constitution was following his conviction that policy must rise from the people through their branch of government. No presidential folk hero has taken this position, but it is hardly a mark of weakness to take a firm view of the nature of the Constitution and to operate from it as a principle.

Jefferson and his followers came to power stimulated by victory over Federalism, rode forward on the momentum of that victory, and stayed united until 1808 or 1809 to forestall a revival of the enemy. In time the momentum died. Jefferson had worked skillfully and lovingly for influence in the Congress; Madison showed less persistence and imagination in promoting his legislative influence. Madison's theories of constitutional government, which emphasized the separation of powers and his philosophy of the polity of

[10] White, *Jeffersonians*, pp. 30, 42–44, 54, 132–133; see also James Sterling Young, *The Washington Community, 1800–1828* (New York, 1966), pp. 229–249.

contending factions, probably served him in good stead as a floor leader in conventions and congresses, but seem to have limited his wish and ability to be a leader of the legislative branch while serving as President.[11]

Most downgraders of Madison have concentrated on his initial appointment of incompetent generals. What happened next? Against the intrigues of his Secretary of War the President promoted proved officers who lost no important battles after mid-1814. Their average age dropped from sixty to thirty-six and their ability improved at the same rate. If he is to be condemned for appointing the old ones, he must be praised for appointing the new.[12]

Madison may properly be described as the President who was subordinated to the Congress by circumstances at least partly beyond his control, who led a third-rate power through an unprecedented national war with only local disasters, who—unlike all presidential folk heroes—faithfully guarded civil liberty, and who ended his administration with more popularity than when he began. He might have found excuse, as some war presidents have, for suppressing newspapers, for ignoring the guarantee of the writ of habeas corpus, for harassing enemy aliens, for interfering with civilian courts, but he guarded civil liberty despite the many provocations he received from New England; his only intervention into the private lives of the thousands of enemy aliens living in the United States was to require them to register themselves. (The aggression against East Florida was a foreign-policy matter, not concerning civil rights, and he recoiled from it quickly when he saw that it would not stand close scrutiny.) His weakness was a failure to understand that in crises the constitutional separation of powers enfeebled the government unless the President could seize and exercise majority-party leadership. Given the circumstances of his election, Madison could only have become the true head of his

11 The point of Madison's constitutional scruples is well made in Abbot Smith, "Mr. Madison's War: An Unsuccessful Experiment in the Conduct of National Policy," *Political Science Quarterly*, LVII (1942), 229–246, in which the word "Experiment" is the precisely correct choice. See also Young, *Washington Community*, pp. 188–191.

12 Those not inclined to collate the multivolume works of Henry Adams and Irving Brant may get the gist of Brant, which agrees with practically everything learned in the past half-century, and which shows Madison as no valley between greatnesses, in Irving Brant, "Madison and the War of 1812," *Virginia Magazine of History and Biography*, LXXIV (1966), 51–67.

party by a successful appeal to the people, a strategem he would
have found personally distasteful and for which he probably lacked
the necessary personal magnetism.

Unlike Madison, Albert Gallatin has generally had a good press.
The Secretary of the Treasury has, however, been overrated in
financial acumen. If his somewhat primitive economic theory had
been carried out with no adaptation to reality, it would have
subordinated the concrete need for a system deriving revenue from
diverse sources to abstract goals, and would have brought the complete collapse of the system and of the administration of the Treasury. He had a fear of speculative finance which gave him a
compulsive drive to combat debt like a conscientious home-mort-
gage borrower. Senator William Branch Giles once openly doubted
that anyone noticed the difference of the burden whether the debt
were $80 million or $40 million. Gallatin's defender, Senator
George W. Campbell of Tennessee, could only say in rebuttal that
the reductions had saved the country $3 million a year in interest
charges, which works out to about fifty cents a head. Of course, debt
is not a matter to be regarded lightly, but the United States in that
decade was what is now called an underdeveloped emerging nation,
and it had vast untapped riches. The hope of being free of debt
should have been well down on the list of national economic
priorities. To Gallatin's credit, in the golden pre-embargo days
when money flowed into the Treasury from customs collectors, he
produced a truly national plan for internal improvements. George
Washington and others had anticipated the idea, but the Secretary
presented the first orderly and comprehensive plan.[13] It is a measure of his philosophy that the Treasury surpluses which encouraged
such planning were the accidental by-products of a world war which
the Americans could not much influence; when the United States
actively tried to influence it, beginning with the embargo, the
surpluses disappeared owing to a doctrinaire reliance on the tariff
as the chief source of public revenue.

Federalism has often been said to be the great source of American

[13] Alexander Balinky, *Albert Gallatin: Fiscal Theories and Policies* (New
Brunswick, 1958) , finds Gallatin's theory of public finance somewhat remote from
reality; the Giles-Campbell exchange appears in *The Debates and Proceedings in
the Congress of the United States* (43 vols., Washington, 1834–56) , 12th Congress,
1st Session, pp. 51–52, 83–84; Carter Goodrich, "National Planning of Internal
Improvements," *Political Science Quarterly*, XLVIII (1948) , 16–28.

nationalism. More precisely, Federalism, as put in force by the acts and judgments of Washington, Alexander Hamilton, and John Marshall, was the creator of a workable central government which legally established its authority over the provinces of a small country. After 1801 the loudest and most self-conscious Federalists were proponents of Little America, while the majority faction of the Democratic-Republicans created an aggressive nationality, proud of sovereign independence in the family of nations, and happy to expand the area of republicanism as an empire for liberty. New England Federalists well illustrated their notion of Little America by their enduring hostility to the American West for generations after the War for Independence.[14]

The intensity of political passions in the first generation of the republic may be more easily understood if we remember that religious controversy had lost much of its attraction, economic theorizing had not yet captured the American imagination, and politics remained as almost the only common focus of public interest. Antipathies generated by partisanship affected almost every human relationship, public or private, and party labels became terms of evaluation. An offensive evaluation of a person or a group might well lead to violence, whether fisticuffs, a duel, or a clash of mobs; the Burr-Hamilton duel was merely the most famous of many such fatal combats.

From 1801 to 1815 there was a great increase in the proportion of eligibles who voted, which was attributable to the fierce competition of parties. The antipathies had been there in the 1790's, but the Federalists were not yet organized as a true party in that decade. It is notable that the increase in voting was greatest where party competition was keenest; one-party districts showed no such increase. It would be improper to credit the increase to the Federalists, since the Republicans showed political creativity first and most Federalist strategems were copies of Republican techniques which had been proved by political test. But the voting totals leaped only where two warmly competing parties interacted—each of them, incidentally, claiming to be the party of the people.

The use of democratic rhetoric by both parties, the invention and

[14] Louis Boudin, *Government by Judiciary* (2 vols., New York, 1932), pp. 267–269, almost incidentally opens this line of thought, which has been but little traveled.

perfecting of techniques of popular appeal, and the stronger organization of each party combined to change the structure of politics.
Party loyalty became an intrinsic good, as did the practice of
adjusting one's principles to the wishes of the people. Aristocratic
corruption—the use of government by the rich to do favors for one
another—was succeeded by the not-necessarily-corrupt spoils system,
used temperately by the Republicans in the national government,
but quite intemperately by state organizations whether Republican
or Federalist. Out-of-office Federalists could be just as ardent in
support of the idea of rotation in office as any politicians since.
Thus Federalism, by 1815, could hardly be recognized externally as
the child of the Federalism of the 1790's, and the hardy legend that
the Federalist band was reduced to a handful of high- and narrow-
minded pamphleteers, out of touch with American life, should be
forgotten. Earlier Federalist leaders had said, in effect, trust us
because we are holier than thou. By the end of Madison's tenure
they had not changed their minds, but a new generation of Federalists disguised their views and said, in effect, trust us because we are
as common as thou. In all of American political history no basic
change occurred as rapidly as the change in the countenance of
conservatism from 1801 to 1815.

The Young Federalist revolution marched with the change of
American society from a hierarchically ordered unity to a society
which elevated individualism as a chief good. The Federalists
adjusted themselves to a change from a system of deference, where
even in democratic colonies and states the voters chose the Best
People, by adopting the concealed principle that the Best People
should rule but must come to power through the whole people.
This revolution began in the eighteenth century (and will have run
its course when all minority groups throw off the shackles of
deference), but the years from 1801 to 1815 were an important and
swift-moving part of that revolution.[15] It was the misfortune of the
obscure and forgotten Young Federalists that their work reached an
anticlimax in the Hartford Convention, the news of the Treaty of
Ghent, and the smashing victories of Plattsburg and New Orleans.

---

[15] David Hackett Fischer, *The Revolution of American Conservatism: The
Federalist Party in the Era of Jeffersonian Democracy* (New York, 1965),
pp. 35–49, 182–199, rediscovers the forgotten Young Federalists; see also Shaw
Livermore, Jr., *The Twilight of Federalism* (Princeton, 1962), pp. 3–14; Lynn W.
Turner, *William Plumer of New Hampshire* (Chapel Hill, 1962), p. 97—
Plumer's defection to Republicanism temporarily stopped the Young Federalist
revival in his state.

III

It is easy to ridicule the judgments of Jefferson and Madison on the problems posed by the great Anglo-French contest, but better solutions (except by hindsight) do not come readily to hand. They worked carefully and thoughtfully, avoiding the absurd extremes of a triangular war or a craven submission to intolerable indignities. Their policies can be better evaluated by those who keep in mind that the United States was a weak power with few choices, and that British leaders, to put it conservatively, were at least equally prone to error in judging the best interests of their own people.

By its end most Americans thought the war had been justified and had achieved a net gain. Wise men did not glorify its military achievements but saw that the war had impressed foreign observers with the fact that the republican experiment was a permanent institution. The American citizenry had gained in self-respect as a people and had proved that their nation could carry on despite sectionalism and factionalism. They became less doctrinaire and more eclectic, and their eclecticism gave American nationality a rough and durable texture.[16]

The Americans learned some statecraft, too. There is nothing like the stress of war to reveal weakness in the body politic. The War of 1812 showed that the administrative structure was not capable of bearing the strain of war. In repairing the administrative weaknesses of the central authority after the war, the Democratic-Republicans strengthened the federal government and provided the political machinery necessary to conquer their own continent. In foreign affairs they had taught Britain that the United States was a difficult enemy and that Canada was vulnerable. This lesson led the British to conclude that quarrels with America could best he resolved at the conference table, however much they privately disliked the United States. Public amity with the United States became the official policy which brought peace ever after, and all later differences have been negotiated peacefully.[17] After all, before the atomic age the United States was as hard to conquer from abroad as Russia was, and for much the same reasons.

---

[16] Paul A. Varg, *Foreign Policies of the Founding Fathers* (East Lansing, Mich., 1963), pp. 300–306, revises earlier judgments of the effects of Republican foreign policy.

[17] White, *Jeffersonians*, pp. 9–12; Marcus Cunliffe, *The Nation Takes Shape, 1789–1837* (Chicago, 1959), pp. 60–61.

Sectionalism has never been wholly absent from the domestic polity of the United States. In the ten years before the Treaty of Ghent, the bond of the sections was relatively weak. National patriotism is not a matter of constitutional law, and the United States was not yet permeated by devotion to the nation. The war stimulated national patriotism everywhere outside of New England, and even there a large minority experienced the feeling of making common cause in the national interest. In apparent danger of destruction, the union, weak as it was or appeared to be, survived attacks upon it from within and without. This survival begat confidence and approval, and two generations would pass before another substantial attempt would be made to dissolve the cement of nationality.

A concrete gain of the war was the release of the American citizens forcibly detained by Britain, whether in the Royal Navy or in British prisons because they refused to serve in the Royal Navy. It is easy to say this was the automatic result of the fall of Bonaparte, but the British victory was not certainly predictable in June, 1812. It was surely possible that Britain and France could agree to an armed peace without victory, a prudent arrangement for any French leader not suffering from victory disease. In such a case the problem of manning the Royal Navy would have remained, at least in the minds of British ministers. Perhaps impressment could have been negotiated apart from war in years to come, but that was not knowable. Against the recovery of the abducted Americans may be balanced the American casualty list, variously estimated at something more or less than two thousand killed and four thousand wounded. A significant difference is that the casualties were all volunteers; of the naval slaves, none.[18]

In summary, the gains of the War of 1812 were economic independence, acceptance as a member of the family of nations, and recognition that republicanism was here to stay. Never again was the American economy regulated by paper weapons drafted abroad, no nation based its policy on the likelihood of the total collapse and dissolution of the United States, nobody regarded republicanism as a passing fad, no country tried to force the United States into a subsidiary place in a system of satellites. Independence had been corroborated, vindicated, confirmed.

[18] The actual number of Americans under arms has been stated as more than half a million, but the figure means little because many militiamen re-enlisted many times, and each enlistment was added separately.

Select Bibliography

Sources

Manuscripts

John Mason Brown Manuscripts, Yale University Library; Gallatin Papers, New-York Historical Society; Griswold Papers, Connecticut Historical Society, Hartford; Jefferson Papers, Library of Congress; Jefferson Photostats, New York Public Library; Letters in Relation to Burr's Conspiracy, Library of Congress (photostatic duplicate in Newberry Library, Chicago); Madison Papers, Library of Congress; Joseph Hopper Nicholson Papers, Library of Congress; University of Virginia Library Manuscripts, Alderman Library, Charlottesville; Wilkinson Papers, Chicago Historical Society.

Official and Other Public Papers

American State Papers, see Lowrie, below.

Annals of Congress, see *Debates and Proceedings in the Congress,* below.

Carter, C. E. (ed.), *The Territorial Papers of the United States* (24 vols., Washington, 1934–52), especially VII.

(Cobbett), *"Hansard's Parliamentary Debates." The Parliamentary History of England . . . to . . . 1803,* 1801–3, XXXVI (1820), followed by *Cobbett's Parliamentary Debates,* I–XXIII (1803–12), after which it is *The Parliamentary Debates* (usually *Hansard,* for short), XXIV–XXXI (1813–15).

Cruikshank, E. A. (ed.), *Documents Relating to the Invasion of Canada and Surrender of Detroit, 1812* (Ottawa, 1912).

——, *Documents Relating to the Invasion of the Niagara Peninsula by the United States Army Commanded by General Jacob Brown in July and August 1814* (Niagara, Ont., 1921).

Debates and Proceedings in the Congress of the United States (42 vols., Washington, 1834–56), often cited as *Annals.*

"Despatches from the United States Consulate in New Orleans," *American Historical Review,* XXXII (1926–27), XXXIII (1927–28). See also Whitaker (ed.), below.

Esarey, Logan (ed.), *Governors' Messages and Letters: Messages and Letters of William Henry Harrison* (Indianapolis, 1922).

"General Court Martial Held at the Royal Barracks, Dublin, for the Trial of Brevet Lieutenant-Colonel Hon. Thomas Mullins . . . ; Dublin . . . 1815,"*Louisiana Historical Quarterly,* IX (1926).

Hart, S. H., and A. B. Hulbert (eds.), *Zebulon Pike's Arkansaw Journal* (Denver, 1932).

Hill, C. E. (ed.), *Leading American Treaties* (New York, 1931; earlier ed., 1922).

Hill, Joseph J. (ed.), "An Unknown Expedition to Santa Fe in 1807," *Mississippi Valley Historical Review,* VI (1919–20), i.e., that of Jacques Clamorgan.

Hoyt, William D., Jr. (ed.), "Civilian Defense in Baltimore, 1814–1815: Minutes of the Committee of Vigilance," *Maryland Historical Magazine,* XXXIX (1944), XL (1945), in four parts.

Hume, E. E. (ed.), "Letters Written During the War of 1812, by the British Naval Commander in American Waters . . ." *William and Mary Quarterly,* Second Series, X (1930), by Admiral Sir David Milne.

"Instructions and Despatches of the British Ghent Commission," Massachusetts Historical Society, *Proceedings,* XLVIII (1914–15).

Knopf, Richard C. (ed.), *Letters to the Secretary of War* (Columbus, Ohio, 1959), i.e., re war in the Northwest.

Knox, Dudley W. (ed.), *Naval Documents Relating to the United States Wars with the Barbary Powers, 1785–1807* (7 vols., Washington, 1935–48).

Lincoln, Charles H. (ed.), "The Hull-Eaton Correspondence During the Expedition Against Tripoli, 1804–1805," American Antiquarian Society, *Proceedings,* New Series, XXI (1911).

Lowrie, Walter *et al.* (eds.), *American State Papers: Documents, Legislative and Executive of the Congress of the United States* (38 vols., Washington, 1832–61), which are divided into ten categories, each of which is numbered in its own sequence of volumes.

Mayo, Bernard (ed.), "Instructions to the British Ministers to the United States, 1791–1812," American Historical Association, *Annual Report 1936,* III (Washington, 1941).

Mullett, Charles F. (ed.), "British Schemes Against Spanish America in 1806," *Hispanic American Historical Review,* XXVII (1947).

Napoleon I, *Correspondance de Napoleon Ier* (32 vols., Paris, 1858–69), XX.

Padgett, James A. (ed.), "The Constitution of the West Florida Republic," *Louisiana Historical Quarterly,* XX (1937).

———, "The Documents Showing that the United States Ultimately Financed the West Florida Revolution of 1810," *ibid.,* XXV (1942).

Richardson, James D. (ed.) , *A Compilation of the Messages and Papers of the Presidents* (20 vols., Washington, 1897–1917) .

Stacey, C. P. (eds.) , "An American Plan for a Canadian Campaign . . . 1815," *American Historical Review,* XLVI (1940–41) .

[Stoddard, Amos,] "Transfer of Upper Louisiana," *Glimpses of the Past,* II (1935) .

Tate, Vernon D. (ed.) , "Spanish Documents Relating to the Voyage of the *Racoon* to Astoria and San Francisco," *Hispanic American Historical Review,* XVIII (1938) .

Thornbrough, Gayle (ed.) , *Letter Book of the Indian Agency at Fort Wayne, 1809–1815* (Indianapolis, 1961) .

Thwaites, Reuben Gold (ed.) , *Original Journals of the Lewis and Clark Expedition, 1804–06* (8 vols., New York, 1904–5) , is the best edition of these records, of which the earliest was *History of the Expedition to the Sources of the Missouri, Thence Across the Rocky Mountains and Down the River Columbia to the Pacific* (2 vols., Philadelphia, 1814) , the so-called "Biddle" edition. The Thwaites texts were reprinted in 1959, and Bernard DeVoto, in 1963, presented an abridgement, *The Journals of Lewis and Clark,* "for the general reader." On the early history of the MSS., see Lester J. Cappon, "Who Is the Author of *History of the Expedition* . . . (1814) ?" *William and Mary Quarterly,* Third Series, XIX (1962) . Louise Phelps Kellogg believed the best short biography of Meriwether Lewis was that written by Jefferson for inclusion in the "Biddle" edition of 1814. See also Jackson, Donald (ed.) , under Private Papers and Memoirs, below.

Webster, C. K. (ed.) , *British Diplomacy, 1813–1815* (New York, 1921) .

Wharton, Francis (ed.) , *A Digest of the International Law of the United States* (3 vols., Washington, 1886) .

Whitaker, Arthur P. (ed.) , "Another Dispatch from the United States Consulate in New Orleans," *American Historical Review,* XXXVIII (1932–33) . See also "Despatches," above.

Wood, William (ed.) , *Select British Documents of the Canadian War of 1812* (4 vols., Toronto, 1920–28) .

Court Cases

The following Court decisions and opinions were among the most important in the constitutional history of the years 1801–15, although some did not achieve final adjudication until years later: American Insurance Company *et al. v.* Canter, 1 Peters 511 (1828) , constitutionality of the power to acquire territory; The Commercen. Lindgren Claimant, 1 Wheaton 382 (1816) ; Ex Parte Bollman, 4 Cranch 74 (1807) , preliminary to Burr trial; Fletcher *v.* Peck, 6 Cranch 87 (1810) , Yazoo affairs; Gibbons *v.* Ogden, 9 Wheaton 1 (1824) , which would seem to permit embargoes; Marbury *v.* Madison, 1 Cranch 137 (1803) ; Martin *v.* Mott, 12 Wheaton 19

(1827), U.S. over militia; Otis *v.* Watkins, 9 Cranch 339 (1815), concerning the embargo, in part; Stuart *v.* Laird, 1 Cranch 298 (1803); U.S. *v.* Judge Peters, 5 Cranch 115 (1809), conflict of federal and state judiciaries.

Private Papers and Memoirs

Abel, Annie H. (ed.), *Tabeau's Narrative of Loisel's Expedition to the Upper Missouri* [1803–5], (Norman, 1939).

Adair, Douglass (ed.), "James Madison's Autobiography," *William and Mary Quarterly,* Third Series, II (1945).

Adams, Charles Francis (ed.), *Memoirs of John Quincy Adams* (12 vols., Philadelphia, 1874–77); Allan Nevins, *Diary* . . . (New York, 1929), presented selections from same.

———, *The Works of John Adams* (10 vols., Boston, 1854–56).

Adams, Henry (ed.), *Documents Relating to New-England Federalism, 1800–1815* (Boston, 1877), indispensable for the senior Federalists and their attitudes.

———, *The Writings of Albert Gallatin* (3 vols., Philadelphia, 1879).

Ames, Seth (ed.), *Works of Fisher Ames* (2 vols., Boston, 1854).

Atherton, Gertrude (ed.), *A Few of Hamilton's Letters* (New York, 1903).

Barnhart, John D. (ed.), "A New Letter About the Massacre at Fort Dearborn," *Indiana Magazine of History,* XLI (1945).

Bassett, John Spencer (ed.), *Correspondence of Andrew Jackson* (7 vols., Washington, 1926–35).

———, *Major Howell Tatum's Journal While Acting Topographical Engineer (1814) to General Jackson* (Northampton, Mass., 1922), mostly on Alabama Valley operations.

[Bayard, James Asheton], "James Asheton Bayard Letters, 1802–1814," New York Public Library, *Bulletin,* IV (1900).

Betts, Edwin Morris (ed.), *Thomas Jefferson's Garden Book, 1766–1824* (Philadelphia, 1944), the sources for Jefferson as scientific farmer.

[Bigelow, Abijah], "Letters of Abijah Bigelow, Member of Congress, to His Wife, 1810–1815," American Antiquarian Society, *Proceedings,* New Series, XL (1930).

Boyd, Julian P. *et al.* (eds.) *The Papers of Thomas Jefferson* (16 vols., Princeton, 1950–).

[Breckinridge, John], "Breckinridge and the Louisiana Purchase," *Magazine of History* (Extra No. 192), XLVIII (1934).

Brown, Dorothy M. (ed.), "Excerpts from Two Pinkney Letter Books [1807–8]," *Maryland Historical Magazine,* LV (1960).

Brown, Everett S. (ed.), *William Plumer's Memorandum of Proceedings in the Senate, 1803–1805* (New York, 1923).

Brown, Stuart G. (ed.), *The Autobiography of James Monroe* (Syracuse, 1959).

Buckley, William E. (ed.), "Letters of Connecticut Federalists, 1814–1815," *New England Quarterly*, III (1930), includes Hartford Convention references.

Cappon, Lester J. (ed.), *The Adams-Jefferson Letters: The Complete Correspondence Between Thomas Jefferson and Abigail and John Adams* (2 vols., Chapel Hill, 1959).

Chinard, Gilbert (ed.), *The Commonplace Book of Thomas Jefferson* (Baltimore, 1927).

Conrad, Henry C. (ed.), "Letters of James Asheton Bayard, 1802–1814," Historical Society of Delaware, *Papers*, XXXI (1901).

Coolidge, Thomas Jefferson (ed.), "The Jefferson Papers," Massachusetts Historical Society, *Proceedings*, Second Series, XII (1897, 1899).

Corbitt, Duvon C., and Lanning, John Tate (eds.), "A Letter of Marque Issued by William Augustus Bowles as Director General of the State of Muskogee," *Journal of Southern History*, XI (1945).

Corner, George W. (ed.), *The Autobiography of Benjamin Rush* (Princeton, 1948), includes his *Commonplace Book* for 1789–1813.

Coues, Elliott (ed.), *The Expeditions of Zebulon Montgomery Pike* (3 vols., New York, 1895), especially valuable because Pike's private papers burned in a fire.

[Dalton, Samuel], "Letters of Samuel Dalton of Salem, an Impressed Seaman, 1803–1814," Essex Institute, *Historical Collections*, LXVIII (1932).

[Darnell, Elias], . . . *Brigadier General Winchester's Campaign Against the British and Indians and His Defeat at Frenchtown* . . . Historical Society of Northwestern Ohio, *Quarterly Bulletin*, III (1931).

Davis, Matthew (ed.), *The Private Journal of Aaron Burr, During His Residence of Four Years in Europe* (2 vols., New York, 1856–58).

Davis, Richard Beale (ed.), *Jeffersonian America: Notes on the United States of America Collected in the Years 1805–6–7 and 11–12 by Augustus John Foster* (San Marino, Calif., 1954).

Diamond, Sigmund (ed.), "Some Jefferson Letters," *Mississippi Valley Historical Review*, XXVIII (1941).

Donnan, Elizabeth (ed.), *Documents Illustrative of the History of the Slave Trade to America* (4 vols., Washington, 1930–35), IV.

———, "The Papers of James A. Bayard," American Historical Association, *Annual Report 1913* (2 vols., Washington, 1915).

Doster, James F. (ed.), "Letters Relating to the Tragedy of Fort Mims: August–September, 1813," *Alabama Review*, XIV (1961).

Douglas, David C. (ed.), *English Historical Documents* (12 vols., New York, 1953); XI, A. Aspinwall and E. A. Smith (eds.).

Einstein, Lewis (ed.), "Recollections of the War of 1812 by George Hay, Eighth Marquess of Tweeddale," *American Historical Review*, XXXII (1926).

Firth, Edith G. (ed.), *The Town of York, 1793–1815, A Collection of Documents of Early Toronto* (Toronto, 1962).

Foner, Philip (ed.), *The Complete Writings of Thomas Paine* (2 vols., New York, 1945).

Ford, Paul L. (ed.), *The Writings of Thomas Jefferson* (10 vols., New York, 1892–99).

Ford, Worthington C. (ed.), "Some Papers of Aaron Burr," American Antiquarian Society, *Proceedings,* New Series, XXIX (1919).

———, *The Writings of John Quincy Adams* (7 vols., New York, 1913–17).

Gibbs, George (ed.), *Memoirs of the Administrations of Washington and John Adams Edited from the Papers of Oliver Wolcott* (2 vols., New York, 1846).

Glover, Richard (ed.), *David Thompson's Narrative, 1784–1812: A New Edition with Added Material* (Toronto, 1962).

Govan, Thomas P. (ed.), "The Death of Joseph Dennie: A Memoir by Nicholas Biddle," *Pennsylvania Magazine of History and Biography,* LXXV (1951).

Green, James A. (ed.), "Journal of Ensign William Schillinger, a Soldier in the War of 1812," *Ohio Archaeological and Historical Quarterly,* XLI (1932).

Hamilton, J. C. (ed.), *History of the Republic of the United States of America as Traced in the Writings of Alexander Hamilton* (7 vols., New York, 1859).

[Hamilton, Robert], "The Expeditions of Major General Samuel Hopkins up the Wabash, 1812," *Indiana Magazine of History,* XLIII (1947).

Hamilton, Stanislaus M. (ed.), *The Writings of James Monroe* (7 vols., New York, 1898–1903), not as thorough and accurate as possible.

Harpster, J. W. (ed.), "Major William Darlington's Diary of Service in the War of 1812," *Western Pennsylvania Historical Magazine,* XX (1937).

Haynes, George Henry (ed.), "Letters of Samuel Taggart, Representative in Congress, 1803–1814," American Antiquarian Society, *Proceedings,* New Series, XXXIII (1923), Parts 1 and 2.

Heaney, Howell J. (ed.), "The Letters of Bushrod Washington (1762–1829)," *American Journal of Legal History,* II (1958).

Hooker, Richard (ed.), "John Marshall on the Judiciary, the Republicans, and Jefferson, March 4, 1801," *American Historical Review,* LIII (1948).

Hopkins, James F. (ed.), *The Papers of Henry Clay* (10 vols., Lexington, Ky., 1959–).

Hopkins, Vivian C. (ed.), "John Jacob Astor and DeWitt Clinton: Correspondence from January 25, 1808 to December 23, 1827," New York Public Library, *Bulletin,* LXVIII (1964).

Horton, John T. (ed.), "An Original Narrative of the Niagara Campaign of 1814," *Niagara Frontier,* XI (1964).

Howe, O. T. (ed.), *Autobiography of Capt. Zachary G. Lamson* (Boston, 1908?), a very illuminating account of commercial difficulties before the War of 1812.

Howland, Felix (ed.), "The Blockade of Tripoli, 1801–1802," United States Naval Institute, *Proceedings*, LXIII (1937), revealing its inadequacy.

Hunt, Gaillard (ed.), *The First Forty Years of Washington Society Portrayed by the Family Letters of Mrs. Samuel Harrison Smith* (Margaret Bayard) . . . (New York, 1906).

———, *The Writings of James Madison* (9 vols., New York, 1900–1910).

Irwin, Ray W. (ed.), "The Capture of Washington in 1814, as Described by Mordecai Booth," *Americana*, XXVIII (1934).

Jackson, Donald (ed.), *Letters of the Lewis and Clark Expedition, with Related Documents, 1783–1854* (Urbana, 1962).

Jefferson, Isaac, "Memoirs of a Monticello Slave, As Dictated to Charles Campbell in the 1840's by Isaac, One of Thomas Jefferson's Slaves," *William and Mary Quarterly*, Third Series, VIII (1951), also printed separately as edited by Rayford W. Logan (Charlottesville, 1951).

Jefferson, Thomas, "Jefferson to William Short on Mr. and Mrs. Merry, 1804," *American Historical Review*, XXXIII (1927–28).

Jennings, Paul, *A Colored Man's Reminiscences of James Madison* (Brooklyn, 1865); Jennings, manumitted by Madison, worked in the federal civil service thereafter.

Jones, Wilbur Devereux (ed.), "A British View of the War of 1812 and the Peace Negotiations," *Mississippi Valley Historical Review*, XLV (1958–59), memoirs of Henry Goulburn.

Kendall, John S. (ed.), "Documents Concerning the West Florida Revolution of 1810," *Louisiana Historical Quarterly*, XVII (1934), thirty-one documents.

Kimball, Marie G. (ed.), "Unpublished Correspondence of Mme. de Staël with Thomas Jefferson," *North American Review*, CCVIII (1918), as late as 1813.

King, Charles, R. (ed.), *The Life and Correspondence of Rufus King* (6 vols., New York, 1894–1900).

Knopf, Richard C. (ed.), *Anecdotes of the Lake Erie Area, War of 1812* (Columbus, Ohio, 1957).

———, *The National Intelligencer Reports the War of 1812 in the Northwest* (2 parts, Columbus, Ohio, 1958).

Latimer, Margaret Kinard (ed.), "Sir Augustus J. Foster in Maryland," *Maryland Historical Magazine*, XLVII (1952).

Latrobe, Charles Joseph, *The Rambler in North America* (2nd ed., 2 vols., New York, 1835), relevant to War of 1812 in Northwest.

[Lear, Tobias], "Mission to Algiers—1815," *American Foreign Service Journal*, XXVIII (No. 3, Mar. 1951), guidance toward the Shaler-Decatur Algerine treaty.

Lipscomb, A. A. *et al.* (eds.), *The Writings of Thomas Jefferson* (19 vols., Washington, 1903–4; index vol., 1905).

Lodge, Henry Cabot (ed.), *The Works of Alexander Hamilton* (12 vols., New York, 1904), superseded by a newly finished edition edited by Harold Syrett *et al.* after this book was written.

Logan, Rayford W. (ed.), see Jefferson, Isaac, above.

McGrane, Reginald C. (ed.), *The Correspondence of Nicholas Biddle . . . 1807–1844* (Boston, 1919).

McPherson, Elizabeth (ed.), "Letters of William Tatham" (Second Installment), *William and Mary Quarterly,* Second Series, XVI (1936), including observations on British ship movements by the father of the topographical and coastal surveys.

Maclay, E. S. (ed.), *Journal of William Maclay* (New York, 1890), of peripheral importance, but characterizes Jefferson.

Malone, Dumas (ed.), *Correspondence Between Thomas Jefferson and Pierre Samuel du Pont de Nemours, 1798–1817* (Boston, 1930).

Mann, Mary Lee (ed.), *A Yankee Jeffersonian: Selections from the Diary and Letters of William Lee of Massachusetts . . . 1796 to 1840* (Cambridge, Mass., 1958).

Mayo, Bernard (ed.), *Thomas Jefferson and His Unknown Brother Randolph, Twenty-eight Letters* (Charlottesville, 1942).

Mazzei, Philip, *Memoirs of the Life and Peregrinations of the Florentine, Philip Mazzei, 1730–1816* (New York, 1942).

Meriwether, Robert L. (ed.), *The Papers of John Calhoun* (3 vols., Columbia, S.C., 1959–).

Morison, Samuel Eliot (ed.), "Two Letters of Harrison Gray Otis on the Hartford Convention, 1814–1815," *Massachusetts Historical Society, Proceedings,* LX (1926–27).

Morris, Richard B. (ed.), *Alexander Hamilton and the Founding of the Nation* (New York, 1957), systematically arranged excerpts.

Munro, Wilfred H. (ed.), "Extracts from the Log Book of the Private Armed Schooner Blockade, Manly Sweet, Commander," Rhode Island Historical Society, *Collections,* XIII (1920).

Munroe, John A. (ed.), "William Plumer's Biographical Sketches of James A. Bayard, Caesar A. Rodney, and Samuel White," *Delaware History,* IV (1951).

Nasatir, Abraham P. (ed.), *Before Lewis and Clark: Documents Illustrating the History of the Missouri, 1785–1804* (2 vols., St. Louis, 1952).

Nolte, Vincent O., *Fifty Years in Both Hemispheres* (New York, 1854), perhaps more entertaining than reliable.

Old Family Letters Copied from the Originals for Alexander Biddle (Philadelphia, 1892).

Padgett, James A. (ed.), "The West Florida Revolution of 1810, as Told in . . . Letters . . ." *Louisiana Historical Quarterly,* XXI (1938).

Paltsits, Victor H. (ed.), "Cruise of the U.S. Brig Argus in 1813; Journal of Surgeon James Inderwick," New York Public Library, *Bulletin,* XXI (1917), also published separately (New York, 1917), 25 pp.

Parker, Wilmond W., and Newton, Earl Williams (eds.), "Letters of the War of 1812 in the Champlain Valley," *Vermont Quarterly,* XII (1944).

Prichard, Walter (ed.), "An Original Letter on the West Florida Revolution of 1810," *Louisiana Historical Quarterly,* XVIII (1935).

Pritchett, John Perry (ed.), "Selkirk's Views on British Policy Toward the Spanish-American Colonies, 1806," *Canadian Historical Review,* XXIV (1943).

Proceedings of the General Court Martial Convened for the Trial of Commodore James Barron . . . January 1808 (Washington, 1822).

[Procter, George], *The Lucubrations of Humphrey Ravelin, Esq., Late Major in the * * * Regiment of Infantry* (London, 1823), a British view of the War of 1812 in the Northwest.

Quaife, Milo (ed.), *The John Askin Papers* (2 vols., Detroit, 1928–31); Askin was a Detroit fur trader.

———, *Southwestern Expedition of Zebulon M. Pike* (Chicago, 1925).

———, *War on the Detroit; the Chronicles of Thomas Verchères de Bourcherville, and, The Capitulation, by an Ohio Volunteer* [James Foster?], (Chicago, 1940), two separate documents.

Ravelin, Humphrey, see Procter, George.

Reinoehl, John H. (ed.), "Some Reflections on the American Trade, 1806," by Jacob Crowninshield, *William and Mary Quarterly,* Third Series, XVI (1959).

Ritchie, Carson I. A., "British Documents on the Louisiana Campaign, 1814–15," *Louisiana Historical Quarterly,* XLIV (1961), which is a commentary on Ritchie (ed.), "Copy of the *Journal of the Operations Against New Orleans in 1814 and 1815,*" by Charles Ramus Forrest; "Journal of Operations in Louisiana, 1814 and 1815," by Alexander Dickson; and five shorter related documents, *ibid.* Dickson was the chief British artillery officer in the Louisiana campaign; these documents require rethinking of the entire story of which the climax is the so-called Battle of New Orleans.

Ritchie, Margaret K. and Carson, I. A. (eds.), "A Laker's Log," *American Neptune,* XVII (1957).

Rives, George Lockhart (ed.), *Selections from the Correspondence of Thomas Barclay* (New York, 1894), British consul at New York during the most troublesome years.

Safford, W. H. (ed.), *The Blennerhassett Papers* (Cincinnati, 1864).

Sargent, Epes, ". . . Account of a British Press Gang in 1803," Essex Institute, *Historical Collections*, LXXXVIII (1952).

Sizer, Theodore (ed.), *The Autobiography of Colonel John Trumbull, Patriot-Artist, 1756–1843* (New Haven, 1953).

Skinner, J. S. (ed.), "Incidents of the War of 1812. From the *Baltimore Patriot*," *Maryland Historical Magazine*, XXXII (1937).

Spivey, Herman E. (ed.), "William Cullen Bryant Changes His Mind," *New England Quarterly*, XXII (1949).

Stacey, C. P. (ed.), "Upper Canada at War, 1814: Captain Armstrong Reports," *Ontario History*, XLVIII (1956).

Steiner, Bernard C. (ed.), "Some Papers of Robert Smith, Secretary of the Navy, 1801–1809, and of State, 1809–1811," *Maryland Historical Magazine*, XX (1925).

Thornbrough, Gayle (ed.), *The Correspondence of John Badollet and Albert Gallatin* (Indianapolis, 1963); Badollet despised William Henry Harrison.

Vane, Charles (ed.), *Memoirs and Correspondence of Viscount Castlereagh, Second Marquess of Londonderry* (12 vols., London, 1848–53), X.

Walker, Henry P. (ed.), "William McLane's Narrative of the Magee-Gutierrez Expedition, 1812–1813," *Southwestern Historical Quarterly*, LXVI (1961–62).

Wallace, S. A. (ed.), "Georgetown Is Saved from the British!" *Social Studies*, XLIII (1952), excerpts from the diary of Mrs. William Thornton.

Warfel, Harry R. (ed.), *Letters of Noah Webster* (New York, 1953).

Warren, Charles (ed.), *Jacobin and Junto; or, Early American Politics as Viewed in the Diary of Dr. Nathaniel Ames, 1758–1822* (Cambridge, Mass., 1931).

"War's Wild Alarm," *Virginia Magazine of History and Biography*, XLIX (1941), documents by and about people of the James Valley in 1813.

[Webster, Daniel], *The Writings and Speeches of Daniel Webster* (18 vols., Boston, 1903).

Wesley, Edgar B. (ed.), "A Letter from Colonel John Allen," *Ohio Archaeological and Historical Quarterly*, XXXVI (1927), who served under Harrison, Aug.–Oct., 1812.

White, M. Catherine (ed.), *David Thompson's Journals Relating to Montana and Adjacent Regions, 1808–1812* (Missoula, Mont., 1950).

Williams, Mentor L. (ed.), "John Kinzie's Narrative of the Fort Dearborn Massacre," Illinois State Historical Society, *Journal*, XLVI (1953).

[Windham, William], *The Windham Papers* (2 vols., Boston, 1913), British sources.

Winston, James E. (ed.), "A Faithful Picture of the Political Situation in New Orleans" (by James Workman or Edward Livingston), *Louisiana Historical Quarterly*, XI (1928), on the Wilkinson quasi terror, 1807.

Contemporary Periodicals, Pamphlets, Books

Albany *Register; The Annual Register* (London), for which, general index, 1758–1819; Boston *Columbian Centinel;* Boston *Repertory;* William Cullen Bryant, *The Embargo* (Boston, 1808, 1809, facsimile reprints of both editions, Gainesville, Fla., 1955); Burlington, Vt., *Centinel;* Zadok Cramer, *The Navigator* (at least twelve eds., title varies, Pittsburgh, 1801–), facsimile reproduction of 8th ed. in Ethel C. Leahy, *Who's Who on the Ohio River* (Cincinnati, 1931); Washington *Daily National Intelligencer; Edinburgh Review,* XIX–XX; George Cary Eggleston (ed.), *American War Ballads and Lyrics* (2 vols., New York, 1889), I; Augustus J. Foster [review of unpublished] "Notes on the United States," in *The Quarterly Review* (London), CXXXVI (1841); *The Gentleman's Magazine* (London), CXIV–CXVII (1812–15); Charles Wilson Hackett (ed.), *Pichardo's Treatise on the Limits of Louisiana and Texas* (4 vols., reprint, Austin, 1931–46); [Alexander Hamilton], "Hamilton on the Louisiana Purchase: A Newly Identified Editorial from the *New-York Evening Post," William and Mary Quarterly,* Third Series, XII (1955); Klinck, Carl F. (ed.), *Tecumseh, Fact and Fiction in Early Records* (Englewood Cliffs, N.J., 1961), containing all the necessary printed contemporary documents; of John Lowell's Yankee-cider-turned-vinegar, the following three are typical specimens: *The New-England Patriot* . . . (San Francisco, reprint, 1940), *Peace Without Dishonor: War Without Hope* . . . (Boston, 1807), *Thoughts Upon the Conduct of Our Administration* . . . (Boston, 1808); *Niles' Weekly Register,* 1811–15, a national newspaper published in Baltimore, the first with a serious intent to be impartial in news presentation and replete with contemporary official documents; William Peden (ed.), *Notes on the State of Virginia,* by Thomas Jefferson (Chapel Hill, 1955); Philadelphia *Aurora;* Timothy Pickering's two polemic publications, *Interesting Correspondence Between* . . . *Governour Sullivan and Col. Pickering* (Boston, 1808), and *A Letter from the Hon. Timothy Pickering* . . . *to his Excellency James Sullivan* (Boston, 1808); John Sampson (ed.), *The Poetical Works of William Blake* (Oxford, 1905); James Stephen, *War in Disguise, or, The Frauds of the Neutral Flags* (London, 1805), by a member of Parliament who was also a master in chancery; Uriah Tracy, "Amendment of the Constitution [1802]," in Frank Moore (ed.), *American Eloquence* (2 vols., New York, 1856–57), I, an excerpt from one of the few who heatedly disliked the republican form of government while holding high office in the United States; Vincennes *Western Sun.*

Secondary Materials

Published Biographies and Biographical Sketches

This group of titles is arranged alphabetically by subject. It includes only secondary materials; sources have been listed above. The biographical literature of the period is profuse, although not proportioned to the importance of the subjects. For senators and representatives, the barest facts, without documentation or bibliographies, may be found in *Biographical Directory of the American Congress, 1774–1961* (Washington, 1961, date varies from Congress to Congress in recent decades; almost any date will do). Much more useful is the *Dictionary of American Biography* (22 vols., or 22 vols. in 11, New York, 1928–58), hereafter cited as *DAB*. Of limited value is J. C. Dent, *Canadian Portrait Gallery* (Toronto, 1880), although a new dictionary of Canadian biography is under construction at this time.

The Secretaries of State of the United States are a special case, and their careers may be traced in Samuel Flagg Bemis (ed.), *The American Secretaries of State and Their Diplomacy* (10 vols. in 5, New York, 1958), namely, Robert R. Livingston, I; Timothy Pickering, II; James Madison, Robert Smith, and James Monroe, III; and Edward Livingston, IV. A similar collection on the Secretaries of the Navy is being assembled under the editorship of Paolo Coletta *et al.,* but is not yet available.

ASTOR, JOHN JACOB. Kenneth W. Porter, *John Jacob Astor, Businessman* (2 vols., Cambridge, Mass., 1931), of which Chaps. VII–VIII deal with Astoria.

BARBÉ-MARBOIS, FRANÇOIS. E. Wilson Lyon, *The Man Who Sold Louisiana: The Career of François Barbé-Marbois* (Norman, Okla., 1942).

BARLOW, JOEL. James Woodress, *A Yankee's Odyssey: The Life of Joel Barlow* (Philadelphia, 1958); T. A. Zunder and S. T. Williams in *DAB;* Irving Brant, "Joel Barlow, Madison's Stubborn Minister," *William and Mary Quarterly,* Third Series, XXV (1958); Robert F. Durden, "Joel Barlow in the French Revolution," *ibid.,* VIII (1951), covering 1788–1805; Joseph Dorfman, "Joel Barlow: Trafficker in Trade and Letters," *Political Science Quarterly,* LIX (1944); Vernon P. Squires, "Joel Barlow—Patriot, Democrat, and Man of Letters," University of North Dakota, *Quarterly Journal,* IX (1918–19), old but not useless.

BARNEY, JOSHUA. Hulbert Footner, *Sailor of Fortune: The Life and Adventures of Commodore Barney, U.S.N.* (New York, 1940).

BARTRAM, JOHN AND WILLIAM. Ernest Earnest, *John and William Bartram* (Philadelphia, 1940).

BAYARD, JAMES A. Morton Borden, *The Federalism of James A. Bayard* (New York, 1955).

BOUDINOT, ELIAS. George Adams Boyd, *Elias Boudinot, Patriot and Statesman, 1740–1821* (Princeton, 1952).

BRACKENRIDGE, HUGH HENRY. Claude Milton Newlin, *The Life and Writings of Hugh Henry Brackenridge* (Princeton, 1932).

BROWN, CHARLES BROCKDEN. David Lee Clark, *Charles Brockden Brown: Pioneer Voice of America* (Durham, N.C., 1952).

BULFINCH, CHARLES. Charles A. Place, *Charles Bulfinch, Architect and Citizen* (Boston, 1925).

BURR, AARON. Nathan Schachner, *Aaron Burr* (New York, 1937), in an exculpatory tone; Samuel H. Wandell and Meade Minnigerode, *Aaron Burr* (2 vols., New York, 1925), perhaps more merciful than just, but carefully studied; I. J. Cox in *DAB;* Gordon L. Thomas, "Aaron Burr's Farewell Address," *Quarterly Journal of Speech*, XXXIX (1953); Julius W. Pratt, "Aaron Burr and the Historians," *New-York History*, XXVI (1945), required reading for the next biographer; Richard B. Morris, in *Fair Trial* (New York, 1953), treats Burr, Chap. V.

CLINTON, DEWITT. Dorothie Bobbé, *DeWitt Clinton* (New York, 1933); D. R. Fox in *DAB.*

DALLAS, ALEXANDER JAMES. Raymond Walters, Jr., *Alexander James Dallas: Lawyer—Politician—Financier, 1759–1817* (Philadelphia, 1943).

DWIGHT, TIMOTHY. C. E. Cuningham, *Timothy Dwight, 1752–1817* (New York, 1942).

EATON, WILLIAM. Meade Minnigerode, *Lives and Times: Four Informal American Biographies* (New York, 1925), including one of Eaton; Louis B. Wright and Julia H. Macleod, "William Eaton's Relations with Aaron Burr," *Mississippi Valley Historical Review*, XXXI (1944–45).

ELLIOTT, MATTHEW. Reginald Horsman, *Matthew Elliott, British Indian Agent* (Detroit, 1964), a careful tracing of western warfare through the Battle of the Thames.

FRENEAU, PHILIP. Lewis Leary, *That Rascal Freneau, A Study in Literary Failure* (New Brunswick, 1941).

GAINES, EDMUND PENDLETON. James W. Silver, *Edmund Pendleton Gaines: Frontier General* (Baton Rouge, 1949).

GALLATIN, ALBERT. Alexander Balinky, *Albert Gallatin: Fiscal Theories and Policies* (New Brunswick, 1958), an estimate by an economist; Raymond Walters, Jr., *Albert Gallatin: Jeffersonian Financier and Diplomat* (New York, 1957), the first life based on the full collection of Gallatin papers in the New-York Historical Society's archives; Henry Adams, *The Life of Albert Gallatin* (Philadelphia, 1879), useful for documents; Balinky, "Albert Gallatin, Naval Foe," *Pennsylvania Magazine of History and Biography*, LXXXII (1958); Jay C. Henlein, "Albert Gallatin: A Pioneer in Public Administration," *William and Mary Quarterly*, Third Series, VII (1950); Walters, "The Making of a Financier: Albert Gallatin in the Pennsylvania Assembly," *Pennsylvania Magazine of History and Biography*, LXX (1946).

GIRARD, STEPHEN. John Bach McMaster, *Life and Times of Stephen Girard* (2 vols., Philadelphia, 1918), II; Kenneth L. Brown, "Stephen Girard, Promoter of the Second Bank of the United States," *Journal of Economic History*, II (1942).

HAMILTON, ALEXANDER. John C. Miller, *Alexander Hamilton: Portrait in Paradox* (New York, 1959); the two other book-length biographies most frequently consulted, by Nathan Schachner (New York, 1946) and Henry Jones Ford (New York, 1920), show poverty of thought in the one and too-frequent inaccuracy in the other; John A. Krout, "Alexander Hamilton's Place in the Founding of the Nation," American Philosophical Society, *Proceedings,* CII (1958); Broadus Mitchell, "The Secret of Alexander Hamilton," *Virginia Quarterly Review,* XXIX (1953).

HARRISON, WILLIAM HENRY. Dorothy Burne Goebel, *William Henry Harrison: A Political Biography* (Indianapolis, 1926); Goebel in *DAB;* Moses Dawson, *Historical Narrative of the Civil and Military Services of Major-General William Henry Harrison* (Cincinnati, 1824), so close to the subject as to be almost primary.

HAWKINS, BENJAMIN. Merritt B. Pound, *Benjamin Hawkins: Indian Agent* (Athens, Ga., 1951).

IRVING, WASHINGTON. Stanley T. Williams, *The Life of Washington Irving* (2 vols., New York, 1935).

JACKSON, ANDREW. Marquis James, *Andrew Jackson: The Border Captain* (Indianapolis, 1933); J. S. Bassett, *The Life of Andrew Jackson* (new ed., 2 vols., New York, 1931); Albert Somit, "Andrew Jackson: Legend and Reality," *Tennessee Historical Quarterly,* VII (1948); James A. Padgett (ed.), "The Difficulties of Andrew Jackson in New Orleans . . ." *Louisiana Historical Quarterly,* XXI (1938).

JEFFERSON, THOMAS. As remarked earlier, Jeffersonian bibliography is a career in itself. The same is almost as true of Jeffersonian bio-bibliography. Below are listed, first, the books about Jefferson which have been most helpful, and then the shorter pieces used. They are in reverse chronological order of publication.

Leonard W. Levy, *Jefferson & Civil Liberties: The Darker Side* (Cambridge, Mass., 1963), the brief of the devil's advocate against canonization, quite useful; Henry Wilder Foote, *The Religion of Thomas Jefferson* (Boston, 1960, reprint of 1947); Merrill D. Peterson, *The Jefferson Image in the American Mind* (New York, 1960), Jefferson as symbol, not person, an illumination brightened by the same author's "Henry Adams on Jefferson the President," *Virginia Quarterly Review,* XXXIX (1963), and "Bowers, Roosevelt, and the 'New Jefferson,'" *ibid.,* XXXIV (1958), which latter describes the apotheosis of partisan Democrat to culture hero; Bernard Mayo, *Myths and Men: Patrick Henry, George Washington, Thomas Jefferson* (Athens, Ga., 1959); Gilbert Chinard, *Thomas Jefferson, The Apostle of Americanism* (2nd ed., Ann Arbor, 1960, from 1929 1st ed.), perhaps the most popular of the lives; Arthur Bestor, David C. Mearns, and Jonathan Daniels, *Three Presidents and Their Books; The Readings of Jefferson; Lincoln; Franklin D. Roosevelt* (Urbana, 1955); Caleb Perry Patterson, *The Constitutional Principles of*

Thomas Jefferson (Austin, 1953), described by one reader as what John Stuart Mill would have liked about Jefferson; Nathan Schachner, *Thomas Jefferson, A Biography* (2 vols. in 1, New York, 1951), giving no impression of profundity; Dumas Malone, *Jefferson and His Time* (4 vols., Boston, 1948–), a continuing multivolume monument, with much remaining to be done, but, meanwhile, see the same author's essay in *DAB;* Max Beloff, *Thomas Jefferson and American Democracy* (London, 1948) ; Saul K. Padover (ed.), *Thomas Jefferson and the National Capital . . . 1783–1818* (Washington, 1946), including the essential documents; Frank Luther Mott, *Jefferson and the Press* (Baton Rouge, 1943) ; Adrienne Koch, *The Philosophy of Thomas Jefferson* (New York, 1943) ; Otto Vossler, *Die amerikanischer Revolutionsideale in ihrem Verhältnis zu den europäischen: Untersuch an Thomas Jefferson,* Beiheft 17, *Historischen Zeitschriften* (München, 1929), perhaps overly oriented toward ideology (the gist of Vossler may be found in Robert R. Palmer, "A Neglected Work: Otto Vossler on Jefferson and the Revolutionary Era," *William and Mary Quarterly,* Third Series, XII [1955]) ; Francis Wrigley Hirst, *The Life and Letters of Thomas Jefferson* (New York, 1926), an English writer's anti-Hamiltonian "corrective"; Allen Johnson, *Jefferson and His Colleagues* (New Haven, 1921), an example of the highest kind of popularization; David Saville Muzzey, *Thomas Jefferson* (New York, 1918) ; Sarah N. Randolph, *The Domestic Life of Thomas Jefferson* (New York, 1871) ; and finally, Theodore Dwight, *The Character of Thomas Jefferson, as Exhibited in His Own Writings* (Boston, 1839), by the Secretary of the Hartford Convention, who feverishly despised the present-day culture hero.

The shorter monographs and essays on Jefferson which have been most useful are arranged below, by decades, in reverse chronological order.

1960's: Fred C. Luebke, "The Origins of Thomas Jefferson's Anti-Clericalism," *Church History,* XXXII (1963) ; Dumas Malone, "The Relevance of Mr. Jefferson," *Virginia Quarterly Review,* XXXVII (1961) ; Merrill D. Peterson, "Thomas Jefferson and the National Purpose," American Philosophical Society, *Proceedings,* CV (1961) ; Milford F. Allen, "Thomas Jefferson and the Louisiana-Arkansas Frontier," *Arkansas Historical Quarterly,* XX (1961) ; Morton Borden, "Thomas Jefferson," in Borden (ed.), *America's Ten Greatest Presidents* (Chicago, 1961).

1950's: H. Trevor Colbourn, "Thomas Jefferson's Use of the Past," *William and Mary Quarterly,* Third Series, XV (1958) ; a chapter on Jefferson in Richard Hofstadter, *The American Political Tradition and the Men Who Made It* (New York, 1958) ; Dwight Boehm and Edward Schwartz, "Jefferson and the Theory of Degeneracy," *American Quar-*

terly, IX (1957); E. Millicent Sowerby, "Thomas Jefferson and His Library," Bibliographical Society of America, *Papers,* L (1956); J. G. de Roulhac Hamilton, "The Pacifism of Thomas Jefferson," *Virginia Quarterly Review,* XXXI (1955); Clinton Rossiter, "Which Jefferson Do You Quote?" *Reporter,* Dec. 15, 1955; H. Hale Bellot, "Thomas Jefferson in American Historiography," Royal Historical Society, *Transactions,* Fifth Series, IV (1954); Claude G. Bowers, "Jefferson and Civil Liberties: Tyranny in America," *Atlantic,* Jan. 1953; Julian P. Boyd, "The Relevance of Thomas Jefferson for the Twentieth Century," *American Scholar,* XXII (1952–53); Adrienne Koch, "Power and Morals and the Founding Fathers: Jefferson," *Review of Politics,* XV (1953); Douglass Adair, "Rumbold's Dying Speech, 1685, and Jefferson's Last Words on Democracy, 1826," *William and Mary Quarterly,* Third Series, IX (1952); Edd Winfield Parks, "Jefferson as a Man of Letters," *Georgia Review,* VI (1952); Van Wyck Brooks, "Thomas Jefferson, Man of Letters," American Academy of Arts and Letters, *Academy Papers,* II (1951).

1940's: (the bicentennial harvest decade): William Peden, "A Book Peddler Invades Monticello," *William and Mary Quarterly,* Third Series, VI (1949), and talks theology with Jefferson; Julian P. Boyd, "Thomas Jefferson's 'Empire of Liberty,'" *Virginia Quarterly Review,* XXIV (1948), and "Thomas Jefferson and the Police State," *North Carolina Historical Review,* XXV (1948); Mina R. Bryan, "Thomas Jefferson Through the Eyes of His Contemporaries," *Princeton University Library Chronicle,* IX (1948); A. Whitney Griswold, "The Agrarian Democracy of Thomas Jefferson," *American Political Science Review,* XL (1946); Philip M. Marsh, "Jefferson and Journalism," *Huntington Library Quarterly,* IX (1946); Carl Becker, "What Is Still Living in the Philosophy of Thomas Jefferson?" American Philosophical Society, *Proceedings,* LXXXVII (1944); Charles A. Browne, "Thomas Jefferson and the Scientific Trends of His Time," *Chronica Botanica,* VIII (1944), by an agricultural chemist; Gilbert Chinard, "Jefferson and the American Philosophical Society," American Philosophical Society, *Proceedings,* LXXXVII (1944); Fiske Kimball, "Jefferson and the Arts," *ibid.,* LXXXVII (1944); William O. Lynch, "Jefferson the Liberal," *Indiana Magazine of History,* XL (1944); Roland S. Morris, "Jefferson as a Lawyer," American Philosophical Society, *Proceedings,* LXXXVII (1944); Harlow Shapley, "Notes on Jefferson as a Natural Philosopher," *ibid.;* M. L. Wilson, "Thomas Jefferson—Farmer," *ibid.;* Louis B. Wright, "Thomas Jefferson and the Classics," *ibid.;* Charles A. Beard, "Thomas Jefferson: A Civilized Man," *Mississippi Valley Historical Review,* XXX (1943–44); Frank P. Bourgin and Charles E. Merriam, "Jefferson as a Planner of National Resources," *Ethics,* LIII (1942–43); Claude G. Bowers, "Jefferson and the Freedom of the Human Spirit," *ibid.,* and "Thomas Jefferson and South America," Pan-American Union, *Bulletin,* LXXVII (1943); Gilbert Chinard, "Jefferson Among the Philosophers," *Ethics,* LIII (1942–43), and "Jefferson's Influence Abroad," *Mississippi Valley Historical Review,* XXX (1943–44); H. M. Kallen, "The Arts and Thomas Jefferson," *Ethics,* LIII (1942–43); George H. Knoles, "The Religious Ideas of Thomas Jefferson," *Mississippi Valley Historical Review,* XXX (1943–44); Herbert W. Schneider, "The Enlightenment in Thomas Jefferson," *Ethics,* LIII (1942–43); Lynn W. Turner, "Thomas Jefferson Through the Eyes of a New Hampshire Politician," *Mississippi Valley Historical Review,* XXX (1943–44), from same MSS. used by E. S. Brown (ed.), listed in section "Private Papers and Memoirs," above; Louis M. Sears, "Democracy as Understood by Thomas Jefferson," *Mid-America,* XXIV (1942); Russell Amos Kirk, "Jefferson and the Faithless," *South Atlantic Quarterly,* XL (1941); Roy J. Honeywell, "President Jefferson and His Successor," *American Historical Review,* XLVI (1940–41), a study not yet assimilated by the historical profession, but which is necessary to understanding the story of the years 1801–17; Joseph J. Spengler, "The Political Economy of Jefferson, Madison, and Adams," in David Kelly Jackson (ed.), *American Studies in Honor of William Kenneth Boyd* (Durham, N.C., 1940).

1930's: Dumas Malone, "Polly Jefferson and Her Father," *Virginia Quarterly Review,* VII (1931).

JOHNSON, WILLIAM. Donald G. Morgan, *Justice William Johnson, the First Dissenter* (Columbia, S.C., 1954); J. G. de R. Hamilton in *DAB;* Henry F. Bedford, "William Johnson and the Marshall Court," *South Carolina Historical Magazine,* LXII (1961).

KENT, JAMES. John T. Horton, *James Kent, A Study in Conservatism, 1763–1847* (New York, 1939).

LATROBE, BENJAMIN HENRY. Talbot F. Hamlin, *Benjamin Henry Latrobe* (New York, 1955), which appeared in preliminary form in *Maryland Magazine of History,* XXXVII (1942).

LIVINGSTON, EDWARD. W. B. Hatcher, *Edward Livingston* (University, La., 1940).

LIVINGSTON, ROBERT R. George Dangerfield, *Chancellor Robert R. Livingston of New York, 1746–1813* (New York, 1960), a master's work; Robert C. Hayes in *DAB.*

LOGAN, GEORGE. Frederick B. Tolles, *George Logan of Philadelphia* (New York, 1953); Deborah Logan, *Memoir of Dr. George Logan of Stenton* (Philadelphia, 1899).

McINTIRE, SAMUEL. Frank Cousins and P. M. Riley, *The Wood Carver of Salem, Samuel McIntire* (Boston, 1916).

MADISON, JAMES. Irving Brant, *James Madison* (6 vols., Indianapolis, 1948–61), with following subtitles and dates of publication: *The Nationalist* (1948), *Father of the Constitution* (1950), *Secretary of State,*

1800–1809 (1953), *The President, 1809–1812* (1956), *Commander-in-Chief, 1812–1836* (1961), with which might be read, for adversary proceeding, reviews by Nathan Schachner, *American Historical Review*, LX (1954), and Charles M. Wiltse, *ibid.*, LXVII (1962). It may also be added that Brant has discarded Henry Adams as a source. Brant went into more detail on specific points in the following essays: "Madison and the War of 1812," *Virginia Magazine of History and Biography*, LXXIV (1966); "Madison and the Empire of Free Men," Illinois State Historical Society, *Journal*, XLVIII (1955); "Madison, the 'North American,' on Federal Power," *American Historical Review*, LX (1954–55); "James Madison and His Times," *ibid.*, LVII (1951–52); "Madison: On the Separation of Church and State," *William and Mary Quarterly*, Third Series, VIII (1951). Other useful studies follow: Ralph L. Ketcham, "James Madison and the Nature of Man," *Journal of the History of Ideas*, XIX (1958), quite good; Arnold A. Rogow, "The Federal Convention: Madison and Yates," *American Historical Review*, LX (1954–55); Adrienne Koch, "James Madison and the Workshop of Liberty," *Review of Politics*, XVI (1954); Neal Riemer, "The Republicanism of James Madison," *Political Science Quarterly*, LXXIX (1954); Theodore Bolton, "The Life Portraits of James Madison," *William and Mary Quarterly*, Third Series, VIII (1951); Abbot E. Smith, *James Madison, Builder, A New Estimate of a Memorable Career* (New York, 1937). Under Jefferson, above, see Honeywell, Spengler.

MARSHALL, JOHN. William W. Crosskey, "Mr. Justice Marshall," in Allison Dunham and Philip B. Kurland (eds.), *Mr. Justice* (Chicago, 1956); W. Melville Jones (ed.), *Chief Justice John Marshall: A Reappraisal* (Ithaca, 1956), containing several perceptive estimates; David Goldsmith Loth, *Chief Justice John Marshall and the Growth of the Republic* (New York, 1949); the main monument is Albert J. Beveridge, *The Life of John Marshall* (4 vols., Boston, 1916–19); Edward S. Corwin, *John Marshall and the Constitution* (New Haven, 1919), much briefer than Beveridge; Beveridge was reviewed by A. C, McLaughlin in American Bar Association, *Journal*, VII (1921), and Robert E. Cushman reviewed both in *Minnesota Law Review*, V (1920); worth seeing is Barbara Barlin, "John Marshall: Usurper or Grantee?" *Social Education*, XXII (1958).

MITCHILL, SAMUEL LATHAM. Edgar F. Smith, *Samuel Latham Mitchill* (New York, 1922); Lyman C. Newell in *DAB*.

MONROE, JAMES. William Penn Cresson, *James Monroe* (Chapel Hill, 1946); Harry Ammon, "James Monroe and the Election of 1808 in Virginia," *William and Mary Quarterly*, Third Series, XX (1963); Dexter Perkins in *DAB*.

OTIS, HARRISON GRAY. Samuel Eliot Morison, *The Life and Letters of Harrison Gray Otis, Federalist, 1765–1848* (2 vols., Boston, 1913), makes the best case for the moderate Federalists of New England, with characteristic grace.

PARSONS, THEOPHILUS. Theophilus Parsons, Jr., *Memoir of Theophilus Parsons* (Boston, 1859); Zechariah Chafee, Jr., in *DAB*.

PEALE, CHARLES WILLSON. Charles Coleman Sellers, *Charles Willson Peale* (2 vols., Philadelphia, 1947).

PERRY, OLIVER HAZARD. Charles J. Dutton, *Oliver Hazard Perry* (New York, 1935).

PIKE, ZEBULON MONTGOMERY. W. Eugene Hollon, *Lost Pathfinder* (Norman, 1949), and "Zebulon Montgomery Pike and the Wilkinson-Burr Conspiracy," American Philosophical Society, *Proceedings*, XCI (1947).

PLUMER, WILLIAM. Lynn W. Turner, *William Plumer of New Hampshire, 1759–1850* (Chapel Hill, 1962).

PRIESTLEY, JOSEPH. Anne Holt, *A Life of Joseph Priestley* (London, 1931).

RANDOLPH, JOHN. William Cabell Bruce, *John Randolph of Roanoke, 1773–1833* (2 vols., New York, 1922), properly described by a critic as "monumental"; Mason Daly, "The Political Oratory of John Randolph of Roanoke," Ph.D. thesis, Northwestern University, described in Northwestern University, *Summaries of Doctoral Dissertations*, XIX (1951).

SACAJAWEA. Grace R. Hebard, *Sacajawea, A Guide and Interpreter of the Lewis and Clark Expedition* (Glendale, Calif., 1933).

SHALER, WILLIAM. Roy Franklin Nichols, *Advance Agents of American Destiny* (Philadelphia, 1956), has a long chapter on this colorful adventurer.

SMITH, SYDNEY. Hesketh Pearson, *The Smith of Smiths* (London, 1934), here inserted not for significance but for the pleasure of exhibiting a great and knowledgeable wit who opposed the ministry which warred against the United States.

STORY, JOSEPH. Mortimer D. Schwartz and John C. Hogan (eds.), *Joseph Story* (New York, 1959); Gerald T. Dunne, "Joseph Story: The Germinal Years," *Harvard Law Review*, LXXV (1961–62); George E. Woodbine in *DAB*.

TAYLOR, JOHN. E. T. Mudge, *The Social Philosophy of John Taylor of Caroline* (New York, 1939); H. H. Simms, *Life of John Taylor* (Richmond, 1932); Grant McConnell, "John Taylor and the Democratic Tradition," *Western Political Quarterly*, IV (1951); Benjamin F. Wright, Jr., "The Philosopher of Jeffersonian Democracy," *American Political Science Review*, XXI (1928).

TECUMSEH. Glenn Tucker, *Tecumseh, Vision of Glory* (Indianapolis, 1956); Benjamin Drake, *Life of Tecumseh* (Cincinnati, 1847), with much from contemporary witnesses; Katharine Elizabeth Crane in *DAB*.

THORNDIKE, ISRAEL. J. D. Forbes, *Israel Thorndike, Federalist Financier* (New York, 1953).

TRUMBULL, JOHN. Alexander Cowie, *John Trumbull: Connecticut Wit* (Chapel Hill, 1936).

WEBSTER, DANIEL. Claude M. Fuess, *Daniel Webster* (2 vols., Boston, 1930).

WEBSTER, NOAH. Harry R. Warfel, *Noah Webster, Schoolmaster to America* (New York, 1936).

WILKINSON, JAMES. James Ripley Jacobs, *Tarnished Warrior* (New York, 1938), which was followed in 1941 by an unnecessary and undocumented life by Thomas Robson Hay and M. R. Werner; Hay, "Some Reflections on the Career of General James Wilkinson," *Mississippi Valley Historical Review*, XXI (1934–35), has an exculpatory tone, as does James Wilkinson, "General James Wilkinson," *Louisiana Historical Quarterly*, 1 (1917), by a descendant; I. J. Cox, "General Wilkinson and His Later Intrigues with the Spaniards," *American Historical Review*, XIX (1913–14).

WILSON, ALEXANDER. Emerson Stringham, *Alexander Wilson, Founder of Scientific Ornithology* (Kerrville, Tex., 1958).

WORTHINGTON, THOMAS. Alfred B. Sears, *Thomas Worthington, Father of Ohio Statehood* (Columbus, 1958).

Short Biographical Sketches and Profiles

The following subjects of short sketches do not seem to have inspired biographers to write magisterial book-length lives. They are arranged alphabetically by surnames. Only those essays which attempt complete portraits are here listed.

Birdsall, Richard D., "The Reverend Thomas Allen: Jeffersonian Calvinist," *New England Quarterly*, XXX (1957).

Douglass, Elisha P., "Fisher Ames, Spokesman for New England Federalism," American Philosophical Society, *Proceedings*, CIII (1959); Samuel Eliot Morison in *DAB*.

Peckham, Howard H., "Commodore Perry's Captive [Captain Barclay, R.N.]," *Ohio History*, LXXII (1963).

Jahoda, Gloria, "John Beckley: Jefferson's Campaign Manager," New York Public Library, *Bulletin*, LXIV (1960); Noble E. Cunningham, Jr., "John Beckley: An Early American Party Manager," *William and Mary Quarterly*, Third Series, XIII (1956); Philip M. Marsh, "John Beckley: Mystery Man of the Early Jeffersonians," *Pennsylvania Magazine of History and Biography*, LXXII (1948).

Harrison, Lowell H., "Attorney General John Breckinridge," Filson Club, *Historical Quarterly*, XXXVI (1962), and "John Breckinridge: Western

Statesman," *Journal of Southern History,* XVIII (1952) ; E. M. Coulter in *DAB.*

Maier, E. F. J., "Mathew Carey, Publicist and Politician," American Catholic Historical Society of Philadelphia, *Records,* XXXIX (1928).

Westcott, Allan, "Commodore Jesse D. Elliott: A Stormy Petral of the Navy," United States Naval Institute, *Proceedings,* LIV (1928), a most unflattering sketch.

Jackson, Donald, "William Ewing, Agricultural Agent to the Indians," *Agricultural History,* XXXI (1957), relevant to the Jeffersonian education of Indians.

LeBreton, Dagmar Renshaw, "The Man Who Won the Battle of New Orleans," *Louisiana Historical Quarterly,* XXXVIII (1955), re Jean Paul Hudry, creole leader.

Cox, Isaac J., "An Early Explorer of the Louisiana Purchase," American Philosophical Society, *Library Bulletin 1946* (Philadelphia, 1947), i.e., George Hunter.

Muller, Charles G., "Commodore and Mrs. Thomas Macdonough," *Delaware History,* IX (1960–61).

Waters, T. C., "Luther Martin," American Bar Association, *Journal,* XIV (1928), two parts; E. S. Delaplaine in *DAB.*

Mindte, R. W., "Another Navy Rodgers," *American Neptune,* XIX (1959), i.e., William Tennant Rodgers, U.S.S. *Peacock,* 1813–15.

Pitcher, M. Avis, "John Smith, First Senator from Ohio and His Connections with Aaron Burr," *Ohio Archaeological and Historical Quarterly,* XLV (1936) ; I. J. Cox in *DAB.*

Davies, George E., "Robert Smith and the Navy," *Maryland Historical Magazine,* XIV (1919).

Dictionary of American Biography is very helpful on the following: George Cabot, Samuel Chase, James Cheetham, DeWitt Clinton, Henry Dearborn, Stephen Decatur, Gabriel Duvall, Roger Griswold, James Hillhouse, Rufus King, John Ledyard, Morgan Lewis, Little Turtle, Henry Brockholst Livingston, William Pinkney, John Rodgers, Caleb Strong, Tenskwatawa (The Prophet), Thomas Todd, and William Peter Van Ness.

General Narratives and Analyses

Many general accounts of the history of the United States or a major part thereof, as well as books tracing the several threads of the story, give considerable attention to the period 1801–15. Among the most useful have been the following:

Abernethy, Thomas P., *The South in the New Nation, 1789–1819* (Baton Rouge, 1961).

Adams, James Truslow, *New England in the Republic, 1776–1850* (Boston, 1926).

Albion, Robert G., and Pope, Jennie Barnes, *Sea Lanes in Wartime, The American Experience* (New York, 1942).

Allen, H. C., *The Anglo-American Relationship Since 1783* (London, 1959).

Ashley, Maurice Percy, *Mr. President, An Introduction to American History* (London, 1948).

Bancroft, Frederic, *Slave Trading in the Old South* (Baltimore, 1931).

Bassett, John Spencer, *The Federalist System, 1789–1801* (New York, 1906).

Beard, Charles A., *Economic Origins of Jeffersonian Democracy* (New York, 1915; reprint, 1956).

———, *The Supreme Court and the Constitution* (New York, 1922; reprint, 1938).

Bemis, Samuel Flagg, *A Diplomatic History of the United States* (rev. ed., New York, 1950).

Bernstein, Harry, *Origins of Inter-American Interest, 1700–1812* (Philadelphia, 1945).

Bidwell, Percy W., and Falconer, John I., *History of Agriculture in the Northern United States, 1620–1860* (Washington, 1925; reprint, 1941).

Binkley, Wilfred E., *American Political Parties, Their Natural History* (3rd ed., New York, 1959).

———, *President and Congress* (Garden City, N.Y., 1947), a complete revision of his earlier *The Powers of the President* (1937).

Boorstin, Daniel J., *The Lost World of Thomas Jefferson* (New York, 1948).

Boudin, Louis, *Government by Judiciary* (2 vols., New York, 1932).

Bowers, Claude G., *Jefferson and Hamilton* (Boston, 1925), quite hostile to Hamilton.

———, *Jefferson in Power* (Boston, 1936), nearly idolatrous.

Briggs, Herbert W., *Doctrine of Continuous Voyage* (Baltimore, 1926).

Brooks, C. E. P., *Climate Through the Ages* (New York, 1949), somewhat dated by recent researches in frigid zones.

Brooks, Robert, *Political Parties and Electoral Problems* (New York, 1923).

Buck, Norman S., *The Development of the Organization of Anglo-American Trade, 1800–1850* (New Haven, 1925).

Buck, Solon Justus and Elizabeth H., *The Planting of Civilization in Western Pennsylvania* (Pittsburgh, 1939).

Burdick, C. K., *The Law of the American Constitution* (New York, 1929).

Channing, Edward, *A History of the United States* (6 vols., New York, 1905–25), IV.

Chappelle, Howard I., *The History of American Sailing Ships* (New York, 1935).

————, *The History of the American Sailing Navy* (New York, 1949) .

Clark, R. C., *History of the Willamette Valley, Oregon* (3 vols., Chicago, 1927) , I.

Clark, Victor S., *History of Manufactures in the United States, 1609–1860* (rev. ed., 3 vols., Washington, 1929) .

Coman, Katherine, *Economic Beginnings of the Far West* (2 vols., New York, 1912) , I.

Commager, Henry Steele, *Majority Rule and Minority Rights* (New York, 1943) , including some useful remarks on judicial deviations from the original course of the U.S.

Conant, C. A., and Nadler, Marcus, *A History of Modern Banks of Issue* (6th ed., New York, 1927) .

Corwin, Edward S., *The President: Office and Powers, 1787–1957, History and Analysis of Practice and Opinion* (4th rev. ed., New York, 1957) .

Cotton, Joseph P., *Constitutional Decisions of John Marshall* (2 vols., New York, 1905) .

Coulter, Ellis Merton, *Georgia, A Short History* (Chapel Hill, 1960) .

Cunliffe, Marcus, *The Nation Takes Shape, 1789–1837* (Chicago, 1959) , a perspicacious treatment of a large subject in small scope (222 pp.) .

Curti, Merle, *Growth of American Thought* (New York, 1943) .

————, *Peace or War: The American Struggle, 1636–1936* (New York, 1936) .

Cushman, H. B., *History of the Choctaw, Chickasaw, and Natchez Indians* (Stillwater, Okla., 1962) .

Dangerfield, George B., *The Era of Good Feelings* (New York, 1952) , which gets off to a running start with the second term of President Madison.

DeVoto, Bernard, *The Course of Empire* (Boston, 1952) , including Lewis and Clark.

Dewey, Davis Rich, *Financial History of the United States* (12th ed., New York, 1936) .

Dorfman, Joseph, *The Economic Mind in American Civilization* (5 vols., New York, 1946–59) , I–II.

Douglass, Elisha P., *Rebels and Democrats* (Chapel Hill, 1955) .

Elliott, R. N., *The Raleigh Register, 1799–1863* (Chapel Hill, 1955) , the attitudes of the leading North Carolina newspaper.

Essary, J. Frederick, *Maryland in National Politics* (Baltimore, 1932) .

Fersh, Seymour H., *The View from the White House: A Study of the Presidential State of the Union Messages* (Washington, 1961) .

Fisher, Godfrey, *Barbary Legend: War, Trade, and Piracy in North Africa, 1415–1830* (New York, 1957) .

Flick, Alexander C. (ed.) , *History of the State of New York* (10 vols., New York, 1933–37) , including the following especially useful essays: Dexter

Perkins, "New York's Participation in the Federal Government," VI; D. T. Lynch, "The Growth of Political Parties, 1777–1828," VI; and Julius W. Pratt, "The War of 1812," V.

Forman, Sidney, *West Point, A History of the United States Military Academy* (New York, 1950).

Fortescue, John W., *History of the British Army* (13 vols., London, 1910–33), X.

Frankfurter, Felix, and Landis, James M., *The Business of the Supreme Court* (New York, 1927).

Franklin, John Hope, *From Slavery to Freedom: A History of American Negroes* (2nd ed. rev., New York, 1960).

Frazier, E. Franklin, *The Negro in the United States* (rev. ed., New York, 1957).

Frederick, John H., *The Development of American Commerce* (New York, 1932).

Fuller, George W., *A History of the Pacific Northwest* (2nd ed. rev., New York, 1945).

Ganoe, William, *The History of the United States Army* (New York, 1942).

Ghent, William J., *The Early Far West . . . 1540–1850* (New York, 1931).

Goodrich, Carter, *Government Promotion of American Canals and Railroads, 1800–1890* (New York, 1960), Chaps. III, IV.

Green, Constance McLaughlin, *American Cities in the Growth of the Nation* (New York, 1957).

——, *Washington, Village and Capital, 1800–1878* (Princeton, 1962).

Hagan, William T., *The Sac and Fox Indians* (Norman, Okla., 1958).

Haines, Charles Grove, *The American Doctrine of Judicial Supremacy* (2nd ed. rev., New York, 1959).

——, and Sherwood, Foster H., *The Role of the Supreme Court in American Government and Politics* (2 vols., Berkeley, 1944–57).

Hammond, Bray, *Banks and Politics in America from the Revolution to the Civil War* (Princeton, 1957).

Hansen, Marcus, L., *The Atlantic Migration, 1607–1860* (Cambridge, Mass., 1940).

Hibbard, B. H., *A History of the Public Land Policies* (New York, 1939).

Hockett, Homer C., *The Constitutional History of the United States* (2 vols., New York, 1939).

Hutchins, John G. B., *The American Maritime Industries and Public Policy, 1789–1914, An Economic History* (Cambridge, Mass., 1941).

Hyde, Charles Cheney, *International Law, Chiefly as Interpreted and Applied by the United States* (2nd rev. ed., Boston, 1945).

Johnson, Emory R. *et al.*, *History of the Domestic and Foreign Commerce of the United States* (2 vols., Washington, 1915), a cumulative work of value, especially, I, Chap. XIX, "Embargo and Coastwise Trade," and II, Chap. XXIII, "Foreign Trade, 1790–1815."

Kass, Alvin, *Politics in New York State, 1800–1830* (Syracuse, 1965).

Kellogg, Louise Phelps, *The British Regime in Wisconsin and the Northwest* (Madison, Wis., 1935).

Knox, Dudley W., *A History of the United States Navy* (New York, 1948).

Landon, Fred, *Western Ontario and the American Frontier* (Toronto, 1941).

Latané, John H., and Wainhouse, David W., *A History of American Foreign Policy, 1776–1940* (New York, 1941).

McCloskey, Robert G., *The American Supreme Court* (Chicago, 1960), questions Marshall's position closely.

McLaughlin, Andrew C., *A Constitutional History of the United States* (New York, 1935).

MacLeod, William Christie, *The American Indian Frontier* (London, 1928), adversely critical of national policy.

Martin, François-Xavier, *The History of Louisiana*, with addenda to the 1827–29 edition (2 vols. in 1, New Orleans, 1882), annals rather than history, but much mined by scholars of each generation.

May, Ernest R. (ed.), *The Ultimate Decision: The President as Commander-in-Chief* (New York, 1960), with a chapter on Madison by Cunliffe.

Merriam, C. E., *A History of American Political Theories* (New York, 1910), including reflections on Jeffersonian theory.

Metcalf, C. H., *A History of the United States Marine Corps* (New York, 1939).

Meyer, B. H. *et al.*, *History of Transportation in the United States before 1860* (Washington, 1917).

Milton, George Fort, *The Use of Presidential Power, 1789–1943* (Boston, 1944).

Nagel, Paul C., *One Nation Indivisible: The Union in American Thought, 1776–1861* (New York, 1964).

Nettels, Curtis P., *The Emergence of a National Economy, 1775–1815* (New York, 1962).

Nevins, Allan, *The Evening Post* (New York, 1922).

Parish, John Carl, *The Emergence of the Idea of Manifest Destiny* (Los Angeles, 1932), a brief 23 pp.

Parrington, Vernon Louis, *Main Currents in American Thought* (3 vols., New York, 1927–30), actually more illustrative of the interesting mind of its author than explicative of its subject.

Peterson, Harold F., *Argentina and the United States, 1810–1960* (New York, 1964).

Phillips, Ulrich Bonnell, *American Negro Slavery* (New York, 1929;

reprint, 1952), the classic which remained uncontroverted so long as the Negro's inferior status seemed comfortably assured in the mind of the white majority.

Phillips, W. A., and Reede, A. H., *Neutrality, Its History, Economics, and Law* (4 vols., New York, 1936), of which II is relevant to this period.

Pollard, James E., *The Presidents and the Press* (New York, 1947).

Potter, E .B., and Nimitz, Chester W. (eds.), *Sea Power* (Englewood Cliffs, N.J., 1960), admittedly a manual of naval history for naval officer candidates, but necessarily included because of its unique and superb bibliographies.

Ratner, Sidney, *American Taxation, Its History as a Social Force in Democracy* (New York, 1942).

Risch, Erna, *Quartermaster Support of the Army: A History of the Corps, 1775–1939* (Washington, 1962).

Robbins, Roy M., *Our Landed Heritage, The Public Domain, 1776–1936* (Princeton, 1942).

Roseboom, Eugene H., *A History of Presidential Elections* (New York, 1964), the best of its genus.

Savage, Carleton (ed.), *Policy of the United States Toward Maritime Commerce in War* (2 vols., Washington, 1934–36), limited mostly to U.S. responses, but valuable, especially, I, Chap. IV.

Spiller, Robert E. *et al.*, *Literary History of the United States* (3 vols., New York, 1948), I.

Sprout, Harold and Margaret, *The Rise of American Naval Power, 1776–1918* (rev. ed., Princeton, 1942), adversely critical of the Jeffersonians.

Stanwood, Edward, *History of the Presidency from 1788 to 1897* (new ed., Boston, 1924).

Swisher, Carl Brent, *American Constitutional Development* (2nd ed., Boston, 1954).

Tansill, Charles Callan, *The United States and Santo Domingo, 1798–1873* (Baltimore, 1938).

Taussig, F. W., *The Tariff History of the United States* (5th ed., New York, 1910), for use as a reference manual of facts.

Tryon, Rolla Milton, *Household Manufactures in the United States, 1640–1860* (Chicago, 1917).

Tsiang, I-Mien, *The Question of Expatriation in America Prior to 1907* (Baltimore, 1942).

Van Alstyne, R. W., *The Rising American Empire* (New York, 1960).

Warren, Charles, *Congress, the Constitution, and the Supreme Court* (new ed., Boston, 1935).

———, *A History of the American Bar* (Boston, 1911), superseded in part by Anton-Hermann Chroust's history of the American legal profession (1966), which appeared too late for use by this author.

——, *The Supreme Court in United States History* (rev. ed., 2 vols., Boston, 1937).

Watson, J. Steven, *The Reign of George III, 1760–1815* (New York, 1960), of less use than might be expected ("United States" does not appear in the index), but it is the only thing of "its kind."

Wecter, Dixon, *The Hero in America* (New York, 1941).

Weinberg, A. K., *Manifest Destiny* (Baltimore, 1935).

Willson, Beckles, *America's Ambassadors to France, 1777–1927* (London, 1928), a labor of love rather than professional, long on narration, short on analysis.

Wiltse, Charles Maurice, *The Jeffersonian Tradition in American Democracy* (Chapel Hill, 1935).

——, *The New Nation, 1800–1845* (New York, 1961), a good but brief treatment of a great theme (194 pp. of text).

Wish, Harvey, *Society and Thought in America* (2 vols., New York, 1950–52), I.

Wissler, Clark, *Indians of the United States* (New York, 1954).

Wittke, Carl, *We Who Built America, The Saga of the Immigrant* (New York, 1939).

Specialized Books

Several useful books give most of their space to the period 1801–15 as part of the general narrative of early American history. There are also many book-length monographs on particular aspects of the years 1801–15 or immediately before. The most useful have been the following:

Abernethy, Thomas Perkins, *The Burr Conspiracy* (New York, 1954), conveniently summarized and brought up to date in his *The South in the New Nation,* above.

Adams, Henry, *History of the United States During the Administrations of Jefferson and Madison* (9 vols., New York, 1889–91), an artistic monument written with rare eloquence, but outdated by the prodigious labors of hundreds of scholars. It should be studied as a piece of American literature, not as a source of historical knowledge. Herbert Agar edited a two-volume condensation, which appeared in 1947 as *The Formative Years.*

Aronson, Sidney H., *Status and Kinship in the Higher Civil Service: Standards of Selection in the Administrations of John Adams, Thomas Jefferson, and Andrew Jackson* (Cambridge, Mass., 1964).

Babcock, Kendric Charles, *The Rise of American Nationality, 1811–1819* (New York, 1906), still has bibliographical uses.

Bakeless, John, *Lewis and Clark, Partners in Discovery* (New York, 1947).

Baldwin, Leland D., *Whiskey Rebels: The Story of a Frontier Uprising* (Pittsburgh, 1939).

Beirne, Francis F., *Shout Treason, The Trial of Aaron Burr* (New York, 1959).

———, *The War of 1812* (New York, 1949), spirited but undocumented.

Bodo, John R., *The Protestant Clergy and Public Issues, 1812–1848* (Princeton, 1954).

Bonnel, Ulane, *La France, les États-Unis, et la Guerre de Course, 1797–1815* (Paris, 1961), uses dated American materials but is also based on French maritime documents not often viewed.

Brebner, John Bartlett, *The Explorers of North America, 1492–1806* (London, 1933).

Brown, Everett S., *Constitutional History of the Louisiana Purchase, 1803–1812* (Berkeley, 1920).

Brown, Ralph Hall, *Mirror for Americans: Likeness of the Eastern Seaboard, 1810* (New York, 1943), the very best thing for re-creating the physical attributes of early America.

Brown, Roger H., *The Republic in Peril: 1812* (New York, 1964), a very satisfactory explanation of why the United States went to war.

Brown, Stuart Gerry, *The First Republicans: Political Philosophy and Public Policy in the Party of Jefferson and Madison* (Syracuse, 1954).

Burt, A. L., *The United States, Great Britain, and British North America from the Revolution to the Establishment of Peace After the War of 1812* (New Haven, 1940), has not been substantially improved upon.

Caldwell, L. K., *The Administrative Theories of Hamilton & Jefferson* (Chicago, 1944).

Chambers, William Nisbet, *Political Parties in a New Nation* (New York, 1963), often and rightly praised.

Channing, Edward, *The Jeffersonian System, 1801–1811* (New York, 1906), superseded by his later work, but useful bibliographically.

Charles, Joseph, *The Origins of the American Party System: Three Essays* (Williamsburg, 1956).

Clauder, Anna Cornelia, *American Commerce as Affected by the Wars of the French Revolution* (Philadelphia, 1932).

Coles, Harry L., *The War of 1812* (Chicago, 1965), briefest and best of the kind.

Condit, Carl W., *American Building Art: The Nineteenth Century* (New York, 1960).

Cox, Isaac Joslin, *The West Florida Controversy, 1798–1813* (Baltimore, 1918), a treatment in exhaustive, and almost exhausting, detail (668 pp.).

Cranwell, John Philips, and Crane, William Bowers, *Men of Marque: A*

History of Private Armed Vessels out of Baltimore During the War of 1812 (New York, 1940) .

Crouzet, François, *L'Économie Britannique et le Blocus Continental, 1806–1813* (2 vols., Paris, 1958) .

Cunningham, Noble E., Jr., *The Jeffersonian Republicans: The Formation of Party Organization, 1789–1801* (Chapel Hill, 1957) .

———, *The Jeffersonian Republicans in Power, Party Operations, 1801–1809* (Chapel Hill, 1963) .

Darling, Arthur Burr, *Our Rising Empire, 1763–1803* (New Haven, 1940) , which includes about 130 pages on the Louisiana Purchase.

Dauer, Manning J., *The Adams Federalists* (Baltimore, 1953) , useful for studying the structure of the Federalist party at the moment of Jefferson's accession.

Doyle, James T., *The Organizational and Operational Administration of the Ohio Militia in the War of 1812* (Columbus, Ohio, 1958) .

Echeverria, Durand, *Mirage in the West: A History of the French Image of American Society to 1815* (Princeton, 1957) , of value for understanding the glaciation of intercultural life.

Engelmann, Fred L., *The Peace of Christmas Eve* (New York, 1962) , a handy summary of familiar knowledge of the Treaty of Ghent.

Fischer, David Hackett, *The Revolution of American Conservatism: The Federalist Party in the Era of Jeffersonian Democracy* (New York, 1965) , a piece of desirable revisionism which discovers a vigorous Young Federalist movement, concealed by the weathered rubble of polemic literature.

Fox, Dixon Ryan, *The Decline of Aristocracy in the Politics of New York* (New York, 1919) , an eroded but still useful book.

Gilpatrick, Delbert H., *Jeffersonian Democracy in North Carolina, 1789–1816* (New York, 1931) .

Gilpin, Alec Richard, *The War of 1812 in the Old Northwest* (East Lansing, Mich., 1958) .

Goetzmann, William H., *Army Exploration in the American West, 1803–1863* (New Haven, 1959) .

Goodman, Paul, *The Democratic-Republicans of Massachusetts: Politics in a Young Republic* (Cambridge, Mass., 1964) , on the years 1785–1815.

Goodwin, Cardinal, *The Trans-Mississippi West, 1803–1853* (New York, 1922) .

Graham, Gerald S., *Sea Power and British North America, 1783–1820, A Study in British Colonial Policy* (Cambridge, Eng., 1941) .

Hallaman, Emmanuel, *The British Invasions of Ohio—1813* (Columbus, Ohio, 1958) .

Harlow, Ralph Volney, *The History of Legislative Methods in the Period before 1825* (New Haven, 1917) .

Hatch, William Stanley, *A Chapter of the History of the War of 1812 in the Northwest* (Cincinnati, 1872) .

Heath, Phoebe Ann, *Napoleon I and the Origins of the Anglo-American War of 1812* (Toulouse, 1929), rather thin treatment of a colossally important subject which someone should try again.

Heckscher, Eli F., *The Continental System, An Economic Interpretation* (Oxford, 1922), considered as European history; the author gives a chronological table, collects all of the British orders, and presents the story with enviable detachment.

Higginbotham, Sanford W., *The Keystone in the Democratic Arch: Pennsylvania Politics, 1800–1816* (Harrisburg, 1952), thorough, but lacking an integrating theme.

Hitsman, J. Mackay, *The Incredible War of 1812* (Toronto, 1965), by which the author means "incredible" in execution, not in cause or effect.

Hoffnagel, Warren Miles, *The Road to Fame—W. H. Harrison and National Policy in the Northwest* . . . (Columbus, Ohio, 1959) .

Horsman, Reginald, *The Causes of the War of 1812* (Philadelphia, 1962), which cannot be ignored.

Howard, Leon, *The Connecticut Wits* (Chicago, 1942) .

Irving, L. Homfray, *Officers of the British Forces in Canada During the War of 1812–15* (Welland, Ont., 1908), useful for identifications.

Irving, Washington, *Astoria, or Anecdotes of an Enterprise Beyond the Rocky Mountains* (Philadelphia, 1836), written from Astor records and still durable.

———, *Knickerbocker's History of New York* (2 vols., New York, 1895, and other printings), includes satires on Wilkinson ("the admirable trumpeter") and Jefferson ("William the Testy") by one who lived through the events.

Irwin, Ray W., *The Diplomatic Relations of the United States with the Barbary Powers, 1776–1816* (Chapel Hill, 1931), definitive and indispensable.

Jacobs, James Ripley, *The Beginning of the United States Army, 1783–1812* (Princeton, 1947) .

James, William, *A Full and Correct Account of the Military Occurrences of the Late War between Great Britain and the United States of America* (2 vols., London, 1818), a British view which provoked much vigorous debate.

Jennings, Walter W., *The American Embargo, 1807–1809* (Iowa City, 1921), with particular reference to its effect on industrialization.

Knopf, Richard C. (ed.), *Return Jonathan Meigs Jr. and the War of 1812* (Columbus, Ohio, 1957) ; Meigs was governor of Ohio.

———, *William Henry Harrison and the War of 1812* (Columbus, Ohio, 1957) .

Koch, Adrienne, *Jefferson and Madison: The Great Collaboration* (New York, 1950).

Labaree, Benjamin W., *Patriots and Partisans: The Merchants of Newburyport, 1764–1815* (Cambridge, Mass., 1962).

Krout, John A., and Fox, Dixon Ryan, *The Completion of Independence, 1790–1830* (New York, 1944), i.e., cultural independence.

Kurtz, Stephen, *The Presidency of John Adams* (Philadelphia, 1957).

LeRoy, Perry, *The Weakness of Discipline and Its Consequent Results in the Northwest During the War of 1812* (Columbus, Ohio, 1958).

Lipsky, George A., *John Quincy Adams, His Theory and Ideas* (New York, 1950).

Livermore, Shaw, Jr., *The Twilight of Federalism: The Disintegration of the Federalist Party, 1815–1830* (Princeton, 1962).

Logan, Rayford W., *The Diplomatic Relations of the United States with Haiti 1776–1891* (Chapel Hill, 1941).

Lossing, Benson J., *The Pictorial Field Book of the War of 1812* (New York, 1869), ultranationalist, but useful for sketches and plans.

Ludlum, David M., *Social Ferment in Vermont, 1791–1850* (New York, 1939), mainly social and intellectual.

Lyon, E. Wilson, *Louisiana in French Diplomacy, 1759–1804* (Norman, Okla., 1934).

McAfee, Robert B., *History of the Late War in the Western Country* (Lexington, Ky., 1816), much based on fresh recollections of participants.

McCaleb, W. F., *The Aaron Burr Conspiracy* (New York, 1903) reprint, 1936), set the tone of discussion in practically all studies until the appearance of Abernethy's work, above; the 1936 printing has additions on the life of Burr by Charles A. Beard in a somewhat frivolous mood.

Magrath, C. Peter, *Yazoo: Law and Politics in the New Republic: The Case of Fletcher v. Peck* (Providence, 1966), appears to be definitive.

Mahan, Alfred Thayer, *The Influence of Sea Power Upon the French Revolution and Europe, 1793–1812* (2 vols., Boston, 1892), and *Sea Power in Its Relation to the War of 1812* (2 vols., Boston, 1905), two innocently tendentious books which have been uncritically drawn upon by practically all writers who have touched on their subjects; most naval histories of the age seem to be distilled Mahan.

Manning, Helen Taft, *The Revolt of French Canada, 1800–1835: A Chapter in the History of the British Commonwealth* (New York, 1962).

Marigny, Bernard, *Reflections on the Campaign of General Jackson in Louisiana in 1814 and '15* (New Orleans, 1848), translated by Grace King for *Louisiana Historical Quarterly*, VI (1923), from which this citation is taken; defends the creoles against baseless innuendoes of disloyalty to the U.S.

Mason, Philip P. (ed.), *After Tippecanoe: Some Aspects of the War of 1812* (East Lansing, 1963), contains six essays, of which the following were especially useful: Thomas D. Clark, "Kentucky in the Northwest Campaign"; W. Kaye Lamb, "Sir Isaac Brock: The Hero of Queenston Heights"; and George F. G. Stanley, "The Contribution of the Canadian Militia During the War."

Miller, John C., *The Federalist Era, 1789–1801* (New York, 1960).

Mirsky, Jeanette, *The Westward Crossings* (New York, 1946), including Lewis and Clark.

Morison, Samuel Eliot, *The Maritime History of Massachusetts, 1783–1860* (rev. ed., Boston, 1941), an excellent work which first appeared in 1921.

Munroe, John A., *Federalist Delaware, 1775–1815* (New Brunswick, 1954).

Nye, Russell Blaine, *The Cultural Life of the New Nation, 1776–1830* (New York, 1960).

Olson, Mancur, Jr., *The Economics of the Wartime Shortage* (Durham, N.C., 1963)

Patrick, Rembert W., *Florida Fiasco: Rampant Rebels on the Georgia-Florida Border, 1810–1815* (Athens, Ga., 1954), concerns not rebels but unprovoked aggressors whose mission was the sole stain on Madison's libertarianism.

Paullin, Charles O. (ed.), *The Battle of Lake Erie* (Cleveland, 1918).

Peake, Ora Brooks, *A History of the United States Indian Factory System, 1795–1822* (Denver, 1954).

Perkins, Bradford, *Castlereagh and Adams, England and the United States, 1812–1823* (Berkeley, 1964), indispensable, as are his *The First Rapprochement: England and the United States, 1795–1805* (Philadelphia, 1955), and *Prologue to War: England and the United States, 1805–1812* (Berkeley, 1961), which together comprise the definitive history of Anglo-American relations in the years covered; we sadly need the same kind of study of Franco-American relations in those years.

Pratt, Julius W., *The Expansionists of 1812* (New York, 1925; reprint, 1949), which adds the territorial dimension to the causes of the War of 1812.

Prucha, Francis Paul, *American Indian Policy in the Formative Years: The Indian Trade and Intercourse Acts, 1790–1834* (Cambridge, Mass., 1962).

Purcell, Richard J., *Connecticut in Transition, 1775–1818* (Washington, 1918).

Renaut, F. P., *La Question de la Louisiane, 1796–1806* (Paris, 1918).

Richardson, John, *War of 1812* (Brockville, Ont., 1842); this contemporary Canadian view also appeared as edited by Alexander Clark Casselman (Toronto, 1902).

Robinson, William A., *Jeffersonian Democracy in New England* (New Haven, 1916).

Rowland, E. O., *Andrew Jackson's Campaign Against the British, or The Mississippi Territory in the War of 1812* (New York, 1926), readable despite its use of the magnolia-cum-chivalry mythos.

Sears, Louis M., *Jefferson and the Embargo* (Durham, N.C., 1927), the principal and durable study.

Shulim, Joseph Isidore, *The Old Dominion and Napoleon Bonaparte: A Study in American Opinion* (New York, 1952).

Smelser, Marshall, *The Congress Founds the Navy, 1787–1798* (Notre Dame, Ind. 1959), legislative history which presents only the surface forensics and polemics of contesting naval theories.

Smith, James E., *One Hundred Years of Hartford's Courant* (New Haven, 1949), a convenient summary of Federalist editorializing.

Sowerby, E. Millicent (comp.), *Catalogue of the Library of Thomas Jefferson* (5 vols., Washington, 1952–59), very revelatory of Jefferson's intellectual formation.

Spiller, Robert E., *The American in England During the First Half Century of Independence* (New York, 1926).

Trent, William P. *et al.*, *The Cambridge History of American Literature* (4 vols., New York, 1917–21), in which, of special value, are Arthur Hobson Quinn, "The Early Drama, 1756–1860"; Samuel Marion Tucker, "The Beginnings of Verse, 1610–1808"; Carl Van Doren, "Fiction I: Brown, Cooper"; George Frisbie Whicher, "Early Essayists"; and Lane Cooper, "Travelers and Observers, 1763–1846." The above are all in Vol. I.

Varg, Paul A., *Foreign Policies of the Founding Fathers* (East Lansing, Mich., 1963), sees a transition to moralizing in foreign policy.

Whitaker, Arthur Preston, *The Mississippi Question, 1795–1803* (New York, 1934).

———, *The United States and the Independence of Latin America, 1800–1830* (Baltimore, 1941).

White, Leonard D., *The Federalists, A Study in Administrative History* (New York, 1948), and, of great value, *The Jeffersonians, A Study in Administrative History, 1801–1829* (New York, 1951), which together tell how the government worked, and why.

White, Patrick C. T., *A Nation on Trial: America and the War of 1812* (New York, 1965).

Williamson, Chilton, *Vermont in Quandary, 1763–1825* (Montpelier, 1949).

Wolfe, John Harold, *Jeffersonian Democracy in South Carolina* (Chapel Hill, 1940).

Wright, Louis B., and Macleod, Julia H., *The First Americans in North Africa: William Eaton's Struggle for a Vigorous Policy Against the Barbary Pirates, 1799–1805* (Princeton, 1945).

Young, D. M., *The Colonial Office in the Early Nineteenth Century* (London, 1961).

Young, James Sterling, *The Washington Community, 1800–1828* (New York, 1966), treats the politicos as a subculture.

Zaslow, Morris, and Turner, Wesley B. (eds.), *The Defended Border: Upper Canada and the War of 1812* (Toronto, 1964), contains twenty-seven articles, mostly on the affairs of present-day Ontario, of which the following are particularly valuable: E. A. Cruikshank, "The County of Norfolk in the War of 1812," and "Sir Gordon Drummond, K.C.B."; J. Mackay Hitsman, "Alarum on Lake Ontario, Winter, 1812–1813"; Victor Lauriston, "The Case for General Procter"; W. R. Riddell, "The Ancaster 'Bloody Assize' of 1814"; C. P. Stacey, "The Defense of Upper Canada, 1812"; R. L. Way, "The Day at Crysler's [sic] Farm"; C. Winton-Clare, "A Shipbuilder's War."

Zimmerman, James F., *Impressment of American Seamen* (New York, 1925), of which the only adverse criticism is that the author used few British sources.

Index

70 71 72 73 10 9 8 7 6 5 4 3 2